WISDOM IN EARLY CONFUCIAN AND ISRAELITE TRADITIONS

Wisdom is an integratal part of all philosophical and religious traditions in the world. Focusing on the concept of wisdom, this book examines the difficulties and problems facing comparative studies of the early Confucian and Israelite traditions by exploring the cosmological and ethical implications of wisdom in the older layers of Christian and Confucian texts. Presenting a detailed discussion of how wisdom was understood in philosophical, religious and social contexts by the writers of the so-called early Confucian and Israelite wisdom texts, this book offers an invaluable contribution to our understanding of the significance of wisdom in the East and West, and to our knowledge of different and yet related ways of life as understood in their literature.

Xinzhong Yao is Professor of Religion and Ethics and Director of the Centre for Chinese Studies, University of Wales, Lampeter. He is also currently a senior fellow at the Ian Ramsey Centre, University of Oxford, and an honorary Professor of Ethics at Hunan Normal University. He has been teaching courses on religion and philosophy in Wales since 1991, and his English publications include *Encyclopedia of Confucianism* (ed., vols 1–2, Routledge, 2003), *An Introduction to Confucianism* (Cambridge University Press, 2000) and *Confucianism and Christianity* (Sussex Academic Press, 1996).

Ashgate World Philosophies Series

The Ashgate World Philosophies Series responds to the remarkable growth of interest among English-language readers in recent years in philosophical traditions outside those of 'the West'. The traditions of Indian, Chinese, and Japanese thought, as well as those of the Islamic world, Latin America, Africa, Aboriginal Australian, Pacific and American Indian peoples, are all attracting lively attention from professional philosophers and students alike, and this Ashgate series provides introductions to these traditions as well as in-depth research into central issues and themes within those traditions. The series is particularly designed for readers whose interests are not adequately addressed by general surveys of 'World Philosophy', and it includes accessible, yet research-led, texts for wider readership and upper-level student use, as well as research monographs. The series embraces a wide variety of titles ranging from introductions on particular world philosophies and informed surveys of the philosophical contributions of geographical regions, to in-depth discussion of a theme, topic, problem or movement and critical appraisals of individual thinkers or schools of thinkers.

Series Editors:

Professor David E. Cooper, University of Durham, UK
Professor Robert C. Solomon, University of Texas, Austin, USA
Professor Kathleen M. Higgins, University of Texas, Austin, USA
Associate Professor Purushottama Bilimoria, Deakin University, Australia

Other titles in this series:

Learning from Chinese Philosophies
Ethics of Interdependent and Contextualised Self
Karyn Lai

Mulla Sadra's Transcendent Philosophy
Muhammad Kamal

The Philosophy of Rabindranath Tagore
Kalyan Sen Gupta

Buddhist Inclusivism
Attitudes Towards Religious Others
Kristin Beise Kiblinger

Buddhism, Virtue and Environment
David E. Cooper and Simon P. James

Wisdom in Early Confucian and Israelite Traditions

XINZHONG YAO

ASHGATE

Published by
Ashgate Publishing Limited
Gower House
Croft Road
Aldershot
Hants GU11 3HR
England

Ashgate Publishing Company
Suite 420
101 Cherry Street
Burlington, VT 05401-4405
USA

Ashgate website: http//www.ashgate.com

British Library Cataloguing in Publication Data
Yao, Xinzhong
  Wisdom in early Confucian and Israelite traditions
  (Ashgate world philosophies series)
  1.Wisdom literature – Criticism, interpretation, etc. 2.Wisdom – Religious
  aspects – Judaism 3.Wisdom – Religious aspects – Christianity 4.Wisdom –
  Religious aspects – Confucianism 5.Wisdom – Religious aspects – Comparative studies
  I.Title
  223

Library of Congress Cataloging-in-Publication Data
Yao, Xinzhong.
  Wisdom in early Confucian and Israelite traditions / Xinzhong Yao.
      p. cm. – (Ashgate world philosophies series)
  Includes bibliographical references and index.
  ISBN 0-7546-0955-3 (hardcover : alk. paper)
  1. Judaism – Relations – Confucianism. 2. Confucianism – Relations – Judaism.
  3. Wisdom – Religious aspects – Comparative studies. 4. Wisdom – Religious
  aspects – Judaism. 5. Wisdom – Religious aspects – Confucianism. 6. Wisdom
  literature – Criticism, interpretation, etc. 7. Philosophy, Confucian. 8. Jewish way
  of life. 9. Confucian ethics. I. Title. II. Series.
  BM536.C66Y36 2006
  181'.112–dc22
                                                                                    2005030619

ISBN-13: 978-0-7546-0955-1
ISBN-10: 0-7546-0955-3

Typeset in Times New Roman by IML Typographers, Birkenhead, Merseyside.
Printed and bound in Great Britain by MPG Books Ltd, Bodmin, Cornwall.

To Keith Ward

Contents

Preface

Soon after the publication of *Confucianism and Christianity – A Comparative study of Jen and Agape*, which explored the paramount principles of Confucianism and Christianity, I became increasingly interested in the study of wisdom in both early Confucian texts and the older layers of the Christian Bible, namely, the biblical Israelite sources. Whereas the first book compared the core of Confucianism and the key ideas of the New Testament, this one is devoted to the study of wisdom as presented in the books of pre-Qin Confucianism and in the 'wisdom literature' preserved in the Old Testament. This comparative study of wisdom in China and Israel is driven primarily by personal interests and theoretical interconnectedness which, I hope, can be discovered within the two traditions, rather than by contemporary concerns. My main intention here is to discover if a common framework of wisdom thinking can be established through examining two paradigms such as were produced in the early Confucian and Hebrew cultures, although I do wish to draw attention to the tranquil and moderate characteristics of the old Confucian and Israelite wisdom in contrast to the disturbing and extreme ways of living that have been adopted in some quarters of the world today and are causing a great deal of violence and confrontation to take place.

Wisdom as an Intellectual and Spiritual Journey

Rich in content and style, the early Israelite wisdom literature and the Confucian classics open up ways for us to appreciate wisdom. My reading of the texts from two seemingly historically unrelated traditions leads me to the conviction that both Israelite and Confucian wisdom is intended as a guide or roadmap for intellectual explorers and spiritual travellers. Understood as such, wisdom is essentially a journey, taken either collectively by a group of people, or individually by a particular person. Life presents us with a great number of tensions, particularly those between individual desires and universal principles, between what we know and what is not yet understood, and between the human and the superhuman or the experiential and the mysterious. Through aiming to overcome these tensions, wisdom enables people to move beyond a focus on the satisfaction of material contemporary needs to a focus on how to complete a higher mission in the world. Also, in dealing with these tensions, wisdom becomes a journey of personal growth, both in intellectual and in spiritual terms: from the experiential accumulation of knowledge and possession of skills that enable us to cope with life, to the mastery of rules, laws and principles that enables us to steer skilfully the voyage of life in social, ethical and political spheres, and finally to the fulfilment of our potentials that enables us to overcome our limitations physical, intellectual and spiritual. This is a development from the limited to the unlimited and from epistemological knowledge to profound understanding, enabling those who have a sincere heart, an insightful intellect and a strong will to reach the spiritual realm, which is the realm of Heaven and Earth for Confucians, and, for the Israelites, the realm of the supreme wisdom of YHWH.

'Confucians' and 'the Israelites'

This book is a hermeneutical examination of Confucian and Israelite wisdom traditions. However, there is no consensus about what 'Confucian' and 'Israelite' mean among scholars as well as general readers; disagreements or debates frequently erupted in history and are still constant topics in modern scholarship. Preferring not to be drawn into such debates, 'Confucians' and the 'Israelites' in this study will simply refer to those teachers or masters who are supposed to be responsible for early Confucian texts and the wisdom literature of the Bible, the people who exemplified, explored or shaped the way of wisdom thinking in that particular period of early China and biblical Israel.

More specifically, by 'Confucians' we mean primarily Confucius and his early followers, those who shared the belief that in ancient writings and culture there was wisdom and that by applying it they would be able to deal with personal and communal life problems, to rectify disorder or chaos of the state and to bring permanent peace and harmony to the world. There have been debates among modern scholars concerning whether or not these people should be called 'Confucians' as a translation of the Chinese character '*ru*', with some scholars pointing out that *ru* or *ru jia* as a special term for 'Confucians' or 'the Confucian school' did not appear until the Formal Han era (206BCE–8CE).[1] 'Confucian', as an adjective in English, was derived from the Latin rendering of Kong Fuzi or Kong Zi (551–479BCE), referring to Master Kong, who was deemed to be the founder of the literati tradition in China. As used in this book, 'Confucianism' refers to the worldview explored by the early *ru* scholars, Confucius and his followers, who were or still are believed to be the authors, compilers, editors or collators of the early texts that are known as 'Confucian books', particularly Mengzi (372?–289? BCE) and Xunzi (313?–238? BCE). Confucianism in this book also refers to the views held by many other so-called 'Confucian' scholars (*ru shi*) whose ideas shaped the particular view of the world in a number of important Confucian texts produced or finalized during the period between the fourth and the second century BCE.

---

[1] Robert Eno: *The Confucian Creation of Heaven: Philosophy and the Defense of Ritual Mastery*, Albany: State University of New York Press, 1990, p.192. Michael Nylan also argues, 'In the pre-Han period, none of the ancient texts that came to be called the "Confucian" Classics (and few of the classical practices) had been identified as the exclusive intellectual property of "Confucians" (Xinzhong Yao, ed. *Routledge/Curzon Encyclopedia of Confucianism*, Routledge, 2003, p.507).

If there are difficulties in pinning down what exactly is meant by 'Confucian', there are even more problems in defining the Israelites. According to Genesis 32:28 of the Old Testament, 'Israel' was a name conferred by YHWH on Jacob, meaning the one who 'contended with God'. It is said in this book that Israel had twelve sons from whom the twelve tribes of Israel are believed to derive. 'Israel', as we use it in this book, does not refer to this part of history, nor to one of the two kingdoms later established in the land of Palestine; it simply means the 'wisdom tradition of the Israelite people' that later became one of the key sources for Judeo-Christian culture. Therefore, by 'the Israelites' or 'Israelite teachers', we intend to denote those people who are implicitly or explicitly recognized as wisdom teachers during the post-exilic period.[2] These 'teachers' may or may not have actually edited, composed or collated particular wisdom texts, but their ideas or teachings certainly played a decisive role in forming and shaping the Israelite tradition of wisdom, as preserved in the current version of the Old Testament.

The Scope of Sources

At the outset, I must briefly clarify the scope of sources to be used in the book. Firstly, this book is attempting a comparative hermeneutics of wisdom as demonstrated in Confucian and Israelite traditions; however, its scope of sources is limited. Chapter 2 gives a detailed explanation of the source books used in this study; thus here it is sufficient to say that this is a study of wisdom in two specifically defined areas, namely, the Israelite wisdom literature represented by a number of texts that were most likely shaped during the so-called post-exilic period or early Hellenistic era and the wisdom thinking in Confucianism of pre-Qin China (namely, before 221BCE). The raw materials that the editors or compilers of these texts drew upon may be traced to a much earlier era, for example, the early period of the Zhou dynasty in the eleventh to ninth centuries BCE for Confucians and the reigns of King David and King Solomon in the tenth century BCE for the Israelites, while further speculations and commentaries on the texts might have been added in a much later age, for example by the syncretic Confucian scholars of the early Formal Han time (206BCE–8CE), or by heavily Hellenized Jews in the first century BCE. However, there is no intention whatsoever of this author to investigate the whole wisdom tradition in ancient Israelite religion or Judaism, nor to explore the overall view of wisdom in China or Confucianism.

Secondly, within the defined areas of Confucian and Israelite wisdom traditions, attention will be confined to a selected group of key texts from each, namely

---

[2] The Hebrew terms for exile, *gōlā, gālūt*, refer to 'captivity' or 'deportation', the chief of which took place in 597BCE and in 587/586BCE. After the Babylonians were defeated in 539BCE, Cyrus the Persian decreed that captured peoples, including the people of Judah, could return to their homeland in the following year. The 'post-exilic age' therefore refers to a historical period of Israel after 538BCE.

Proverbs, Job, Ecclesiastes, the Wisdom of Solomon and the Book of Ben Sira from the Hebrew and Greek wisdom literature, and the *Analects*, the *Book of Mengzi*, the *Book of Xunzi*, the *Book of Changes* and the *Doctrine of the Mean* from the Confucian classics. I will work on them with the presumption that within each group there is an interpretive structure of the core and the extended wisdom texts. For Confucianism, the core of Confucian wisdom is the *Analects of Confucius*, which is first extended through the books of Mengzi and Xunzi, and then elaborated in the *Book of Changes* and the *Doctrine of the Mean*. There is also a similar structure among Israelite wisdom texts, but the logical connections between the different layers are much less obvious. My understanding of biblical Israelite wisdom is that the core is the book of Proverbs, and the books of Job and Ecclesiastes are taken as a supplement to, or extension of, proverbial wisdom, while the final two books constitute the third layer that provides later deliberations, often under the influence of Greek philosophy and religion. Having said this, I must also clarify that this structure is only an interpretation from my own hermeneutical contextualization, and is not intended to be historically real, or to reflect the literature structure of textual criticism and redaction.

The Chinese source books for key Confucian classics are from the *Shisan jing zhushu* or *Annotations and Commentaries on the Thirteen Classics* (ed. Li Xueqin, Beijing: Beijing University Press, 1999), and *Zhuzi jicheng* (Beijing: Zhonghua Shuju, 1954). Their English translations are based on the following publications but with my own modifications on occasion: *Confucius – The Analects* (trans. D.C. Lau, London: Penguin Classics, 1979); *Mencius* (trans. D.C. Lau, London: Penguin Books, 1970); *Xunzi – A Translation and Study of the Complete Works* (trans. John Knoblock, Stanford: Stanford University Press, vols 1–3, 1988, 1990, 1994); *I Ching or the Book of Changes*, The Richard Wilhelm translation, English translation by Cary F. Baynes (London: Arkam, 1967) and *Zhouyi: the Book of Changes – A New Translation with Commentary* (trans. Richard Rutt, Richmond, Surrey: The Curzon Press, 1996); the *Great Learning* and the *Doctrine of the Mean* (in *A Source Book in Chinese Philosophy*, translated and compiled by Wing-tsit Chan, Princeton: Princeton University Press, 1963, pp. 84–114). Other sources in the Chinese tradition that will be occasionally used include two key Daoist texts, *Lao Tzu: Tao Te Ching* (trans. D.C. Lau, Penguin Books, 1969) and *The Complete Works of Chuang Tzu* (trans. Burton Watson, New York: Columbia University Press, 1968). Quotations from these books will be referred to by parenthetical references and abbreviated in parentheses respectively as *Analects*, Mengzi, Xunzi, Yijing, Daxue, Zhongyong, Daode jing and Zhuangzi, while for all other books footnotes will be provided for information on their sources.

While recognizing a wide range of sources that contain wisdom materials in ancient Israel, our research will mainly be confined to the above sources and will make use of other source books or passages only when necessary. References to the five key wisdom texts will be given in abbreviations in brackets: Proverbs (Prov.), Job (Job), Ecclesiastes (Eccl.), the Wisdom of Solomon (Wisd.), and the Book of Ben Sira (Sir.). Quotations from these texts are drawn primarily from the following books: *The New Oxford Annotated Bible with the Apocrypha* (Revised Standard Version, ed. Herbert G. May and Bruce M. Metzger, New York: Oxford University Press, 1977), and *The Holy Bible* (New International Version, Thompson Chain Reference Edition, by International Bible Society, Sevenoaks: Hodder and Stoughton Ltd, 1984).

Comparative as it is, this book does not claim that the author is also an OT scholar or an expert on Hebrew or Israelite religion. I prefer to see myself as a learner of Hebrew wisdom, with a strong interest in certain aspects of its religious and philosophical worldview. My understanding of key Hebrew words and passages is formulated primarily under the influence of a number of academic publications, such as the *Theological Dictionary of the Old Testament* (ed. G. Johnnes Botterweck and Helmer Ringgren, trans. David E. Green, vols I–VI, Grand Rapids, Michigan: William B. Eerdmans Publishing Company, 1980–1990), *The Oxford Companion to the Bible* (ed. Bruce M. Metzger and Michael D. Coogan, New York and Oxford: Oxford University Press, 1993), and *Eerdmans Dictionary of the Bible* (editor-in-chief: David Noel Freedman, Grand Rapids, Michigan/Cambridge, England: William B. Eerdmans Publishing Company, 2000). Among numerous modern books and articles I have consulted on Israelite wisdom, I would like particularly to mention the scholarship of Katharine Dell, whose insightful views have guided me through the maze of the so-called 'wisdom literature'. My own reconstruction of Israelite wisdom is greatly indebted to her argument that 'Tension between the human and divine is at the centre of an understanding of wisdom, and the wisdom enterprise is to be characterised by this tension between the two emphases.'[3]

Structure of this Book

The shape of this book has been dictated to a great extent by my hermeneutical reading of wisdom as a personal journey towards intellectual and spiritual maturity. Chapter 1 of the book is an introduction that deals with the issues raised by methodological considerations and initial probing into the nature of wisdom, while Chapter 2 examines the scope, contents and dates of the texts from early Israel and Confucianism that are taken as the source materials for this book. The selection of five texts from each tradition has been made not only because these five texts have been generally accepted as key 'wisdom sources' in their own traditions, but also because the five Confucian and Israelite texts have a great many similarities in terms of their formation dates, composition styles and didactic methods.

The first two chapters together provide a background for further study, and set up the central theme of the comparison, namely that Confucian wisdom is primarily anthropocentric while Israelite wisdom is essentially theocentric, which is clearly

---

[3] Katherine Dell: *'Get Wisdom, Get Insight': An Introduction to Israel's Wisdom Literature*, Macon: Smyth & Helwys Publishing, Inc., 2000, p.6.

demonstrated either through similarities or in divergence. Chapter 3 discusses the epistemological issues surrounding wisdom, exploring the following questions: Is wisdom a kind of knowledge and if so what kind of knowledge is it? Can this knowledge be passed on or taught and how is it transmitted between generations? There is no doubt that knowledge is the constituent element of wisdom, yet many traditions have categorically denied the function of knowledge in the working of wisdom, or at least have not identified knowledge with wisdom. This must indicate that there are different kinds of knowledge, and that some are of a wisdom nature and can lead to wisdom, while others are not and cannot. Is the knowledge that leads to wisdom innate or learned from *posterior* experience? By exploring the connection between knowledge and wisdom we will also touch on issues of the nature and function of education. If wisdom is a kind of knowledge, then it must be transmittable and learnable, from which arises the importance of education in wisdom transmission.

Chapter 4 considers wisdom as a way of life, and examine its usefulness, meaning and value as a guide and for formalizing a particular course in life. Is wisdom a 'way'? If it is, then what is meant by the 'way' in Confucian and Hebrew texts? As a way of life, wisdom is primarily concerned with the practical dimensions of life, and invests a range of meanings to this. A meaningful life cannot be divorced from necessary skills and abilities and both Israelite and Confucian texts have demonstrated that a person who is not capable of doing practical things may not be expected to be wise, and that a highly wise person must also be able to master important issues or questions that have arisen from personal and communal complexities. As a way of life, wisdom also manifests itself in more personal matters, particularly in a person's attitude towards wealth and poverty, towards making friends and towards leading a joyful life.

Chapter 5 deals with the moral or ethical contents of wisdom. Ethical consideration is fundamental to the Confucian view of the world, and is also very important in the Israelite tradition. Wisdom is not only shrewdness or judiciousness; rather it is revealed as a way of behaving and thinking, the constancy of which leads to what we call 'virtue', an excellence resulting from proper cultivation or moral training. Virtue is ethical, but is not merely ethical in its narrow sense. For Confucians ethical virtue is an important path to the ideal and is therefore taken as the foundation on which the whole moral universe can be established and, for the Israelites, virtue primarily belongs to the divine, and by extension becomes human goodness; the tension between the human dimension and the divine content drives the Israelites to search for wisdom in righteousness. However differently virtue is defined and interpreted, Confucians and the Israelites attach it to their models of the ideal person, the wise and righteous in Israel and the person of wisdom and gentility (or the 'gentleman' in its original meaning) in Confucianism. These models or images provide a basic prototype for Confucians and the Israelites to follow and imitate during their journey to wisdom.

Wisdom in early Confucian and Israelite traditions is not confined to personal issues, but is also developed through dealing with familial, political and juridical issues, in which the wise choose a quite different way from that of the foolish. However divergent Confucian views of wisdom are from the Israelite ones, they share a fundamental belief in the value of family and community that are hierarchical in structure and patriarchal in function. Chapter 6 is intended to examine how wisdom operates in familial and political contexts. In terms of the family the meaning and implication of parent–child and husband–wife relationships for wisdom will be discussed, while in political wisdom, we will examine the reason, meaning and function of 'revering tradition' and 'ordering society' in the context of wisdom. Confucian political hierarchy is primarily moral, with the top of this hierarchy being the sage–king who rules the world through moral influence and example, while the Israelites place human politics and wise kingship on the foundation of the righteousness and wisdom of YHWH.

Chapter 7 explores the sacredness of wisdom; for the early Confucian masters and Israelite sages, wisdom cannot be separated from their understanding of the sacred or the divine. At first glance it seems that Confucian and Israelite teachers are the same in their search for the sacred nature of wisdom, as they both connect wisdom with the divine. However, their understanding of the divine is very different, with the Israelite YHWH and the Confucian Heaven operating in different ways as far as wisdom is concerned. The sacredness of wisdom can also be found in a human appreciation of the spirits that help people to cultivate reverence within, and in their understanding of the order behind the disorder and of human destiny in this world.

In the eighth chapter, the conclusion, we will give an overall view of what has been discussed and examined, and of what makes the Confucian view of wisdom differ from and yet relate to the Israelite wisdom doctrine, by which a common framework of these two wisdom traditions is laid down. It will also finalize our thesis suggested in this Preface, that wisdom is a personal journey with multifaceted purposes and functions, but is aimed at breaking through human finitude. Throughout the journey, humanity in general, and individuals in particular, gradually grasp the dialectic of the changing and unchanging faces of wisdom, its universal and particular presentations, and its secular and spiritual orientations. In so doing are eventually able to transcend individual human limitations and understand the process of creation and regeneration. It is at this point that early Israelites and Confucians depart from one another. The Israelites are 'theo-optimistic' rather than confident in humans themselves, because they believe that humans cannot understand the mysteries of the world unless they have been enabled to do so by divine wisdom. For Confucians, ultimate wisdom arises from daily experience and knowledge, and by performing one's duties in society and cultivating one's character in learning and practice, one is able to penetrate the mysterious surface and grasp the final truth, gaining ultimate wisdom, transcendent and eternal, and partaking in the power of Heaven and Earth.

Transliteration

There are two major systems currently in use for transliterating Chinese characters into English, namely, the well known but outdated Wade–Giles or modified Wade–Giles system, and the *pinyin* system. Considering the increasing popularity of the latter among scholars as well as readers, this book will primarily use the *pinyin* system, retaining the Wade–Giles transcription only for the names of some authors or in quotations. To make it convenient for readers, a glossary of Chinese characters with their *pinyin* spellings and English meanings or references will be provided at the end of the book.

In transliterating Hebrew words, the traditional system has been broadly followed. Note that the six consonants b g d k p t are pronounced in the normal English way, but if underlined as <u>b</u> <u>g</u> <u>d</u> <u>k</u> <u>p</u> <u>t</u> they are softer in sound, with four of them being pronounced differently (to our ears): <u>b</u> = v, <u>d</u> = *th*e, <u>p</u> = f, <u>t</u> = *th*in. S and ś sound the same as English s; s = hi*ss*; š =*sh*all. A glossary of spellings, Hebrew words and English meanings or references is given as Appendix II.

A number of articles, inspired by the process of writing this book, have been published in academic journals, for example *The Journal of Chinese Philosophy* and *Dao: A Journal of Comparative Philosophy*, and I would like to thank the editors for their permission for parts of these articles to be included in this book. The writing of this book was only made possible with the support of the Department of Theology and Religious Studies, University of Wales, Lampeter. I have benefited intellectually from many of my colleagues or former colleagues in Wales and special thanks are due to Professor D.P. Davies and Canon Peter Morris for their reading of the manuscript, and for their insightful comments and suggestions, some of which have been adopted in the book. I also wish to thank Professor Dan Cohn-Sherbok for allowing me to sit in his biblical Hebrew classes, and Kar Yong Lim for his assistance in constructing the glossary of Hebrew words. Finally I would like to dedicate this book to Emeritus Professor Keith Ward, University of Oxford, for his wisdom and for the leading role he has played in the development of comparative studies of cultural and religious traditions.

CHAPTER ONE

Wisdom in a Comparative Perspective

Wisdom lies at the centre of all philosophical and religious traditions. Philosophy comes directly from the love and pursuit (*philia*) of wisdom (*sophia*) concerning the nature and meaning of existence, reality, knowledge and goodness, while religion in essence is a search for wisdom on how to transcend our limitations: physical, intellectual or spiritual.[1] On the surface, wisdom appears to be simply a collection of proverbs, maxims and aphorisms arising from past life experiences that are in turn used to guide individual human beings or particular groups or communities on how to deal with daily matters, and to help them to determine what measures can be best adopted to cope with life situations. This is so-called 'practical wisdom', a kind of wisdom closely associated with skill, know-how and shrewdness by which people can perform their duties well and solve their problems satisfactorily. There is another, deeper meaning of wisdom, however, about the nature, the ultimate meaning and the hidden 'pattern' of the world, society and individual life. It is named variously 'intellectual wisdom', 'transcendental wisdom' or 'great wisdom'. Whatever name it is given, wisdom at the higher level often presents itself either as an almost intuitive understanding of the seemingly unconceivable, or as a kind of insight that penetrates the surface of phenomena and grasps the essence of existence, or as a predictive vision of the fortune or misfortune of people and about the good or bad result of a particular event or action.

The so-called 'higher' wisdom itself appears to be a paradox. It is a kind of knowledge, but it is not an ordinary kind of knowledge. It is associated with life experiences, but it also frequently requires us to sever links with experience. It permeates religious, social and personal matters, but it often does not come to the front; rather, it hides itself in the somewhat mysterious revelation of the patterns by which people and events shape themselves. While appreciating the differences between the 'lower' and the 'higher', we must understand that practical or intellectual, apparent or hidden, 'small' or 'great' are merely theoretical divisions, and do not make any difference to real wisdom. Wisdom as a whole deals both with

---

[1] The meanings of 'religion' from its Latin roots as given in dictionaries are, for example, *'religare'* (to bind back), *'religio'* (reverence, binding), and *'religere'* (to re-read, to ponder). In a typical English context, the word from such a root normally indicates a kind of bond between God and human beings, and implies the human understanding of, and relation to, the divine, while the divine is primarily understood as 'supernatural' and 'superhuman'. Religion as traditionally and narrowly understood has been dramatically extended by modern scholars. When discussing religion and human nature, for example, Keith Ward points out that most religions 'relate human life in some way to a supramaterial realm of spirit or mind, whether spirit is conceived as one or many, as substantial or as in continual flux' (Keith Ward: *Religion & Human Nature*, Oxford: Oxford University Press, 1998, p.1). However, in this book the author attempts to expand the reference of religion further, not only to the outer boundaries of theocentric systems but also to the essence of non-theocentric doctrines, defining religion as an enterprise of seeking to break through human limitations: physical (longevity or immortality), intellectual (sagehood) and spiritual (godliness).

practical matters and with more fundamental and philosophical issues. It is an important part of the meaning and value of life, and is one of the chief reasons enabling the continuity of humanity both as the race and as individual persons.

Questions concerning the nature, source and functioning of human wisdom have attracted the attention of many scholars from different disciplines. However, studies of wisdom are often engaged as a purely textual examination of one single tradition and do not pay sufficient attention to the variety of philosophical implications in a comparative perspective. Different from them in one way or another, this book is primarily a philosophical attempt at a synthetic study, in the sense that it is intended to examine the theoretical structure and philosophical application of wisdom in the early Confucian and Israelite traditions. On the one hand, it is a textual study by nature, since it draws extensively upon a number of historically and theoretically important texts or 'books' contained in the Confucian classics and preserved in the Hebrew Bible or in ancient Greek deuterocanonical texts that are specifically concerned with wisdom issues. On the other hand, it is an attempt to study wisdom in a comparative perspective and to set early Confucian and Israelite wisdom in a hermeneutical framework. To understand clearly what ancient Confucian and Israelite wisdom is, we have to resort to extant documentary materials, which preserve or partially convey the form of wisdom thinking in early China and Israel, and to the examination of the structural characteristics of particular messages, the semantic environment of special characters or graphs, and the contextual meanings of specific passages.

Early Confucian and Israelite Traditions

In the remote past the world saw the rise of different civilizations, particularly in India, Greece, Israel and China, each of which became the source of a particular cultural tradition from which arose creative thinking that reached its peak during what Karl Jaspers names the 'Axial Age', a period ranging between around 800 to 200BCE.[2] Acknowledging that the definition of the 'Axial Age' might be of relevance to our mapping of various wisdom traditions, we must add that the human search for wisdom was not confined to this period; it extended back into the past, and forwards into later history. It is less appropriate too to term this search a 'period', because we can hardly give any precise starting and ending date; rather, the human search for wisdom is more like a great river, running ceaselessly through time and space, or like a long chain with each period or age of human history functioning as a link of it, comparatively either more crucial or more ordinary. It is through these links, however, that the continuity of human civilization was forged and the diversity of the human way of life developed. To understand human history, philosophy and

---

[2] Karl Jaspers: *The Origin and Goal of History*, New Haven: Yale University Press, 1953.

culture, we must study the sources, particularities and commonalities of wisdom as manifested in each culture or tradition of human beings.

What are of most interest here are two particular traditions from two different sources, namely the early Israelite tradition and the early Confucian tradition. These two traditions are both philosophical and religious. Modern scholarship tends to distinguish clearly the religious from the philosophical, the sacred from the profane. One potential challenge to the theme of this book would be the argument that wisdom in ancient Israel is primarily religious, while Confucian thought is essentially secular or ethical. This is a narrow vision of the history of ideas. As a matter of fact, the distinctions cannot be applied to ancient systems of thought at all, either in Israel or in China. In classical China there was no special word for 'religion' or 'philosophy'. Rather, different characters were used to denote different aspects of a particular tradition: *zong* links ancestors with their descendants, *jiao* points to the transmission of ancient teachings, and *Dao* denotes its (mysterious) essence or unfathomable doctrine. None of these words distinguishes between religious and philosophical, educational and political, ethical and ritualistic. They refer to the same and whole system that operates in history and society, a system that is to a great extent moralized.

Ancient Israelites and Greeks did not think the distinction so important either that they should use a word to denote what we mean by religion today; as Paul Griffiths has rightly observed, 'there is no significant biblical term (in Hebrew or Greek) naturally and consistently rendered by *religio* (in Latin) or *religion* (in English)'.[3] As in the Confucian tradition, however, we can read discourses in the Israelite tradition covering all areas of life, both religious and secular, philosophical speculative and religious prescriptive. We do not deny that these discourses are essentially religious by nature, because their underlying theme is 'the fear of the LORD' (Prov. 9:10), and their purpose and contents are determined by the faith in the LORD's creation and activity: 'faith in the stability of the elementary relationships between man and woman, faith in the similarity of men and of their reactions, faith in the reliability of the orders which support human life and thus, implicitly or explicitly, faith in God who put these orders into operation'.[4] However, this does not mean that early Israelite thinkers deliberately excluded intellectual reasoning and philosophical examining of a general nature from their discourses. We have clear evidence to show that, in the early Israelite tradition, just as in many other ancient cultures, faith and knowledge are not separable, and divine experiences are also experiences of the world.

The Confucian and Israelite wisdom thinking is nevertheless different from what

---

[3] Paul J. Griffiths: *Problems of Religious Diversity*, Oxford and Malden: Blackwell Publishers, Inc. 2001, p.3. The usual Greek word for cultic or ceremonial actions that express reverence for the gods is *thrēskeia*, although it often bears a negative sense when used of deviant or suspect cults. Another word *eusebeia* refers to 'piety', reverence for the gods and for the social or moral order which they uphold. This word is translated in Proverbs 1:7 as 'the fear of the LORD'.

[4] Gerhard von Rad: *Wisdom in Israel*, trans. James D. Martin, Nashville: Abingdon, 1972, pp.62–3.

we know as 'philosophy' proper in the West. In the Western intellectual tradition developed from ancient Greeks, philosophy is defined clearly as a form of analytical and synthetical reasoning. Judged by this criterion, we have to say that most Confucian and Israelite wisdom texts do not have a systematic treatment of their subject matter. Their way of thinking is in general engaged in brief and somewhat disconnected sayings, expressed in the form of aphorisms, apothegms or allusions and illustrations. There are plenty of statements that are suggestive rather than articulative. However, this difference does not automatically disqualify them from being philosophical. Suggestive statements and brief dialogues do not necessarily mean that they lack philosophical reasoning and intellectual depth. Rather this only indicates that they pursue truth in a different manner, a manner different from a narrow sense of 'philosophical'. To reveal the distinctive methodology as used in ancient Confucian and Israelite tradition, we must make a careful intellectual reconstruction of what has been taken as Confucian and Israelite wisdom and of how this wisdom has been reached and employed.

The reason we have chosen these two wisdom traditions for comparison is threefold. First, they stand as two major influences on human civilizations. The early Israelite wisdom tradition, as contained in the Christian Bible essentially as the Old Testament, has not only moulded the mindset of Jews, Christians and Muslims, but also as part of 'Western' civilization has fundamentally shaped the modern world, while the early Confucian ideas and ideals became the backbone of Chinese culture, sufficiently powerful to determine the way of life in East Asia. Secondly, both have bequeathed rich resources concerning wisdom. Some people tend to talk about wisdom as purely concerned with practical matters, having little to do with religious faith, philosophical reasoning and psychological emotions. In fact, as we have argued, wisdom in early Israel and China is by nature both social, political and educational and religious, philosophical and psychological. It arises from, and is indeed the refined or examined form of, an experiential accumulation of believing, knowing, reasoning and feeling. Thirdly, in their concept of wisdom a cosmic ethic tendency is demonstrated. In some streams of modern (Western) philosophy wisdom is distinguished from knowledge and from cosmology, but that way of making distinctions does not sit well with the early Hebrew and Chinese conception, in which wisdom is closely related to, or fundamentally based on, knowledge and experience, and is directly concerned with human reflection on, and experience of, the cosmic order.

Wisdom in Early Confucian and Israelite Traditions

Wisdom and the search for wisdom occupy a particular position in the Confucian and Judeo-Christian enterprises. In his typology of world religions Hans Küng classifies Judaism, Christianity and Islam as *prophetic religions*, while Chinese religions, including Confucianism, are seen as *religions of wisdom*, but he also stresses that 'there is a wisdom literature' in the former and that the latter have 'something akin to *prophetic*' features.[5] On the basis of an understanding of philosophy and religion as various kinds of 'teaching', some modern New Confucians consider all philosophical and religious systems in the world to be 'wisdom or intellectual traditions' (*zhi de chuantong*), and thus establish a particular framework for comparative studies, especially between Confucianism and the Judeo-Christian tradition. In both cases, wisdom is singled out as characteristic of philosophies and religions East and West, but its cosmological and ethical implications for philosophical pursuit and religious endeavour have yet to be examined. Through examining the particular expressions of wisdom by comparing these two traditions, we will be in a better position to answer such questions as what is meant by 'wisdom' and to what extent wisdom underlies philosophical and religious pursuits characteristic of the Confucian and Israelite way of life.

Wisdom undoubtedly plays an important role in philosophical contemplation and religious practices in ancient China and Israel, where the so-called 'great wisdom' and 'small wisdom' have been in interaction since the very beginning. At one level, wisdom of a practical application has been highly appreciated in the Confucian and Judeo-Christian traditions; this is typically manifested in the form of advice or instructions, maxims and proverbs contained in such classics as the *Analects* of Confucius and the Proverbs of the Hebrew Scriptures. These wise, and frequently insightful, sayings reflect what can be termed the 'reasoned search for specific ways to ensure personal well-being in everyday life, to make sense of extreme adversity and vexing anomalies'.[6] They have had an appeal for thousands of years and are still being used by a large number of people in looking for a solution to the paradoxes and perplexities of life. Unlike many current studies of wisdom, however, our study of wisdom will not be confined to practical issues. To appreciate fully such 'wisdom thinking or tradition', we will have to investigate what wisdom on a higher level or, in other words, 'great wisdom' is generated, applied and reasoned, and how it has become the backbone of the worldview concerning metaphysical, ethical and political matters, which has informed the Chinese and Israelite peoples in their search for a breakthrough in the face of human finitude.

Wisdom cannot be separated from other aspects of thought in early Israel and China either. The connection between wise teachings and theological matters has added a profound 'sacred' meaning to wisdom. Early Confucian and Israelite traditions both confirm that there is a sacred dimension of wisdom, but they each in their discourses adopt a particular path to the sacredness of wisdom.[7] Israelite wisdom is part of an overall theology, although with its own characteristics, and the

---

[5] Hans Küng and Julia Ching: *Christianity and Chinese Religions*, New York: Doubleday and London: Collins Publishers, 1989, pp.xv, xvi.

[6] James L. Crenshaw: *Old Testament Wisdom: An Introduction,* revised and enlarged, Louisville: Westminster John Knox Press, 1998, p.3.

[7] For a fuller discussion of the sacredness of wisdom in the Israelite and Confucian traditions, and the differences between them as demonstrated in their wisdom texts, please refer to Chapter 7.

wisdom teaching is presented as a testimony to faith in YHWH or the Lord. 'Fear of the LORD' is fundamental to the Israelite tradition, and is also a key to its wisdom literature, as it is stated clearly that 'To God belong wisdom and power' (Job 12:13). As a way of encoding a lived experience, the sayings of the sages or wise men recorded their encounters with reality and their insights into the world and human beings. The understanding that wisdom is a 'path to life' (Prov. 10:17) connects Israelite wisdom with their ethics. While some sages deplored the fact that wrongdoers enjoyed a luxurious life, while the righteous suffered bad fortune, the majority of them proclaimed a just retribution when the good would be rewarded and the evil punished, which has become one of the pillars supporting the Israelite view of the world and life.

Wisdom in early Israelite tradition is a paradigm of cosmology, knowledge and ethics, which is both deeply formative of subsequent traditions and yet distinct from them. It has been recognized among modern scholars that many of the themes embedded in wisdom literature were not picked up in later debates and remain tied to a cosmological ethics predicated upon the divine order of the world. The chief critical questions which have arisen in recent debates regarding the Hebrew sapiential tradition, and which may offer a fresh analytical perspective on wisdom in the Confucian tradition, centre on the nature of knowledge, the relation between human knowing and the divine or cosmic order, and the social locus of the tradition of insight and teaching represented in the wisdom books. They provide a valuable resource for a comparative study with classical Confucianism which itself looks to a cosmological and ethical grounding for wisdom and has proved resistant to the kinds of metaphysical developments which were to become characteristic of the Neo-Confucian tradition in later China's intellectual history.

Wisdom in ancient China and Israel can be set against the background of education, because most Confucian and Israelite authors or compilers of the so-called 'wisdom texts' were originally educators, and the teachings on wisdom had their root in an educational context. Various scholars have traced the origins of the Confucians (*ru*) to a government office (*situ zhi guan*, Ministry of Education) during the early Zhou dynasty (1045?–256BCE), whose function was to 'assist the ruler to follow the way of the yin-yang and to enlighten [the people] by education'.[8] Along with the decline of cultic practices and the rise of rationalism during the Spring and Autumn period (770–476BCE), a large number of *ru* departed from the officially assigned profession, and entered various areas of social life. The *ru* became distinctive for their skills in various kinds of ritual, and in official and private education. The character *ru* was then gradually extended to become a specific term for those who had skills of ritual, history, poetry, music, mathematics and archery, and who lived off their knowledge of all kinds of ceremonies and of many other subjects.[9]

---

[8] *Hanshu*, Beijing: Zhonghua Shuju, 1998, p.1728.

[9] Chen Lai: *Gudai Zongjiao yu Lunli – Rujia Sixiang de Genyuan* (Ancient Religion and Ethics – The Origin of the Confucian Thought), Beijing: Sanlian Shudian, 1996, p.350.

The case for ancient Israel is more complicated. Ludwig Köhler confirms that although 'What we think of as school and schooling was alien to the Hebrew even until the latest period', wisdom and practical training did exist, developing from familial training provided by parents, and dealing 'with the rights which belong to each man as regards pieces of land, pastures, inheritances and such like', and concerning 'the rites, the abstentions and actions which accompanied sacrificial festivals; participation in the covenant community; the sentences, customs and traditions in cases of disagreement, and their adjustment, and those appropriate to misdemeanours and crimes and their atonement; the ordering and controlling of public affairs', covering 'every conceivable aspect and manifestation of common life'.[10] When and how this training tradition developed into formal education and even became the privilege of wisdom schools, however, is a matter open to debate. The *Theological Dictionary of the Old Testament* confirms that 'After the beginning of the monarchy, it is commonly understood that the root *ḥkm* refers above all to the academic wisdom of the court and the ideals of the class entrusted with it', and 'According to the list in 1 K. 5:9–12(4:29–34), Solomon's wisdom was demonstrated in the "literary" field: v.12(32) represents the King as the author of 3000 proverbs and 1005 songs; v.13(33), by contrast, suggests encyclopaedic scholarship in prose, involving lists introducing an organization of natural phenomena.'[11] Katharine Dell also observes that 'The wisdom enterprise clearly has its own distinctive character and this had led many to assume that a separate group of sages existed, quite distinct from other groups such as prophets and priests, even though existing alongside them.'[12] In a variety of early Hebrew writings, wisdom is indeed often associated with courtiers and royal counsellors (2 Samuel 15–17; Daniel 1–6), and with teachers (Prov. 9:9–12; Jeremiah 8:8–9). However, no consensus so far has been reached among modern scholars concerning whether or not there was a wisdom movement in ancient Israel and whether or not wisdom texts were composed by the royal court or teachers. For example, while James Crenshaw is convinced that 'the several arguments seem to justify the conclusion that a group of professional sages existed in ancient Israel',[13] Roger Whybray argues that wisdom texts were the product of an

---

[10] Ludwig Köhler: *Hebrew Man*, trans. Peter R. Ackroyd, London: SCM Press, 1956, pp.76–9.

[11] *Theological Dictionary of the Old Testament*, ed. G. Johnnes Botterweck and Helmer Ringgren, trans. David E. Green, vol. IV, Grand Rapids, Michigan: William B. Eerdmans Publishing Company, 1980, pp.373, 375.

[12] Katharine Dell: *'Get Wisdom, Get Insight': An Introduction to Israel's Wisdom Literature*, Macon: Smyth & Helwys Publishing, Inc., 2000, p.10. Dell seems to attempt a different interpretation, namely to 'see wisdom as a wider thought-world, not confined to intellectuals and therefore not restricted to a school context. Wisdom could be seen as basic education undertaken in families, in the home or in local schools, and hence being a major formative influence on all kinds of oral transmission, influencing other areas of Israelite life …'. On the other hand, wisdom can also be 'regarded as a formative literary influence at, say, the time of the monarchy or as a later literary redaction of earlier material primarily in the post-exilic period' (p.11).

[13] James Crenshaw 1998, p.21.

ongoing intellectual tradition in ancient Israel rather than a distinct group of sages who were teachers and court counsellors, and particularly criticizes the 'royal court' theory as too dependent upon presuppositions derived from non-biblical sources and not supported by the internal evidence itself.[14]

Another important feature of Confucian and Israelite wisdom education is its radiation from court education to private schools. Confucians drew upon earlier court education materials and edited them into textbooks for their own use.[15] Modern scholars in general recognize the role played by King Solomon and his court in the initial formation of the wisdom tradition in Israel, and have conjectured that a formal and sustained 'group' of 'wise men' flourished under the patronage of the king.[16] If this is correct, court settings were most probably the background of the majority of the earlier wise sayings in Hebrew wisdom literature that were late circulated among 'wise men' and their audience, and it is suggested that wisdom in ancient Israel 'stands for skill learned from others, and is associated above all with training and schools'.[17] It seems clear that the origin of Confucianism and the source of Israelite wisdom converged in that both were the product of intensive intellectual activities involving both state and private education. Using or collecting raw materials from these activities, Confucian and Israelite teachers of a later age constructed or reshaped an understanding of wisdom, and extended the education of wise teachings to a wider range of social classes. Through editing and interpreting, they created

---

[14] Roger N. Whybray: *The Intellectual Tradition of the Old Testament,* Berlin and New York: W. de Gruyter, 1974, and *Wealth and Poverty in the Book of Proverbs*, JSOT Press, Sheffield, 1990.

[15] Most of the Confucian classics had clear court education sources. Part of the *Book of Changes* was the notes made by court diviners who conducted divination on behalf of the king. The *Book of Documents* contains a great number of statements made by kings or high officials. While a substantial part of the *Book of Poetry* was collected from common people, there are a good number of poems that are actually hymns for court ceremonies. The core of the *Spring and Autumn Annals* was based on the official chronicle of the State of Lu during the period from 721 to 481BCE. All these point to an affinity between Confucian texts and official documents either of the Zhou court or of the courts of feudal states, and to a successive linkage between Confucian masters and their predecessors such as court officials or educators.

[16] For example, James M. Efird states that 'Most studies of the wisdom movement point to the person of Solomon as the one who gave impetus to this phenomenon in Israelite thought … and it is quite probable that the court of Solomon was the place where the first formal and sustained group of "wise men" flourished in Israel's history' (James M. Efird: *Biblical Books of Wisdom*, Eugene: Wipf and Stock Publishers, 2001, pp.14–15). When discussing 'the influence of a wider thought-world on the development of Israelite wisdom', Katharine Dell argues for caution: 'while the court of Solomon seems a likely contender in Israel for such activity, we should not forget the "men of Hezekiah" (Prov. 25:1) and other possible later court contexts. There may alternatively have been a slower infiltration of wisdom ideas into the early thought of Israel than simply cultural interchange at a court level … which led indirectly to wisdom influence in the form of experiential knowledge and ethical norms'. However, Dell does not deny the connection between wisdom tradition and court settings, acknowledging that 'A more sophisticated and literary tradition however also emerged, one that was the preserve of a more literate class, and it is this tradition that may have flourished in either court, temple or school in an Israelite context' (Katharine Dell, 2000, pp.109–10).

[17] *Eerdmans Dictionary of the Bible* (David Noel Freedman, editor-in-chief), Grand Rapids, Michigan/Cambridge, UK: William B. Eerdmans Publishing Company, 2000, p.1328.

'new' wisdom traditions, either oral or written, for educating the young and transmitting the tradition, suitable both for (formal) education and for community learning.

Studies of Confucian and Israelite Wisdom

Until relatively recently, however, wisdom, either as a literary genre or as a tradition or way of thinking did not attract much attention within traditional Judeo-Christian scholarship on the Old Testament where the central concerns were, in terms of priority, the Torah and Prophets for Judaism, and the fulfilment of ancient prophecy in Jesus Christ and the law for Christians. Early modern Western theologians generally overlooked it, believing that the wisdom books of the Old Testament offered little, if anything at all, for a systematic discussion of sin, grace and redemption. Wisdom came to the centre of Christian scholarship only about 40 to 50 years ago. Since then, the study of biblical literature has gradually generated an active interest in wisdom, and attracted considerable attention from various kinds of scholars: theologians, philosophers and historians. This development has even been called the 'rediscovery of the Hebrew wisdom tradition' and judged as 'having particular value for the spiritual quest of our time'. Gerhard von Rad marked the beginning of this new interest; in his work, *Wisdom in Israel* (Nashville: Abingdon, 1972) he pioneered a new direction for the study of biblical wisdom. This was followed by Roger N. Whybray's *The Intellectual Tradition in the Old Testament* (Berlin and New York: de Gruyter, 1974), James Crenshaw's *Studies in Ancient Israelite Wisdom* (New York: Ktav Publishing House, Inc., 1976), a collection entitled *Wisdom and Knowledge: Papin Festschrift* (ed. J. Armenti, Philadelphia: Villanova Press, 1976), and Roland E. Murphy's *Wisdom Literature* (in the series of *The Forms of the Old Testament Literature*, Volume XIII, Grand Rapids: William B. Eerdmans Publishing Company, 1981). More recent publications on the topic include *Wisdom in Ancient Israel* (ed. John Day, Robert P. Gordon and H.G.M. Williamson, Cambridge: Cambridge University Press, 1995), Stuart Weeks's *Early Israelite Wisdom* (Oxford: Clarendon, 1994), Roland E. Murphy's *The Tree of Life: An Exploration of Biblical Wisdom Literature* (2nd edn, Grand Rapids: Eerdmans Publishing Company, 1996), James Crenshaw's *Old Testament Wisdom: An Introduction* (revised and enlarged, Louisville: Westminster John Knox Press, 1998), Richard J. Clifford's *The Wisdom Literature* (Nashville: Abingdon, 1998), and Katharine Dell's *'Get Wisdom, Get Insight': An Introduction to Israel's Wisdom Literature* (Macon: Smyth & Helwys Publishing, Inc., 2000), to name but a few. These researches have substantially deepened our knowledge, and extended our understanding, of wisdom in ancient Israel.

Parallel to this, there is also progress in the study of Confucian wisdom as embodied in a religious and intellectual tradition. Earlier views from a Christian lens have been challenged and substantially revised, and a more general description focusing on beliefs and practices surrounding the sacred is now widely preferred. Various translations and textual studies with detailed comments on the Confucian classics have enabled English readers to examine more clearly the wisdom of the Confucian masters, particularly the *Analects of Confucius* and *Mencius* (trans. D.C. Lau, Penguin Classics, 1979, 1970), *Transmitters and Creators: Chinese Commentators and Commentaries on the 'Analects'* (John Makeham, Harvard University Asia Center/Harvard East Asian Monographs, 2004), *Xunzi: A Translation and Study of the Complete Works* (trans. John Knoblock, Stanford University Press, vols 1–3, 1988–94), *Ta Hsüeh* and *Chung Yung* (*The Highest Order of Cultivation* and *On the Practice of the Mean*, trans. Andrew Plaks, Penguin Classics, 2003); and *Zhouyi: the Book of Changes* (trans. Richard Rutt, Curzon Press, 1996). Scholarly studies of Confucianism as a highly moralized intellectual tradition have also gained momentum in recent years, and a number of books have in one way or another explored the wisdom dimension of early Confucianism, highlighting its characteristics and special features in comparison with other wisdom thinking ways, either in China or in the world.[18]

As far as comparative studies of wisdom are concerned, there are a number of approaches by which we can come to the issue of significance. It can be done through bringing together two different key concepts in two different traditions, as I have attempted in one of my earlier publications *Confucianism and Christianity – A Comparative Study of Jen and Agape*. It can also be engaged through a comparison between two pieces of classical texts or two leading figures from the two sides, as has been attempted in a recent publication on the Greek *siren* and the Chinese sage, Part I of which is a comparison between the Confucian *Classic of Poetry* and the Greek *Odyssey*, while Part II explores the similarities and divergences between Thucydides and Sima Qian.[19] In terms of comparison between early Hebrew and Confucian texts, we may gain some insight from H.H. Rowley, who delivered his Jordan lectures in comparative religion at SOAS, London in 1954 and then published them as a book entitled *Prophecy and Religion in Ancient China and Israel*. This book starts with 'The Nature of Prophecy', followed by chapters on 'The Prophet as Statesman', 'The

---

[18] The following are of particular value for a study of wisdom in classical Confucianism: *Confucianism: The Dynamics of Tradition* (ed. Irene Eber, Macmillan, 1986); *Thinking Through Confucius* (David Hall and Roger Ames, Albany: State University of New York Press, 1987); *Confucian Ethics of the Axial Age – A Reconstruction under the Aspect of the Breakthrough Toward Postconventional Thinking* (Heiner Roetz, Albany: State University of New York Press, 1993); *The Ways of Confucianism – Investigations in Chinese Philosophy* (David Nivison, Chicago: Open Court, 1996); *Mysticism and Kingship in China: The Heart of Chinese Wisdom* (Julia Ching, Cambridge University Press, 1997); *Transformation of the Confucian Way* (John Berthrong, Westview, 1998); *An Introduction to Confucianism* (Xinzhong Yao, Cambridge University Press, 2000); *The Way of Virtue: The Ancient Wisdom of Confucius Adapted for a New Age* (James Vollbracht, Humanics New Age, 1997) and *Confucius and the Analects: New Essays* (Bryan Van Norden, Oxford University Press, 2001).

[19] Steven Shankam and Stephen Durrant: *The Siren and the Sage – Knowledge and Wisdom in Ancient Greece and China*, London and New York: Cassell, 2000.

Prophet as Reformer', 'The Prophet and the Golden Age', and 'The Prophet and Worship', and finishes with a chapter on 'The Prophet and God', which elaborates on the divine destiny of Israelite prophets and Chinese Sages.[20] Although some of his views have been challenged by a number of scholars who point out that one of the reasons why Rowley unfortunately wrongly associated Chinese sages with prophets rather than with the wise is that he failed 'to appreciate wisdom';[21] the way he approaches the theme is inspiring: he examines religious and intellectual prophecy in biblical Israel and classical China, not as a simple and static phenomenon, but as a dialectic relationship with important social, moral and religious dimensions. Recent years have also seen a number of comparative studies which, although mostly general in nature, are partly concerned with wisdom issues in Confucianism and/or ancient Israel. Focusing on Israelite wisdom in the Old Testament, John Eaton's *The Contemplative Face of Old Testament Wisdom in the Context of World Religions* (London and Philadelphia: SCM Press and Trinity Press International, 1989) places the biblical texts in parallel with similar sayings and ideas from other traditions in the world. Ray Billington's *East of Existentialism – The Tao of the West* (London: Unwin Hyman, 1990) sheds light on the thinking in the East and West on the most fundamental issues. *Christianity and Chinese Religions* (Hans Küng and Julia Ching, New York: Doubleday, 1989) engages in a series of dialogues between Chinese religions including Confucianism, and Christianity including ancient Israelite ideas.

Defining Wisdom

An examination of two different types of wisdom thinking enables us to have a better understanding of the nature of wisdom. What is wisdom? Where does it come from? What functions has it played in scriptural traditions? Many scholars have already devoted great effort to uncovering answers to these questions, and ventured a number of new approaches or new perspectives. They define wisdom either specifically as the ability to cope with life problems, or as enlightened understanding arising from intellectual contemplation, or as practical knowledge of the laws of life and of the world based on experience, or as the quest for self-understanding and for mastery of the world, or seeing it more generally in terms of a philosophical way of thinking or of a religious principle of living.

As far as the study of wisdom is concerned, Confucianism has certain advantages over the Israelite tradition. Confucianism has been considered a tradition of wisdom, the teachings of which are of paramount importance to the way of life. Any study of

---

[20] H.H. Rowley: *Prophecy and Religion in Ancient China and Israel,* University of London/The Athlone Press, 1956.

[21] Nathaniel Yung-tse Yen: 'Prophet sage and wise man: a comparative study of intellectual tradition in ancient China and Israel'. PhD thesis, Drew University, Madison, 1977, p.307.

Confucian texts cannot but involve their wisdom teachings. On reflecting on Confucian discussions of wisdom as contained in its early texts, we learn that Confucian wisdom is characterized by four features. First, wisdom is either related to knowledge or is derived from the higher grade of knowledge. The epistemological foundation enables Confucian wisdom to be differentiated from the mystic understanding of wisdom that attributes wisdom solely to mysterious intuition or sudden enlightenment. Secondly, wisdom is closely related to, or even determined by, virtue, frequently represented by benevolence or humaneness (*ren*), the chief of Confucian virtues. Wisdom and benevolence or humaneness together constitute the Confucian ideal which is in contrast to a theocentric one that normally confines wisdom to the revelation of God or gods. Thirdly, wisdom is expected to bring joy to the people, for only a person of wisdom is believed to be able to enjoy real pleasure and have real joy. The joyful character makes Confucian wisdom diverge from that of ascetics who believe that wisdom comes only from enduring physical and mental suffering. Fourthly, wisdom has a fundamental similarity to the way of water, constantly running, and prompts people to act according to the Way, which demonstrates that Confucian wisdom differs from some naturalist doctrines that define wisdom as completely following the way of nature and as leading a submissive and quiet course of life.

Although wisdom is of paramount importance for Confucianism as a whole, ironically the wisdom nature of Confucian teachings has not led to substantial researches in the modern era that focus on the Confucian paradigm of wisdom itself. In this respect, a great deal of groundbreaking work has been done in terms of the Israelite wisdom literature, as contained in the Old Testament of the Bible. As far as the nature of wisdom in the Old Testament is concerned, prominent opinions range from 'practical knowledge of the laws of life and of the world, based on experience',[22] to 'a set of ideas, or an attitude to life', or 'innate intelligence'.[23] Concerning its source, a variety of suggestions have been put forward such as that wisdom comes from 'the quest of self-understanding in terms of relationships',[24] or that it results 'from the effort to discover order in human life'.[25] These scholarly opinions attempt to pin biblical wisdom on a map either of human intelligence or of human responses to the call from God. Typically Israelite thinking is dominated by salvation history; the world's creation by YHWH, the teachings of Patriarchs, the Exodus experience and the Sinai covenant are all parts of the narrative about divine intervention and about the warning of the disaster or punishment if YHWH is betrayed. However, as many scholars have pointed out, in the texts of wisdom the

---

[22] Gerhard von Rad: *Old Testament Theology*, vol. 1, New York: Harper & Row, 1967, p.418.

[23] Whybray, 1974, pp.72, 7.

[24] James Crenshaw: *Stdies in Ancient Israelite Wisdom*, New York: Ktav Publishing House Inc., 1976, p.484.

[25] John G. Gammie, Walter A. Brueggemann, W. Lee Humphreys and James M. Ward (eds): *Israelite Wisdom: Theological and Literary Essays in Honor of Samuel Terrien*, Missoula, Montana: Scholars Press, 1978, p.35.

elements of historical narrative are notably absent.[26] Rather, the texts are mostly devoted to the daily events of an individual life, in contrast to the central theme in other texts, namely the salvation history of the Israelite people.[27] One interpretation of this absence is that Israel inherited her wisdom thought from a wide range of thinking on wisdom and the texts written in her canon reflect more an international than a national character. However, it can also be interpreted in another way, a more theologically coherent way. The divine intervention is *hidden* in the texts of wisdom, in contrast to other types of Hebrew Scriptures where it is highlighted. In this sense these texts did not depart from salvation narratives, but skilfully wove them into the solution of more practical matters and daily events. The focus is on the 'worldly sphere', in which humans have a more independent role, to enable them to think of their own life, and to draw their own lessons from successes and failures.

Based on these researches, this book aims to examine wisdom from a comparative perspective. From this perspective wisdom can be defined in terms of knowledge, ability/skill and insight, but it can also be taken as a way of life and a path to human destiny. It is derived from human observation of the world, natural or social, but it is also the result of human reflection on the hidden 'laws' that are only manifested through the sequences of events, and through the function of social institutions.

From a comparative perspective, this book sees wisdom as a threefold enterprise. First, wisdom is a thinking way, in which human relationships with the external world, with other people in a social context and with spiritual authority are contemplated, speculated upon and analysed. Wisdom thinking is distinct from other kinds of thinking in the sense that it searches for the best way to cope with life based on wisely calculating all factors involved and anticipating the possible consequences, spiritual or material, bad or good, as guidelines for action. Secondly, wisdom is a tradition that grows in the transmission of past knowledge and experience. Wisdom tradition is enriched through each generation that adds its own knowledge and experience to the enterprise. Wisdom tradition defines the way of life, in the sense that it has been formalized as legal codes, mores and customs, which have a disciplining and forceful power to impose on individuals in choosing particular courses of action. Thirdly, wisdom is a kind of literature or text that theoretically reflects wisdom thinking and records wisdom tradition in a condensed form. A wisdom text is normally the result of several generations' efforts in collecting,

---

[26] 'In any attempt to outline a discussion of Biblical faith it is the wisdom literature which offers the chief difficulty because it does not fit into the type of faith exhibited in the historical and prophetic literatures. In it there is no explicit history, election or covenant' (E. Wright: *God Who Acts*, London: SCM Press, 1952, p.105).

[27] 'Within Proverbs, Job, and Ecclesiastes one looks in vain for the dominant themes of Yahwistic thought: the exodus from Egypt, election of Israel, the Davidic covenant, the Mosaic legislation, the patriarchal narratives, the divine control of history, the movement toward a glorious moment when right will triumph. Instead, the reader encounters in these three books *a different world of thought*, one that stands apart so impressively that some scholars have described that literary corpus as an alien body within the Bible' (James Crenshaw, 1998, p.21).

editing or compiling existing materials, written or oral, and it presents a loosely or a systematically compiled 'book' that is normally intended to be a textbook for education or as general reading for the public.

The division of wisdom into the above mentioned three types is made from the point of view of form. In fact these forms are intertwined and must be seen as three facets of the same wisdom. Therefore, to study wisdom, we will also have to go to the content and context in which wisdom exists and operates. From this viewpoint, wisdom can be understood as a reflection on the world order that makes insightful knowledge meaningful and possible, and as an intellectual development that springs from a careful combination of internal intelligence and external investigation.

Wisdom and the World Order

The world we live in is full of mysteries and wonders, to which there are no ready answers or explanations. Are these mysteries and wonders the reflection of an original universal order, to which we have no easy access? If there is such an order, why did it come into being, and how does it work? Is the order essentially of a divine or a natural origin and nature? Investigation into these questions and into the ways to cope with the world and how to make use of natural and social 'laws' or 'orders' for human purposes marked the beginning of human civilization and is the power driving humans to search for 'wisdom'. Wisdom is a collective term, covering many facets or dimensions of human knowledge, understanding, insight, skill and ability. It may refer to the accumulated knowledge and experience, by which some people become 'wise'; it may also imply special skills and abilities through which some complete their tasks more quickly, efficiently and successfully. Whatever form it may take, it is most likely based on an understanding that there is a final order or pattern in the physical or metaphysical world that determines the sequence of events and the different stages of development or evolution. While in Confucianism the order or Way is either moral or natural, which in the work of Xunzi is described as *tian xing you chang* 'There is a constant order in the course of Heaven' (Xunzi, 17:1), in Israel the order is primarily associated with the Lord and his creation, depicted in the 'Torah' (*tōrā*) as the divine law or instruction according to which Israel was to live as stipulated in the covenant. For the Israelites the world order was created by YHWH, eternal and unchangeable, as it is said in the Book of ben Sira that 'He arranged his works in an eternal order' (Sir. 16:27), and will be continually so as he wishes, as evidenced in Genesis where YHWH promised that 'While the earth remains, seedtime and harvest, cold and heat, summer and winter, day and night, shall not cease' (Genesis 8:22). This is, in a theological language, an echo of what is said as the 'constancy' of the world in Confucianism.

It is clear that both Confucians and the Israelites are confident that if this so-called 'constant order' or 'eternal order' is discerned, then rules and regulations can be established, and that by following the rules and regulations, people will find it much easier to cope with life's problems and to deal with similar situations. Those who have discovered the order are then called teachers of wisdom or 'wise men', and those who have skilfully established and employed the 'rules' and 'regulations' are revered as 'sages', 'kings' or 'sage–kings'. Rules and regulations are then morally justified and become ethical, just and righteous; people are expected to follow them and to implement them, for doing so is promised certain awards and rewards, in terms either of material happiness or of spiritual benefit.

However, as in today's world, life in ancient Israel and China did not always appear to be as simple as this. Those who followed the 'good' rules were not always able to lead a successful career, or, even worse they frequently suffered undeserved punishments, while those who disregarded rules might have enjoyed a rich and glorious life. This touches the second level of the meaning for the world order. How to apprehend the seemingly 'disordered order'? Those who attempt to reflect on such a 'disordered order' or 'unjustified justice' aim to explain why this should have happened, and how humans can derive meaning and value from it. Their discoveries may thus become recognized as 'wisdom' or 'insight' of a higher rank.

Different societies and cultures have developed different ways to carry out the investigation and to formalize their own 'rules', which lead to different 'forms' or 'types' of wisdom. However, underlying all these forms, is an attempt to unlock the secrets of the world and life, and to discover or understand the 'order' that regulates the world. Through the lines and paragraphs of Israelite wisdom texts and Confucian classics we can read a fundamental belief that there is a world order, an order to natural events and to the day-to-day activities of human beings that is like an invisible hand predetermining current situations and the future. Both Israelite and Confucian thinkers believed that the knowledge of this order enabled them to have insights into seemingly disorganized things and matters, to grasp the laws of the natural and the social world, and to discharge their duties successfully. The authors of the so-called 'wisdom texts' strongly opposed the disorder currently prevailing in life, having serious concerns about the chaos or disruption that was dominant in their times. They attempted to make sense of the disorder, and to take wisdom as a way, a particularly effective way so it was believed, to the order, or to the restoration of the order, of the world.

Can this order be fully understood or followed? On different grounds most Israelite teachers and Confucian masters generally believed that, however hidden and complicated, the order could be known in one way or another. At the same time they were fully aware of the elements of mystery and uncertainty. While some Confucians attributed the unknown to the Way or the Destiny that was beyond ordinary comprehension, most of them would admit that eventually 'learning below will be able to penetrate what is above' (*Analects*, 14:35). For some of the Israelite sages, this question had more serious consequences for their interpretation of wisdom. Believing that the order was bestowed by YHWH the Lord, they wondered if, without divine revelation, humans would ever be able to 'penetrate' the designs of God, know the depth of the order, and this led some of them finally to admit that the creator and the created order were 'great beyond our knowledge' (Job 36:26).

A good understanding of the world order is, at least partly, conditional upon intellectual training, the exercises of which enable humans to sharpen their faculties and to discover the sequence of events and phenomena. Through the Confucian and Israelite discourses wisdom has become a living tradition and a body of literature, and is closely associated with a particular understanding of reality. In Confucian and Israelite wisdom exercises, the ultimate reality is twofold: the religious and the intellectual. The former, whether called God's creation, the Order, the Torah, *Tian* or the Mandate of Heaven, is believed to be 'out there', challenging humans to search for and to find it, or compelling them simply to hold it in awe and to conform to it, while the latter, whether termed Wisdom or Truth or Law, is attainable only in acknowledging, and contemplating upon, the universal order or the way. In this sense, wisdom is a reward for those who have found harmony or union with the ultimate reality.

The special requirement for wisdom transmission called into being a particular group of people, 'teachers' of biblical Israel and 'masters' (*zi*) in pre-Qin China. As wisdom teachers, these people were believed to be able to communicate messages between the divine and the secular realms, and between the sacred past and the disoriented present, in which the sacredness of wisdom is portrayed and manifested. In Israel, a wisdom teacher is an intermediary whose function is to carry wisdom teaching back and forth between his audience below and the deity above. For this we can call him a 'vertical messenger'. However, there is another function a teacher is expected to perform, that is, to preserve and then deliver the teachings and lessons of the past to the present day. For this we may call him a 'horizontal messenger'. This double role is also performed by Confucian masters who not only communicate between 'what is below' and 'what is above', but also between the ancient and the present, by which wisdom traditions are formulated and transmitted.

Wisdom as the Refining of Life Experience

If there is a 'world order', universal and comprehensive, then what can humans do to conform to it? Questions have been raised with regard to the relation between knowledge, experience and wisdom within the Judeo-Christian tradition, and wisdom as such is defined by some scholars as 'practical knowledge' which plays out in the domain of justice and ethics. Personified wisdom is described in terms of dwelling together with prudence, and possessing knowledge and discretion (Prov. 8:12), which is an integral part of wisdom's association with the deity and its presence at the creation of the universe (Prov. 8:28). It is therefore acknowledged that wisdom comes not only from one's relationships with the divine, but also with one's ancestors and with others. In Proverbs both terms, *tōrā* and *miṣwāh*, are used to denote not only the law and commandment of YHWH but also the teaching and instruction of the father and mother, the representations of experience (Prov. 1:8; 7:1–2). Confucians search for the way of harmony between the cosmological 'order' and human order in the collected wisdom of the society, manifested as *li* (moral codes, customs and laws), and use them as yardsticks to distinguish good from evil, right from wrong, proper from improper. The experiential dimension of wisdom underlies an extremely reverent attitude towards the experience of the past, which are manifested in the sacred and memorable events of history for Israelites and the golden time of the ancients for Confucians. As part of wisdom experience is both outward and inward. Outwardly, experience leads to knowledge and understanding concerning external matters and relationships; inwardly, experience enriches one's inner world and leads an intelligent and ethical character. In both Confucian and Israelite traditions wisdom as inward experience is taken as a conscious activity by which humans learn how to make a better self and how best to associate themselves with the external world. Confucius' 'looking within and examining one's self' (*nei zi xing*, *Analects*, 4:17), Mengzi's 'self-examination' (*fan shen*, Mengzi, 4A:4) and Zhongyong's 'self-completion' (*cheng ji*, Zhongyong, 25) are all different types of inner experiencing. This is also echoed in Israelite wisdom texts where it is taught that 'Before you speak, learn', 'Before judgment, examine yourself', 'Before making a vow, prepare yourself' (Sir. 18:19–23). What is expressed through 'self-learning', 'self-examination' and 'self-preparation' is ways to increase one's inward experience and therefore 'wisdom'.

Wisdom is therefore more than a tradition and literature; it is an attitude towards life and a special experience of life that arises from intelligent reflection on the human past, in terms either of individuals or of the race, and is furthered by conscious activities in the social and the natural world. Traditional and modern studies of wisdom confirm that wisdom is somehow related to individual humans' or collective humanity's ageing process, where occasional intellectual understandings and experiential discoveries are brought together in rational activities to form 'moral and spiritual integrity, humility and compassion, or insight into the pragmatic, subjective, and psychological dimensions of life' which are commonly recognized as the core of wisdom.[28] This point has also been confirmed in both Confucian and Israelite traditions. Early Confucians held that wisdom is an integrated process of outer, objective and logical knowledge and inner, subjective and organic growth, which is well illustrated in Confucius's self-description, where his life is divided into five stages and each of them makes a distinctive contribution to the maturity of his wisdom and integrity (*Analects*, 2:4). In conventional Hebrew wisdom, one's becoming wise is closely associated with age: 'Age should speak; advanced years should teach wisdom' (Job 32:7). However, there is something more in Confucian and Israelite wisdom thinking than experience gained through leading a long life. For Confucius, wisdom is more than just becoming older, and the aged are not necessarily wiser than the young. In fact longevity is not associated with the wise; rather it is the by-product of a benevolent life. There is also an admirable quality in the young and

---

[28] Gisela Labouvie-Vief: 'Wisdom as integrated thought: historical and developmental perspectives', in Robert J. Sternberg (ed.), *Wisdom: its nature, origins, and development*, Cambridge University Press, 1990, p.52.

'we should hold the young in awe' (*Analects*, 9:23). For Israelites, age does not account for human wisdom either, because 'It is not only the old who are wise, not only the aged who understand what is right'; rather, 'it is the spirit in a man, the breath of the Almighty, that gives him understanding' (Job 32:7–9). As accumulated life experience, wisdom is expressed through the medium of language. Both life and language are multifaceted, as is wisdom. It is well-known that, in the European tradition, Greek terms for wisdom refer to different aspects of intellectual, moral and ordinary life, and all are very much intellectually oriented. *Sophia* refers to the gifts of a philosopher who has devoted himself to a contemplative life in pursuit of truth. *Phronesis*, or practical wisdom, refers to the quality of a statesman who is able to locate the prudent course of action and resist the urgings of the passions and the deceptions of the senses. *Episteme* refers to a form of scientific knowledge developed in those who know the nature of things and the principles governing their behaviour.[29] There are also a number of Hebrew words that are equivalent to what we call 'wisdom'; *bīnā* (understanding, intelligence), *ḥākam* (to become wise; in certain forms to make wise), *ḥākmā, hokmōt* (wisdom, skill), *śākal* (to become wise or intelligent; to have insight).[30] The root word for wisdom most frequently used in the Hebrew texts is *hkm*, which, according to R.N. Whybray, 'refers to innate intelligence of a quite general kind',[31] and which 'is expressed in a variety of abilities or skills'. Anyone who possessed these skills would be 'considered wise'.[32] The close relationship between intellectual knowledge and wisdom can be seen from the fact that the Hebrew word *da'at* (knowledge), which is derived from the root *yd'* (to know), has a close association with wisdom thinking in the Hebrew scriptures where it occurs 90 times, of which '40 times in Proverbs, 11 in Job, 8 in Ecclesiastes'.[33]

The ancient Chinese developed a fundamentally different system of writing language that originated from pictographic images and was intended to make connections between internal conception and external phenomena.[34] In earlier

---

[29] Robert J. Sternberg (ed.), *Wisdom: its nature, origins, and development,* Cambridge University Press, 1990, p.14.

[30] Robert Young: *Analytical Concordance to the Holy Bible*, 8th edn, London: United Society for Christian Literature, Lutterworth Press, 1939, pp.1059–60.

[31] R.N. Whybray, 1974, p.7.

[32] Dianne Bergant: *What are they saying about wisdom literature?* New York/Ramsey: Paulist Press, 1984, p.7.

[33] *Theological Dictionary of the Old Testament*, vol. V, 1986, p.453. 'In the Greek Bible, da'at has 21 equivalents: *gnōsis* (29 times) and *epígnōsis* (5 times), *aíshēsis* (19 times), *sýnesis* (6 times) and *epistēmē* (5 times), *boulē/boúlēma* (3 times), *sophía* (twice), and *noús, paideía, and phrónēsis* once each' (*ibid*).

[34] According to Xu Shen (30?–124?), the author of the first etymological dictionary of Chinese characters (around the year of 120), original characters were simply imitations of natural things: 'the images in the sky', 'the patterns on the earth', and 'the patterns of birds and beasts' (Duan Yucai: *Shuowen jiezi zhu* (A Commentary on Explaining Simple Graphs and Analysing Compound Characters), Hangzhou: Zhejiang Guji Chubanshe, 1998, p.753).

writing systems, such as oracle-bone inscriptions (around 13 to 15 centuries BCE) and bronze inscriptions (12 to 9 centuries BCE), the character for wisdom is a word for knowledge, also pronounced as '*zhi*', composed of a *zhi* (knowledge), a *bai* (whiteness) and a *yu* (air).[35] In later texts, this character is simplified as a word for knowledge that is also pronounced *zhi*, composed of an arrow (*shi*) and a mouth (*kou*), symbolizing that one grasps the principle or reason (*li*) of an event or phenomenon as swiftly as an arrow flies. Wisdom is believed to be an extension of knowledge. In later dictionaries a definition of *zhi* is made in association with knowledge: 'Wisdom means knowledge, [and the man of wisdom] refers to the one who has nothing unknown.'[36] Because of the identity between wisdom and knowledge, in most early Chinese philosophical and religious texts, wisdom (*zhi*) is not separated from knowledge (*zhi*), which indicates that, in the mind of the ancient Chinese, wisdom is primarily derived from knowledge, or results from the extension of knowledge. This etymological identification points the Chinese concept of wisdom in a heavily intellectual direction.

Both Confucian and Israelite traditions hold that wisdom is either related to knowledge or is derived from a higher grade of knowledge. This is an intensive processing, involving such intellectual activities as those described in one Israelite text of wisdom: 'meditating on wisdom', 'reasoning', 'reflecting on the ways of wisdom in the mind', 'pondering her secrets', 'pursuing wisdom like a hunter' (Sir. 14:20–22), or as those taught in the *Doctrine of the Mean*: 'studying extensively, inquiring accurately, thinking carefully, sifting clearly and practising earnestly' (Zhongyong, 20). This solid epistemological foundation essentially associates the discovery or attainment of wisdom with intellectual achievements, making their concept of wisdom differ from the mystic perception that relates wisdom only to mysterious intuition or sudden enlightenment. Human intellectuality grows in particular cultures and is nurtured through different language systems. Therefore, apart from the examination of these two key words individually, we will also need to look at pairs of words in their association rather than separation, particularly knowledge (*da'at* and *zhi*), wisdom (*ḥokmā* and *zhi*), wise (*ḥākām* and *zhe* or *zhizhe*) and righteous (*ṣaddīq* and *yi*). Since these key words represent the abstract of what is meant in each tradition, we will be able to make meaningful contrasts or comparison of Confucian and Israelite wisdom by bringing them together and examining the one in light of the other.

Wisdom in Perceived Relationships

To know is to make a connection, and to be wise is to interpret intellectually and to

---

[35] *Hanyu da zidian* (*A Great Dictionary of Chinese Characters*), ed. *Hanyu dazidian bianji weiyuanhui*, Sichuan Dictionary Publishing House and Hubei Dictionary Publishing House, 1993, p.638; also in *Shuowen jiezi zhu*, pp.137, 227.

[36] *Hanyu da zidian*, 1993, p.638.

make use of connections skilfully. Wisdom is thus essentially concerned with relationships, and is meaningful only in the context of interrelatedness. In many philosophical and religious systems, relationship is primarily defined by the three objects we attempt to grasp intelligently and interpret wisely; the world, society, and the self, by which we gain three kinds of conventional wisdom: natural, social, and personal. Just as the world, society and the self cannot be totally separated from each other, wisdom of any particular tradition contains all three aspects of insight, knowledge or intuition, and equips us with efficient tools to understand, interpret and regulate our relationship with the natural environment, social institutions and individuals (including both the self and the others). To fully understand the nature and function of wisdom, we will analyse below these three kinds of wisdom one by one.

The first relationship humans attempt to establish and understand is between themselves and the outside world (the cosmos, the universe, nature, natural phenomena and so on). Concerning the natural world, wisdom questions the origin, nature and order of the world in which we live and act. The order of the world may refer to the order of creation in a theistic tradition, or to the natural or moral way in other kinds of traditions. Whether of a divine nature or not, the order or the way is believed to underlie all phenomena, and to demand human conformity. In this sense our knowledge and insight about it may be called 'cosmic wisdom' that searches for answers to the deepest and most fundamental metaphysical questions; or 'natura wisdom' that is drawn from knowledge concerning first the relationship between individual events and the natural order, and secondly the way humans should behave in relation to things and the environment.

The second object of human enquiry is society, including its political, juridical, ethical and communal aspects. This is essentially our relationship with other people, either as collective communities or as political entities. Understanding this relation enables us to gain so-called 'social wisdom' and leads to the formation of ethical norms, moral establishments, legal systems and political infrastructures, by which a particular social order is prescribed for all people to follow. These are all practical matters we have to master. Therefore social wisdom is also called practical wisdom, involving skills and abilities to cope with the demands of life, and experience and knowledge to deal with emerging problems. 'Skill' is a word with many implications and meanings.[37] It refers to the so-called 'soft' skills such as 'smart' attitudes, skilful approaches, and prudent ways to control difficult situations. It also refers to 'hard' skills that are used physically and manually to overcome problems and complete particular tasks. Confucians place a stress on both meanings of skill, and exhort their students and audience to learn about it to sort out complicated situations. The Hebrew

---

[37] For a more detailed discussion of skill, see Section 2 of Chapter 4, where we will examine what scope the ancient Confucians and Israelite teachers have defined for skills and what short-term or long-term influence they have taken into account in their evaluating the implication and meaning of skills for the Confucian and Israelite way of life.

wisdom texts also talk about skills as part of practical wisdom. The book of Proverbs not only highlights the skills enabling one to shun dangers, but also suggests that with good practical skills a wise man is able to complete concrete tasks such as building a house (Prov. 24:3).

In dealing with ethical, legal and political matters we gain a particular kind of social wisdom that comes from reflection on, and evaluation of, governing practices in relation to the people and state, and is applied to solve legal and political problems. It has been agreed that the majority of Confucian and Israelite wisdom teachings are aimed at the ruling class or the young generation who will come to govern. Therefore, how to deal skilfully with legal problems and how to balance the advantage and disadvantage of political relationships is an important part of Confucian and Israelite wisdom. The key to legal and political wisdom is maintaining a sound social order by which peace and harmony can last. How to govern well is one of the fundamental issues for Confucians, because they took it as their primary mission to advise the heads of states on policy and political ideology. The government wisdom Confucians advocated was moralist by nature, because it suggested that, if we made use of moral influence in a proper way, then order and peace would come naturally. To the question of what to do to win the support of the common people, for example, Confucius replied, 'Raise the straight and set them over the crooked and the common people will look up to you. Raise the crooked and set them over the straight and the common people will not look up to you' (*Analects*, 2:19). Political wisdom in ancient Israel was primarily concerned with how to deal with juridical cases, to ensure that the wise would be rewarded and the fool must suffer the consequences of his foolishness. Therefore how to maintain social justice becomes central to the Israelite governing wisdom. This highly praised wisdom in political and legal matters can be illustrated by Solomon's judgment in a case where two women were competing for one baby.[38]

The third object of human inquiry is how to deal with individuals. This is further divided into two aspects: one concerns personal relationships revealed as one and others, male and female, young and old, superior and inferior, and so on, and the other concerns how to deal with one's self, involving the knowledge and understanding of the internal world of human individuals with both its rational and irrational elements. In the first aspect, personal relationships are necessary for human survival and happiness but at the same time they create great difficulties for individuals to cope with. Generation after generation has acquired fundamental insights into these relationships, and etched them into the collective memory through careful formulation of wise sayings and instructions. In both Hebrew and Confucian

---

[38] He then gave an order: 'Cut the living baby in two and give half to one and half to the other.' The woman whose son was alive was filled with compassion for her son and said to the king, 'Please, my lord, give her the living baby! Don't kill him!' But the other said, 'Neither I nor you shall have him. Cut him in two!' Then the king gave his ruling: 'Give the living baby to the first woman. Do not kill him; she is his mother.' When all Israel heard the verdict the king had given, they held the king in awe, because they saw that he had wisdom from God to administer justice' (1 Kings 4:25–8).

texts we find a great many sayings concerned with these aspects, providing us with wise teachings about how to treat a particular person in a fruitful way and how to deal with others by mutually beneficial methods. The second aspect of personal wisdom concerns how a particular individual thinks, how he or she is motivated and responds wisely in the face of choices, and what kind of choices each of us should make in a particular situation and at a particular time, by which one's personal character is formed and known.[39] In a sense, there are more problems when we come to know ourselves intelligently than to understand external phenomena, because most of us find it extremely difficult to form a balanced opinion when introspecting the inner self, and many of us have a strong bias about our own image, strongly affected by our own feelings, emotions and views. It is in this sense that Socrates places 'knowing yourself' at the centre of philosophical wisdom, and some Daoist masters elevate the wisdom of knowing oneself above knowing others: 'He who knows others is wise; he who knows himself is enlightened' (Daode jing, Chapter 33). Personal wisdom requires one to appreciate what one can and what one cannot do. Anyone who attempts to do what is beyond his ability is bound to fail, while one who knows his limitations will act with caution and finally achieve success. It is evident that Confucian and Israelite teachers studied the inner qualities in detail. For them, self-control is the key to living a peaceful life, as it says in the book of Proverbs: 'One who is slow to anger is better than the mighty, and one whose temper is controlled than one who captures a city' (Prov. 16:32). These qualities often lead one to modesty or even humility, which is defined as one of the most important elements in wisdom. Since a person of wisdom knows his limits, he does not waste his time in complaining about his situation. Rather he is content with what he has, the quality that has become central to the inner quality of Confucian gentlemen who, as it is believed, will find peace within while being misjudged by others, because only those who do not take offence when others have failed to appreciate their abilities are recognized as 'gentlemen' (*Analects*, 1:1).

Wisdom as a Sacred Enterprise

In many ancient philosophical and religious systems, apart from conventional interpretations, wisdom is also related to the ultimate reality, either called the spiritual being or the mystic power. In the Judeo-Christian tradition, the ultimate reality is the Creator or God, the understanding of whom leads to what James Crenshaw defines as 'theological wisdom'.[40] Theological wisdom comes from reflection upon one's relationship with the transcendental power. In ancient Israel this is primarily

---

[39] The goal of all wisdom is the formation of character. For a more informed discussion of this aspect of wisdom, see Philip Ivanhoe: *Confucian Moral Self Cultivation*, New York: Peter Lang, 1993, and William P. Brown: *Character in Crisis: A Fresh Approach to the Wisdom Literature of the Old Testament*, Grand Rapids, Michigan: William B. Eerdmans Publishing Company, 1996.

[40] James Crenshaw, 1976, p.ix.

concerned with the acknowledgment of the divine source of wisdom: 'Where then does wisdom come from? And where is the place of understanding? It is hidden from the eyes of all living, and concealed from the birds of air' (Job 28:20–22). The hiddenness of wisdom does not mean that wisdom is not possible for humans, but implies that YHWH alone has access to wisdom and humans will not have wisdom unless YHWH gives it to them: 'I went about seeking how to get her for myself … But I perceived that I would not possess wisdom unless God gave her to me' (Wisd. 8:18–21). The second aspect of Israelite theological wisdom is concerned with questions of theodicy, how to vindicate the justice of YHWH, in the face of prevailing injustice and disorder. According to the so-called 'Deuteronomic theology', if one obeys YHWH and his laws, one will be rewarded with good life, protection, riches, honours, health and so on. If one disobeys, then one will be punished. However, it is not always so in reality, since good people can suffer and the wicked often live an easy life. To explain this, wisdom thinkers, particularly the author of the book of Job, expounded upon the human relation with YHWH, and developed speculative wisdom in Hebrew thought.

Similar developments also happened at roughly the same period in China when questions concerning divine justice were raised because good people suffered greatly from the consequences of natural and social disasters. A reflection on them is recorded in some poems of the *Book of Poetry*, where people complained that Heaven did not care about the injustice they suffered. Rationalism arising particularly during the seventh and fifth centuries BCE, however, redirected the thinking of Chinese thinkers, and turned them away from questioning the justice or injustice of Heaven to the examination of human ways: 'The Way of Heaven is distant, while the way of humans is near.'[41] Under such an influence, Confucian masters committed themselves to the questions of whether humans had fulfilled their own duties in the world. Instead of expounding upon metaphysical questions concerning divine justice, they explored what humans should do to be in conformity with the heavenly order. However, this does not mean that within classical Confucianism there is no speculation on the transcendental. In thinking of the human relation to Heaven, Confucius outlined a special 'theological wisdom', as follows: what Heaven endowed could not be taken away by humans (*Analects*, 7:23); humans had a mission entrusted by Heaven and it was their primary duty to carry it out (*Analects*, 9:5); Heaven could not be cheated, and one who was against the will of Heaven would have nowhere to pray for (*Analects*, 3:13). These have provided Confucian wisdom with a sacred ground on which all other human relationships are interpreted and exercised.

Wisdom in Hermeneutic Reconstruction

Many ways and approaches are available for our study of wisdom in the early

---

[41] Fung Yu-lan: *A History of Chinese Philosophy*, vol. 1, trans. Derk Bodde, Princeton: Princeton University Press, 1952, p.32.

Israelite and Confucian traditions: theological, historical, socio-anthropological and philosophical. Before proceeding with our comparative study, therefore, we must first consider carefully the tools we are going to use.

Traditionally in the West there are two kinds of methodological paradigms employed within the study of religious traditions. The first may be termed 'textual study' as it focuses on sacred scriptures or texts, taking extant writings as transparent blueprints of a particular tradition that inform us of religious leaders' authentic teachings and early followers' practices. This paradigm was nurtured and fundamentally shaped by the understanding during the medieval period that the Christian Bible was the only source of truth, and that only by studying the passages of biblical texts were we able to grasp the messages from Jesus Christ and his disciples. For a long time it was indeed the case that the study of biblical passages facilitated the transmission of religious, philosophical and historical knowledge. However, religious texts do not necessarily provide us with a true picture of the origin and early developments of a religion. Although believers may have been convinced that a particular text is full of religious visions, it is frequently the case that the text itself was produced or edited or even compiled during a later period and demonstrates a significant difference from the earlier period in terms of philosophical and religious views of the world and life. Therefore studies of this text most likely point to certain beliefs and ideals reflected in later authors' or compilers' own experience and values.

Having seen the problems of textual studies, a number of scholars, for example, Mircea Eliade (1907–1986) and Ninian Smart (1927–2001), advanced a new approach to the study of religious traditions, which was generally accepted as the phenomenological paradigm. When applied to the study of religion, phenomenology focuses on the dimensions of religion that can be categorized, observed and recorded, and separates what religion is from the observer's own religious experience. On the one hand, it aims to describe faithfully what people believe and how they behave, by which we can understand the sacred message and meaning of particular rituals or texts of a religious tradition. On the other hand, however, since it desires quasi-scientific 'objectivity' and values the 'distance' between the observer and the observed, the phenomenological paradigm tends, as its critics have argued, to be content with an uncritical perspective on any kind of religious ideas and practices.

A third paradigm arises from the application of hermeneutics to the study of religious and philosophical traditions, and is what we are going to take for the study of wisdom in early Confucian and Israelite traditions. Disregarding subjective readings of the text and objective descriptions of the sacred and the contemplative, a hermeneutical paradigm is aimed at an interpretive reconstruction of what wisdom is according to certain texts. Fundamentally hermeneutical, our paradigm also recognizes that the message of Confucian and Israelite texts lies in their existential appeal, and their meaning is wrapped in a form of discourse that is an expression of the time in which the texts were written.

Hermeneutics is a theory of interpretation and also has an origin in biblical studies.

Different from earlier biblical interpretation methods such as grammatical, philological, historical and linguistic inquiries, however, the new hermeneutical philosophy confirms that interpretation is not intended to be a total 'unearthing' of original authors' thoughts and ideas, and that all different interpretations are closely related to the interpreters' own experience and their personal reading of particular texts. Furthermore, it does not confine interpretation to one's personal life experience; rather it attempts to reveal the connection between interpretation and one's experience of, and reading into, the ultimate reality and truth. In the light of the *Yin–Yang* polarity philosophy, Chung-ying Cheng elevates this new method of interpretation to the ontometaphysical level, and calls it an 'onto-hermeneutical enterprise' embracing both Gadamerian subject-oriented reflective insights and the analytical constructive theories into an integrated theory of human understanding relative to our interpretation of human existence and reality.[42]

Both Confucianism and the Judeo-Christian tradition are essentially traditions of interpretation, a combination of the original ideas and later expansions, each generation of which often comes to a new view or understanding of earlier ideas and theories through interpreting and reinterpreting the classical writings, and in the process a huge number of commentaries and sub-commentaries have been generated. But our hermeneutical approach is not confined merely to historical and allegorical interpretation. It is characterized by the following features. First, it searches for meaning and answers through a meaningful combination of the particular and the general, and in the interaction between a passage of a text and the sense of the whole text, and between interpretative ideas and creative experience. Hermeneutics reveals that our interpretation of a particular message is meaningful only when we have a general sense of the situation overall, while the meaning of the whole text is relevant only when we have 'fore-projected' an initial meaning from a particular message. This is sometimes termed Heidegger's 'hermeneutic circle'.[43] The importance of this interdependence between the whole and the particular and between the interpreted meaning and fore-projection is that through this circle and indeed through going through this circle repeatedly it has become possible for us to reconstruct our knowledge concerning a particular message or text.

The second feature of our hermeneutical paradigm is that it seeks to shed new light

---

[42] 'This notion of hermeneutics could also ascend to the level where ontological reference to both the subject and the object in a unified experience of the ultimate reality is required to be made clear' (Chung-ying Cheng: 'Inquiring into the Primary Model: *Yijing* and Structure of Chinese Hermeneutic Tradition', *Journal of Chinese Philosophy*, 30, no. 3–4, 2003).

[43] We cannot understand a whole (for example, a text) unless we understand its parts, or the parts unless we understand the whole. This has been illustrated in the following passage from Heidegger: 'in the circle is hidden a positive possibility of the most primordial kind of knowing. To be sure, we genuinely take hold of this possibility only when, in our interpretation, we have understood that our first, last, and constant task in interpreting is never to allow our fore-having, fore-sight, and fore-conception to be presented to us by fancies and popular conceptions, but rather to make the scientific theme secure by working out these fore-structures in terms of the things themselves' (Martin Heidegger: *Being and Time*, trans. John Macquarrie and Edward Robinson, Oxford: Blackwell, 1978, p.195).

on questions about meaning and understanding in Confucian and Israelite wisdom contexts, by looking at the Israelite wisdom texts in the light of Confucian understanding and by interpreting Confucian wisdom in the light of Israelite views. In this sense we can say that our hermeneutical interpretation is selective, in that a particular example of wisdom thinking in one tradition is meaningful to us only if it can be reflected in our comparative framework, either in contrast or in parallel. This is based on another hermeneutical principle, that 'human understanding takes its direction from the fore-understanding deriving from its particular existential situation, and this fore-understanding stakes out the thematic framework and parameters of every interpretation.'[44] The Confucian–Israelite inter-interpretation, that is, their mutually being the interpretive 'other', is our framework and parameter for this study, and therefore our 'fore-understanding'. The value of this inter-interpretation is that it allows presuppositions which are implicit and unobserved within one system to come into view through juxtaposition with those of the other system. Placing texts in the narrative context of their occurrence, the comparative hermeneutics involves their decontextualizing in one context and their recontextualizing in another.

Thirdly, our hermeneutical approach aims to understand Confucian and Israelite writings not only as historical documents of the past but also as living discourses that continue to address the central concerns of these two traditions, which involves another hermeneutical circle of Heidegger: as living discourses we inevitably bring presuppositions to what we interpret, while the central concerns of Confucian and Israelite wisdom enables us to set boundaries to restrict arbitrariness in our interpretation. In the process of recontextualization, the texts are not simply taken as what they were, but also as what they should be, with each being placed in parallel to the other. A hermeneutical paradigm such as this one requires a distance from both of the traditions that are to be compared, so that our interpretation of the ideas contained in one does not become exclusively apologetic for the other, and yet at the same time it requires that the distance should not be so great that a reconstruction has to be based on purely subjective imagination. To reconstruct hermeneutically the wisdom world of ancient Israel and China through interpreting and reinterpreting classical passages, the paradigm requires us to place ourselves in the time and cultural setting when and where the wisdom teaching was made and instruction given, and to evaluate those teachings in relation to the world in which the Confucian and Israelite teachers lived and operated.

While placing an emphasis on Confucian–Israelite interconnection, we must point out that our hermeneutical comparison must not be undertaken simply to find chance parallels between two different systems; it is more important to search for the underlying reasons for the parallels, and to test the hypothesis about philosophical and religious divergence and convergence. This can be done at two levels, meta-

---

[44] Jean Grondin: *Introduction to Philosophical Hermeneutics*, New Haven: Yale University Press, 1994, p.92.

theoretical and normative. At the meta-theoretical level, an interphilosophical and interreligious examination involves an analytical and hermeneutical discussion as to what wisdom is, while, at the normative level, it needs to investigate the possibility of a substantial consistency with subtle differences in the way that wisdom functions in different cultural contexts, and to examine the particular source, reason and principle of the commonly accepted wisdom teachings regarding how people manage to live a good and wise life.

Hermeneutics presupposes philological, textual study. A comparative framework cannot be established until we have completed critical studies of a number of key texts important for early Israelite and Confucian understanding, and have considered their metaphysical, epistemological, ethical and political implications by placing texts in the narrative context of their occurrence. One of the main thrusts of our hermeneutical textual studies is to offer a cross-examination of early Israelite and Confucian discourses, to reveal the particularity of their understanding of knowledge and wisdom, and to enable a dialogical comparison to be generated through the interaction of texts. To engage in such a hermeneutical comparison of texts, special attention in this book will be given to the following three tasks. First, we will search as thoroughly as possible for comparability between the early Israelite and Confucian understandings as manifested in proverbs and the patterns of didactic teachings on wisdom, and the differences in emphasis, conception and expression which can only be fully appreciated by putting them back in the respective contexts of the historical and cultural circumstances each had. In so doing it will become possible for us to see connections between unrelated issues and fields, and differences between seemingly similar areas. Secondly, we will investigate how and why different focuses converge and parallel discussions diverge from one another, and their implications for comparative studies of these two religio-ethical–philosophical traditions. Through this investigation it will become clear that wisdom does not exist independent of epistemology, ethics, politics, education and so on; rather in their interaction wisdom has become part of culture and civilization, providing humans with tools and paths to fulfil their responsibilities. Thirdly, on the basis of such investigations, it will become evident that Chinese and Judeo-Christian wisdom draws heavily upon early Confucian and Israelite ways of thinking. These ways of thinking provide paradigms that develop through time and will continue to develop in cross-cultural exchange in the life of both the East and the West.

CHAPTER TWO

Confucian and Israelite Sources

Our hermeneutical reconstruction is based on detailed comparative studies of wisdom texts in the early Confucian and Israelite traditions. This will inevitably involve at least two risks. First, our inability to be a specialist on both traditions may lead to a tendency to interpret one through the lens of the other, and consequently our comparative study which has certain requirements of objectivity could become biased and selective. To a certain degree, hermeneutics allows a kind of interpretive 'bias' or 'selection', as long as it is derived from our interpretative framework and is enabled throughout textual studies in a consistent way. Wisdom exists not merely as a collection of knowledge and experience but also as an underlying idea, central to the way of thinking of each tradition and related to many other theological and philosophical premises. To ensure that our study has taken into account both wisdom's particularity and its commonality, we will have not only to grasp its contents and extensions, but also to examine it against a particular theoretical foundation and cultural setting.

Secondly, while our hermeneutical comparison permits us to take a 'partial' stance as regards the Confucian and Israelite understandings of wisdom which has sufficiently relieved our interpretation from being totally arbitrary, we would still run the risk of overstretching the scope of one particular piece of research if no proper boundaries were set. Each of the two wisdom traditions covers a diverse area in terms of wisdom thinking and application, and contains numerous streams of thought involving a dynamic process of reinterpretation. Explicit or implicit statements made in different parts of the sacred texts would most likely lead our interpretation in a different direction, and commentaries provided by later commentators and scholars, although very helpful for our appreciation, would probably direct us to reading ideas of their own time into the original texts. To begin our study, therefore, we must consider carefully these methodological problems and set an appropriate boundary for our own purpose.

Research Boundaries and Sourcebooks

Although any interpretive comparison of two different traditions or sets of ideas can tend to simplify one or even both of them, we are mindful of this becoming oversimplification. To pursue effective research involving wisdom in the early Confucian and Israelite traditions, we must set research boundaries at the outset. This book is an attempt to approach the early Israelite and early Confucian understandings of wisdom from a comparative hermeneutical perspective. It is not intended in any sense to be a full historical and cultural study, even if the historical and cultural settings are important for our understanding of wisdom. Nor is it intended to be a comprehensive treatment of Israelite and Confucian doctrines as a whole, even if Israelite theology and Confucian ethics are the theoretical foundation on which our research must be based. Rather, it is a study of wisdom through a limited number of texts, focusing on selected works on each side, which came into their present form during roughly the same period, namely, from the sixth to the first century BCE, although some of their material has no doubt drawn upon much earlier sources.

Whether or not there is a definitive group of writings in each tradition that can be accepted as wisdom texts, and whether or not the primary audience of the Confucian and Israelite texts we are going to study was made up of princes and state administrators (as indicated clearly in the Confucian *Great Learning* and the Hebrew book of Proverbs), are questions open to debate. While there is less disputation in terms of Confucian texts, how to select Israelite wisdom texts has been vigorously debated among modern biblical scholars. Some scholars believe that there was a particular group of people (profession) 'the wise (*hākām*)', whose social function can be differentiated from those of the prophet and the priest, and whose productivity has bequeathed to us clearly defined wisdom texts. Others tend to define the wisdom literature from the point of view of literary style: there is a genre particularly used in the texts of which wisdom is the centre. Again others argue that only those materials comprising non-revelatory speeches and experiences are of a wisdom nature.

We will not enter debates of this kind. Rather we will take into account the forms, contents and contexts of the books in Hebrew as well as in Greek that are generally considered to have been recordings of wisdom thinking in the early Israelite tradition. We shall draw our sources primarily from those 'books' as included in various versions of the Christian Bible, particularly Proverbs, Job and Ecclesiastes which are in the Hebrew Bible, and the Book of Ben Sira and the Wisdom of Solomon in the Greek Bible, that is, the collection later known as the so-called apocryphal (for Jews and Protestants) or deuterocanonical (for Roman Catholics) texts. These are together generally accepted as key texts of the wisdom literature of ancient Israel,[1] partly because in these books early teachings are collected to form a particular kind of literature focusing on how to think and act wisely in the face of religious, social and personal problems, and partly because the Hebrew root word for wisdom (*hkm*) 'occurs in one form or another 318 times' in the Old Testament, and 'over half of these (183) are found in Proverbs, Job and Ecclesiastes' in the Hebrew Bible, while in the two deuterocanonic/apocryphal books, 'forms of the Greek word *sophos* or *sophia* occur over 100 times'.[2] Other texts preserved in the Old Testament of the

---

[1] The scope of biblical wisdom is disputed, and some scholars have extended it to almost all books in the Old Testament, such as Genesis 1–11, 37–50, Exodus 32, Deuteronomy, Amos, Micah, Isaiah, Jonah, Habakkuk, Esther, 2 Samuel 9–20, 1 Kings 1–2, and a good number of Psalms and so on. However, what we offer here is an attempt to set a boundary for this search. While admitting that other biblical texts do contain vocabulary and ideas similar to those found in the five selected books, we will not enter the debate concerning which texts are more wisdom oriented or which are less.

[2] *The Anchor Bible Dictionary* (editor-in-chief: David Noel Freedman, New York: Doubleday, 1992), vol. VI, p.920.

Christian Bible such as Psalms, 1 Kings and Song of Songs, are to be consulted when necessary to support what we illustrate in the above-mentioned five 'books'. As far as these five books are concerned, we are not going to take them absolutely equally. Rather we concentrate our attention on the first three, namely, Hebrew texts, taking them as the core of Israelite wisdom, while the two that were composed under the influence of Greek philosophy will be used to supplement our positions.

For the early Confucian understanding of wisdom we will go to the primary sources of the *Analects of Confucius*, the *Book of Mengzi*, the *Book of Xunzi,* and the *Book of Changes* and the *Doctrine of the Mean* that were recomposed or compiled during the period of so-called 'classical' Confucianism when a new vision of the world and life was propagated through interpreting old traditions.[3] Other texts in the Confucian classics of an earlier or later date, particularly the *Book of Poetry*, the *Book of Documents*, the *Book of Rites* and the *Great Learning*, are also very important for the Confucian understanding of wisdom, and will therefore be considered as necessarily supplementary to our interpretation. Unlike the books or texts in the early Israelite tradition, however, none of these books or texts is ever specifically defined as 'wisdom literature'. Rather they are part of *the* sourcebooks of the Confucian tradition, and we single them out not because their central themes are the narrowly defined idea of wisdom, but because they provide us with a particular understanding in Confucian discourses concerning what a wise person is and how to lead a wise way of life. As far as the contents, style and genre are concerned, the Confucian texts are not too far away from the Israelite wisdom literature, because they are also the record of sayings or teachings; some contain aphorisms, while others are more or less systematic treatises or didactic discourses intersected by proverbs and quotations from older traditions.

Although it is not really our concern in this study to establish when a particular book or its chapters were written or what their cultural settings were, we are required by our hermeneutical presuppositions to gain some historical sense of the texts we are studying by looking into the date and authorship of each of them. This will enable us to see that both groups of texts were written or composed, or their final versions edited, during roughly the same period, namely from the sixth to the first century BCE.[4] However, the task of dating texts and ascertaining their authorship is not as easy as it appears to be. In both traditional China and Israel, people tended to attribute an entire book or text to one single master or prophet or historical figure of a much

---

[3] In the way that we differentiate the three 'core texts' from the other two for Israelite texts, we will concentrate our attention on the first three major Confucian books, namely the *Analects*, *Mengzi* and *Xunzi*, while taking the other two as supplementary sources.

[4] Whether or not all the extant versions of the five Israelite texts and the five Confucian writings came from this period is a question of debate. For example, some OT scholars have dated the Wisdom of Solomon Book of Ben Sira 'to around the second quarter of the first century CE, as it was probably written during the reign of Caligula' (Pablo A. Torijano: *Solomon The Esoteric King – From King to Magus, Development of a Tradition*, Leiden Brill, 2002, p.90), while some Sinologists have placed the final composition of the *Doctrine of the Mean* in the first century CE.

earlier date. For example, the natural author of the *Book of Mengzi* was thought to be Mengzi (372?–289? BCE), the second sage in the Confucian tradition, although in fact it might have been recorded or compiled by his discipline or later followers; the *Doctrine of the Mean* was said to have been composed by Zi Si (483–402? BCE), the grandson of Confucius, but most modern scholars would like to put the formation of this text in a much later historical context. Similar situations can also be found on the Israelite side: the Proverbs and the Wisdom of Solomon were once considered to have been the work of King Solomon or his court teachers, but few modern scholars still hang onto this view.

In some cases there was a close association between the book and the ideas or thought of that particular person, but in others the supposed link has on closer scrutiny become very loose, for the following reasons. First, most ancient teachers or masters did not write down their own thoughts and teachings. For instance, Confucius said clearly that 'he transmitted, but did not compose (write)' (*shu er bu zuo, Analects*, 7:1). Instead his interpretation of texts and his comments on events were noted and then transmitted by his students; the oral transmission was not compiled into a written work until long after his passing away. Secondly, most ancient books, both in Israel and in the Confucian tradition, were compiled by a group of authors, rather than by a single hand, and were further edited and re-edited, probably for several generations. The *Book of Changes* offers a striking example. If we take its text (*jing*) and the commentaries (*zhuan*) into consideration together, the extant book was the result of collecting, compiling and editing the material over a period of almost seven centuries. Much the same can be said about the Israelite book of Proverbs in that part of these proverbs (particularly Prov. 10:1–22:16) can be dated back to the tenth century BCE, some (for example, Prov. 25–9) were copied by the 'men of Hezekiah' (a seventh-century BCE king of Israel), while others were derived from later sixth- or fifth-century BCE.

Wisdom thinking in early Israel and China was never isolated from other sources and influences. The Confucian concept of wisdom, especially in the *Doctrine of the Mean* and the *Book of Changes*, was no doubt partially indebted to the Daoist view of the world. These books were finalized during the end of the Warring States period (475–221BCE) or even later, when syncretic philosophy dominated the Chinese world of thought. Dao or the Way is commonly known as the cornerstone of philosophical and religious Daoism, which, according to its famous text, the *Daode jing*, is the mystical source from which all things and all phenomena came into being and which exists before and after the formation of Heaven and Earth, standing alone and never changing, and yet functioning as the way guiding humans through to their destiny. This understanding of the Way has clearly left marks on the author(s) of the *Doctrine of the Mean* where the Way, when identified with 'Centrality and Harmony' (*zhong he*), appears to be something like an ontological substance, representing the 'hidden and secret ultimate reality', which when realized to the full, can 'establish the foundation of the cosmic order and sustain the regenerative processes of all the myriad creatures' (Zhongyong, 1). The Confucian Mean is also reminiscent of the

Daoist Way when it is identified with the Way of Heaven and Earth as that which is broad, massive, lofty, brilliant, unbounded in distance and in time, and which 'engenders all existing things with unfathomable fecundity' (Zhongyong, 26).

Some modern biblical scholars have argued that the wisdom literature of Proverbs, Ecclesiastes and Job is alien to the rest of the holy scriptures of Israel. Their argument is based partly on what is missing from the books: the promises to the ancestors, the Exodus from Egypt and the Mosaic covenant, the centrality of Jerusalem and the Davidic dynasty, and so on. The argument that wisdom texts do not deal with these topics becomes immediately less convincing when we include the Book of Ben Sira and the Wisdom of Solomon in the group, because in these two texts there is a deliberate combination of secular wise teachings and traditional Yahwism.[5] Apart from this, there is also a distinctive style of writing and content. Mainly collections of sayings or retelling old stories, these texts explore the path by which humans can find knowledge that enriches life or makes life bearable or enjoyable, which also demonstrates a feature different from that of narratives in other parts of the scripture. These distinct characters prompt us to think of other possible explanations. One is that the wisdom literature was more exposed to influence from outside Israel. It is generally understood that the belief in the world order in the wisdom literature of Israel was under the influence of the Egyptian concept of *ma'at* that was believed to regulate the cosmic world, the social world and the world of the gods; some scholars have made a connection between this belief and the Hebrew *ṣᵉdāqā* (righteousness, justice) and *ḥokmā* (wisdom). Scholars have also noted a similarity between the wise teachings of the Israelite tradition and those Egyptian texts that were used in the education of royal princes and state officials. They contend therefore that the authors of Israelite wisdom texts were certainly familiar with such Egyptian 'teachings' or 'instructions' (*seboyit*) as follows:

> The rules cover such areas as truth and integrity, generosity and moderation, proper and timely speech, the need to 'hear' (and obey), a correct relationship with officials, women, one's household and friends … The model person is a 'silent' one. Silence is a sign of self-control and thoughtfulness, a characteristic of one who is master of the situation.[6]

The influence of the Greek culture should not be neglected either, since the Greek *sophia* plays a role in later Israelite wisdom texts as important as the Hebrew word *ḥokmā*. The received version of the two texts we are going to study, the Book of Ben Sira and the Wisdom of Solomon, were generally addressing Jews living in a Greek cultural setting. Therefore, although they are intensely Israelite books, they can be fully understood only in the light of Hellenistic philosophical and religious views.

---

[5] Bruce M. Metzger and Michael D. Coogan (eds): *The Oxford Companion to the Bible*, New York and Oxford: Oxford University Press, 1993, p.801.

[6] *The Anchor Bible Dictionary*, vol. VI, p.929.

The Five Confucian texts

In the Confucian tradition the canon is composed of thirteen classics, ranging from collections of ancient poems and historical documents to later doctrinal illustration and expansion. Of these thirteen texts and other Confucian philosophical writings we have selected five books as our primary sources of study.

Analects of Confucius

The first of these is the *Analects of Confucius* composed of 20 books or sections and about 500 chapters or paragraphs. The *Analects* is a translation of the Chinese title *lun yu*, literally meaning 'discussion or conversations', composed of not only the sayings of Confucius the Master but also many of the utterances of his disciples. It is alleged that these conversations and sayings were recorded by some disciples and after the death of the Master these disciples and their students put together their notes to make a compilation, which they transmitted in their own master–disciple lineages. It was most plausible that different versions of the *Analects* were not combined into one 'authentic' text until several centuries had passed, which made it possible or even highly likely that some later insertions or alterations found their way into the final version as we have it today. For example, having examined the contents and styles of recorded conversations, Arthur Waley claimed, 'Books XVI–XVII are not from a source close to the earliest Confucian students, and Book XVIII and parts of Book XIV are even later, because they contain many anti-Confucian stories, similar to those prevalent in Taoist works.'[7]

In his own examination of the book, D.C. Lau divided the *Analects* into three strata:

> The first stratum consists of the books which are well ordered and in which no sayings of disciples are included. The next consists of Book I (and possibly Book II) and Book VIII. Although these books show a lack of internal organization of the chapters and contain sayings of disciples, they, nevertheless, do not use '*K'ung Tzu*' for Confucius. Finally, there is the stratum consisting of Book X and the last five chapters. These are interlinked through a number of features and are likely to be much later in date than the bulk of the work.[8]

As a compilation of sayings and stories this book lacks a logical connection between its various sections or books, and does not have, as many later books do, a central theme running through the chapters. However, in most cases it provides us with an original 'Confucian' discourse on many topics and issues, if by 'Confucian' we mean a particular way of thinking that is found in early *ru* scholars' exploration of political and ethical truth and wisdom, and there is no doubt that the *Analects* are the primary

---

[7] Arthur Waley: *The Analects of Confucius*, London: Allen & Unwin 1938, p.21.

[8] *Confucius: The Analects (Lun yü)*, translated with an introduction by D.C. Lau, Harmondsworth: Penguin Books, 1979, p.232.

source for our knowledge of the life and teachings of Confucius. It is in this book that we find a rich resource of Confucian understanding of wisdom, with many of the sayings probably collected from past experiences but reinterpreted in Confucius's and his immediate disciples' own views.

Mengzi

The *Book of Mengzi* was possibly edited and compiled by the disciples of Mengzi (Master Meng, or Meng Ke, 372?–289?BCE). Unlike the case of the *Analects* where no consensus has been reached among modern scholars concerning whether or not all the sayings recorded in the book truly reflect the real Confucius and his thought, the *Book of Mengzi* has been generally recognized as 'a perfect reproduction of the teaching' of the Confucian philosopher whose name it bears. Mengzi was undoubtedly a well-known philosopher, or, better, Confucian thinker during the Warring States period (475–221BCE). However, from the facts that the author of *Shiji* (the *Records of the Historian*) places his biography in the section of *lie zhuan* (Individual Biographies) where Mengzi is said to 'have composed (*zuo*)' the book of seven chapters,[9] that his writings are not listed in the section of Confucian classics (including the *Analects of Confucius*) but rather are placed together with other scholars' writings in *Hanshu* (the *History of the Former Han Dynasty*),[10] and that it was not officially recognized as one of the Confucian classics until the Song Dynasty (976–1279CE), we can assume that he was not particularly prominent in the Confucian tradition until a much later age. The *Book of Mengzi* was possibly not a subject of classical learning (*jing xue*) throughout the Han Dynasty (206BCE–220CE), and what Zhao Qi (108?–201CE, the author of the existent earliest commentary on the *Book of Mengzi*) claimed for the Han official post of academicians (*bo shi*) on the learning of the book has not been confirmed by other sources.

The book comprises seven sections or chapters, each of which is further divided into two parts. In this book, Mengzi, by engaging in argument with (real or imagined) representatives of other schools or in conversations with kings, ministers and his own students, expounds his theories, such as the original goodness of human nature, the unity of humans with Heaven, the possibility for everybody to become a sage, humane government and so on and so forth. Mengzi's idea of wisdom is closely associated with his doctrine of benevolence and righteousness, which according to him are the foundation of the whole world. Wisdom is clearly listed as one of the five cardinal virtues (benevolence, righteousness, propriety, wisdom and trustfulness), and by interacting with the other four, wisdom leads people to knowledge of Heaven and to the service of Heaven, the highest achievement human beings are expected to experience in their engaging the ultimate reality.

---

[9] Si Maqian: *Shiji* (*The Records of the Historian*), Beijing: Zhonghua Shuju, 1997, p.2343.

[10] In the list, the *Book of Mengzi* is said to comprise 11 chapters rather than seven chapters as we have in the extant version (*Hanshu*, Beijing: Zhonghua Shuju, 1997, p.1725).

Xunzi

The *Book of Xunzi* was a compilation of treatises by another distinguished Confucian philosopher, Xun Kuang (313?–238?BCE). Xunzi, Master Xun, was a well known writer on ritual, moral and political matters, and his writings were widely circulated even in his own lifetime. Despite the fact that few scholars would express any doubt that the treatises contained in the book bearing his name were mostly authentic, the book itself was not formed until the Han dynasty, when Liu Xiang (77–6BCE), the librarian of the Imperial archives came to collect together available essays that were believed to have been from Xunzi, and then sifted and edited them into a compilation that comes down to us as 'the *Book of Xunzi*'.

Deeply dissatisfied with current scholarship, Confucian or otherwise, Xunzi attacked the then popular Confucian propagators as 'following the model of the ancient kings in a fragmentary way', arguing that 'being mysterious and enigmatic, they lack a satisfactory theoretical basis'. He also criticized those who elevated traditional doctrines rather than the spirit of Confucius as 'stupid and delusive scholars' or 'base and mean scholars' (Xunzi, 6:7, 13). At the same time Xunzi attempted to construct a comprehensive and inclusive system that synthesized a variety of philosophical and ethical traditions. For example, his discussion of Heaven as Nature shows a clear understanding of Daoist metaphysics, and his interest in logic shows familiarity with the School of Logicians, while his views on education indicate an affinity with the *Great Learning* which is supposed to have been composed by Zengzi (505–432BCE), one of the Confucius's disciples. Xunzi placed his greatest emphasis on ritual/propriety (*li*) rather than on humaneness (*ren*, Confucius) or righteousness (*yi*, Mengzi), and this naturally prompted him to give more attention to penal laws than to moral models, which leads his political philosophy to the ideas of legalism. On the basis of a naturalistic and intellectualistic philosophy, Xunzi developed the Confucian understanding of wisdom both as the ultimate goal and as the necessary path for people to follow. He powerfully argued that humans were all born with the same nature and it was learning that set them apart: 'Those who undertake learning become men; those who neglect it become as wild beasts' (Xunzi, 1:8). For Xunzi, Confucian wisdom starts with scholarly study and ends with one becoming a sage. To become a sage, one must constantly accumulate knowledge and virtues 'to make whole one's inner power', 'to acquire a divine clarity of intelligence' and 'to fully realise a sagelike mind' (Xunzi, 1:6).

Doctrine of the Mean

The extant version of the *Doctrine of the Mean* (*Zhongyong*) was found as the thirty-first chapter of a loosely compiled anthology of treatises on rituals (*Liji, the Records on Rites* or *Book of Rites*) that did not acquire its current form until some time around the first century BCE. From the early records we learn that the *Doctrine of the Mean* was said to have been composed around the fifth century BCE by the grandson of

Confucius, Zi Si (483–403?BCE), but it is most likely that it was re-edited during the time of the Qin and the early Han Dynasty (221BCE–8CE).

This treatise is probably the first Confucian writing to provide us with a metaphysical outline of a moral universe that sustains the interaction between personal cultivation and the ultimate reality. It expounds upon a cosmic order that underlies all other social and political orders, the knowledge of which enables people to be in conformity with universal principles. In terms of personal development, it places less emphasis on learning and education but more on self-cultivation, which it argues will lead one to becoming a sage. In this process, it insists, one must stick to the Way, the Middle Way, the way of centrality and harmony. By following the Middle Way it does not mean simply pursuing a middle course, a central line exactly between two extremes; rather it is said to be following the harmonious process of the moralized universe. In order to follow the 'Way of the Mean', one has to keep one's mind sincere. Compared with external knowledge about things, events and phenomena, inner qualities are more important for the formation of wisdom. Of the inner qualities, sincerity (*cheng*) is particularly highlighted as the link between the Way of Heaven and the way of humans, enabling people to extend and develop their nature: those who possess sincerity achieve what is right without effort, understand without thinking, and therefore naturally and easily embody the Way. Sages are those who, by their sincerity, have had ultimate wisdom; by their sincerity and wisdom sages 'co-create' the world together with Heaven and Earth. This internalized theory of wisdom was later accepted as orthodox Confucianism, and the goal of the 'triad' (Heaven, Earth and Sages) became the supreme ideal for many Confucians.

Book of Changes

The *Book of Changes* or *Yijing* comprises two parts, the text and the commentaries. The text (*jing*) is the much earlier part, the product of ancient practices in relation to divination, which we might trace to the later Shang (1600?–1045?BCE) or early Zhou dynasty (1045?–256BCE). Central to the text are the eight patterns or trigrammes of three lines, each of which is either broken (- -) or unbroken (–), symbolising respectively the cosmic *yin* and *yang* powers. It is believed that the eight trigrammes represent eight phenomena of the world, supplementary to each other: heaven and earth, fire and water, wind and thunder, mountain and lake. By adding one trigramme to the other, there are a total of sixty-four hexagrams, each of which has a name, tribute, image and commentary. By consulting them one may expect to gain foreknowledge of the future. Traditionally it was believed that these trigrammes were invented, and brief texts attached to them, by the sage–kings of antiquity, but recent scholarship has disputed this, arguing that this part of the book was produced over a long period, probably in the early time (the ninth to the seventh centuries BCE) of the Zhou era, during which materials from various sources were collected by an unknown number of learned diviners and ritual masters to form a more or less recognized manual, available to court ritual masters and other professionals.

The second part of the book is composed of ten pieces of commentaries, also called the 'Ten Wings'. Traditionally these commentaries were attributed to Confucius, who was said not only to have edited the book but also to have transmitted the book with his commentaries to his disciples. Confucius was said to be so fond of the text that he wore out the leather bindings of his copy three times.[11] This tradition has again been refuted by modern scholars. It is now agreed that the commentaries were actually added to the text probably towards the end of the Warring States period (475–221BCE) or even as late as the early period of the Qin and Former Han dynasties, although there are surely some elements that came from Confucius or his school. Disregarding debates its date and authorship, this book is of special importance for our understanding of Confucian wisdom, because it provides us with an insight into the way Confucians constructed a relationship between knowledge and the secrets of the universe, and between human endeavour and their ultimate destiny.

The Five Israelite Texts

To date each of the Israelite wisdom books or set them in a particular historical setting is as difficult as, if not more difficult than, what we have attempted with the Confucian classics. Scholars of the Old Testament have made great efforts to examine the so-called 'wisdom literature' in the Israelite tradition and found that 'Israel's proverbs do not contain a single reference to a recognizable historical person or event, with the exception of the editorial superscriptions that mention Solomon and Hezekiah's officials'.[12]

This fact has led many people to believe that wisdom did not become a formal part of Israel's intellectual environment until the reign of King Solomon (961–922BCE), although it has also been pointed out that 'the genre of wisdom forms an important bridge between the ancient Near Eastern world and the religion of Israel'[13] at an earlier age. As far as the texts themselves are concerned, a large number of passages were traditionally attributed to the court of Solomon; for example, passages from Proverbs, Ecclesiastes and the Wisdom of Solomon implicitly or explicitly indicate that they were of Solomonic origin.[14] If this was right, then it seems right to say that after this splendid start, wisdom clearly 'became sidetracked because of the excess practiced by Solomon and his court, which ultimately led to the split of the kingdom

---

[11] Si Maqian: *Shiji*, p.1937.

[12] James L. Crenshaw: *Old testament Wisdom: An Introduction*, revised and enlarged, Louisville: Westminster John Knox Press, 1998, p.66.

[13] Katharine Dell: *'Get Wisdom, Get Insight' – An Introduction to Israel's Wisdom Literature*, Macon, Smyth & Helugs Publishing, Inc., 2000, p.109.

[14] These claims, however, are difficult to prove. Modern scholarship has suggested that they were attributed to Solomon probably because he was traditionally known as the paragon of wisdom: 'God gave Solomon wisdom and very great insight, and a breadth of understanding as measureless as the sand on the seashore. Solomon's wisdom was greater than the wisdom of all the men of the East, and greater than all the wisdom of Egypt' (I Kings 4:29–30).

into northern Israel and southern Judah (around 921BC)'.[15] The second surge of wisdom literature came only several centuries later when people reflected on their history, personal as well as national, and pondered questions concerning their relationship with YHWH, the community and other people. Therefore we have reasons to assume that, although some of the materials used in the extant books may have been of an earlier date, in the present form these books were all the products of the post-exilic period. There are significant differences between the pre-exilic and post-exilic periods, in terms of the theological recognition of human value and the position of humans in the world. Various proposals have been made concerning the date, authorship, structure and major themes for each of these texts. To make full use of their scholarly achievement, we will briefly examine them below and highlight some problematic issues for our study.

Proverbs

Like the *Book of Poetry* in the Confucian tradition, where poems and hymns of an earlier era were collected and edited into one of the key textbooks for education, the book of Proverbs was a collection of aphorisms and sayings of the past, some of which may have been transmitted through oral traditions for a long time before being written down. Modern scholars confirm, however, that the final edition was not made until after the exile, probably between the fifth and the third century BCE. In terms of content, the book can be roughly divided into two major parts: 'a series of didactic discourses comprising parental instructions and speeches by personified Wisdom' (Chapters 1–9) and 'collections of chiefly short proverbial sayings' (Chapters 10–31). It has been suggested that the first part was of a later date and, being more theological, was probably intended as an introductory work to the second part. The beginning of Chapter 10 states that the following are the proverbs of Solomon. Whether or not this statement is true, the majority of modern scholars agree that Chapters 10:1–22:16 represent the earliest material in the wisdom corpus and may have come from oral traditions of the pre-exilic period, while Chapters 22:17–24:22 show some similarities with the Egyptian Instruction of Amenemope and indicate an international context of cultural exchanges.

It was not unusual for proverbs and sayings from a diversity of sources to be collated and edited into a textbook for education so that people might attain well-instructed teaching on intelligence, righteousness, justice and probity (Prov. 1:3). As a book of refining and sifting past experiences, Proverbs is full of witty comments on human relationships in daily life and vivid analogies between nature and human experience, intended to reveal to the reader the patterns, principles and orders that govern the world, by which individual humans can see the truths behind phenomena and can make sense of their own lives. As far as its nature is

---

[15] James M. Efird: *Biblical Books of Wisdom – A Study of Proverbs, Job, Ecclesiastes, and other Wisdom Literature in the Bible*, Valley Forge, PA: Judson Press, 1983, p.15.

concerned, the book may well be regarded as *the* wisdom book in the Hebrew scriptures, and scholars have calculated that the Hebrew word for wisdom (*ḥokmā*) occurs in it thirty-nine times and the adjective for 'wise' (*ḥākām*) forty-seven times.[16] Its importance to the formation and transmission of Israelite wisdom can only be compared with that of the *Analects* for Confucian wisdom, and the study of it will no doubt shed light on our search for the true characteristics of conventional wisdom in ancient Israel.

Diverse as its themes are, the book in general demonstrates a moral optimism about the end of human efforts, based on the belief in the causal relationship between what people do and what they receive, as well as a positive attitude towards wisdom based on an understanding of the world order. It states confidently that from truths and wisdom collected from keen observation of life experiences in the past, a wide range of people will benefit: 'The simple will be endowed with shrewdness, the young with knowledge and discretion. By listening to them the wise will increase their learning, and those with understanding will acquire skill' (Prov. 1:4–5).

There are great advantages when wisdom teaching is applied to life situations, for people are often misled by their unjustified desires and tend to make unwise choices. However, conventional wisdom does have its limitations and can lead to many contradictions when used to solve problems of a diverse nature. Identifying wisdom with skill or ability, for example, it seems this book simply confirms that to learn about wisdom means to become equipped with the skills necessary to live a good and successful life. However, for a scholar trained in modern Western philosophy, a question immediately arises from this equation: how can the practical skills and abilities that are factual promote the values of 'righteousness, justice and equity' that are in the realm of value? Another example is that in some sections of this book wisdom is equated with shrewdness, in contrast to the simple. The preference of shrewdness to simplicity can be true only at the secular level, and will immediately create a tension when it is associated with the theological premise that 'the fear of the Lord is the foundation of knowledge' (Prov. 1:7). Does the fear (or faith) come from simplicity or from shrewdness which is supposed to have resulted from a complicated mind, or neither of these? If simplicity is a precondition of accepting the faith, then, by the reasoning of logic, we will have to say that wisdom (if equal to shrewdness) is an obstacle for, rather than a bridge to, faith, which poses a direct opposition to the majority of wisdom teachings we have found in the book. All these questions indicate that as a loosely compiled text without being theologically and philosophically refined, the content of the Proverbs is very diverse, and its sayings may well be found both supplementary and contradictory to one another.

---

[16] R.N. Whybray: *Proverbs*, New Century Bible Commentary, London: Marshall Pickering/Grand Rapids, Michigan: William B. Eerdmans Publishing Company, 1994, p.3.

Ecclesiastes

Modern scholarship confirms that the book of Ecclesiastes was not written before the exile, and that it may have been completed as late as the third century BCE, probably between 225 and 250BCE.[17] It is a philosophical discourse on religious, social and ethical issues, in the form of speeches by a character called Qoheleth, which denotes a teacher or speaker of an assembly and is directly translated as 'Preacher' in some English versions of the book. Qoheleth claims to be the king (in Chapters 1 and 2), ruling Israel from Jerusalem, but his real identity is impossible to verify.

Whoever the author might be, this book is unique among Hebrew wisdom texts and in many aspects can be seen as an antithesis of the main theme of the Proverbs. The author demonstrates a strong scepticism about the functionality of wisdom and reveals the irreconcilable tension between conventional wisdom and the perceived reality, and the unbridgeable disparity between faith and experience. In his discussion Qoheleth expresses his doubt about traditional wisdom teaching and suggests that seeking wisdom and truth is meaningless and is like chasing after wind.[18] He describes the world as changeless but mysterious, and argues that human beings are not able to grasp or understand the deliberate design of YHWH in his creation.

Uniquely Ecclesiastes provides us with evidence of a worldview that echoes the Buddhist understanding that all is empty, far removed from the theological orientation governing most books of the Hebrew Scriptures. A central theme of the book is that 'All is vanity (*hebel*)', a theme repeated several times. Here *hebel*, literarily probably meaning 'a breath of wind', is used metaphysically, 'to suggest transience, uselessness, or deceptiveness'.[19] Extending this to the social realm, Qoheleth sees the prevalence of injustice, where the honest suffer whilst the dishonest enjoy life and possess power (Eccl. 4:1). Reflecting upon his own life experiences and observations, he is convinced that the future is unpredictable, and that the best way of living is to be content with whatever one can get. The more one seeks, the unhappier one will be.

Despite the lack of any immediate punishment of the wicked, the author, being pragmatic, reckons that it is still safer to 'stand in fear before God' than to become a total anarchist or doubter. While admitting that wisdom cannot guide us through the mystic path of life, the author has no intention to promote immoral and unwise behaviour, reckoning that wisdom might be just more profitable than folly and that the wise man is more likely to be respected than the fool. Being wise or not, the author argues, this will not change one's destiny, because 'one and the same fate

---

[17] *The Anchor Bible Dictionary*, vol. II, p.273.

[18] It has been suggested that there are four thematic teachings within the book: (1) wisdom could not achieve its goal; (2) a remote God ruled over a crooked world; (3) death did not take virtue or vice into consideration, and (4) enjoyment is the wisest course of action during youth (*The Anchor Bible Dictionary*, pp.275–7).

[19] John Barton and John Muddiman (eds): *The Oxford Bible Commentary*, Oxford University Press, 2001, p.423.

overtakes them both' (Eccl. 2:14). This leads him to fatalism: nothing will make any difference and all efforts are futile; whatever we do, the result is the same. From this the author concludes that the world and beyond are unknowable to the human mind, and that human intelligence is not capable of understanding or even sensing what has happened, is happening and will happen in the world.

Job

Different from the Proverbs that propagates conventional wisdom based on the belief in the world order, and from Ecclesiastes that adopts a cynical attitude towards life based on the belief that YHWH and his design are unknowable, the book of Job takes a much more critical line towards conventional wisdom and seeks to find answers to the seemingly unjust reality. Being of a well-developed literary style, it contains few wise sayings that characterize Israelite wisdom tradition. This causes some modern scholars to doubt whether it should be included in the Hebrew wisdom literature. In any case it seems right to say that, depending on how we define wisdom literature, the nature of Job is between a wisdom text and a non-wisdom text, as Katharine Dell has rightly pointed out, the book of Job shares the same intellectual and spiritual quest as other wisdom books if we follow a broad definition, while we should 'have some profound reservations about simply assuming that Job is "wisdom literature", as narrowly defined'.[20]

As far as its contents are concerned, there is evidence that part of Job was adapted from an earlier source, while some materials were added much later. Most scholars would agree that an unknown author produced the book by using an ancient story about a righteous man who encountered horrible calamities as a central theme and then supplementing it with poetic dialogues in the post-exilic era, probably between the fourth and the third century BCE, in order to speak to the nation during that period of harsh conditions.[21] This righteous man is named Job, who, as we are told, lived a blameless and righteous life, but whose motives for being righteous were suspect. A series of tests were imposed by YHWH, causing the loss of property and children, and his being possessed by serious diseases. These tragedies changed Job from a contented into a complaining man, and his complaints led to debates and arguments between him and his friends. The whole book is rather like a drama depicting the cyclical relationship between a human and YHWH, from being obedient, to resentful, and finally to repentant.

The central theme of the book is undoubtedly theological, but it also raises many philosophical and ethical questions concerning conventional wisdom; for example,

---

[20] Katharine Dell, 2000, p.43.

[21] The structure of the book is that it opens with a prosaic prologue and ends with a short epilogue, with lengthy poetic dialogues in between. The two different styles and the many inconsistencies between them have led some modern scholars to wonder if the book itself was composed by more than one author, although no conclusive opinion has been agreed.

whether one's being good or not should depend upon good reward. It can be argued in the first place that, although challenging the traditional framework of justice and wisdom, the book does not vary too much from the Israelite view of the theological implications of humanity in relationship with YHWH. As in many other biblical wisdom texts, the author insists that only YHWH can reveal 'the secrets of wisdom' (Job 11:6), and that to HIM 'belong wisdom and power' (Job 12:13). Secondly, the book of Job does not totally cast away traditional wisdom either. Through exchanges between Job and his friends, the book confirms conventional views of the wise way of living and behaving; for example, the link between intelligence and wisdom (Job 12:2), and between wisdom and the aged (Job 12:12). It also provides some other types of wisdom teaching, showing the reader how the wise would think or make choices in perplexity and dilemmas; for example, one should think of one's good past when faced with troubles in the present, and one must keep to one's way even when encountering temporary difficulties. Many of the sayings contrast the wise and the foolish, confirming and reconfirming that a truthful way of life is the only wise choice.

Book of Ben Sira

The longest of the so-called apocryphal books in the Greek Bible, the Book of Ben Sira or the Wisdom of Jesus the Son of Sirach, consists of several short treatises, presenting the most comprehensive example of wisdom literature preserved in the Bible, the contents of which 'are clearly sapiential, following the line of Proverbs, Job or the deuterocanonical *Wisdom of Solomon*', containing moral, cultic and ethical maxims, folk proverbs, psalms of praise and lament, theological and philosophical reflections, and pointed observations about life and customs of the day.[22] Unlike many other books of proverbs in the Bible which were written or compiled by different authors over a longer or shorter period, the Book of Ben Sira seems for certain to have come from a single hand, a professional scribe (*sōpēr*), a known wise man or sage (*ḥākām*), named Joshua ben Sira (the Hebrew name of Jesus the Son of Sirach). It was composed originally in Hebrew probably between 200 and 180BCE, but was translated by the author's grandson and published in Greek after 117BCE. It did not gain a place in the Hebrew Bible, but as a Greek text it was cherished as part of the Greek Scriptures of the early churches; hence there are two different recensions of both the Hebrew and Greek texts, although the Hebrew text that we possess does not comprise the whole book.[23] The later Protestant churches include it in the Apocrypha, and use its Latin name of Ecclesiaticus, 'the Church Book'.

Unlike other books on wisdom that do not refer to the distinctive traditions of

---

[22] Pablo A. Torijano, 2002, p.33.

[23] P.W.Skehan and A. Di Lella: *The Wisdom of Ben Sira*, Garden City, New York: Doubleday, 1987, pp.3–92.

Israel but are mainly concerned with human life, the Book of Ben Sira pays great attention to Israel's history, status and Scriptures, confirming that wisdom has been expressed in the 'book of the covenant of the Most High God, the law that Moses commanded us' (Sir. 24:23).

The themes it attempts to develop are of two kinds, expanding upon traditional and practical wisdom, such as relations with women, behaviour at banquets, and theological reflections on wisdom and on the problem of theodicy. It reconfirms the Israelite conviction that 'The whole wisdom is fear of the Lord, and in all wisdom there is the fulfilment of the law' (Sir. 19:20). This leads some scholars to believe that the Book of Ben Sira 'first made the link between wisdom and Torah, the Law', although others such as Katherine Dell reject this claim, arguing that 'a close relationship exists between wisdom and law in Deuteronomy and in a few contenders for the wisdom psalms category'.[24]

Being a wisdom teacher himself, the author appraises highly the value and importance of reverence towards received tradition, and towards the elders who transmit it. In explaining the world, the author betrays a clear influence of Hellenistic philosophy when he goes as far as proposing that the world is constituted of complementary pairs, so that evil is necessarily the opposite of good, and as such contributes to the harmony of the cosmos: 'Good is the opposite of evil, and life the opposite of death; so the sinner is the opposite of the godly. Look upon all the works of the Most High; they likewise are in pairs, on the opposite of the other' (Sir. 33:14–15).[25] He is also more confident than the author(s) of Ecclesiastes that human beings are able to know the right behaviour at the right time. Acknowledging that human experience is not sufficient on its own to understand God's will, and therefore might not always be able to make a right choice, he nevertheless suggests that, except for the limit of the divine ('the fear of God is the beginning of wisdom', Sir. 1:16, 27), humans do not have other limits in their knowledge. This causes a tension between self-reliance and praying for divine guidance, but the wisdom of the Book of Ben Sira is developed precisely through the interaction between human attempts to master life and human piety towards God.

---

[24] Katharine Dell, 2000, p.112.

[25] This view is similar to that of later Confucians in China, influenced by *yin–yang* philosophy. Based on the belief that human nature is originally good and that evil is a deviation from the good, Neo-Confucians consider good and evil to be related concepts. The relation between good and evil is compared to that of the *yang* and the *yin*, the binary forces of the universe, not in the sense that good is the *yang* and evil is the *yin*, but in that 'Among all things, there is none that does not have its opposite. Thus for the *yin* there is the *yang*, and for goodness there is evil. When the *yang* waxes, the *yin* wanes, and when goodness increases, evil diminishes' (Cheng Hao, quoted in Fung Y-Lan: *A History of Chinese Philosophy*, 1953, p.518). In this sense they believe that 'The goodness and evil of the world are both equally Heavenly principles. To say that something is evil does not mean that it is inherently so. It is so merely because it either goes too far or does not go far enough' (ibid.).

Wisdom of Solomon

Although some traditional wisdom materials of the Hebrew origin from an earlier date have been present in the Wisdom of Solomon, the book is not found in the Hebrew Bible, and more recent scholarship suggests that it 'was written in Greek by a learned and profoundly Hellenized Jew of Alexandria, after that city's conquest by Rome in 30BCE'.[26] The difficulties in defining particular passages make other scholars more hesitant to provide a clear date; rather they place its composition in the period from 100BCE to 100CE, because of its links to Hellenistic philosophy, literature and science, although there is a wide debate with regard to the degree and extent of this influence. In any case we can safely say that the Wisdom of Solomon is the latest one of the group of texts we take into account when examining Israelite wisdom.

The nineteen chapters of the book can be roughly divided into five parts. The first part is mainly about 'wisdom and human destiny' and is addressed to the 'rulers of the earth', reminding them that 'we are born by mere chance, and hereafter we shall be as though we had never been', and only 'in the memory of virtue is immortality' (Wisd. 2:2; 4:1). The second part is in praise of wisdom with Solomon as the speaker telling the mighty of the earth to 'get wisdom' and describing how wisdom can do and renew 'all things', is 'more beautiful than the sun and excels every constellation of the stars' and is 'superior' to the light and 'orders all things well' (Wisd. 7:27–30). The third part is concerned with wisdom in Israel's history, claiming that 'Wisdom protected the first-formed father of the world' and 'gave him strength to rule all things', and that 'Wisdom rescued from troubles those who served her' (Wisd. 10:1, 9). The fourth and fifth parts deal respectively with an indictment of idolatry (Chapters 13–15) and with Israel and the Egyptians (Chapters 16–19).

Although much less proverbial or didactic than the book of Proverbs, the Wisdom of Solomon is conspicuous in providing wise teachings that can be used as guidance for human life. The concept of wisdom is central to the text, where it occurs twenty-nine times in the first ten chapters but only twice in the last nine. The book is an exhortatory discourse, urging listeners to be wise rather than stupid. By being 'wise' is meant setting one's mind upon God in the right way. It is particularly concerned with the divine implications for the rulers of the earth, reminding them that their 'authority was bestowed by the Lord' (Wisd. 6:3). Unlike the author of Ecclesiastes, where Qoheleth suggests that people should take pleasure as much as they can, because life is short and humans can do nothing to change their fate, the Wisdom of Solomon condemns the hedonistic way of life and shows how wrong such people are because 'they failed to understand God's hidden plan' (Wisd. 2:21). The author highly praises the glory of wisdom and personifies the concept of wisdom: 'Wisdom shines brightly and never fades' (Wisd. 6:12), and believes that anyone who sincerely seeks wisdom will find her. It is also emphasized that 'the beginning of wisdom is the

---

[26] *The Anchor Bible Dictionary*, vol. VI, p.120.

most sincere desire for instruction' (Wisd. 6:17), thus laying responsibility for being wise on the shoulders of individuals. However, in the end God is the sole source of wisdom, and provides humans with 'knowledge of the structure of the world and the operation of the elements' (Wisd. 7:15–21). This leads the author to claim that wisdom was present at the world's creation, and that it is God's holy spirit who comes down to teach humans what is pleasing to God and has brought them salvation (Wisd. 9:13–18).

Influenced heavily by Greek philosophy of the soul and the body, the author of the book takes wisdom as the spirit of immortality. God created humans in his own image and their soul in the image of the divine Wisdom. However, whether or not one can enjoy immortality depends upon whether or not one behaves wisely and righteously, because to follow the laws of wisdom is 'a warrant of immortality' (Wisd. 6:18). In this sense wisdom has become knowledge of secrets, especially cosmic secrets, which comes from God's divine foreknowledge (Wisd. 7:7–8).

Wisdom Mentalities behind the Texts

We have argued in the previous chapter that wisdom as presented in early Confucian and Israelite texts is not merely a collection of clever sayings or proverbs, but also a reflection on the cosmic order or the way of the world, an intellectual enterprise concerning the art of life, and a reconstructed relationship between oneself and nature, society, legal and moral systems and transcendental powers. Having examined the key texts on wisdom in early Confucian and Israelite traditions we can now further say that it is this sense of wisdom that is extended and enlarged throughout all these texts, but in obviously different ways. The difference in expression and expansion reflects two mentalities that were rooted and nourished in ancient Israelite and Chinese cultures, respectively. The mentality of wisdom is extremely complicated and delicate, and a sweeping comparison between Confucian and Israelite wisdom mentalities requires more extensive study than we can afford here. However, to illustrate the differences and similarities between Confucian and Israelite texts, it may help to make the following points.

The etymological root of Israelite wisdom, *ḥokmā*, is skill and ability, while the root meaning of Confucian wisdom, *zhi*, comes from the character for knowledge. The two different root meanings of 'wisdom' determine, in a conventional way of wisdom thinking, that the expectation on wisdom in Confucian and Israelite texts differs: Confucian masters expect wisdom to grow from one's intellectual development and therefore place great emphasis on education that is believed to bring people to maturity, while Israelite teachers associate wisdom with skills and abilities whereby how to sort out daily issues becomes an essential part of wisdom literature. Although both Confucian and Israelite teachings stress that wisdom must be practised in personal and social life, their routes to this end are different. Passages from the Confucian classics have painted us a more intellectually oriented mentality which is preoccupied with the nature and function of knowledge. No question is raised concerning the origin of knowledge, or about why the sages are able to have it. Rather, great efforts are made to search for answers to questions concerning how to understand the world we live in intelligently and how to behave and act wisely in a particular natural and human environment. Because of this intellectual orientation, Confucian masters addressed primarily kings or dukes or 'gentlemen' who were more educated and intellectually capable of accepting knowledge and politically able to carry it out in the human world. This shows a difference from Israelite teachers whose teachings are addressed to all the people, including the 'kings of the earth' as well as local folk, but primarily to the young who tend to make stupid choices owing to lack of experience and skill. For wisdom means primarily the acquisition of life skills in coping with actual problems, through leading 'a disciplined and prudent life' and doing 'what is right and just and fair' (Prov. 1:3), and this applies to all human beings, both those of high rank and the lowly.

Emphasizing the practical dimension, both Confucian and Israelite texts demonstrate a clear tendency towards ethicism in their wisdom elaboration. In Israelite wisdom literature, the 'wise' (*ḥākām, sophos*) has become an ethical term rather than a cognitive judgment. The contrast between the wise and the foolish is not that the former have knowledge while the latter have not, but that the former are diligent, prudent and faithful, while the latter are lazy, reckless and deceptive. Therefore the contrast between the wise and the foolish naturally becomes one between the righteous and the wicked. Confucian masters substantialize wisdom with intellectual development, but this intellectual capacity is not considered to be purely cognitive either. Like the Israelite teachers, the Confucian masters essentially moralized the wise, and differentiated between the true 'wise' and the superficial 'clever'. The former are virtuous, although they are slow to speak (*ne, Analects,* 13:27), while the latter are immoral, although they seem always to manage 'clever talking' (*qiao yan, Analects,* 1:3). What is meant by the wise, *zhizhe,* therefore, involves both intellectual and ethical achievement.

Both the Hebrew word *ḥokmā* and the Greek word *sophia* are feminine nouns, and the femininity of the Israelite wisdom is clearly expressed in a number of texts, where wisdom is said to be a lady who speaks as a prophet (Prov. 1:20–33) and can employ a messenger (Prov. 9:1–6). Wisdom is closer than a woman; she is a 'sister' (Prov. 7:4), who is in an intimate relationship with a man in the same way as a wife or lover (Prov. 8:6–14). This kind of personification and feminization of wisdom is not seen at all in the Confucian texts. There is no gender distinction between Chinese characters, and no attempt has ever been made to associate wisdom with the virtues of women. Instead, we may speculate that, since the character for knowledge (also pronounced *zhi*) is composed of an arrow and a mouth, it may be intended to symbolize the masculine virtue demonstrated in warfare and competition. Modern scholarship has confirmed that the deified feminine wisdom in the Israelite texts is in some way related to the Egyptian goddess *Ma'at* (Truth), and to *Asherah* (the Canannite fertility goddess) in that wisdom is said to be the tree of life (Prov. 3:8) and Asherah's primary symbol was also a tree of life,[27] and the femininity of Israelite wisdom demonstrates again the intercultural influence upon the Israelite view of the world. No Confucian works have ever indicated that wisdom is a kind of god or goddess. It is indeed the fact that in Chinese history the worship of fertility gods or goddesses is completely confined to folklore. One of the reasons for this might be the highly rational tendency of Confucian philosophy which was nurtured and strengthened in a social environment of the heavily patriarchal society in which there was little place left for goddesses, although some traces of an earlier matriarchal tradition were preserved in Daoist works, such as *Daode jing*.

An implication of wisdom being feminine is that she is associated with God and God's creation. Some modern scholars favour the assumption that 'Lady Wisdom represents an irruption in the Bible of the persistent but biblically suppressed Israelite worship of a female counterpart to Yahweh.'[28] Whether or not there was a time when a goddess was worshipped in Israel is beyond the scope of our research. However, the feminine wisdom in its wisdom literature re-emphasizes that the religious mentality of ancient Israel is preoccupied with the divine source of wisdom, and provides a theological justification for the premise that the 'fear of God is the source of wisdom' which runs through virtually all wisdom literature. Although somehow diverging from other biblical writings in terms of the lack of emphasis on the divine history of Israel, the Israelite wisdom literature does not depart from the fundamental conviction of all biblical texts: wisdom must be founded on faith in God. In this sense we can see that wisdom thinking and discourse in the Israelite literature are in each and every case based on a logical reasoning: wisdom is needed in daily life and functions well in secular events, because YHWH intends it to be this way; YHWH's wisdom illustrates the secrets and mysteries of the universe so that humans are able to understand them; therefore having faith in YHWH is the only way to wisdom and to a wise life. There is also a sense of wonder about wisdom in the Confucian texts. Wisdom is said to enable humans to penetrate all mysteries and impart to them the deepest knowledge of Heaven and Earth. Wisdom thus contains the measure of Heaven and Earth and enables us to comprehend their Way and Order.[29] Nevertheless, however mysterious wisdom is, it is still a kind of knowledge, and is substantially different from the Israelite wisdom that is essentially rooted in the creation and the divine order.

The divine nature of wisdom leads Israelite teachers in the direction of a theological absolutism that wisdom is unconditional and never changes, and that with wisdom humans will surely be protected and guided by YHWH (Prov. 3:26). Wisdom the Goddess spoke about her presence at the beginning of creation. With divine power wisdom is categorical: 'blessed are those who keep my ways; listen to

---

[27] *The Oxford Companion to the Bible*, p.800.

[28] *The Oxford Companion to the Bible*, p.801.

[29] *I Ching or the Book of Changes*, The Richard Wilhelm translation, rendered into English by Cary F. Baynes, London: Arkana, 1967, p.293.

my instruction and be wise'; 'whoever finds me finds life and receives favour from God', but 'whoever fails to find me harms himself' (Prov. 8:22–35). Since they do not give wisdom a divine status in their writings, in contrast, Confucian masters had to measure their advice according to the conditions they taught. Times are changing, and so are the requirements for wise action. While the order of the universe demands conformity, it allows freedom, since change is the nature of the order. 'Heaven and earth change and transform; and the holy sage imitates them.'[30] In the Confucian classics the search for wisdom is not simply conducted in obedience to divine commands, but is a constant activity concerning different aspects of the world: 'contemplating the signs in the heavens' and 'examining the symbols of the earth' will enable us to know the circumstances, while 'going back to the beginning of things and pursuing them to the end' will enable us to know the secrets of life and death.[31] This changing nature and intellectual approach underlie the mentality of the Confucian wisdom.

Structuring the Texts

Even from a select number of texts, we have already seen that such texts are in reality of various kinds. Structuring wisdom texts is, however, more complicated than simply putting them into different categories. Each of the texts contains distinct themes and/or genres that are closely associated, and are presented in different styles that are employed interchangeably. To impose a structure on them essentially means hermeneutically restructuring all the texts. There are a number of methods to do this, but a method that is suitable for Israelite texts might not necessarily be applicable to the Confucian classics.

Wisdom is, in one sense, an ability to see and to cope with present and future events based on life experiences, either religious or non-religious. In this respect, wisdom texts as contained in the corpus of Confucian classics and Israelite Scriptures can be fitted into a structure of three tiers. First, in the form of collections of wise sayings and aphorisms, the lessons of past life experiences, either in local communities or in royal courts, were refined into the texts as experimental teachings for students and the general public, containing instructions on how to deal with both typical and untypical life situations, and giving guidance on present choices and actions. This kind of teaching took place when parents guided their children or when teachers educated their students. The *Analects of Confucius* (16:4–8) provides us with many pieces of advice or admonishments on what kinds of friends we should make, what kinds of pleasure we should pursue, what kinds of discipline we must place on ourselves at different ages, and so on. These are clearly the products of the

------

[30] *I Ching or the Book of Changes*, p.320.
[31] *I Ching or the Book of Changes*, p.293.

wise thinking that comes from serious reflection on past experiences, personal as well as social; this is of value in enabling us to live by the wise way of life and to choose a right course of action. On the Israelite side, Proverbs 10–30 talk about the good and bad consequences of diligence and laziness, and about the ways a righteous and wise man speaks and behaves, in contrast to the ways of a wicked and foolish man. All these can be placed in the first tier of wisdom writings in the Israelite and Confucian traditions, representing the initial efforts to grasp the secrets and mysteries of the world and life.

In the second tier, a particular text or parts of it are concerned with how to understand and control the future or future events, in which by employing particular knowledge of the secular and spiritual worlds, individuals or particular groups of people, especially magicians, court counsellors and teachers, associated the past with the future, and highlighted a particular course of action to deal with the possible situation lying ahead. In ancient Israel wisdom teachers or sages were generically associated with prophets, and they were believed to have the ability to predict or project the future and provide good advice on future action. Although most Confucians of the later period were too rational to consult oracles for the future or to read signs to justify choices, the early masters inherited the tradition that the future could be known by observing and examining auspicious and inauspicious signs and symbols. When Confucius did not see auspicious omens, for example, he lamented that the ideal he strove for would fail to be realized: 'The Phoenix does not appear nor does the River offer up its Chart. It is all over with me!' (*Analects*, 9:9) However, there is a substantial difference between wisdom advice and fortune-telling in both traditions. Wisdom teaching was given as the result of understanding past experience, while fortune-telling was to interpret dreams or portents to generate visions about the future. Based on experience, Confucian and Israelite wisdom teachers advised people to follow certain routes of action or to avoid certain other courses so that they could reap their harvest successfully or reach their final destination. This demonstrates a fundamental difference from those who were either called 'prophets' or 'diviners'.[32] Prophets and diviners are intermediates between the human and the spiritual worlds, and their prediction of the future is a reflection of the divine will, not of human wisdom.

In the third tier, the texts seek answers to more subtle and deeper questions concerning the meaning and significance of theological and cosmological issues, and elaborate on speculations and contemplations that conventional wisdom has provided. In relating wisdom to the power of YHWH or his creation, the Israelite sages admit there are fundamental weaknesses in the human search for ultimate wisdom: humans can find hidden treasures in the earth, but cannot find wisdom. Only

---

[32] 'But the most common designation: *nābî'*, usually translated as "prophet", is of uncertain derivation … Prophets were men or women believed to be recipients through audition, vision, or dream of divine messages that they passed on to others by means of speech or symbolic action' (*The Oxford Companion to the Bible*, p.620).

YHWH can do that, because he sees everything. It was in the creation of the wind and the rain that YHWH became actively involved with wisdom: seeing, appraising, establishing and searching her out (Job 28). It is asserted that being with the creator from the beginning of the world and in the process of creation, wisdom is capable of unlocking the secrets of the cosmic and human order (Prov. 8:22–36). There is also a recognition among Confucians that not every human is able to understand the mysterious nature of the universe and history. Confucius left matters of cosmic significance to Destiny, which was believed to determine the way of humans: 'It is Destiny if the Way prevails; it is equally Destiny if the Way falls into disuse' (*Analects*, 12:36). However, taking a more positive stand than the Israelites, Confucians attempt to unlock the secrets of the Destiny. It seems that Confucius came to the question of destiny with confidence when he said that 'A man has no way of becoming a gentleman unless he understands Destiny' (*Analects*, 20:3); in other words Confucius believed that a true gentleman should have understood Destiny. However, different from the Israelites who claimed that only by having faith in YHWH could humans have knowledge of the creation order, Confucius insisted that to understand Destiny one must be fully developed in terms of intellect and virtue. This is why Confucius said of himself that he did not understand the Destiny of Heaven until he was fifty years old (*Analects*, 2:4).

Between these three tiers there is a tension both in the Israelite literature and in Confucian classics. This tension is manifested in two kinds of discourse on wisdom that are supposed to be interdependent, but which from time to time conflict with each other. In Israelite texts they are discourses on both the divine and the secular wisdom. The former is more fundamental: wisdom must be founded on the 'fear of YHWH', and is believed to be the 'gift of YHWH' and as a personified deity to mediate YHWH's creation in relation to human beings. This is the foundation of Israelite wisdom tradition, and determines its character and features. The latter concerns how we humans should lead a wise life, and deal with everyday matters arising in family and community, and with personal relationships. On being further stretched, these two themes develop into two orientations: the so-called 'Yahwism' that dominated later Israelite traditions, and the secular moralism that originated in community life and gained momentum in practical areas, which in the words of Katherine Dell represent 'an ongoing tension between the human-sided wisdom and the God-given dimension'.[33] Although efforts were not spared to harmonize these two orientations, the tension between them can nevertheless be seen in certain contexts. In different situations they further reflected two opposite attitudes towards the destiny of human beings: the optimistic and the pessimistic. Holding faith in the creative order of YHWH, writers or compilers of the texts were often confident that, mysterious as nature and society were, humans had the ability and capability to interpret and understand the order behind them, and were able to solve problems with the guidance

---

[33] Katharine Dell, 2000, p.50.

of the divine wisdom. However, in the post-exilic era, a pessimistic tendency took over in Israelite thought, when people no longer had confidence in the human capacity for reasoning and understanding. This pessimistic tone is clearly reflected in the books of Job and Ecclesiastes.

There is little evidence that the tension as expressed in Israelite literature between the divine and the secular dimensions of wisdom plays an important role in the Confucian classics. For Confucians wisdom is the fruit of extensive knowledge about the world and life, and is therefore embedded in human intelligence and rediscovered in the longing for answers to fundamental questions concerning the Way of Heaven and the way of human society. Confucian masters felt dismayed at what they saw in their lifetime – 'the Way does not prevail' (*Analects*, 5:7) – and they deplored the inability to grasp the deepest secrets and mystery of the universe. However, instead of aligning themselves with the divine power and searching for a rational tool to correct the irrational reality in transcendental wisdom, Confucians looked to the past for a solution. A worthy teacher of wisdom was said to be the one 'who understands the new through reviewing the old' (*Analects*, 2:11). In establishing golden rules in antiquity, and connecting the present with the past, Confucian masters built an intellectual bridge over the gap between the wise and the ignorant, between the intelligent and the foolish, and between the enlightened and the unenlightened.

Wisdom Teaching and Persuasion Styles

Ancient masters, teachers and authors were well known for their literary elegance and philosophical innovation. Each of them normally had a group of disciples who followed him, studied with him and probably travelled alongside him. The master became the recognized head of a distinctive school, of which the disciples were the first generation students. After the death of the master, these students would normally establish their own 'sub-schools', of which they in turn became masters, and transmitted the teaching they had learned from their master to second and third generations.

From a historical perspective, however, this description is probably more applicable to the case of Confucianism than to that of Israel. What was true of both, however, was that, in the process of transmitting knowledge and wisdom, the masters or teachers not only needed to argue against rival groups, but also to attract more people to join their own ranks, in order to survive and expand. The nature of wisdom transmission required that charismatic masters demonstrated in a variety of ways to the reader or audience that their teaching was more substantial than that of others, and that their solutions were more effective for philosophical, religious, social and personal problems. Indeed wisdom enables their teaching to be effective and their words attractive, as it is said in Hebrew proverbs, 'The wise of heart is called a man of discernment, and pleasant speech increases persuasiveness ...The mind of the wise makes his speech judicious, and adds persuasiveness to his lips' (Prov. 16:21, 23).

Competition with other schools or teachers also forced Confucian and Israelite wisdom masters to advance various skills of persuasion and debate, and they were fully aware that persuasion did not always have to be explicitly disputing, nor must it be coercive. To attract their readers or audience to what they believed to be true wisdom and to divert them from so-called 'false doctrines', these masters and teachers implicitly or explicitly employed a number of styles and techniques to present their teachings.

In describing basic wisdom genres of the Old Testament, Roland Murphy draws our attention to the three types of sayings that are widely applied in the books: the proverbs that 'draw a conclusion from experience and formulate it in a pithy, succinct way', the experiential saying that 'merely presents some aspects of reality … and leaves the practical conclusion(s) for the hearer/reader to draw', and the dialectic (or learned) saying that 'goes beyond a mere statement about reality; it characterizes a certain act or attitude in such a way as to influence human conduct'.[34] We will not go in the direction of literature style analysis as Murphy has done. What we are interested in here is how the writers or collectors of the wisdom texts in both the Confucian and Israelite traditions tried to 'sell' their teaching. In this respect we find that analogies are extensively employed in oral tradition as well as in written literature, and with a light touch they carry with them the power of argument and persuasion. By using as an example a well-known thing or event or a noted regular pattern in the social and natural world, the nature or result of which is easily understood and seen, an analogy builds up a close connection between it and what the teacher wants to illustrate, from which a particular lesson or instruction is implicitly or explicitly drawn. Such an analogy can arouse strong emotional and cognitive responses in the audience.

It was perhaps because of its effectiveness that Confucian masters and Israelite teachers were particularly fond of analogy, and indeed many of the analogies found in the wisdom literature of ancient Israel and Confucian texts are short, expressed in pithy form but full of insights into human affairs, either religious and social, or personal. To clearly see the nature of an action or event, these masters and teachers frequently present their understanding by comparing it to something else; for example, by extending their reasoning from birds' behaviour to human attitude, from plants' life to human choices, or from social matters of a secular nature to religious issues of spiritual significance. In Israelite proverbs, the glory of YHWH is sometimes likened to that of the king (Prov. 25:2), to illustrate the absolute power of YHWH who rules the universe in the same way as a king rules the state, and to suggest that, just as the subjects who disobeyed the king would be punished, the people who violated YHWH's discipline and departed from his will would suffer the consequences. The 'way' of animals or birds or insects could also be taken as

---

34 Roland E. Murphy: *Wisdom Literature – Job, Proverbs, Ruth, Canticles, Ecclesiastes, and Esther, The Forms of the Old Testament Literature*, series vol. XIII, Grand Rapids, Michigan: Wm. B. Eerdmans Publishing Company, 1981, p.4.

teaching on human behaviour, and the reader or audience were taught to 'ask the animals, and they will teach you, or the birds of the air, and they will tell you' (Job 12:7). In order to inspire people to go for wisdom rather than to follow a stupid course of life, the author of the Wisdom of Solomon illustrates the pursuit of wisdom as longing for love: 'Wisdom I loved; I sought her out when I was young and longed to win her for my bride; I was in love with her beauty' (Wisd. 8:2). The implication of this teaching is that, without a longing and sincere heart, it will not be possible for wisdom to come to one's embrace and one will therefore remain outside of her door.

Confucian masters were originally private teachers, and acted from time to time as counsellors at the court. Their audience was primarily the educated upper class, heads of states or general intellectuals. They either taught at a fixed place where they and their disciples studied, discussed and debated together, or went from state to state to seek a willing ear.

Confucius was a great master of analogy, and valued highly the 'ability to take as analogy what is near at hand' (*Analects*, 6:30). Many of his illustrations are indeed still of significance and value even in today's idiomatic language and conventional thinking. In his conversations he frequently made use of a variety of simple and easy-to-see examples to explain or illustrate what he intended to teach. He once compared a good government to the north pole star which was at that time believed to be located at the centre of the universe with all other stars moving around it: 'The rule of virtue can be compared to the Pole Star which commands the homage of the multitude of stars without leaving its place' (*Analects*, 2:1). The implication of this analogy is that a good government does not need to resort to force or punishment, but through virtue it will naturally command the loyalty of the people. On another occasion he used the relation between the wind and the grass to illustrate this point, and to propagate his teaching on how peace and morality can be realized by moral influence. For him, the virtue of the upper class is like the wind, while the virtue of ordinary people is like grass. Since the wind blows over the grass and the latter is surely to bend, then, if the people who rule are virtuous and behave morally, the people who are governed will naturally follow suit (*Analects*, 12:19). One day he was annoyed when one of his students slept in the daytime, and therefore compared him to a piece of rotten wood and a wall of dried dung. Just as the rotten wood cannot be carved, and the wall of dried dung cannot be trowelled, a lazy person like that student is not worth teaching (*Analects*, 5:10). The power of these analogies for this student and indeed for all others was much stronger than a simple condemnation.

Other Confucians also made use of various kinds of analogies in their teachings. For example, in his conversation with King Hui of Liang, Mengzi made use of an analogy to explain why the king, although believing that he had done a great many good things for his people, was not able to make his state stronger. To explain that his behaviour was not substantially different from that of other kings or dukes, Mengzi told him an imagined story: when the army was overwhelmed by the rival state on the battlefield, some soldiers fled, abandoning their armour and trailing their weapons. One of them stopped after a hundred paces, another after fifty paces. The one who ran only fifty paces laughed at the one who ran a hundred. As a matter of fact both of them were deserting their own course, and the difference between them was no more than that one ran away a hundred paces while the other only fifty (Mengzi, 1A:3). By this Mengzi taught the king that, in order for the people to come to him and for the state to increase in wealth and to become stronger, it is not enough for him just to do similar things to the rulers among his neighbours. He must practise a substantially benevolent government.

Another persuasive tool frequently employed in Confucian classics and Israelite texts is comparative contrast. Differing from an analogy that compares two similar things or events and draws out lessons from the parallel, a contrast places two diametrically different things alongside one another. The value of a good choice is magnified when it is compared with a stupid one, while the stupidity of one's behaviour can be seen more clearly when it is in contrast to the shining character of the wise. This is particularly widely used in proverbs. In the wisdom literature, the word 'proverb' is a translation of the Hebrew term *māšāl*, the etymological origin of which is associated with 'comparison' and 'rule of power',[35] and indeed many of the proverbs contain a metaphor or simile to make a contrast. We read a variety of comparisons and parallels between the wise and the foolish, between a shrewdly chosen action and a stupid decision, or between a tendency to goodness and a trend to disaster. For example, Proverbs 10:5 contrasts the diligent and the lazy, and gives different moral evaluations of them: 'He who gathers crops in summer is a wise son; but he who sleeps during harvest is a disgraceful son.' Frequently there is no need to say more about the two extremes, since the contrasting results are themselves sufficiently illuminating. It is through such a comparison that a tacit conclusion is arrived at in order to influence people's minds and to change their choice of action in the future.

The same technique is also favoured in Confucian classics, and comparison and contrast themselves lead to convincing teaching. Confucius compared 'a gentleman' and 'a small man', in which he praised highly the valuable and noble character of the former and condemned or ridiculed the character of the latter: for example, 'The gentleman is at ease without being arrogant; the small man is arrogant without being at ease' (*Analects*, 13:26). He called people to study to improve their character and disliked those who studied in order to show off: 'The scholars of antiquity studied to improve themselves; while people today study to impress others' (*Analects*, 14:24).

What has been discussed above demonstrates that neither language nor cultural differences have turned Confucian texts and Israelite writings into completely different and unrelated wisdom teachings. Instead, the fundamental commonality of intellectual pursuit and social cohesion have generated numerous similarities between what is considered to be wise in the Israelite tradition and what is believed to be intelligent by Confucian scholars. On many occasions we find that a great number of moral and religious teachings given in the two traditions have a common

---

[35] *The Anchor Bible Dictionary*, vol. VI, p.921.

mentality, although on many others they diverge significantly. However, we must be aware that, just as differences should not be taken as a total opposition, similarities are not always sufficient to justify identity. To fully appreciate the difference of such similarities we must examine their respective epistemological, philosophical and ethical grounds and applications. This is what we are going to do in the next few chapters.

CHAPTER THREE

Knowledge and Wisdom

There is a fundamentally epistemological dimension to wisdom, where wisdom presents itself as a form of knowledge, concerning the laws or causal relationships of the natural, human and spiritual worlds, expressed in collected and accumulated truths obtained through repeated observation and logical reasoning. Like information and skills acquired through experience and/or education, knowledge expands people's view and provides them with flexibility and options in dealing with problems, enabling informed decisions and choices of the most likely successful course of action. Both Israelite and Confucian teachers confirm that wisdom is based on, or comprises, or is derived from, knowledge, but they differ in emphasis, especially in dealing with the source and nature of knowledge, and with the question about which element of knowledge plays a decisive role in forming wisdom. In Confucianism the emphasis is placed on knowledge of the Way, and discussion is engaged on whether this kind of knowledge is *a priori* or *a posteriori* or, in other words, innate or learned, whether humans are capable of knowledge of the Way, and how it can be transmitted. There is a different orientation in the Israelite epistemology of wisdom where attention is paid to the establishment of the belief that the divine is the only source of insight and understanding, and to finding a solution to the question of how to solve the tension between divine knowledge and secular knowledge. Despite its theocentric orientation, Israelite teachers nevertheless acknowledge that knowledge is accumulated experience and can guide action, and stress that instructions from teachers must be heeded and applied in life situations. To establish a paradigm on wisdom and knowledge in a comparative perspective, we will in this chapter explore the issue of knowledge, and learn what kind of knowledge is taken to be the most important element of wisdom in the Confucian and Israelite traditions.

Ordinary and Wisdom Knowledge

In epistemological terms, knowledge is in general defined as 'true and justified beliefs' as opposed to untested opinions.[1] However, this does not mean that all forms

---

[1] Definition of knowledge varies and scholars have proposed various ways to differentiate knowledge, opinion and wisdom. The classical definition of knowledge as 'justified true beliefs' given by Plato is still influential, although some modern philosophers, such as Karl Popper and Frege, tend to use 'true propositions' to indicate that the nature of knowledge lies in the subject's attitude and knowledge is not necessarily dependent on what is believed. A modern Chinese philosopher, Feng Qi (1915–95), attempted this through the formation of perspectives: 'opinion is from my perspective, knowledge is from the perspective of the object, and wisdom is from the perspective of *dao*'. For him human knowing is a process of progressing from 'ignorance to knowledge and from knowledge to wisdom' (Huang Yong: 'Feng Qi', in *Contemporary Chinese Philosophy*, ed. Chung-ying Cheng and Nicholas Bunnin, Malden, Massachusetts and Oxford: Blackwell, 2002, pp.213–14).

of knowledge are of the same nature and function for human wisdom. Knowledge in fact is of various kinds and of a wide range, and can be classified into different categories according to different criteria. There are differences between good and bad knowledge, between profound and superficial knowledge, between general (theoretical) and specific (practical) knowledge, and ultimately between ordinary knowledge and wisdom knowledge. In early Daoism, wisdom or knowledge of the Way, is differentiated from ordinary knowledge. Laozi, an earlier contemporary of Confucius and the supposed compiler of the *Daode jing*, argues that wisdom must not be judged by the accumulation of experience and information, because wisdom is not determined by the number of things and events one knows, but by understanding of, and insight into, *dao* (the Way); he thereby concludes that 'He who knows has no wide [knowledge]; he who has wide [knowledge] does not know' (Daode jing, 81). He even goes further to contrast the way of accumulating knowledge and the way of practising the Way: practising learning we must increase [our knowledge] day by day; practising the Way, we must decrease [our knowledge] day by day' (Chapter 48). Zhuangzi (399?–295?BCE), the second most prominent figure within philosophical Daoism, claims that wisdom enables us to understand that we are part of the great unity (the universe). He further differentiates 'great wisdom that is all embracing' from 'small wisdom that is discriminative', believing that the highest wisdom belongs to those who 'know to stop at what they do not know'.[2]

Most Confucian masters tend to use easily understood language to illustrate differences between ordinary knowledge about things and events, and profound knowledge about the causes of phenomena, and to explain the different functions of these two layers or types of knowledge, one enabling us to know phenomena, and the other facilitating our understanding of the laws underlying the phenomena or the causes of events or affairs. In a sense knowledge of phenomena is gathered primarily in personal experience, observation and data collection, while profound knowledge can be acquired only after refining raw materials of knowledge in critical thinking, reasoning and interpreting. Unlike their counterparts in Daoism, however, the early Confucian masters did not exclude either of these two types of knowledge from their concept of wisdom, believing that knowledge of phenomena provides a necessary access to the understanding of deeper causes. This is in line with the general view of knowledge in ancient China, as we have argued in the first chapter, that Chinese thinkers and intellectuals in general did not distinguish knowledge and wisdom; rather, they identified knowledge and wisdom by using the same word for both. Because of the unity of knowledge and wisdom, Confucians believe that, for the sages as well as for ordinary people, investigating (*ge*) things and affairs, observing (*guan*) events and examining (*shen*) the signs and images are the only way to gain knowledge of Heaven and Earth, and to understand the Way of the universe. In the *Great Learning*, investigating things and events (*ge wu*) is the prerequisite for

---

[2] My translation. See *The Complete Works of Chuang Tzu*, trans. Burton Watson, New York: Columbia University Press, 1968, pp.37, 44.

extending knowledge. In the *Analects*, it is said that, by observing one's words and behaviour (*ting qi yan guan qi xing*), one is able to understand what kind of person one is. And in one of the *Lüshi Chunqiu*'s essays, it is clearly stated, 'To gain foreknowledge one must first examine the internal and external signs [of things and events] (*shen zheng biao*). [It would be impossible] to have foreknowledge without [knowing] internal and external signs, Yao and Shun [the sage–kings] and ordinary people are the same in this respect'.[3]

In the Great Commentary of the *Book of Changes*, this is further expanded in order to show how the ancient sage was able to gain the ultimate knowledge of great mysteries:

> Looking upward, [the sage] observes the signs of Heaven; looking down, [he] examines the lines of the Earth. Thus he knows the causes of the dark and the light. Tracing things to their beginning, and following them to their end, he thus knows the reasons of life and death. Examining how vital essence (*jing*) and vital energy (*qi*) are transformed into things, and how wandering souls lead to changes, thus he knows the conditions and characteristics of ghosts and spirits.[4]

In its ultimate meaning, Confucian knowledge is intended to provide a solution to the problems caused by human finitude rather than a power to 'master nature' (to use Francis Bacon's terminology[5]). Therefore, in Confucianism knowledge becomes an important element of its overall strategy for dealing with human finitude. As part of the solution, ordinary knowledge is closely related to wisdom knowledge, or more precisely, knowledge (*zhi*) is believed to be none other than wisdom (*zhi*). The primary 'object' of wisdom knowledge is the ultimate reality or law, referred to as *tian* (Heaven), *ming* (the Mandate of Heaven or destiny), or *dao* (the Way). However, as the cause and the effect are entwined, knowledge of the cause and knowledge of things are always mutually dependent. Heaven or the Way is not something totally external to human existence. It exists in the interaction between humanity and the (physical and metaphysical) universe, in the intercommunication between individuals and the Ultimate. Therefore, to unlock the secrets of the universe is equivalent to uncovering the meaning of personal life, which is well summarized in the *Doctrine of the Mean* as follows: 'What Heaven (T'ien, Nature) imparts to man is called human nature. To follow our nature is called the Way (Tao). Cultivating the Way is called education' (Zhongyong, 1).[6]

---

[3] *Lüshi Chunqiu*, 20:8, in *Zhuzi Jicheng*, Beijing: Zhonghua Shuju, 1954, vol. 6, p.272. We have reasons to believe that this essay was composed under the influence of Confucian philosophical views of knowledge.

[4] My translation. See *I Ching or the Book of Changes*, The Richard Wilhelm translation, rendered into English by Cary F. Baynes, London: Arkana, 1967, p.294.

[5] Francis Bacon searched for ways to give humans the 'mastery over nature, a mastery that would enable man to transform the quality of his life on earth' (Maurice Cranston: 'Bacon, Francis', in *The Encyclopaedia of Philosophy*, vols 1–2, ed. Paul Edwards, London: Macmillan, 1976, p.236).

[6] Wing-tsit Chan (trans.): *A Source Book in Chinese Philosophy*, Princeton: Princeton University Press, 1963, p.98.

In Israelite scriptures, wisdom knowledge is also carefully distinguished from knowledge of a specific nature. The words for 'knowledge' and 'knowing' in Israelite scriptures are *yāda'* (Hebrew) and *ginōskō* (Greek) and are used in two different senses, one referring to experiential and relational knowledge, and the other to rational discourse and insight into the nature of reality. In the experiential and relational sense, 'knowing' something means one has experienced it or has been in a relation with it. However, in wisdom literature, knowledge is used more in the sense of insight, as we can see from Job 12:3 and Ecclesiastes 1:16, where knowing something means having grasped its essence.[7]

Unlike Confucians, however, Israelite teachers emphasized more the gap than the affinity between these two types of knowledge, in line with their theocentric perception of the opposition between the secular and the divine. There is a general consensus among early Israelite teachers that human experience and personal reflection have their limitations and that these limitations cannot be easily overcome because of the complexity of the phenomenal world and the profundity of the 'world order'. The limitations first arise from the finitude of human intelligence. Human wonder at the secrets of the natural world often leads to their longing for knowledge of natural events, but natural events and things are believed to be far more complicated than humans can grasp or understand:

> Three things are too wonderful for me; four I do not understand: the way of an
> eagle in the sky, the way of a snake on a rock, the way of a ship on the high seas,
> and the way of a man with a girl. (Prov. 30:18–19)

The gap between human knowledge and the order of the world also comes from the finitude of human life. Humans are mortals, whilst the world order was created by YHWH who 'does great things beyond understanding' (Job 9:10), which, for example, makes Job wonder, 'how can a mortal be just before YHWH?' (Job 9:2). Based on the conviction that nobody would have presumed to understand the 'whole world of YHWH', the wisdom of the Israelites draws a clear line between what humans can know and what they cannot, while admitting that, by means of one's knowledge of the patterns and regularities of phenomena, one would make wise decisions about what one should do and what one should not. To acknowledge the limits is also to admit the hiddenness and unfathomablity of divine wisdom, the inexpressible otherness and the mystery that is beyond human intelligence. This is an area where humans must wait for the revelation of the superhuman, because it is in the divine sphere.

In the Confucian tradition the limitedness of human understanding is tackled at two levels. At the level of ordinary knowledge, everyone, however clever they may be, lacks knowledge of something. Therefore the wise are those who admit frankly that they know what they know and they do not know what they do not know. This is

---

[7] *Eerdmans Dictionary of the Bible* (David Noel Freedman, editor-in-chief), Grand Rapids, Michigan: William B. Eerdmans Publishing Company, 2000, p.777.

exactly what Confucius taught his disciples. When one of his students, Zi You (506–? BCE) asked about what it means to know, 'The Master said: 'You, let me tell you what is knowledge. To say you know when you know, and to say you do not when you do not, that is knowledge' (*Analects*, 2:17). At the level of wisdom knowledge, Confucians demonstrate a more positive character than early Israelites about the role and function of ordinary knowledge in forming wisdom, believing that by observing the 'signs of Heaven' and the 'patterns of the Earth' humans can have a holistic understanding of the universe, that is, gain wisdom knowledge. However, the difference between Confucian and Israelite views is not as substantial as it appears. Early Israelite teachers did not totally divorce 'knowledge' per se from their perspective on wisdom either. Knowledge (*da'at* is derived from the root *yd'*, to know) is associated with insight and understanding. Coming from the root *byn* (to understand) are the substantives *bīnāh*, insight, understanding, and *t^ebūnā*, 'understanding, knowledge'.[8] To understand (*byn*) is thus connected with 'to know' (*yd'*): 'What do you know that we do not know? What do you understand that we do not?' (Job 15:9). Knowing is therefore taken as a path to understanding and insight which are in turn part of wisdom knowledge.

The difference between wisdom knowledge and ordinary knowledge has another dimension, namely, that between superficial knowledge and true knowledge. Confucius categorically excludes cunning or discerning from wisdom knowledge. A similar idea can also be observed in the Israelite wisdom tradition, that such discerning would stop people from gaining real knowledge. Only by reproving a person of discerning (*nābōn*), will he 'gain' knowledge (*yābīn da'at*) (Prov. 19:25). Like Confucians, the Israelite teachers also associate superficial knowledge with the intention of making a good profit, while associating true knowledge with the intention of improving one's character. Learning the words of the wise will improve one's character, but those who always think of making a profitable choice in a particular situation are foolish; the simple ones can gain prudence, while foolish men can understand discretion (*'ormā*) (Prov. 8:5).

True knowledge or insightful understanding is concerned with the deeper meaning and mysterious nature of life and the world, and with the fundamental order hidden within the universe that sustains the cosmos. While Confucians are positive that what we have observed will in the long run lead us to the deep cause of the universe or the world order, the Israelite teachers are more suspicious about this possibility and do

---

[8] The Hebrew root of understanding (*byn*) is connected with the substantive *bayin*, 'interval, space, between'; its original meaning was 'to distinguish, separate', 'to understand', 'to perceive (see)', 'to have insight', and its synonyms include *ḥākam*, to be wise, and *śākal*, to be prudent (*Theological Dictionary of the Old Testament*, ed. G. Johannes Botterweck and Helmer Ringgren, trans. John T. Willis, vol. II, Grand Rapids, Michigan: William B. Eerdmans Publishing Company, 1977, pp.99–100). Both *bīnā* and *t^ebūnā* are closely connected to wisdom thought: 'Of the 42 times *tebhunah* occurs in the OT, it appears 19 times in Proverbs and 4 times in Job; 22 times it is explicitly connected with *chokhmah*, "wisdom" … Both *binah* and *tebhunah* appear as synonyms of *chokhmah*, "wisdom", with all the nuances of meaning of which it is capable' (ibid. pp.106–7).

not believe that we humans are ever capable of knowing the fundamental law of creation. For them, knowledge of the world order can come only as a gift of YHWH for human beings, and therefore is subject to his will. However, at this point we can nevertheless perceive something important for our comparison with the Confucian view. While Israelite teachers believe that YHWH holds the ultimate veto over human efforts in understanding the order, it is equally believed that he does not exercise the right of veto arbitrarily. This has in effect left some room for human knowledge and experience to function. Believing that wisdom means discovering the 'rational rule' of the order, the Israelites think this discovery will enable the wise to secure their existence by acting in harmony with the order.[9] However, despite this leaning towards humanistic epistemology, the Israelite perspective on wisdom is fundamentally theocentric, the prerequisite of which is that the order or principle reflects the will of YHWH, and that only the divine can truly have it and give it to humans. We as ordinary people know little, or nothing, about it, because only he who weighs the heart can 'perceive' it, and he who keeps watching over the soul 'knows' it (Prov. 24:12).

Like Confucian masters, who differentiate knowledge about events and affairs from profound knowledge of the Way and attribute the latter to the sages only, the Israelites classify knowledge into two categories: one is human understanding and the deeds resulting from this understanding, and the other is divine knowledge, or the knowledge of YHWH concerning the world order, life and death, which the prophets may be able to convey to us. However, we find a significant difference here between Confucians and Israelite teachers concerning how and why some specifically defined people can find true knowledge. The Confucians believe that the sage is able to find truth through ordinary experiences such as observation, because his understanding has penetrated the deepest mysteries of the universe and his reasoning has revealed the most profound reasons for the evolution of phenomena. The Israelites, however, believe that only the faithful will have bestowed on them this kind of knowledge. In the book of Genesis we already read that knowledge of good and evil and of life and death can only be a gift from YHWH. In the mouth of the serpent it is said that the fruit of the tree in the midst of the garden will open humans' eyes, making them like God knowing good and evil; in other words, making them wise. Disobeying YHWH's will, Adam and Eve took the fruit and gained part of YHWH's wisdom, and this then led to their punishment of being banished from the garden (Genesis 3:4–19). The divine nature of wisdom knowledge is vividly illustrated in a passage of the book of Ezekiel where, on seeing a great many skeletons, YHWH asked Ezekiel if these bones could live, to which Ezekiel replied, 'O Sovereign Lord, you alone know' (Ezekiel 37:3). This indicates that YHWH is believed not only to be able to give life, but also to be the sole source of knowledge about life and death. This understanding is demonstrated in all wisdom texts and becomes a central theme running through Israelite wisdom thinking.

---

[9] James L. Crenshaw: *Old Testament Wisdom: An Introduction*, revised and enlarged, Louisville: Westminster John Knox Press, 1998, p.55.

The Confucian differentiation of ordinary knowledge and wisdom knowledge is to justify the progress of human knowing through learning and education, not to separate them into two realms. Therefore it is more important for Confucians to associate the two types of knowledge than to disconnect them. The association of ordinary knowledge and wisdom knowledge has convinced Confucian masters that through education and training everybody would be able to gain wisdom, to know and understand the world order, and to act properly in accord with the universal principle. There is a fundamental unity between the Confucian Ultimate (Heaven) and human affairs, and between self-knowledge and knowledge of the Ultimate. It is in this sense that Mengzi formulates a well-cherished pathway to knowledge of Heaven, arguing that the way to the unlimited is to be found in one's own heart/mind, and 'by knowing one's own nature one knows Heaven, and by retaining one's heart and nurturing one's nature one is serving Heaven' (Mengzi, 7A:1).

The separation of human knowledge from YHWH's knowledge, however, causes a problem for Israelite teachers, and makes them less positive about the prospect that humans can progress from ordinary knowledge to wisdom. On the one hand, they acknowledge the link between knowledge and wisdom, and that, like an inheritance, 'wisdom is a good thing and benefits those who see the sun'; 'the advantage of knowledge is this: that wisdom preserves the life of its possessor' (Eccl. 7:11–12). On the other hand, admitting that wisdom is so profound and mysterious that humans are not able to grasp it, some of the teachers come to a totally sceptical view of human capability of attaining wisdom knowledge: 'I am determined to be wise – but this was beyond me. Whatever wisdom may be, it is far off and most profound – who can discover it?' (Eccl. 7:23). The authors of these Israelite texts teach people cynically not to trust those who claim they have knowledge, because 'even if a wise man claims he knows, he cannot really comprehend it' (Eccl. 8:17). This inevitably leads to an exclusively theistic perspective on wisdom knowledge, that only the creator fully knows the created, that wisdom knowledge is possessed only by the divine, and that the only teaching teachers should give is that there is no need to look for profound knowledge, since it is only by believing in YHWH that knowledge will come:

> The Lord gives wisdom, and from his mouth come knowledge and understanding … Then you will understand what is right and just and fair – every good path. For wisdom will enter your heart, and knowledge will be pleasant to your soul. Discretion will protect you, and understanding will guard you. (Prov. 2:6–11)

On the positive side, we can see from these passages that, even for those most cynical teachers in ancient Israel, knowledge is valuable for, or is an integral part of, wisdom. However, embedded in a theistic tradition, these teachers make a great effort to prove that every kind of knowledge, particular and general alike, is meaningful only if its divine source is acknowledged and confirmed.

Natural and Social Knowledge

Although there are many types of knowledge open to people, the most common are natural knowledge or knowledge about the natural world, and social knowledge or knowledge concerning the human self and human communities. Natural knowledge is probably the first type of information humans came to acquire consciously and possess intelligently, finally leading to what we know today as science and technology. Humans live in the natural environment, surrounded by natural objects and phenomena such as wind, rain, hills and mountains, rivers and seas, animals and plants; their life depends upon environmental conditions, and at the same time is disciplined by natural laws, that is, the laws governing all movements, growth and death in the universe. The knowledge of these two aspects of the natural world, natural conditions and natural laws, is therefore essential for humans to survive and prosper.

For humans, the natural world is like the mother providing the necessities of life, such as land, water, air, light and changes of seasons, indispensable prerequisites for the existence and functioning of human beings and human communities. The Judeo-Christian understanding of the human–nature relation can be seen from the order of creation where the creation sequence of light, sky, land, seas, plants, living creatures and finally humans, indicates that humans rely on the natural world for living (for example, fruits, birds and beasts for food). This is, in theological terms, an acknowledgment of the dependence of humans on nature. Confucian masters clearly attribute all human relationships and values to the existence and functioning of the natural world (heaven and earth), and base human wisdom on knowledge of natural laws, as stated in the *Book of Changes*:

> After there are heaven and earth, there are individual things. After individual things have come into being, there are two sexes. After there are male and female, there is the relationship between husband and wife. After the relationship between husband and wife exists, there is the relationship between father and son. After the relationship between father and son exists, there is the relationship between prince and servitor. After the relationship between prince and servitor exists, there is the difference between superior and inferior. After the difference between superior and inferior exists, the rules or propriety and of right can operate.[10]

However, there is the other side of the nature–human relation. Nature is constantly changing; some changes are benign and enable humans to enjoy the benefits of seasons, while others are violent and render humans at the mercy of the nature 'tyrant'. Do such changes follow certain patterns, which humans can know and act upon for their own benefit? The need to know about natural changes in order to reap a harvest or to avoid evil consequences is the first motivation in searching for natural

---

[10] *I Ching or the Book of Changes*, pp.540–41.

knowledge. Knowledge of animals, plants, changes of seasons, wind and rain, flooding and drought and so on is the basis on which the complicated structure of human wisdom is established. This is why both Confucian and Israelite masters urged people to pay attention to the observation of natural phenomena, to understanding living creatures, and to acquiring familiarity with the circumstances they happened to be in.

On the surface it seems that ancient Israelites believed that the first kind of knowledge humans possessed was of a moral nature (good and evil), not about the natural world. In the book of Genesis it is claimed that the first man and woman did not have knowledge until they ate the fruit of the tree of the knowledge of good and evil, when their eyes 'were opened, and they realised that they were naked…' (Genesis 3:7). However, being charged with the responsibility of managing the natural world, human beings must possess a certain degree of knowledge about what they are responsible for before they can fulfil their God-given task. Natural creatures are therefore one of the important sources of wisdom knowledge, and in the book of Job we read that animals and plants can give testimony to the wisdom and might of YHWH: 'ask the beasts, and they will teach you; the birds of the air, and they will tell you; or the plants of the earth, and they will teach you; and the fish of the sea will declare to you' (Job 12:7–8).

To understand a particular natural condition is not only to know its phenomenal expressions, but also to know the connection between different phases of its changes, something more permanently underlying the changeable sequences of events. This seemingly unchangeable essence is called by the Confucians the Way of Heaven and Earth, and by the Israelites 'the eternal order' of creation (Sir. 16:27). However, Confucius was fully aware that the complicity of the Way of Heaven was far beyond human intelligence and therefore refrained from talking about it (*Analects*, 5:13). For ancient Israelites the creation order was full of mysteries, beyond their comprehension. In fact the Hebrew word, *ōlām*, referring to the world, probably 'means something hidden, unknown, mysterious', and according to Ludwig Köhler, 'to the Hebrew the whole world is mysterious. He neither understands it, nor does he penetrate it and examine it.'[11] However this did not prevent the Israelites from gaining knowledge of the natural order through observing individual natural phenomena, which according to the Wisdom of Solomon, includes

> A knowledge of the structure of the world and the operation of the elements; the beginning and end of epochs and their middle course; the alternating cycles of the years and the constellations; the nature of living creatures and behaviour of wild beasts; the violent force of winds and human thought; the varieties of plants and the virtues of roots. (Wisd. 7:17–20)

Observation of natural phenomena is one of the important sources of knowledge for

---

[11] Ludwig Köhler: *Hebrew Man*, trans. Peter R. Ackroyd, London: SCM Press, 1956, p.132.

the Israelites, and Solomon's wisdom is said to have been displayed in his discourses on trees, plants, animals and reptiles (1Kings 5:13). Modern scholars have speculated on the reason why knowledge of the natural world is emphasized in ancient Israel. For some this was because 'Israel's sages believed that the movements of heavenly bodies, the activities of weather, and the actions of animals contained hidden knowledge about ways of coping with life. By studying these phenomena, one discovered truth that, by analogy, applied to human conduct.'[12]

Knowledge concerning the natural world is also an important element of Confucian wisdom. The sayings in the *Analects* are primarily concerned with social, political and moral matters, but this does not mean that Confucius had no interest in natural phenomena. He once wondered what was the reason for 'young plants that fail to produce blossoms and blossoms that fail to produce fruits' (*Analects*, 9:22). He also observed 'the four seasons going round and a hundred things coming into being' (17:19), underlying which, he implied, there must be an order. Acknowledging that the natural world has its own laws, Mengzi suggested that by weighing we came to know what things were light and what heavy, and by measuring, we gained knowledge of what things were long and what short, so much so that 'The relationships of all things may be thus determined' (Mengzi, 1A:7). Xunzi naturalized the concept of Heaven as Nature. For him all mysteries of Heaven and Earth (literally meaning the universe) could be explained by the sequences of natural events, and it was in the knowledge of nature that we gained our wisdom to interpret the seemingly uninterpretable, and to control violent natural forces such as weather and flood.

The relation between humans and nature was perceived differently in Confucian and Israelite traditions, which had a direct effect on their perception of natural knowledge and wisdom. In Israel, humans were created in the image of the creator, who then gave two commissions to his final creation: 'Be fruitful and multiply, and fill the earth and subdue it' (Genesis 1:28). The command that humans must subdue the earth directed human activities and attitudes towards nature, producing both benefits and damage to human life, and generated a view that, the more powerful one was in subduing nature, the wiser one would be considered to be. This has eventually created huge tension between humans and nature and brought about disasters to the environment. In the Confucian metaphysical world, humans were part of nature, and confined by the same laws as all other natural phenomena were. In the Confucian discourse of nature wisdom we can see an eco-ethical discipline requiring us to respect nature, follow natural laws and protect the natural environment. Underlying such a discipline is a deep wisdom that sees humans and nature as one unity and maintains that humans must co-exist with the natural environment.

However insightful Confucian and Israelite natural wisdom was, knowledge of nature in ancient China and Israel was not primarily scientifically oriented, but

---

[12] John Barton and John Muddiman (eds): *The Oxford Bible Commentary*, Oxford University Press, 2001, p.340.

something based on empirical observation by which the behaviour and characteristics of plants and animals could be used to form paradigms which illustrate human life and experience. Their intention was that certain regular patterns in the natural world should be employed as guidelines for human behaviour. Knowledge about natural events and phenomena was taken as the source of analogies to further understanding and to master life. Israelite teachers frequently drew wise teachings from animal behaviour; for example, they taught that 'Four things on earth are small, yet they are extremely wise': ants, conies, locusts and lizards (Prov. 30:24–8). Similarly Confucius took plants as a parable for a strong and righteous human character: 'Only when the cold season comes is the point brought home that the pine and the cypress are the last to lose their leaves' (*Analects*, 9:28).

For many Confucians knowledge of natural law (the Way of Heaven, *tian*) is an important pathway to knowledge of the spiritual ultimate (*tian*). Human knowledge about nature and natural creatures was possible because, like humans, all natural existences were believed to have been produced by Heaven and to have a common nature with humans. This is what Mengzi says about the 'one root' (*yi ben*): 'Heaven gives birth to all things in such a way that they have one root' (Mengzi, 3A:5), and the 'one root' underlies all bio-diversity and is fundamental to human knowledge of nature. As the ultimate source of natural beings, things and events, the Confucian *tian* does not speak, but reveals the secrets of the universe through changes of seasons and regularities of phenomena, as Mengzi explains: 'Heaven does not speak but reveals itself through its acts and deeds' (Mengzi, 5A:5). Therefore it is important for us to study natural 'acts' and 'deeds', from which we draw our knowledge of nature and by which we will be able to make wise choices. It is by this kind of knowledge and action that we find how Confucian sages would rule the world, and the *Doctrine of the Mean* proclaims the virtue of Confucius as that 'He conformed with the natural order governing the revolution of the seasons in heaven above, and followed the principles governing land and water below.'[13]

Knowledge about the value and laws of nature leads to an awareness of protecting the natural environment. Environmental ethics is therefore an important part of ancient Confucian and Israelite wisdom. Confucians realized the interreliance between nature and humans, and that protecting the environment is to protect human interests, as Mengzi clearly pointed out: 'If you do not interfere with the busy seasons in the fields, then there will be more grain than the people can eat; if you do not allow nets with too fine a mesh to be used in large ponds, then there will be more fish and turtles than they can eat; if hatchets and axes are permitted in the forests on the hills only in the proper seasons, then there will be more timber than they can use' (Mengzi, 1A:3). Xunzi suggested two ways to maintain harmonious relations between humans and nature. One is to act in accordance with the course of nature. For example, 'plowing in spring, weeding in summer, harvesting in autumn and storing up in winter' are in accordance with natural order and thus people will have plenty of grain

---

[13] *A Source Book in Chinese Philosophy*, pp.111–12.

for food. The other is to protect the natural environment by following the order and law of nature. For example, the season of spring is the time when all things grow, so that all kinds of activities against growth must be forbidden in this season, or in Xunzi's words, 'axes and halberds are not permitted in the mountain forest' and 'nets and poisons are not permitted in the marshes' (Knoblock, Xunzi, vol. 2, 1990, p.105).

The case for an Israelite environmental ethics is more complicated. For some scholars, the cycle of nature was only a stage for YHWH's historical drama of salvation, and the biblical views of the natural world include 'mastery over nature' and 'subjugation to nature'. However, more recent scholarship confirms that the natural world played a significant role in the formation and expression of the religion of Israel, and the Israelite texts contain multiple views of nature, of which 'harmony with nature' is 'the most frequently expressed value', which assumes that 'humans and nature are united in a precarious balance so that human actions cause consequences in nature which inevitably affect humans themselves'.[14]

It is apparent that both Confucians and the Israelites built their environmental ethics on a theological ground, and the interaffecting relation between humans and nature is presided over by Heaven or YHWH. For Confucians, Heaven would make known its approval or otherwise of human affairs by manifesting blessings or condemnations in the form of, for instance, a good harvest or natural disasters. This was later developed into a sophisticated doctrine during the Han Dynasty that failure to fulfil human duties would annoy Heaven and Heaven would first warn and then reprimand them by sending down the visitations (*zai*) and prodigies (*yi*) 'to warn the human sovereign of his behaviour, to command him to repent on his wrongdoing and to cultivate his virtue'.[15] The Israelites linked the conditions of the natural world with the people's faithfulness to the divine commandments: 'If the Israelites follow God's commandments, then Yahweh will send the rains so that the land abundantly yields its products. Otherwise, God will withhold the rains and the land will become desolate, resulting in the people's death.'[16]

Social knowledge primarily exists in the form of insights into human nature, history, culture and various kinds of human relationships, represented by, in modern terms, psychological, historical, sociological, economic, political, legal, ethical and anthropological knowledge.[17] Both natural and social knowledge are based on observation and experience, and are essentially scientific by nature. Both require a

---

[14] *Eerdmans Dictionary of the Bible*, p.949.

[15] *Baihutong Shuzheng*, 1994, Beijing: Zhonghua Shuju, p.267.

[16] David Noel Freedman, 2000, p.949.

[17] A distinction between what we mean by social knowledge and modern disciplines such as 'social epistemology' or 'sociology of knowledge' should be made here. Social epistemology is the conceptual and normative study of the relevance to knowledge of social relations, interests and institutions, while the sociology of knowledge is an empirical study of the contingent social conditions or causes of what is commonly taken to be knowledge (*Concise Routledge Encyclopedia of Philosophy*, London: Routledge, 2000, p.836).

certain degree of objectivity and preciseness, for which the will and emotion of the observer must be kept away from the presentation of data and statistics. However, hermeneutics rejects the traditional view of knowledge that totally separates the observer and the observed; rather it allows the interaction between them to take place in searching for and interpreting information. There is a difference in terms of subjectivity and objectivity in the formation of natural and social knowledge. Natural phenomena and natural laws do not depend on human consciousness and activity, and knowledge of them is therefore pursued with much less 'subjective' deliberation than social knowledge where the observed are motivated and influenced by conscious decisions of human beings. Traditional epistemology therefore tends to promote the view that natural knowledge constitutes a pure, value-free method of obtaining knowledge about the natural world. This does not sit well with modern hermeneutical understanding, nor is it suitable for our interpretation of Confucian and Israelite wisdom knowledge. As we have observed above, in the Confucian and Israelite traditions natural and social knowledge are intertwined and there is no such perception as that natural knowledge can function independently. Both Confucian and Israelite epistemological vision supports a methodology that refrains from ruling out the influence of social and cultural values in the very structuring of natural knowledge, and that reveals how human assumptions laden with social values affect the description, presentation and interpretation of data.

As far as the skill of coping with life problems is concerned, society is more complicated than nature and therefore requires a wider range of knowledge to deal with. Compared with natural knowledge, therefore, social knowledge is more closely related to, and more important for the formation of, wisdom. To live a good and pleasant life, people have to deal skilfully with various kinds of social conflicts, and to make delicate choices in the face of multiple options; in other words, a profound understanding of human nature and social structures is a prerequisite for treating other people properly and resolving personal problems adequately. Only by this understanding can we establish norms, rules and principles as guidelines for our behaviour and attitudes.

A great number of wise teachings found in Confucian and Israelite wisdom texts are concerned with the way secular or divine history is interpreted to provide a blueprint for social and political infrastructure, how particular individuals should lead a life in the context of complicated social relationships, and how to act and behave under the guidance of wisdom knowledge about these relationships. For Confucius, history was successive links of ages or generations, and from our observation of what was added and what was omitted we would grasp the change and continuity (*Analects*, 2:23). Confucian knowledge is essentially a deep understanding of human destiny and a mastering of social conventions and communication tools: 'A man has no way of becoming a gentleman unless he understand Destiny; he has no way of taking his stand unless he understands the rites; he has no way of judging men unless he understands words' (*Analects*, 20:3). In this sense, social knowledge includes not only knowledge of history, but also knowledge of religious rites. The knowledge of religious rites goes beyond what is on the surface; it is related to our understanding of human destiny as well as human living. When being asked about what is intended by a specific sacrifice, Confucius confessed that he did not understand, but he indicated that its knowledge was extremely important because he said that 'whoever understands it will be able to manage the Empire as easily as if he had it here', pointing to his palm (*Analects*, 3:11). Apart from knowledge of history and rites, Confucians considered central to wisdom the knowledge of humans, both as a race and as individuals. In ethical terms, knowledge of humans indicates an understanding of human nature and destiny, which is what is said about 'knowing our own nature' leading to our knowledge of Heaven (Mengzi, 7A:1). In political terms, knowledge of humans also points to the knowledge of all the people's needs and how they can be appointed to proper positions and, in one of the Confucian classics, the *Book of Documents*, it is stated that 'when a sovereign knows men, he is wise and can put men into their proper offices'.[18]

Israelite epistemology is built upon divine knowledge and wisdom. Human history is a testimony of YHWH's creation and personal experience is the evidence of divine guidance: 'The king's heart is a stream of water in the hand of the LORD; he turns it wherever it will. Every way of a man is right in his own eyes, but the LORD weighs the heart' (Prov. 21:1–2). From this conviction Israelite teachers drew a fundamental wisdom that a human is worthy of humanity because of the wisdom of YHWH, 'for even if one is perfect among the sons of men, yet without the wisdom that comes from thee he will be regarded as nothing' (Wisd. 9:6).

All kinds of knowledge can be traced to their sources in human nature and human history and are developed for the sake of their function in giving us adjustment to, and power over, the conditions under which we live. The branches of social knowledge correspond to the divisions of social existence and the depth arises from the capacities of the human mind and the interaction between these capacities and the social conditions. There are also the 'hard' and the 'soft' dimensions of social knowledge. Charles Horton Cooley, in his famous article 'The Roots of Social Knowledge', suggests that knowledge can be classified into two categories, one is from the development of sense contacts into knowledge of things, including its refinement into mensurative science, which he calls 'spatial or material knowledge', and the other is developed from contact with the minds of other humans, through communication, which sets going a process of thought and sentiment similar to theirs and enables us to understand them by sharing their states of mind, which he calls 'personal' or 'social' knowledge.[19] What he meant by 'social knowledge' is essentially centred on human relations, and arises from personal contact with the 'objects' we come to observe and study. In comparison, Confucian and Israelite

---

[18] James Legge (trans.): *The Chinese Classics: Vol III, The Shoo King or the Book of Historical Documents*, London: Trubner & Co., 1865, p.70.

[19] Charles Horton Cooley: 'The Roots of Social Knowledge', *American Journal of Sociology, 32*, 1926–7, pp.59–79.

teachers emphasized more 'soft' or personal knowledge than 'hard' or mensurative knowledge. It is clear that for the Israelites all knowing or knowledge can be gained only through entering personal relations. To know YHWH is to be in relationship with the divine creator; to know another person or nation is to have a relationship with that person or nation (Exodus 1:8; 1 Kings 1:4).

From an ethical point of view, Confucians linked moral knowledge and moral behaviour. Aristotle pointed out, '*knowing* about them [just and good acts] does not make us any more capable of *doing* them',[20] and Confucians were also confronted by the problems caused by the discrepancy between knowing and acting. An advantage Confucians have over Aristotlean ethics in solving these problems seems to be that Confucians in general do not place intellectual activity above practical wisdom, and do not therefore refer to wisdom either as a state of the mind or a behaviour pattern or an attribute of the soul, but as the whole process of self-cultivation guided by an insightful understanding of universal principles. Confucian self-cultivation can thus only be defined as the daily renewal of one's virtue (*ri xin*), which involves not only intellectual comprehension but also practical knowledge and action. In other words, Confucian wisdom is clearly reflected in the organic growth of a wise and good person. Identifying knowledge and moral action, it seems that Confucians have bypassed the barrier between knowing and doing. For some of them, to know (good) is to be good and virtuous, and to be good and virtuous is, in the case of family relationships, to follow one's parents' teaching, as stated in the Confucian *Analects*: 'If, for three years, he makes no changes to his father's ways, he can be said to be a good son' (*Analects*, 1:11).

Factual and Predictive Knowledge

Knowledge can be employed in different ways and can fulfil different purposes. Some knowledge provides us with information about the world in which we live, and by it we know what rules or norms we should follow in daily life and how to make decisions on specific occasions. Since this kind of knowledge is primarily descriptive and exists in the form of information about facts referring to something that exists, it may be called factual knowledge, similar to what Cooley terms 'spatial or material knowledge'. Factual knowledge is knowledge of natural, social and historical facts and tells us about a specific matter or event or situation in a particular time and space. Factual knowledge consists of statements concerning what has happened, existed and functioned.

Does this kind of knowledge entail evaluation of the fact described, or any motivation or guideline for undertaking a particular course of action? This has been a debated question open to various explanations in modern epistemology. Developing from the Humean thesis that cognitive states cannot suffice for action unless

---

[20] Aristotle: *Ethics*, trans. J.A.K. Thomson, Harmondsworth: Penguin, 1976, p.221.

combined with desires, many twentieth century meta-philosophers in the West tend to distinguish fact from value, and to separate factual statements from value judgments. Insisting that values such as good cannot be analytically reduced to a natural property and that no states of affairs themsleves in the world can be said to be values, some of these scholars categorically exclude (ethical and religious) value statements such as 'altruism is good' from knowledge. Ethical realism argues against this kind of ethical non-cognitivism, suggesting that there are facts of the matter about which actions are right and which wrong, and about which things are good and which bad, although it is conceded that value facts are somehow different from other sorts of facts, and that value statements are constitutent elements for a special kind of knowledge.

While we would not wish to be drawn into the debates between ethical realism and anti-realism, and deliberation over the distinction between values and facts, or between statements and judgments, we find the view that value judgments and statements are concerned with facts and are therefore part of our knowledge more fitted to the wisdom world of Israelite and Confucian traditions. In a sense, Confucian and Israelite wisdom exists in the statements and judgments about social, ethical and religious facts, which were and still are taken as solid knowledge, with particular meanings for the people who listen to them and who take them as spiritual and ethical mentors. When Confucius said that benevolence was to love others and wisdom was to know others (*Analects*, 12:22), or when authors of the Hebrew wisdom texts categorically stated that 'The fear of the Lord is the beginning of wisdom, and knowledge of the Holy One is understanding' (Prov. 9:10), they were making informative statements describing their experience and insights, which inform us about what values are placed on objects and what knowledge is manifested through these sentences.

Not all knowledge in wisdom is factual. There is another kind of knowledge, not about what has happened, but about what will probably happen. Just as there are two kinds of factual statements (about physical and ethical facts), there are two kinds of statements about what will happen, the causal and the possible. The causal future must come if and when certain conditions and causes are present, while the possible future may come. In a causal situation, we know what a certain future will be by knowing its existing conditions and causes. Therefore, factual knowledge about what has happened is part of future knowledge about what is going to be. In a possible situation, factual knowledge alone is not enough for us to know the future. We have to make reference to uncertain factors, which present more than one possibility for the future. Knowing these possibilities is not in itself sufficient for us to gain future knowledge. We have to predicate rightly which one is most likely, to enable us to make a particular choice, to undertake a particular course of action and to make life comprehensible and manageable. Since this knowledge is primarily about what is yet to happen, it may be called 'predictive knowledge', knowledge that informs us about the possible occurrence of a particular event or action in the future.

In the Israelite tradition there is a fundamental belief that the future is in the hands of YHWH, not of humans. Therefore predictive knowledge often appears in the form of prophecy which is seen as a manifestation of the divine will, and as a pronouncement of the divine planning, prophetic knowledge has thus become an important part of wisdom. However, prophecy is not the only form of predictive knowledge, and one's predicating ability does not necessarily involve mysteries or divine power. Future knowledge may be simply a further extension of what one has known. Many Israelite wise teachings, such as those contained in the book of Proverbs, were derived from past experience. They are predictive because their outline of a certain future is derived from the 'practical knowledge of the laws of life and of the world, based on experience'.[21] Like their views on the nature and function of factual knowledge, some Israelite teachers were uncertain as to whether or not humans were able to predict the future. Acknowledging that the design of YHWH was beyond human intelligence, they claimed that 'Since no-one knows the future, who can tell him what is to come?' (Eccl. 8:7).

In his study *Prophecy and Religion in Ancient China and Israel*, H.H. Rowley claims that 'prophecy is something intimately associated in our thought with the Old Testament, whereas there are no claims to a comparable prophetic character amongst the sages of China'.[22] If by 'prophecy' in the Old Testament he means something ecstatic, or words embodying a living force able to control events, or the ability to speak on behalf of YHWH,[23] then he is probably right, because few Confucians would claim that they were such 'prophets'. However, if we interpret this word in a more epistemological sense – indeed as Rowley's own assertion admits that 'the Old Testament prophets were both forthtellers and foretellers',[24] then his generalization concerning China is misleading, because both Confucians and Daoists at an early stage were keen to explore the nature and function of foreknowledge or prediction of the future. In this respect, Confucians are more positive about human ability and capability to know their own future than Israelite wisdom teachers. Confucius believed that the future could be known, but only if the past had been known well. One day his disciple Zi Zhang (503–? BCE) asked him if ten generations hence could be predicted, Confucius replied,

> The Yin (dynasty) built on the rites of the Xia (dynasty). What was added and what was omitted can be known. The Zhou (dynasty) built on the rites of the Yin. What was added and what was omitted can be known. Should there be a successor to the Zhou, even a hundred generations hence can be known. (*Analects*, 2:23)

---

[21] G. von Rad: *Old Testament Theology*, vol. 1, Edinburgh and London: Oliver and Boyd: SCM Press, 1962, p.418.

[22] H.H. Rowley: *Prophecy and Religion in Ancient China and Israel*, University of London/The Athlone Press, 1956, p.2.

[23] 'Prophecy is a declaration, a forthtelling, of the will of God – not a foretelling. Prediction is not in any sense an essential element of prophecy, though it may intervenes as an accident' (R.H. Charles: *Critical and Exegetical Commentary on the Book of Daniel*, Oxford: Clarendon Press, 1929, p.xxvi).

[24] H.H. Rowley, 1956, p.3.

It is clear for Confucius that predictive knowledge is only part of historical knowledge and does not involve anything divine or mysterious; it is based on reasoning from what has happened to what may happen. In broadly defined Confucian traditions predictive knowledge or foreknowledge plays an important role in their perception of wisdom. Later Confucians significantly increased the mystical element of knowledge in their understanding of future knowledge, emphasizing that the essence of knowledge is to predict or foresee (*yu* or *xianzhi*) human destiny, and that wisdom is embodied in foreknowledge.

After Confucius, predictive knowledge or foreknowledge became more and more appealing to Confucians, and various terms such as foreknowledge (*xianzhi* or *xianshi*) and advanced knowledge (*qianzhi* and *qianshi*) began to appear in late fourth-century BCE works.[25] Mengzi, for example, argues that, when produced by Heaven, people are differentiated into two categories: those who first attain understanding or have awareness in advance (*xianzhi*) and those who come later to understand (*houzhi*). He claims that it is the heavenly bestowed duty of the former to awaken the latter, and that those who are the first to awaken have a duty to awaken those who are slow to awaken (Mengzi, 5A:7; 5B:1). Xunzi does not explicitly acknowledge the existence of foreknowledge.[26] However, he states the following as the important part of a government:

> The official tasks of the hunchbacked shamanesses and lame shamans include examining the influences of the Yin and Yang principles, prognosticating the significance of mysterious vapors and halos, penetrating the tortoise shell with the heated rod and arranging the milfoil for divination, presiding at ceremonies exorcising and summoning the Five Omens, and knowing whether the portents are good or evil, auspicious or inauspicious. (Xunzi, 9:17)

This does indicate that Xunzi leaves some space for foreknowledge to operate in his moral system. When he criticizes the last kings of the Xia and Shang dynasties, he also uses the term '*xianzhi*', prescient awareness or foreknowledge, believing that the failure of these wicked kings was due to their lack of intelligence and moral quality: 'they were not themselves prescient of their bad end, and no one was able to

---

[25] In the *Daode jing*, foreknowledge or advanced apprehension (*qianshi*) is not much appreciated, and is compared to 'the flower of Dao' which once blossoming is coming to the end of life: 'foreknowledge is the flowers of Dao and the beginning of stupidity' (Chapter 38). This is to say that Dao is not something we can predict, and any attempt to know Dao in advance is doomed to fail. Unlike Daoists, Confucians took a more positive attitude towards foreknowledge, in which they invested much value of sageness.

[26] Xunzi in general opposed divination and religious prayer as the way to predict the future: 'If you pray for rain and there is rain, what of that? I say there is no special relationship – as when you do not pray for rain and there is rain. When the sun and moon are eclipsed, we attempt to save them; when Heaven sends drought, we pray for them; and before we decide any important undertaking, we divine with bone and milfoil. We do these things not because we believe that such ceremonies will produce the results we seek, but because we want to embellish such occasions with ceremony. Thus the gentleman considers such ceremonies as embellishment, bu the Hundred Clans consider them supernatural. To consider them embellishment is fortunate; to consider them supernatural is unfortunate' (Xunzi, 17:8).

remonstrate with them' (Xunzi, 21:3). In this kind of statement Xunzi implies that some individuals of sufficient intelligence and moral virtue can possess predictive knowledge of their own future.

The *Doctrine of the Mean* goes further in this direction, defining predictive ability as the essence of perfect virtue, and arguing that once they reach the highest level, people of perfect sincerity are able to know in advance:

> It is characteristic of absolute sincerity to be able to foreknow (*qian zhi*). When a nation or family is about to flourish, there are sure to be lucky omens (*zhen xiang*). When a nation or family is about to perish, there are sure to be unlucky omens. These omens are revealed in divination and in the movements of the four limbs. When calamity or blessing is about to come, it can surely know beforehand (*xian zhi*) if it is good, and it can also surely know beforehand if it is evil. Therefore he who has absolute sincerity (*zhi cheng*) is like a spirit (*shen*).[27]

Thus foreknowledge is a by-product of one's achievement in moral cultivation and a significant association between foreknowledge and sageness is forged. The wisdom knowledge that provides a solution to our finitude and leads us to understanding our ultimate destiny is the knowledge of the sage. In the *Book of Changes*, this kind of knowledge is said to enable one to stay in the divine realm, knowing the future and storing up the past;[28] in other words, it enables one to become a sage. The knowledge of the sage is believed to have been embodied in the Confucian classics. For example, it is confirmed that the *Book of Changes* 'illustrates the past and interprets the future', and discloses 'that which is hidden and opens that which is dark'.[29] By studying these classics, it is argued, one would gain ultimate knowledge, and with this ultimate knowledge one would be able to penetrate outer layers of things and events, understand their deeper cause and essence, act wisely and make wise and prudent choices. In terms of the practical sense of wisdom knowledge, the *Book of Changes* defines it as discovering potential risks and knowing when and where to stop: 'To see the danger and to stand still, that is called wisdom knowledge.'[30] It is claimed that a Confucian gentlemen observes the figures and meditates on the judgments, that he can undertake something he contemplates and ponder on the oracles, and that through this he will be 'blessed by Heaven' and obtain 'good fortune'.[31]

It is evident that under the influence of Daoist mysticism, Confucians of the late Warring States period (475–221BCE), the Qin (221–206BCE) and the Former Han (206BCE–8CE) dynasties greatly increased the stake of foreknowledge in their

---

[27] Zhongyong, 24; in *A Source Book in Chinese Philosophy*, p.108.

[28] My translation, see *I Ching or the Book of Changes*, p.317.

[29] *I Ching or the Book of Changes*, p.344.

[30] *I Ching or the Book of Changes*, p.580. Note that knowing when to stop is considered a sign of wisdom both in the *Book of Changes* and in the *Book of Zhuangzi* (See *The Complete Works of Chuang Tzu*, 1968, pp.37, 44).

[31] *I Ching or the Book of Changes*, p.290.

understanding of wisdom and made wisdom knowledge a mystical approach to one's own and the state's destiny. Even Confucius, who always claimed to be merely an untiring learner, was said to be able to divine the origin of strange animals or a giant human skeleton.[32] Most Confucian followers believed that wisdom knowledge was wisdom because it would enable one to gain an understanding of the secrets of the universe, to foresee the future, and to transcend one's own limitations, that is, to become a sage. Therefore, foreknowledge is what differentiates the sage from ordinary people, as is confirmed in a miscellaneous collection of treatises that took its final form as a syncretic and encyclopaedic compendium in 239BCE, the *Lüshi Chunqiu* (*The Spring and Autumn Annals by Mr. Lü*): 'That by which the sage surpasses other men is his foreknowledge.'[33] The difference between the knowledge of ordinary people and the knowledge of the sage is further illustrated in the *History of the Former Han Dynasty* as the contrast between factual knowledge and predictive knowledge: ordinary people 'know what has happened', but the sage 'knows what will happen'.[34]

However, further slippage into the mystification of the sage's knowledge caused a powerful counter-movement both within the Confucian tradition and in the Chinese intellectual world. As early as in the latter part of the Warring States period there had already been an attempt to 'demystify' foreknowledge by interpreting human destiny through the interchange of the Five Agents (*wu xing*), as we can see in other essays of *The Spring and Autumn Annals by Mr. Lü*, where human ability in reading and shaping future events is said to have come from the determining presence of the Five Agents shaping all things in the cosmos. According to one of its treatises, 'The natural occurrence of fortune and misfortune is considered by the masses to be a matter of destiny', but the wise now understand the authority of the Five Agents by which they know what is to come and what is to go.[35] Wang Chong (27–100?), an independent and rational thinker of the Later Han Dynasty (25–220CE), for example, in his fight against all mysticism and superstitions, debunked the apparently current notion that sages had special divine (*shen*) qualities that helped them see the future: 'The Confucians talk about Sages, saying that they can know a thousand years into the future and ten thousand generations into the past ... I say this is all empty [talk].'[36] This marked the turning point when the Confucian wisdom tradition started to depart from the mysticism of predictive knowledge, with most Confucians stepping once more into the rational realm of thought.

---

[32] Hsien-yi Yang and Gladys Yang (trans.): *Selections from Records of the Historian,* Beijing: Foreign Languages Press, 1979, pp.1–28.

[33] *Lüshi Chunqiu,*20: 8, in *Zhuzi Jicheng*, p.272. While little evidence shows that all these treatises are of a Confucian nature, we can be confident that some of them were indeed heavily influenced by the Confucian teachings prevailing at that time and therefore reflected to certain degree the general trend within the Confucian tradition.

[34] *Hanshu* (*History of the Former Han Dynasty*), Beijing: Zhonghua Shuju, 1997, p.2252.

[35] *Lüshi Chunqiu,* 13:2, in John Knoblock and Jeffrey Riegel (trans.), *The Annals of Lü Buwei,* Stanford: Stanford University Press, 2000, pp.283–4.

[36] Huang Hui: *Lunhen jiaoshi*, Beijing: Zhonghua Shuju, 1990, Section 78, in vol. 4, pp.1069, 1070.

In summary, we may say that both Israelite and Confucian teachers are concerned with the future, and take it as one of their tasks to gain knowledge about what can possibly happen, in terms either of personal fortune or of political conditions. The convergence of these two traditions can be seen in the fact that the Chinese translation of 'prophets' is '*xian zhi*', those who know beforehand or who have possessed foreknowledge, which, as quoted above, is first used in the *Book of Mengzi* for people who know in advance. However, the difference between Israelite authors and Confucian masters lies not in whether or not they believe there is foreknowledge or in whether or not the future can be known; rather their divergence lies in their understanding of the nature and function of prediction of the future; one is religious and the other essentially epistemological and ethical. The Israelites had no doubt that true prophetic words could come only from YHWH and that prophets and wisdom teachers were charged with the mission to pass these words on. For Confucians, however, prediction must be based on factual or causal knowledge, and one's ability to know the future results from one's understanding of the moral laws of the universe, from one's accumulation of factual knowledge, and most importantly from the cultivation of one's character that, on reaching the ultimate, would enable one to know the underlying order of the affairs and events.[37] In both traditions prediction of the future later lost its importance. In Israel, prophecy gradually gave way to Yahwism that forbade people to speak on behalf of the LORD, and finally came to an end following the appearance of Christianity. Meanwhile in China, foreknowledge mysticism was mistrusted and attacked by rational Confucians, and gradually became the preserve of religious Daoists.

Source of Knowledge and Innate Faculty

Wisdom is based on knowledge which enables its possessor to be of wide learning, to be competent in task-completion and to cope skilfully with the problems of life. According to contemporary studies of wisdom, a wise person is one who possesses multidimensional qualities. For example, Holliday and Chandler argue that 'any

---

[37] The primary means by which Confucians come to predict the future is of a spiritual and moral nature. Both for a state and for individuals, their future is determined by the Way of Heaven that is to award the good and to punish the bad, and if one understands this Way then the future can be known. For example, in the Book of History we read that 'The way of Heaven is to bless the good, and make the bad miserable. It sent down calamities on (the House) of Hsia, to make manifest its guilt ... High Heaven truly showed its favour to the inferior people, and the criminal has been degraded and subjected' (*The Sacred Books of China: the Texts of Confucianism*, trans. James Legge, Part I, in *The Sacred Books of the East*, ed. F. Max Müller, vol. 3. First published Oxford: Clarendon Press, 1879, reprinted Delhi: Motilal Banarsidass, 1970, p.90). The moral force that operates in the world is that the good will lead to flourishing, happiness and harmony, while the evil or bad will lead to self-destruction, ruin and disorders, as is said in *Zuo's Commentary on the Spring and Autumn Annals* that 'Those who pursue evil courses will eventually encompass their own ruin' (*The Chinese Classics*, vol. V, trans. James Legge, London: Trubner & Co., 1872, p.5).

adequate concept of this notion of wisdom must redefine mature cognitive development in terms which overspill the usual boundaries of empirical-analytical knowledge to include practical and emancipatory achievements ...'[38] Sternberg concludes that a wise individual is generally recognized by his reasoning ability, superior intellectual functioning, and good pragmatic judgment and skills of reflection that allow him or her to profit from past mistakes.[39]

Where do this ability, capability and knowledge come from? Empiricist philosophy rejects the possibility of *a priori* ideas, or innate knowledge, and sees knowledge as coming from our life experience. John Locke (1632–1704) describes it this way:

> Let us then suppose the mind to be, as we say, white paper, void of all characters, without any ideas, How comes it to be furnished? ... Whence has it all the materials of reason and knowledge? To this I answer, in one word, from experience.[40]

Experience is of a variety of types: sensory, aesthetic, moral, religious, and so on. Whatever experience is, it is gained from our contact with objects, either through stimulation of the five senses, or in a mode of consciousness in which something seems to be presented to the subject.[41] Therefore if we say that knowledge comes from experience, we are confirming that all kinds of knowledge are acquired *a posteriori*. Are there any forms of knowledge that do not rely on experience? No doubt logical truths and mathematical assertions are *a priori* knowledge, in the sense that they do not change according to subjects' consciousness or experience. However, the emphasis of Confucian and Israelite wisdom texts is not on this kind of knowledge. Rather, Confucian masters and Israelite teachers give priority to exploration of the interaction between what we have had, either in terms of religious revelation, or as an inborn faculty, and what we can have, such as religious experience, moral knowledge and practical skills. They debate among themselves whether or not wisdom can arise from the interaction between *a priori* knowing faculty and *a posteriori* experience.

Confucians in general tend to demystify the origin of knowledge, and place the formation of wisdom knowledge in the epistemological processes, regarding the deeper understanding of causes and the future as coming from observing and reasoning. However, different opinions have been put forward with regard to whether or not some knowledge is innate, and whether or not there is an inborn faculty that is capable of knowing before learning and experiencing. Confucius rejected the claim

---

[38] S.G. Holliday and M.J. Chandler, *Wisdom: Exploration in adult competence*, Basle: Karger, 1986, p.32.

[39] R.J. Sternberg, 'Implicit theories of intelligence, creativity, and wisdom', *Journal of Personality and Social Psychology*, 1985, 49 (3), pp.607–27.

[40] John Locke: *An Essay Concerning Human Understanding*, Harmondsworth: Penguin, 1997, Book II, Chapter 1, p.45.

[41] See 'Empiricism', in *Concise Routledge Encyclopedia of Philosophy*, p.239.

that he was innately wise. Instead, he stated that his knowledge was not something with which he was born; it came from his love of ancient culture and from tirelessly seeking the truth (*Analects*, 7:20), that is, that knowledge came from *a posteriori* experience and effort. However, it seems that he had no intention to carry this 'empiricism' through all his understanding of knowledge, and on occasions he mentioned that there were different kinds of people in terms of their knowledge:

> Those who are born with knowledge are the highest. Next come those who attain knowledge through study. Next again come those who turn to study only after having been vexed by difficulties. The common people, in so far as they make no effort to study even after having been vexed by difficulties, are the lowest. (*Analects*, 16:9)

This clearly indicates that Confucius was ambiguous concerning the existence of any innate capability of wisdom. Although he denied that he was born with knowledge, he believed that *a priori* knowledge was possible and it was not susceptible to change. He considered humans to have been born with differences of intelligence. There were people of high intelligence (*shang zhi*) and people of low foolishness (*xia yu*), and the difference between them did not change over time (*Analects*, 17:3). By this he implied that the people of high intelligence possessed wisdom knowledge, while the people of low foolishness could not possibly gain this kind of knowledge. On the other hand, however, Confucius did not totally attribute wisdom knowledge to one's innate capability. He implied that all people, even those of low intelligence, had been endowed with an innate faculty to study, so that, if those people who did not possess innate knowledge were willing to study, then they were able to gain knowledge and become wise. The difference in people's levels of knowledge was therefore mostly due to acquired attitude and intention, rather than an innate capability.

The ambiguity concerning the source of knowledge gives further evidence that Confucius shifted between an apriorist and an empiricist position. Consequently, for him knowledge can either be *a priori* possession or come from *a posteriori* studies and practices. However, in the balance between the innate faculty and learned experience, as we observe, Confucius leaned heavily towards the empiricist position, and did not totally abandon his emphasis on learning even when admitting that there were people of innate knowledge. Basically he took the view that true knowledge was the result both of learning (training) in various subjects and of cultivating innate qualities. Acknowledging the dual source of knowledge, but crediting the formation of knowledge to the learning process, is also reflected in almost all other Confucian works, albeit in different forms. Mengzi, for example, insisted that there was an innate element of *zhi* (knowledge) or *liangzhi* (good knowledge) in all humans: 'Benevolence, dutifulness, observance of the rites, and wisdom are not welded on to me from the outside; they are in me originally' (Mengzi, 6A:6). However, on the other hand, Mengzi equally insisted that humans must make great efforts to 'seek' to manifest this 'innately' potential knowledge: 'Seek and you will find it; let go and you will lose it' (Mengzi, 6A:6), and he agreed with Zi Gong (520–?BCE), one of the closest disciples of Confucius, that 'Not to tire of learning is wisdom' (Mengzi, 2A:2). This indicates that, for Mengzi, although humans are born with the capability of being good and wise, they must cultivate and practise it in order to gain full knowledge.

Xunzi seemed to be a total empiricist in terms of knowledge, as he clearly stated that knowledge was not innate and it came only from constant learning: 'Learning must never be concluded' (Xunzi, 1:1). To gain knowledge, as Xunzi argues, we must engage in enquiries and studies. Like Confucius, Xunzi contrasted the gentleman and the small man. However, there was nothing innate to differentiate a gentleman from a small man except that, while the latter was lazy and did not study, the former always engaged himself in study: 'When he does not know, he asks others; when he lacks an ability, he studies' (Xunzi, 6:12). However, Xunzi did not totally deny the role played by one's inborn capability. Insisting that humans were born with an evil nature, he believed that human nature could be changed by 'undergoing the transforming influence of teachers and laws' and 'being guided by propriety and righteousness' (Xunzi, 23:1), for 'only through learning, involving conscious effort, can the original nature of man be overcome'.[42] It was clear to him that, to do so, humans must have been born with ability to learn and intelligence to understand, and that, possessing the faculty of intelligence, humans could consider 'the long view of things and thinking of the consequences of their actions' (Xunzi, 4:11).

Epistemological dualists are often perplexed at the question: Is knowledge simply an innate endowment, or is it an acquired set of ideas resulting from personal or collective experiences? In contrast to them, however, early Confucians do not see any conflict between the two sources of knowledge; rather they search for the effective inter-action between them, implying that wisdom comes only from an effective combination of the innate and the learned. For Israelite wisdom teachers the matter is more complicated, although most of them, like Confucians, also hold that knowledge is possible only when people combine their internal faculties and learned experiences. To explain this point more clearly, we will examine the concept of 'heart/mind' (*lēb* in Hebrew and *xin* in Chinese). The heart/mind is of particular importance for wisdom because it is the seat of memory, making it possible to incorporate particular apperceptions into a larger realm of experience, providing the basis for judgment and responsible action with respect to what is perceived. In Confucian and Hebrew texts, the heart/mind is both the faculty of knowing and the organ of perception. In general Confucian philosophers talk about *xin* (heart/mind) not as a physical but as an intellectual organ, the faculty of which is defined as 'thinking' (Mengzi, 6A:15). For Xunzi, knowing the Way is of the ultimate importance, and in response to the question of what humans use to know the Way, his answer is categorical: it is the heart/mind (*Xunzi*, 21:8). Most Israelite writers also

---

⁴² John Knoblock: *Xunzi: A Translation and Study of the Complete Works*, vol. 1, Stanford: Stanford University Press, 1988, p.131.

define *lēb* (the heart) in the epistemic sense as an organ of perception and knowledge, supporting understanding and decision on the basis of what is perceived (Exodus 7:23).

For Israelite teachers, various objects of perception become concentrated in the heart/mind to form insight into the true nature of the world, and they believe that it is on such a basis that people can consciously frame their lives.[43] This we can see in the following passage, 'Know then in your heart that, as a man disciplines his son, the Lord your God disciplines you' (Deuteronomy 8:5). Like one's sense organs that perceive, the heart/mind is capable of understanding: 'making your ear attentive to wisdom and inclining your heart to understanding' (Prov. 2:2), and people can turn their heart/mind 'to know and to search out and to seek wisdom' (Prov. 7:25). The book of Job talks about the heart/mind by which knowledge is possible (Job 12:3). The heart/mind is taken as a storehouse for knowledge and as a refinery for processing raw experiences, just as in the book of Proverbs people are taught to keep wise instructions within their heart (Prov. 4:21), and write them on the tablet of the heart (Prov. 7:3). The heart/mind has judging and discerning functions, enabling people to reflect on a multitude of heterogeneous perceptions, and then focus on true values. Only by laying the truth in the heart can people become faithful and righteous: 'know therefore this day, and lay it to your heart, that the Lord is God in heaven above and on the earth beneath' (Deuteronomy 4:39). The heart is therefore the organ of judging and understanding, and in certain conditions even the heart/mind of the rash will be able to make good judgment (Isaiah 32:4).

Despite the importance of the heart/mind for knowledge, Israelite teachers provide us with a very different perception of the formation of knowledge. Owing to the fact that the heart/mind has stored up the seeds or beginning of knowledge, and can process the raw materials of experience, some Confucians view it as the source of true knowledge, believing that, if cultivated properly, and if necessary conditions are met, the heart/mind can alone lead to wisdom. Israelite teachers deliberate on the nature and function of the heart/mind within their theistic epistemological framework, and some of them are indeed deeply sceptical as to whether the human heart/mind alone is able to generate knowledge. The reason that the human heart/mind is capable of knowledge and understanding is repeatedly said to be that YHWH has inscribed his law or *Torah* in the minds of the Israelite people, and has written it on their hearts (Jeremiah 31:33). All religious knowledge and values are from YHWH, as the author of Ecclesiastes asserts, 'YHWH has set eternity in the hearts of men' (Eccl. 3:11). This is, in theological terms, a statement that the knowledge of YHWH's law and eternity cannot come from our experience; nor does it arise from any innate faculty. Rather, true knowledge and wisdom exist in the hearts/minds of the people, because YHWH has inscribed them there.

The belief that knowledge has a kind of divine or spiritual foundation and that knowledge is possible only when it is installed into the heart/mind by the spiritual

---

[43] *Theological Dictionary of the Old Testament*, vol. V, 1986, pp.462–3.

ultimate is not totally alien to some of the early Confucians. If we change YHWH here to Heaven (*Tian*) in a Confucian context, we will have interesting parallels and divergences between early Israelite and Chinese epistemologies. Mengzi says that wisdom is what the heart/mind already has, and is not something added to us from outside, and Israelites believe that the hearts of humans have been inscribed with knowledge of law, and that true knowledge and wisdom is possible only because it is set there by YHWH. It seems that the key divergence between them is that Mengzi believes that the human heart/mind is where the root of wisdom lies, while the Israelites argue that it remains blank until YHWH has inscribed his wisdom on it. However, if we further analyse where the innate wisdom of Mengzi comes from, then we can see that for Mengzi wisdom does not come from the organ itself, but from Heaven; and that it is Heaven which has bestowed the beginnings of wisdom in the heart/mind of humans. In the light of this we may conclude that the difference between Mengzi and the Israelites is not that the one believes wisdom comes from outside humans, and the other argues that it is what humans already have, because both confirm that wisdom comes from the ultimate and divine source. The real difference between them is rather that Mengzi is confident that the beginning of wisdom comes along with human life (endowed by Heaven), which, if properly cultivated (by humans), will grow into wisdom, while the Israelites believe that wisdom is inscribed in human hearts by YHWH, which arises only when humans show their faith in the creator.

Learning and Transmission of Knowledge

Whether they insist that wisdom is inscribed onto the heart/mind by YHWH or argue that its beginning or root has already existed in our innate nature, Confucians and Israelite teachers do not totally deny the important role played by experience and learning in the formation of wisdom knowledge. A significant amount of space in wisdom texts is allocated to teaching about how we can get true knowledge and how we can transmit this knowledge. The Israelite faith that YHWH has inscribed true knowledge in the hearts of the people does not mean that people can sit around doing nothing, waiting for its manifestation and then becoming wise. On the contrary, Israelite authors repeatedly remind their readers and audience that people can be wise only if they actively pursue knowledge through education and training. Knowledge is transmitted from generation to generation, and humans must learn how to cope with life and to impose a kind of order on the myriad experiences that surround them. The teaching of the wise is thus compared with a fountain of life thanks to which one may avoid the snares of death (Prov. 13:14). In the mouth of King Solomon, the book of Proverbs lists the following conditions for gaining knowledge:

> If you accept my words and store up my commands within you, turning your ear
> to wisdom and applying your heart to understanding, and if you call out for
> insight and cry aloud for understanding, and if you look for it as for silver and
> search for it as if hidden treasure, then you will understand the fear of the Lord
> and find the knowledge (*da'at*) of God. (Prov. 2:1–5)

In this passage it is made clear that to have the ultimate knowledge, one must be willing to do and be capable of doing the following: accepting the instructions of wisdom teachers, searching for wisdom with a strong will and determination, and intensively and extensively looking for understanding and insight. Elsewhere it is also said that, to gain knowledge and understanding, it is important to make a personal effort, for example, to 'hold fast to' the wise teaching, to 'get wisdom and get insight' (Prov. 4:4–5), and to 'preserve' it or, in a metaphorical language, 'buy the truth and do not sell it; get wisdom, discipline and understanding' (Prov. 23:23). There is no doubt in the minds of the wisdom teachers that knowledge is not there for people simply to pick up because wisdom knowledge is hidden rather than on the surface, and the searcher is faced with great difficulties in seeking it out, just like the one who goes after the truth of YHWH: 'I go forward, but he is not there; and backward, but I cannot perceive him; on the left hand I seek him, but I cannot behold him; I turn to the right hand, but I cannot see him' (Job 23:8–9). Therefore true knowledge must be 'sought' and laboriously 'searched out' (Eccl. 7:25), and only comes as a result of systematic searching, trying, making effort, testing and discerning (Job 34:4).[44]

It is also clear to the Israelite teachers that knowledge is possible only when both the internal and the external requirements have been satisfied. Certain conditions are necessary for perception and knowledge to take place; these include not only the perceiving faculty (the heart/mind) and personal effort (learning and accepting training), but also the object (what we are intended to know and understand). The object of perception and knowledge must be in existence because human minds cannot perceive nothingness. An object must also be fundamentally perceptible, that is, it must be within the grasp of the knowers: before them, before their eyes, immediately with them, because humans cannot know without directly coming upon a thing, and only YHWH can know from afar (Psalm 138:6; 139:2). If these conditions are satisfied, then it is presumed that all people are able to understand and to gain knowledge about things, events and phenomena, just as Eliphaz the Temanite confronts Job with questions: 'What do you know that we do not know? What insights do you have that we do not have?' (Job 15:9).

Since humans must make an effort to get knowledge and become wise, however, Israelite teachers in effect imply that education and training are of the greatest importance and, in the words of the book of Proverbs, lack of education and training is the cause of death: 'He dies for lack of discipline, and because of his great folly he is lost' (Prov. 5:23). To be educated and trained, students or the audience must have a certain level of intelligence to understand the principles and reasons of matters and events, and different grades of intelligence enable people to have different kinds of knowledge. This leads some of them to a position similar to that of Confucius: that people are of different grades in terms of their intelligence and sensitivity in the process of learning and education. It is stated that, although the highest truth is clear,

---

[44] *Theological Dictionary of the Old Testament*, vol. V, p.463.

the dull or senseless cannot know, and the stupid cannot understand (Psalm 92:6), and that, although all the people have their own minds, the function of these minds is quite different: 'The lips of the wise spread knowledge; not so the minds of fools' (Prov. 15:7). The grades of intelligence are demonstrated in the difference of the minds as well as the difference of the characters, so that we have not only the contrast between the wise and the stupid, but also that between the righteous and the wicked. Can the stupid and wicked be transformed into the wise and the righteous by *a posteriori* efforts? It seems that, like Confucians, Israelite teachers are also ambiguous in their response. On the one hand, they make it clear that 'to understand' or to 'know' is the faculty of the wise, not that of the wicked: 'None of the wicked shall understand' (Daniel 12:10), because 'Wisdom is too high for a fool' (Prov. 24:7). But on the other, as we have demonstrated above, some of them argue for the possibility that anyone can become wiser and more righteous by learning and listening to the teachings of wise teachers.

How then can one become wiser? For most Confucians and Israelites, an effective way to transform the stupid to become wise is by learning, and so education is of special significance for the formation and transmission of knowledge. Whether or not they believe that human beings are innately intelligent, Confucian masters argue that humans must learn before having knowledge. The *Great Learning* makes use of an ancient poem to illustrate how a person can be cultivated by learning: a person who is engaged in learning is likened to a jewel that shines after being cut and polished (Daxue, 3). Learning in Confucian contexts is a multi-facet process, and is an underlying basis for all other moral virtues and qualities (*Analects*, 17:8). First, learning has a significant dimension of practice. For Confucius, learning must be practised from time to time (*Analects*, 1:1), and what we have learned is not knowledge until it can be applied in daily life. One of his disciples, Zi Xia (507?–? BCE), defines learning as 'appreciating the people of excellence' in contrast to appreciating beautiful women, 'exerting oneself to the utmost in the service of one's parents', 'offering oneself to the services of the ruler', and 'in dealing with friends being trustworthy in what has been said'. He finally comes to a conclusion that such a person is really learned, even though he says that he has not been properly educated (*Analects*, 1:7).

Secondly, learning is also meant to be the study of classical texts which are believed to contain the wisdom of the ancients. It is clear that Confucians emphasize the study of books because they believe that it is the only way to comprehend the complicated nature of life and to cope with difficult situations. The books of the ancients are therefore taken as manuals or handbooks that make the process of knowing and understanding an easy and straightforward task. The commentary of the *Book of Changes* has illustrated this vividly to us:

> The creative knows the beginnings; the receptive completes the finished things. The Creative knows through the easy. The Receptive can do things through the simple. What is easy is easy to know; what is simple is easy to follow. He who is

easy to know attains fealty. He who is easy to follow attains works ... By means of the easy and the simple we grasp the laws of the whole world. When the laws of the whole world are grasped, therein lies perfection.[45]

Therefore whether or not one has studied the books has become one of the important Confucian criteria for judging one's ability. The son of Confucius related a story about his father's teaching. Once his father asked him whether or not he had studied the *Book of Poetry*, and taught him that, unless he had studied it, he would be ill-equipped to speak; on another occasion Confucius taught his son that, unless he had studied the rites he would be ill-equipped to take his stand (*Analects*, 16:13).

Thirdly, important as reading books and accepting instructions may be, Confucians do not regard learning as passive acceptance of what one is taught, and so they add an important internal element to the learning process: eagerness to learn or love of learning (*hao xue*). Confucius stresses the importance of being eager to learn, and distinguishes himself from other people in terms suggesting that other people are not as eager to learn as he is (*Analects*, 5:28). He praises highly his favourite student, Yan Hui (521–481BCE), for his eagerness to learn (*Analects*, 6:3; 11:7). Xunzi also sees 'love of learning' as one of the necessary qualities for becoming a gentleman (Xunzi, 2:12).

Fourthly, learning is always closely associated with thinking. From his own experience Confucius knows that learning is more important for the formation of knowledge than thinking: 'I once spent all day thinking without taking food and all night without going to bed, but I found that I gained nothing from it. It would have been better for me to have spent the time in learning' (*Analects*, 15:31). However, Confucius is clearly aware of the dangers of separating studying and thinking, believing that a one-sided approach cannot lead to knowledge: 'If one is engaged in learning but does not think, then one will be bewildered; if on the other hand one thinks but does not engage oneself in learning, one will be in peril' (*Analects*, 2:15). Gaining knowledge through learning and thinking is a long process, and we should not expect to become learned within a short period and by initial efforts. Confucius describes himself as 'a man who learns without flagging and teaches without growing weary' (*Analects*, 7:2), qualities which have since been praised as the highest manifestation of education.

It is apparent that for Confucians learning is the cause, while knowledge is the result. Most of the Israelite teachers would also agree with this, arguing that people have knowledge, not because they are innately wise, but because they are willing to learn from past proverbs and teachings. The beginning of the book of Proverbs states that by understanding proverbs and parables people may attain wisdom and discipline, understand words of insight and do what is right and just and fair; by holding fast to the teachings of the old, the simple may gain prudence and the wise increase their learning (Prov. 1:2–6). One's learning may be increased by taking

---

⁴⁵ *I Ching or the Book of Changes*, pp.285–7.

instruction and by receiving education from teachers (Prov. 9:9). Study is regarded as the pathway to wisdom, and only those who have gained knowledge can speak properly and wisely. It is for this reason that the Book of Ben Sira teaches the audience, 'Before you speak, learn' (Sir. 18:19).

Knowledge is learned not only through life experience, but also in the process of education and training. Confucius regards himself as a learner who is 'in love with ancient studies', and as a teacher who never turned away anyone coming earnestly to learn and in educating students he never grows weary (*Analects*, 7:2). In transmitting wisdom, Confucian teaching aims not only to pass on knowledge, but also to initiate students' responses, and Confucian teachers expect students to understand all other parts when they have understood one, as Confucius once remarks:

> I will not explain to one who is not trying to make things clear to himself. And if I explain a quarter and the man does not go back and reflect and think over the implications in the remaining three quarters for himself, I will not bother to teach him again. (*Analects*, 7:8)

From these remarks we may see clearly that for Confucians knowledge can be transmitted through education and training, from earlier to later generations, and from teachers to students. However this transmission requires not only the availability of ancient knowledge and the diligence of teachers, but also the attentive hearts of the students.

For the Israelites it also seems true that wisdom can be taught to those who are willing to accept. 'Hear, my son, and accept my words, that the years of your life may be many. I have taught you the way of wisdom; I have led you in the paths of uprightness' (Prov. 4:10–11). It seems that Israelite teachers recognize the importance of the transmission chain through generations, as we can see from the following passage: 'for I give you good precepts: do not forsake my teaching. When I was a son with my father, tender, the only one in the sight of my mother, he taught me, and said to me, "Let your heart hold fast my words; keep my commandments and live; do not forget, and do not turn away from the word of my mouth"' (Prov. 4:2–5). However, there is a clear difference between the Confucian transmission of knowledge and the Israelite process of learning. For Confucians, the transmission is a process of normal education, either by means of textual studies or through the teaching given by teachers, and different teacher–student transmission lines thus developed later into distinct schools (*jia*).

In contrast to Confucians who develop along the line of intellectual education and philosophical training, the Israelites adopt a spiritual understanding of knowledge transmission, recognizing that in wisdom 'there is a spirit that is intelligent, holy, unique, manifold, subtle, mobile, clear, unpolluted, distinct, invulnerable, loving the good, keen, irresistible, beneficent, humane, steadfast, sure, free from anxiety, all powerful, overseeing all, and penetrating through all spirits'. In this way, they state that wisdom is essentially divine, and that the transmission cannot be achieved by conventional and intellectual education. Neither can wisdom transmission be achieved purely through philosophical deliberation; it must involve wisdom herself: 'I learned both what is secret and what is manifest, for wisdom, the fashioner of all things, taught me' (Wisd. 7:21–2).

To summarize what we have discussed above, we may conclude that the discipline of wisdom in the Confucian and Israelite traditions has a significant epistemological dimension and wisdom is based on the formation of knowledge. Knowledge for both Confucians and Israelites is of a complicated nature, composed of ordinary and wisdom, natural and social, factual and predictive, and learned and innate dimensions. A significant difference between wisdom teachers of the Confucian and Israelite traditions and modern dualists can be discerned in that the former do not believe that knowledge is derived from the separating of the internal and the external, the learned and the innate, and the particular and the general elements. In one way or another they argue that the two sources and two functions of knowledge must be properly combined, so that we can have knowledge and wisdom.

From the comparative perspective, we have also observed that Confucians approach the epistemological issues of knowledge in a way quite different from that of the Israelite teachers. Confucians base the formation of knowledge on conventional educational grounds, in which humans gain knowledge from both life experience and reasoning faculties. Therefore Confucians are optimistic in relation to the final wisdom knowledge: as long as we learn, we can understand the 'secrets' and 'mysteries', the law or order of the world. Based on a fundamentally theocentric ground, however, the Israelites are less confident about the prospect of humans having full knowledge of the world. Rather, they believe that final knowledge is in the hands of the creator, and that humans can gain access to wisdom only when wisdom reveals herself to us. This difference leads not only to divergence in their understanding of knowledge but also to different patterns of life in which Confucians and the Israelites formed distinct ways of life.

CHAPTER FOUR

Wisdom as the Way of Life

Wisdom exists in the form of knowledge and wisdom knowledge involves experience, rationality and insight. In all traditions, wisdom knowledge has a very practical implication, intended not only to increase people's intellectual capacity but also to guide people in their daily life. Wisdom can therefore be defined as the 'way of life' for people to follow. A way of life is forged in personal and communal environments. At the personal level, wisdom knowledge outlines the wise way of life and prescribes how each human individual should think and behave in a particular time and on a specific occasion, expressed through a series of imperatives in positive and negative forms. Thinking and behaving wisely are influenced not only by changing psychological faculties such as temperament and emotion, but also by more equable qualities such as reason and character. Therefore which way one follows in life often indicates the level of wisdom one is at.

In the communal respect, wisdom becomes a particular way of life through dealing with a variety of interpersonal relationships. How one treats other people and the social and natural environment reflects one's experience and knowledge and is influenced by one's vision of life, and in turn determines the formation of personal character and identity as well as one's position in community. In this sense, wisdom is not merely wise rules governing one's life – the way of life as determined in particular social contexts – more importantly, it is a way of dynamic living, the way of life in formation through one's choices and tendencies. While the way to lead a wise course of life is manifested through many dimensions of personal and social experience (moral, ethical, political and so on), this chapter will concentrate only on the personal aspect, namely, how the Israelite and Confucian wisdom texts define the 'wise way' which is composed of life attitudes and personal qualities, and is manifested in the requirements for a wise individual intending to run a successful course of personal life. We leave the moral and social dimensions of the way to the next chapter.

Way of Wisdom

The 'way' as used in this chapter is both a philosophized term referring to the truth or principle that is believed to sustain the metaphysical, physical and social worlds, and also a figurative word referring to the journey one follows in life, including its method, style and manner by which one leads a desired course of life. There are a number of more figurative words, such as 'road', 'path' or 'street' that have been used to express the same meaning and reference, of which the most commonly used in classical China and ancient Israel are '*dao*' and '*derek*'.

Dao in Chinese is primarily a path. According to the *Shuowen jiezi zhu*, *dao* is the path along which one walks (*Dao, suo xing dao ye*) and by which one reaches one's destination (*yi da wei zhi dao*).[1] An earlier form of this character in the bronze inscriptions appears to be composed of three parts: *jie* (street), *shou* (head) and *zu* (foot), from which we can see several significant characteristics of ancient Chinese community life: the leader (head) as a pathfinder or a pioneer takes his followers to walk along the path to their destination. However, as the 'head' also denotes a self-conscious person, the character of '*dao*' may also refer to the way in which an individual follows his or her own path of life. Modern scholars have employed various means to introduce their own definitions or interpretations of *dao*. For some, *dao* is none other than a personal way of life, and must be realized through fulfilling certain criteria of a more meaningful life. But for others, *dao* primarily refers to the interactive relationship between the self and the metaphysical and transcendental reality, and should therefore be understood or reached only through 'an omnipresent ubiquitous awareness'. In this sense Thomas In-sing Leung's etymological analysis sheds new light on the meaning of *dao* as invoking a form of movement to point to an infinite process.[2]

Perhaps the best-known usage of *dao* is in Daoism, and some people mistakenly think that *dao* is only applicable to the Daoist tradition.[3] As a matter of fact, *dao* is a word common to all philosophical and religious schools of China, for each of them claims *dao* as the foundation of their theory and practice. Mozi argues for his principle of 'universal love and mutual benefit' as *sheng wang zhi dao* ('the way of the sage–kings') and 'the principle of governing the empire' (*zhi guo zhi li*).[4] The teaching of Confucius is said to be '*fuzi zhi dao*' (the Way of the Master) and Neo-Confucians name their doctrines '*dao xue*', the learning of the Way.[5] After being introduced in China, Buddhism is also taken as a form of *Dao*, and the Eightfold Path to the Buddhahood is translated as the Eight Orthodox *Dao* (*ba zheng dao*). Even for imported religions such as Christianity, *dao* is also used to render their key terms; for example, 'In the beginning was the Word (*Logos*)' of the first Chapter of the Gospel

---

[1] Duan Yucai: *Shuowen jiezi zhu*, Hangzhou: Zhejiang Gubi Chubanshex, 1998, p.75. From the primary meaning of 'path', *dao* is extended to refer to other things such as methods, arts, the essence or original status of the universe, principles or laws, doctrines, ethical principles, speaking and so on (see *Hanyu da zidian*, 1993, pp.1608–9).

[2] Thomas In-sing Leung: 'Tao and Logos', *Journal of Chinese Philosophy*, 25, pp.131–46.

[3] Although '*dao*' has a variety of meanings and references in Daoism, the Daoist '*dao*' is primarily, at least in early Daoist philosophies, 'the way in which the universe work[s]' (Joseph Needham: *Science and Civilization in China: volume 2: History of Scientific Thought*, Cambridge: Cambridge University Press, 1956, p.36).

[4] Mozi, Chapter 15, see Wing-tsit Chan (ed.): *A Source Book in Chinese Philosophy*, Princeton: Princeton University Press, 1963, p.217.

[5] Scholars have pointed out that, in terms of an historical order, Daoists might have transformed the Confucian interpretation of Dao as 'moral doctrine' to a notion as a 'metaphysical monistic absolute' (Chad Hansen: *A Daoist Theory of Chinese Thought: A Philosophical Interpretation*, New York: Oxford University Press, 1992, p.13).

according to John is often translated in Chinese as '*Tai chu you Dao*, In the beginning there was the *Dao*.' As *dao* is commonly used in different philosophical and religious traditions, modern scholars have suggested that *dao* be seen as a shared concept that has an intrinsic meaning and understanding for Chinese society and that defeats any in-depth translation.[6]

Dao can be both the universal Way and particular ways. As the Way, *dao* refers to the highest level of cosmic existence and the deepest possible understanding of it that humans are capable of. Many great thinkers have pointed out that being profound and subtle, the Way is incomprehensible to an ordinary mind. In the *Daode Jing*, for example, it is said that 'The Dao that can be spoken of is not the constant Dao', and the author of this classic confesses that he calls it Dao because he does not know its name.[7] Confucians have also noted the ineffable character of the metaphysical *dao*. For them, the highest truth lies in the Way of Heaven (*tian dao*), which Confucius himself did not often talk about (*Analects*, 5:13), probably because of its subtlety and profoundness that are beyond what an ordinary language could describe. However, in contrast to Daoists, Confucians do not think that the Way must be separated from the way of individuals' life: 'The Way cannot be separated from [humans] for a moment. What can be separated [from humans] is not the Way' (Zhongyong, 1).[8] The reason why the Way is part of our life but is difficult to be fully grasped is said to be that we often deviate from the Middle Way (*zhong dao*): 'I know why the Way [Dao] is not understood. The Worthy go beyond it and the unworthy do not come up to it' (Zhongyong, 4).[9]

Compared with the use of *dao* to refer to the ultimate truth and supreme reality, *dao* is referred to more frequently in the Confucian texts as the ways, particular and specific paths and methods by which a thing manifests itself and a person makes his/her own life. In this sense, everything and everybody has its/his own *dao*. In the *Analects of Confucius*, we encounter a variety of this kind of uses. For example, there is the *dao* of the great learning (*da xue zhi dao*);[10] a father has a father's *dao* (*fu zhi dao*, *Analects*, 1:11); former kings had their *dao* (*xian wang zhi dao*, 1:12); a gentleman has a gentleman's *dao* (*jun zi zhi dao*, 5:16); and a good man has the *dao* of a good man (*shan ren zhi dao*, 11:20). However, it seems that distinctive as they are from each other, all these ways are the same in essence; that is, in all particular ways there is a universal core that makes a particular way partake of the highest truth and reality. As the truth for human living, *dao* can be taken and can also be abandoned. In an ideal society, those who follow *dao* are promoted to the position of ruling, while those who abuse *dao* should be demoted or even executed (*Analects*, 12:19). *Dao* is also the right way of life, and those who have taken *dao* should be regarded as a model by which we correct ourselves (*Analects*, 1:14). *Dao* is the

---

[6] Da Liu: *The Tao and Chinese Culture*, London: Routledge and Kegan Paul, 1981, p.1.

[7] *Dao de Jing*, Chapters 1 and 25, see *A Source Book in Chinese Philosophy*, pp.139, 152.

[8] *A Source Book in Chinese Philosophy*, p.98.

[9] *A Source Book in Chinese Philosophy*, p.99.

[10] *The Great Learning*, The Text, see *A Source Book in Chinese Philosophy*, p.86.

righteous goal of life that must be realized by practising what is right (*Analects*, 16:11) but it also refers to minor arts (*xiao dao*) that have their worthwhile aspects in our life (*Analects*, 19:4).

There are a number of words in Hebrew wisdom texts referring to 'road', 'street' or 'path' that can be used figuratively as the way, for example, *derek* (a road), *šūq* (a street in the city), *ḥūṣ* (a narrow lane), *mesillā* (a prepared road leading across country), *hālik/haִlīkā* (the path that people take), *ma'gāal* (highway), *nātīb/netִībā* (path), *'ōrach* (way), and so on. But of all the words, the most frequently used and most significant is *derek*, which, according to the *Theological Dictionary of the Old Testament*, 'occurs 706 or 710 times in the OT', and whose meanings range from 'road', 'journey', 'custom' and 'behaviour', to 'condition' and 'situation'.[11] It is more often used figuratively for human activity in general: a *derek* 'is not a road or way that has come into existence without people moving on it, but is that on which and in which people move'.[12] It is suggested that in its figurative usage *derek* means

> conduct and destiny, the living of life and the course of life in the sense of prosperity or adversity in a causal relationship … The way of uprightness and the way of security and prosperity are the same (Prov. 3.23) … Evil behavior and an evil condition go together.[13]

As we have noted above, the Confucian *dao* carries with it in most cases a laudatory meaning of righteousness and truth. It has an intrinsic moral value and does not need an ethical adjective if it is used for a desirable quality.[14] The value of *dao* in a Confucian context is often manifested in condemnation of those 'having no *dao*' (*wu dao*) or 'having lost *dao*' (*shi dao*), referring to a variety of people who do not possess the truth or who behave in an unjust, immoral and unrighteous way (Zhongyong, 33).[15] As the ideal way of life, *dao* must be sought after (*mou*), and humans should be concerned (*you*) if they cannot attain to *dao* (*Analects*, 15:32). Therefore for

---

[11] The meanings of *derek* are more widely ranged than human behaviour: 'Three things are too wonderful for me; four I do not understand: the way (*derek*) of an eagle in the sky, the way of a serpent on a rock, the way of a ship on the high seas, and the way of a man with a maiden' (Prov. 30:18–19). Crenshaw uses this paragraph to examine the double sense of *Derek* that is used in wisdom literature: path and sovereignty, which leads him to the exploration of the value of wisdom for the journey of life: 'for at birth everyone had embarked on a journey that led to a full life or, lamentably, to premature departure. Useful road maps existed; they were the fruit of long effort. Those who relied on their own ingenuity soon became hopelessly lost along winding footpaths', while 'the wise journeyed toward their ultimate destination with sure confidence that they would reach that place safely, whereas fools would lose their way' (James Crenshaw: *Old Testament Wisdom: An Introduction*, Louisville, Kentucky, Westminster John Knox Press, 1998, p.67).

[12] *Theological Dictionary of the Old Testament*, vol. III, 1978, pp.277–82.

[13] *Theological Dictionary of the Old Testament*, ed. G. Johannes Botterweck and Heilmer Ringgzen, trans. John T. Willis, Grand Rapids, Michigan: William B. Eerdman Publishing Company, 1977, vol. III, p.272.

[14] In the *Book of Xunzi*, there are also phrases such as '*zheng dao* 正道', the right or correct way (Xunzi, 22:8), but the adjective 'correct' here only indicates the nature of the way, and does not make it the right way.

[15] *A Source Book in Chinese Philosophy*, pp.112–13.

Confucians it is worrisome and even dangerous if the Way does not prevail in the state or in the world (*dao bu xing*). It is even more so for the state if those in authority do not follow *dao*, because they believe that, 'If those in authority have lost the Way, the common people will be rootless' (*Analects*, 19:19).

Differently from the Confucian *dao* that is mostly used in an ethically laudatory sense, however, the Hebrew *derek* can be both ethical and ethically neutral (as the course of life). With an added ethical value it refers both to morally responsible 'conduct' (the good way) and immoral behaviour (the way of evildoers or an evil way, see Prov. 28:10). As a word for the ethically right way, it is frequently associated with the root *tmm* (complete, blameless and integrity, see Prov. 10:9; 13:6; 28:6) or with *yšr* (upright and righteous, see Prov. 14:12; 21:29; 29:27), denoting both an ethically perfect quality and the resultant condition of unimpaired prosperity (Prov. 10:9; 13:6; 28:6). Therefore, there are two kinds of *derek*; one is good and the other bad. The good way is the *derek* of those who are faithful and righteous, and it is the same as the way of good people, the way of wisdom and the path of the righteous (Prov. 2:20; 4:11, 18), while the bad way is the *derek* of evildoers or the wicked which is compared to 'deep darkness' (Prov. 4:19; 15:9). The good way is said to have the power of the *tāmīm*, 'blameless', and *ṣᵉdāqā* (righteousness) that can smooth the *derek* and keeps death at a distance.[16] As part of the theocentric doctrine, the Israelite understanding of *derek* is based on the belief that the final judgment on the ways lies with YHWH: 'For a man's ways are before the eyes of the LORD, and he watches all his paths' (Prov. 5:21). The good way pleases YHWH, while the evil ways make him angry: 'The way of the wicked is an abomination to the LORD, but he loves him who pursues righteousness', and 'When a man's ways please the LORD, he makes even his enemies to be at peace with him' (Prov. 15:9; 16:7).

Although the Confucian *dao* is used most frequently to refer to the right course of life or action, this does not exempt it from being abused or distorted by those whose morality is low. Thus there comes a contrast between the way of a superior person (*jun zi zhi dao*) and the way of an inferior person (*xiao ren zhi dao*) in the *Doctrine of the Mean*. Therefore, while admitting that *dao* is right by definition and there are no grades of quality between this and that right way, Confucians nevertheless insist that different people take the way differently. Confucius does not believe that people should take counsel together if they have followed different principles (*dao*) of life (*Analects*, 15:40). *Dao* is the same but its manifestations are different, and the problem is in humans rather than in *dao* itself. To fully appreciate *dao* and to wisely follow it, people have to cultivate it (*xiu dao*; Zhongyong, 1) or study it (*xue dao*; *Analects*, 17:4). This does not mean, however, that Confucians suggest that the Way can be modified or transformed; rather they mean that we must 'believe in the Way' with all our heart (*Analects*, 19:2) and cultivate our own character in order to be closer to the Way or to be part of it. In this sense Confucians integrate the internal and the external, rather than separating them.

---

[16] *Theological Dictionary of the Old Testament*, vol. III, p.287.

The ways in which the word *derek* is used in Hebrew texts are characteristic of Israelite theology. Since *derek* can be both ethical and ethically neutral, there is a division between the good *derek* and the bad *derek*. Good or bad, a *derek* is not subject to personal choices. An individual must follow a good course of life, but this does not imply that he is required to pursue a course of internal transformation or cultivation as Confucians claim is necessary; rather, it requires 'faith' in the righteousness of YHWH, which is the only guarantee for one to choose the righteous way and desert the 'evil' way. The dualism of the good and the evil determines the significance for the Israelites of separating the way of YHWH from the way of evildoers, and to emphasize discerning and understanding rather than learning and self-cultivation.

However, the existence of two kinds of *derek* does not mean that the Israelite way of life is purely a religious matter without moral meaning and value. In the Hebrew texts *derek* is associated with the heart, and is under the control of the heart. The course of action will in turn have an effect on the determination of the heart. It is clearly stated that *derek* 'originates in the heart (*lēb*) as the centre of rational planning (Prov. 16:9; 23:19) and it leads to an action which in turn reacts upon the *lēb* (14:14)'.[17] The heart not only must choose a *derek* but also must understand it, because if one does not understand then one will wander in the path of one's life (Prov. 5:6). The Israelite teachers constantly remind their audience that they must pay great attention to guarding or keeping the course of the chosen way, because this is essential for a happy and good life: 'Happy are those who keep my ways' and 'He who guards his way preserves his life' (Prov. 8:32; 16:17). It is important that, as soon as one has chosen the way, one does all one can to make it secure and firm because 'A man who wanders from the way of understanding will rest in the assembly of the dead' (Prov. 21:16).

It is clear that Confucian *dao* and Israelite *derek* contain both spiritual and secular meanings. The way of life is not simply a matter of secular concern; it is rooted in the understanding of the spiritual ultimate. In Confucianism the way of life is primarily based on, or rooted in, the Way of Heaven. Without a full understanding of the Way or the Mandate of Heaven, Confucians claim, it is not possible for us to establish our way of life and make a wise choice in our living. The Hebrew *derek* also refers both to the divine way and to the righteous and wise path by which one goes ahead with one's plan for life. However, while acknowledging the spiritual foundation of the Confucian and the Israelite way of life, we must appreciate that *dao* and *derek* are more commonly associated with secular ways of life than with the spiritual principle of living. In the *Analects*, *dao* is seldom used to refer to the Way of Heaven. In fact one of the disciples of Confucius even said that it was rare for them to hear about the Way of Heaven from their master. The same can also be said about the Hebrew wisdom texts. It has been noted that in the wisdom literature *derek* is used in the sense of the divine way very rarely; instead it is closely in association with moral qualities such as righteousness and wisdom.

---

[17] *Theological Dictionary of the Old Testament*, vol. III, pp.286–7.

Both Confucians and Israelites confirm that the spiritual Way and the secular ways are not in two totally different realms and that they must be put together if we are to understand the true way of life. However, interrelated as the moral meaning and the religious meaning of the way are believed to be, the approaches to the interrelationship made by Confucians and Israelites are nevertheless different. For the Israelites, in order to be in the Way of YHWH, humans must follow divine commandments and walk in the righteous way, as is taught in the Proverbs, an upright way, *derek*, is pleasing to YHWH and 'The LORD is a stronghold to him whose way is upright, but destruction to evildoers' (Prov. 10:29). However, in determining the meaning and value of the Israelite way of life we see an ambiguity concerning the question of whether a *derek* is righteous because YHWH is delighted in it, or YHWH is happy with it because it is righteous. This ambiguity can be clarified only by referring to the overall theology of the Israelites, in which YHWH is the creator, not only of the physical world, but also of the meaning and value of the existence of the human world. Thus this frequently leads to the admission of human ignorance of their own way of life: 'A man's steps are ordered by the LORD; how then can man understand his way? (Prov. 20:24). The Israelite answer to the above question can be and can only be that the direction and the righteous nature of a *derek* are determined by YHWH and must be tested by the faith of those who have chosen it.

This ambiguity does not appear to be of significance in a Confucian context. It is a fundamental belief among Confucians that the Way of Heaven and the ways of humans are two in one: the Way underlies what we should pursue in life, and what we should pursue in life must reflect the requirement of the Way. However, the route they follow to integrate these two dimensions is quite different from that of the Israelites. For Confucians, human nature, the Way and Heaven are interrelated or even interlocked or interdependent, as is stated in the *Doctrine of the Mean*: 'What Heaven imparts to humans is called human nature. To follow this nature is called the Way. Cultivating the Way is called education' (Zhongyong, 1).[18] Zhu Xi (1130–1200), the greatest representative of Neo-Confucianism in the twelfth century, comments on this sentence that it is intended to illustrate that the roots of the Way are originally from Heaven and they will not therefore be subject to change.[19] Owing to the interrelatedness, however, the heavenly root of the Way must be cultivated in the human heart, which is called 'education' or 'self-cultivation' in which wisdom grows and leads us to the right path of life. Through internal cultivation the Way that seems to be outside of us becomes internalized as our existence, or the Way that is not yet manifest in our nature becomes illustrious. In other words, the religious meaning and the moral value, the physical and the moral worlds are integrated in the process of human moral efforts, in which there is no difference between the outside and the inside, and between the transcendent and the immanent.

---

[18] *A Source Book in Chinese Philosophy*, p.98.
[19] Zhu Xi: *Sishu zhangju jizhu*, Beijing: Zhonghua Shuju, 1983, p.17.

The Confucian *dao* cannot automatically enhance humans' intellectual and moral power without human efforts; rather it requires to be extended or enlarged by human intelligence and morality: 'It is humans who can make the Way great. It is not the Way that can make humans great' (*Analects*, 15:29). This understanding may not be so unique to Confucians as it appears to be, because we can observed in the Hebrew texts the same teaching, that one's *derek* requires one's personal efforts. However, an underlying difference between the Confucian *dao* of self-reliance and the Israelite *derek* of the divine guidance is prominent. As the most fundamental element of the Israelite way of life, one's *derek* must be guided by 'instruction' in wisdom (Prov. 4:10; 6:20–23; 7:1–5; 28:6–10), and one must bind the *Torah* (*tōrā*, the law) upon one's 'heart', act accordingly, and experience it 'as an illuminating revelation of the way of life'.[20]

Wisdom and the Practical Life

Having examined the uses of, and references to, *dao* in early Confucian texts and *derek* in Israelite wisdom literature, we can now say with confidence that both the Confucian and the Israelite way of life are closely related to, or even derived from, their concept of wisdom. Wisdom is first of all the search for the meaning of life, and different types of understanding often lead to different perceptions of the way of life, which in turn define its value and meaning differently. The meaning of life thus stands at the core of Confucian and Israelite wisdom reflection. Where does the meaning come from? What determines the course of living? The Confucian and Israelite answers to these questions will be examined below in association with their views on life's meaning, practical skills and abilities, and the way of communication.

The Meaning of Life

Both in Confucianism and in the Israelite tradition, the search for the meaning of life is central to wisdom thinking. However, being wise does not mean merely following sound advice and behaving prudently. It is the pursuit of a meaningful life, a course of life that carries with it significant spiritual value. A life that lacks meaning is often compared with a tree without roots that is definitely going to wither, or as a stream without fountainhead that will doubtless die out.

The fundamental doctrine of Confucian and Israelite traditions is that the meaning of life is rooted in its spiritual value. A way of life cannot be meaningful unless it is ensured in one way or another by the ultimate spiritual power, YHWH in the Israelite tradition and *Tian* (Heaven) in Confucianism. For the Israelites the primary teaching about the wise way of life is 'Trust in the LORD with all your heart, and do not rely on your own insight. In all your ways acknowledge him, and he will make straight your paths' (Prov. 3:5–6). For Confucians, Heaven plays a key role in determining

---

[20] *Theological Dictionary of the Old Testament*, vol. III, p.287.

the course of life, without which, as it is believed, humans both as a nation and as individuals will not be able to lead a life full of meaning and value. With his trust in Heaven, for example, Confucius dismisses the relevance of the fact that nobody understands him; rather he claims that he does not complain against Heaven, nor against other humans because he believes that he will be fully understood by Heaven (*Analects*, 14:35).

However, the spiritual meaning of life is manifested differently in Confucianism and the Israelite religion. Believing that all values are directly derived from faith and that meaning is a gift from the spiritual other, the Israelites rely on YHWH for steering the ship of life, and insist that without his blessing there would have not been meaning in life at all. Therefore, for the Israelites the meaning of life starts with humility before YHWH, not with confidence in humanity. Regarding humility as the way to wisdom and as the source of the meaning of life, they place it in parallel with the fear of YHWH: 'The fear of the LORD is instruction in wisdom, and humility goes before honour' (Prov. 15:33), because YHWH delivers the humble and brings down the haughty (1 Samuel 2:7), and accords blessings to the former, including honour (Prov. 15:33), life and sometimes wealth (Prov. 22:4). In wisdom texts, humility is often connected with low social–economic stature, with individuals or groups who are in affliction, poverty and suffering (Job 22:9). For Israelite teachers, humility is not only a path to safety but also the guarantee of wisdom: 'when pride comes, then comes disgrace, but with the humble is wisdom' (Prov. 11:2). As a manifestation of the divine, wisdom is the first created and has the power and ability to determine the right way. Wisdom walks in the way of righteousness and in the paths of justice (Prov. 8:20), and he who walks in her way will find well-being both in terms of spiritual value and in terms of secular meaning. As far as the secular meaning of life is concerned, the Israelite teachers place an emphasis on learning, which is to devote oneself to the study of the law of the Most High, seek out the wisdom of all the ancients, be concerned with prophecies, preserve the discourse of noble men, penetrate the subtleties of parables, seek out the hidden meanings of the proverbs (Sir. 39:1–3). With all this learning and wisdom, one is able to have a successful career, such as to serve among great men, appear before rulers, and travel through the lands of foreign nations (Sir. 39:4).

In different terms, the Confucian secular perception of life also contains a strong spiritual sense. To lead the right way of life, individuals must first seek to cultivate their character, by which they are able to serve their parents and understand other people. However, whether or not they can fulfil these moral duties successfully depends on whether or not they know the will of Heaven, as the *Doctrine of the Mean* explains:

> A noble person cannot but cultivate his person. As he thinks about cultivating his person, he cannot but serve his parents. As he thinks about serving his parents, he cannot but know other human beings. As he thinks about knowing other human beings, he cannot but know Heaven. (Zhongyong, 20)[21]

---

[21] *Sources of Chinese Tradition*, 2nd edn, vol. 1, compiled by Wm Theodore de Bary and Irene Bloom, New York: Columbia University Press, 1999, p.336.

It seems apparent that, for the author(s) of this text, knowing Heaven is both the end and the precondition of one's cultivation, namely, the source and guarantee of the value and noble meaning of life. However, in contrast to the Israelites of the theocentric religion, Confucians develop in the direction of a humanistic tradition and do not attribute the meaning of life solely to faith in Heaven. Heaven's role in bringing out the meaning of life is distantly indirect, and is played through moral and social mediation. Although providing necessary justification for a wise and meaningful course of life, Confucian Heaven does not endow the value for life as a spiritual gift. Rather, each individual must make his or her life meaningful unaided. An important part of these efforts is in one's conscious interaction with Heaven, by which the spiritual value is manifested through leading a distinct course of living. For rationalistic Confucians, this interaction must be carried out in real terms, namely between individuals and their communities and between a human person and the external world. For idealistic Confucianism it can be made in the cultivation of the human heart/mind and in the development of moral and spiritual qualities that are believed to be innate to human existence. Again in the *Doctrine of the Mean* we read that humans become part of Heaven by cultivating 'sincerity': 'Sincerity is the Way of Heaven. To think how to be sincere is the way of humans. One who is sincere attains centrality without striving, apprehends without thinking' (Zhongyong, 22).[22] In this sense the human way of life has become a process of realizing the spiritual value within, and has carried with it the ultimate meaning.

Can humans fully realize the meaning of their life? Is there any contradiction between spiritual pursuits and the earthly life? Although Israelite and Confucian teachers are in general optimistic about the meaning of life and about the unity between spiritual and secular values, they are also fully aware of the tension between them, and are concerned about the incomprehensibility of spiritual destiny. The Israelites have a clear perception of the unbridgeable gap between human pursuit and the intention of YHWH, while Confucians are worried about their inability to reverse the trend that the Way fails to prevail in human society. Comparatively speaking, the Israelites are more sensitive to this issue than the Confucians, because for them the belief in a moral order that has been established and is continually guaranteed by YHWH is the foundation of all their teaching, and as soon as this order is perceived as having collapsed, life will become meaningless and valueless, as in the case of Job who, after suffering what he believes to be unjust punishments, comes to curse the day of his birth (Job 3:1) and to question whether there is any meaning or value in life at all: 'I loathe my life' (Job 10:1).

Seeing that the human mind cannot grasp the order of YHWH and human wisdom cannot change what life is, some Israelite authors even go for an extremely pessimistic view about the meaning of life. For example, Qoheleth in the book of Ecclesiastes points out that the infathomability of YHWH's intention and activity is a barrier to a deep understanding of life, and that humans do not have access to the

---

[22] *Sources of Chinese Tradition*, 2nd edn, vol. 1, p.338.

knowledge of YHWH and cannot therefore achieve any security, either material or spiritual (Eccl. 11:9–10). This has deprived life of any value, and all that humans do is therefore meaningless. Qoheleth tells his audience cynically that the claim about human wisdom's power to make secure one's existence has no validity, and whatever an individual has done, death cancels all his gains and renders life absurd: 'I have seen everything that is done under the sun; and behold, all is vanity and striving after wind' (Eccl. 1:14).

In comparison with the pessimistic Israelites, Confucians are moderate in their view of human failure, and tend to believe that humans are capable of overcoming the gap between human wisdom and the ultimate meaning of life. Acknowledging that every being has its potential in terms of spiritual value and moral power, Confucians are nevertheless aware that this potential may not be fully realized, either because of the unpredictability of destiny or because of our weakness in carrying out self-cultivation. On the one hand, Confucius is deeply concerned that failure to cultivate virtue and to practise what is right makes one's life less valuable and meaningful. On the other, he does not attribute the failure totally to the nature of humans, or to the limitations Heaven has placed on human beings; rather he says that this happens because of moral shortcomings: some of us are too lazy and tend to set limits for ourselves before we even start (*Analects*, 6:12). Since the reason for humans to have a less meaningful life is moral weakness, it is natural for Confucians to believe that by overcoming it and by addressing the shortcomings all humans are able to make a change in the course of an unsuccessful life, and that the meaning of life can be realized only through the process of making efforts, the best guarantee of a meaningful life. In this sense, Confucians consider the way of life as a personal choice: the wise way of life marks the wisdom of a person, while the stupid or foolish would follow a foolish way. The necessary condition for a life to be valuable is that we learn, and are properly trained about, how to make wise choices, and this requires other means, particularly moral and ethical norms and disciplines, to help individuals in their choosing.

Entwined with the search for the meaning of life is concern about death. Worries about death are one of the main causes not only of psychological stresses and physical problems, but also of a distorted view of life itself, having a direct effect on the way of life. Therefore a correct attitude toward death is a necessary part of wisdom. In the Hebrew literature life and death are deemed to be a matter solely determined by YHWH, about which humans should not be worried: 'Naked I came from my mother's womb, and naked shall I return; the LORD gave, and the LORD has taken away' (Job 1:21). There is no disputing that, when Job made the above remarks, he was under extreme stress as he and his life were thoroughly turned upside down in a series of disasters. However, this view can be verified in many other texts where YHWH is said to be both the creator and the terminator of life. 'Choosing life' is a fundamental requirement of the Israelite doctrine (Deuteronomy 30:19) and YHWH is believed to have the 'power over life and death' (Wisd. 16:13).

Confucians hold that life and death are of spiritual significance and therefore must be treated with utmost sincerity and reverence. Everyone has an allotted span of life, some longer and some shorter. This is predetermined by Destiny (*Analects*, 12:5). It is natural that everybody wants to live and does not want to die (Mengzi, 6A:10), and it is therefore natural that when death comes relatives grieve. Confucian wisdom is to teach people to take a natural view of life and death. 'Death has always been with us since the beginning of time' (*Analects*, 12:7). Strongly disagreeing with religious mysticism that strives for longevity or immorality, however, Confucius does not believe that there are such beings as immortals; rather he regards those who refuse to die when old as a pest (*Analects*, 14:43). On the one hand, Confucius calls people to treat death as a natural phenomenon, and to understand life rather than death (*Analects*, 11:12). On the other, he places a high value on the ritual of serving the dead, and requires the people 'to serve the dead as if they were served while alive' (Zhongyong, 19). This kind of service is to hold in memory the moral virtue and achievements of the past generations and to urge the living to follow the footsteps of the dead and to carry on their unfinished enterprises. In this way, Confucius nurtures a moral view of life and death: in living one is honoured; and in death one is mourned (*Analects*, 19:25).

Is there any eternal element in human life? We have already noted that Confucians do not in general believe life can be immortal, though their virtue and achievement can. The same can be said also of the Israelite view. David believed that to die was the way of all the earth (1 Kings 2:1–2), and most Israelite sages 'reckoned with death as a real factor' and 'entertained no hope of life beyond'.[23] Influenced by Greek beliefs in eternity of the soul, some later Israelite teachers seem to have come to this issue from a different approach and take a comparatively more positive view of immortality. For them, life is created by YHWH and humans are made in the image of his own eternity. Death entered the world through the devil's envy, but the souls of the righteous are believed to be 'in the hands of YHWH' and 'no torment will ever touch them' (Wisd. 2:24; 3:1). However, as in Confucianism, physical immortality is never taken seriously in the Israelite wisdom tradition; eternity is in general defined by virtue and faith, 'for in the memory of virtue is immortality' (Wisd. 4:1). Life can be prolonged in a literal sense, and this can be done through wisdom in the sense that wisdom is life or the tree of life, and by taking wise counsel 'the years of your life may be many' (Prov. 4:10). Israelite wisdom has also pointed us in the direction of being righteous for the meaning of life: 'In the path of righteousness is life, but the way of error leads to death' (Prov. 12:28).

As discussed above, the dominant Israelite view of life is concerned with the same aspects as those with which Confucians engage; the meaning must be generated in the real course of life through physical existence and activity guided by wisdom, not in the life after death or immortal life. However, there are also fundamental differences between them, in which we can see clearly that the Israelites are confident that the

---

[23] James L. Crenshaw:, 1998, p.66.

religious pious will lead a blessed life, meaningful materially and physically, while Confucians declare that life is full of meaning and value only if an individual strives personally to become morally good.

Skills and Practical Abilities

Being the source of spiritual value and the guarantee of life's meaning, wisdom also has a practical dimension that makes the way of life both secularly and spiritually meaningful. Confucians and the Israelites tend to define the meaning of life in a moral sense and distinguish the right way from the unjust and evil way, confirming that the former leads to a meaningful and valuable destination, while the latter directs one to a dark and meaningless destiny. Therefore, the Confucian and Israelite way of life is an ethical way, denoting a significant moral meaning with an added ethical value. The Confucian way of life is metaphorically compared to a tree that is destined to be alive and to grow only if the roots are firmly grounded in moral disciplines and ethical principles. The roots are goodness and virtues, and it is only in goodness and virtue that the right way of life can be well established (*Analects*, 1:2). Therefore wisdom is associated with benevolence, truthfulness, fidelity, kindness and honesty, which are constant topics in Confucian classics and Hebrew texts such as Proverbs and Ecclesiastes where we can find a striking parallel between *hkm* (wisdom) and *sdq* ('righteousness').

As an individual, each human being has to explore his/her own way of life, and to find meaning in it. To lead a meaningful life, we not only need spiritual faith and moral cultivation; we are also required to solve day-to-day problems by employing certain skills and abilities by which life difficulties can be solved and complicated situations can be understood. A person is wise, not only because he/she has faith or is engaged in moral cultivation, but also because he/she has skilfully followed the right course of action that makes life secure and safe, while a foolish person does the contrary. On many occasions, being wise or foolish is judged not only by one's knowledge and understanding, but also by one's practical skills.

Both Confucians and the Israelites associate wisdom with skill and ability, and value highly their importance for the meaning of life. However, as far as the source of skill and ability is concerned, there is a substantial difference between the Confucian and Israelite views, and this difference reveals to us, from a different point of view, the key divergence between a humanistic doctrine and a theocentric religion. For the Israelites, skill and ability, like all other aspects of life, are primarily a gift from YHWH who alone determines that some people are more skilful than others, as Moses related in the story of Baz'alel, in which YHWH was said to have 'filled him with the Spirit of God, with ability, with intelligence, with knowledge, and with all craftsmanship', and to have filled him and Oho'liab of the tribe of Dan 'with ability to do every sort of work done by a craftsman or by a designer or by an embroiderer in blue and purple and scarlet stuff and fine twined linen, or by a weaver – by any sort of workman or skilled designer' (Exodus 35:30–31, 34–5).

In contrast, Confucians consider Heaven to be the source of abilities only in a metaphorical sense, taking Heaven as an inspiring power while regarding practical skills and abilities as coming from people's learning, practice and effort. One of Confucius's contemporaries commented that Confucius was surely a sage; otherwise why should he be skilled in so many things? For this Confucius did not go to Heaven or Heaven's mission to give an account of his skill and ability; rather he described himself as someone who grew up in humble conditions and therefore became skilled in many menial things, and this enabled him to have many practical accomplishments in regard to everyday matters (*Analects*, 9:6).

Despite this underlying difference in Confucian and Israelite views, life was not dramatically different in China from that in Israel. The Chinese and the Israelites were faced with the same problems in life and their wisdom was demonstrated in solving these problems through the same or similar skills and abilities. These skills and abilities included not only those of a manual and technical nature, but also those of dealing with other people and managing social projects. A distinction is often made in Greek philosophy between specific mental abilities or skills and wisdom, the former enabling one to be literate and adept, the latter enabling one to love harmony, beauty and truth, in which a specific character emerges with a principle of self-control, and to be able to subordinate passion and desire to the authority of reason. In Confucian and Israelite traditions, however, wisdom grows in personal experience, and wisdom and skills, reason and passion are not excluded from each other. For example, Confucius admits that he does not possess knowledge, but by using proper methods (skills) he can answer various questions (*Analects*, 9:8).

Skills and abilities as emphasized in Confucian texts and the Israelite wisdom literature can be roughly classified into two categories, 'hard' or specific, and 'soft' or general. 'Hard' and specific skills and abilities refer to those that enable us to be capable of a particular task, while 'soft' and general skills and abilities refer to those that enable us to be respected in the community and therefore to have a successful career. Although a competent person is likely able to complete all his tasks more easily, general abilities cannot replace specific skills, and labour division requires each of us to be skilled in a limited number of areas. The *Xunzi* talks about 'the hundred skills' (*bai ji*) that are required to nurture the needs of a single individual; it also points out, however, that even the most able people cannot be universally skilled (Xunzi, 10:1). For the Israelites, wisdom is practical, a skill in action that includes both hard and soft aspects. In the Hebrew Scriptures, wisdom is the word that designates the skills of craftsman (for example, in Exodus 31:6; 1 King 7:14; Isaiah 40:20), and is displayed in the skill with which a man fulfils an office or a responsibility.[24] There are a variety of skills that are associated with wisdom; for example, the skills and abilities in running the state (Genesis 41:39), the prudence of the chieftain of a tribe or the leader of community (Deuteronomy 1:13, 15), the ability to render a just judgment in a legal case (1 Kings 3:28), and the medical skill of a physician (Sir. 38:3).

---

[24] John L. McKenzie, S.J.: *Dictionary of the Bible*, London/Dublin: Geoffrey Chapman, 1980, p.930.

Both specific and general skills and abilities are highly valued in Confucian and Israelite considerations of human life. Skills such as that of a metalworker, a carpenter or a weaver (Exodus 35:35), and abilities such as that of drawing squares or circles like a carpenter, that of adjusting the pitch of the five notes like a musician, or that of ruling the empire like sage–kings (Mengzi, 4A:1) are appreciated as essential to a successful career. Therefore talking in a practical sense, Confucians and Israelites take the view that how to pursue a meaningful life depends to a great extent on what skills and abilities one possesses. 'Skill will bring success' (Eccl. 10:10), and a man skilful in his work will stand before the king (Prov. 22:9). For them it is apparent that a skilful person copes with life more easily and more successfully, while an incapable person is always frustrated by failure to solve his own problems. Confucius taught his students that lack of skill and ability would lead to disappointment in life and therefore 'It is not the failure of others to appreciate your abilities that should trouble you, but rather your own lack of them' (*Analects*, 14:30). In this sense, one's practical ability is often taken to be the scale measuring one's wisdom, because skill and ability are not only manifested as specific tools in managing one's work, such as those of a sailor, but also can become the life skill that determines which course of life one can lead and what purpose one can achieve. This life skill is like that of steering, enabling one to manage a real situation such as controlling an actual boat, as well as to steer successfully through life in a more general sense.

In many contexts, life skill seems to be intended to deal only with one's particular job and with other people one happens to be associated with. In many others, however, we find the Confucians and the Israelites are also deeply concerned with the skill and ability in dealing with oneself, particularly when engaging in a wide range of ethical, legal and political responsibilities. Life skill and ability present themselves as manners and attitudes essential to the wise way of life, such as thoughtfully discerning one's way (Prov. 14:8) and skilfully practising what is right in order to realize the way (*Analects*, 16:11). Practice can be of different kinds and be engaged in different circumstances. For instance, it has been recognized that an artisan in any of the hundred crafts must master his trade by staying in his workshop, while for a gentleman the only means by which he can perfect his way is through learning (*Analects*, 19:7). To illustrate the importance of practising a variety of skills for completing tasks, for example, Confucius compared the cultivation of political skills to the sharpening of tools of a craftsman. 'A craftsman who wishes to practise his craft well must first sharpen his tools.' Likewise, a gentleman who wishes to be capable of governing the world must skilfully 'seek the patronage of the most distinguished Counsellors', and 'make friends with the most benevolent gentlemen' (*Analects*, 15:10).

Skilfully dealing with others and with oneself requires a balanced attitude and manner. Therefore the mean or the Middle Way is important. Confucius has no doubt that going beyond and falling short are equally wrong (*Analects*, 11:16), and Xunzi also makes it clear that 'Pride and excess bring disaster for man. Respectfulness and moderation ward off five weapons' (Xunzi, 4:1). Using the principle of the Middle Way and moderation, Israelite teachers recommend it as a necessary ability for the wise to keep their temper under control, because they are fully aware of the danger of losing one's temper. 'A man of wrath stirs up strife, and a man given to anger causes much transgression' (Prov. 29:22). In contrast, a balanced character would easily dissolve conflict; as it is claimed in the book of Proverbs, 'he who is slow to anger quiets contention' (Prov. 15:18).

Speaking and Silence

Wisdom as the practical way of life is expressed through communication skill and ability. However, it seems to be a common feature among all sapiential traditions that a wise way of living must be ensured by silence rather than through speaking. In Daoism there is a strong disdain towards the talkative, and the *Daode jing* points out, 'The one who knows does not speak; the one who speaks does not know' (Daode jing, 56). A similar attitude is also taken by Confucius, who does not think that wisdom comes from one's manipulating words.[25] Confucius describes himself in learning as 'quietly storing up knowledge in my mind' (*Analects*, 7:2), and praises those who do not have a big mouth as virtuous, because 'A person of benevolence loathes to speak' (*Analects*, 12:3). In the same vein, Israelite wisdom teachers also praise silence highly: 'Silence is a sign of self-control and thoughtfulness, a characteristic of one who is master of the situation',[26] and they place wisdom in sharp contrast to the loquacious. A man of knowledge is described as the one who 'restrains his words' (Prov. 17:27). One of the Israelite contrasts between the wise and the ignorant or fools is that the former learn but do not speak, while the latter speak recklessly, which causes them much harm: 'Wise men lay up knowledge, but the babbling of a fool brings ruin near' (Prov. 10:14). A significant sign of a wise man is that he 'remains silent' (Prov. 11:12), learns before speaking (Sir. 18:19), and keeps silent because he knows when to speak (Sir. 20:6).

Confucian and Israelite teachers repeatedly told their students that the wise spoke only when it was necessary, and, when they spoke, they told only what was necessary. Their caution over using language and words arises from both theoretical and practical considerations. First, it is related to the Confucian and Israelite

---

[25] Although both praise silence and disregard speech, the difference between Confucius and Daoists should not be overlooked. Neo-Daoists such as Wang Bi (226–49) attempted to blur the line and regarded Confucius as a more sublime sage than Laozi, the supposed author of the *Daode jing*, as he transmitted wisdom without writing anything and devoted his life to 'remembering silently' (Liu, I-ching: *Shih-shuo hsin-yu: A new account of tales of the world*, trans. Richard B. Mather, Minneapolis: University of Minesota Press, 1976, p.96). This is a misinterpretation of Confucius, because Confucius' silence is praised in a moral sense, intended to emphasize that inner cultivation is more important than seeking external reputation, and to shun damage caused by imprudent comments, while for Daoists, silence is the nature of Dao and is therefore the metaphysical source of wisdom.

[26] David Noel Freedman (ed.): *The Anchor Bible Dictionary*, New York: Doubleday, 1992, vol. VI, p.929.

understanding of the metaphysical universe. For Confucians, the Way of Heaven guides humans but does not tell them what they should do. 'What does Heaven ever say? Yet there are the four seasons going round and there are the hundred things coming into being' (*Analects*, 17:19). Mengzi also emphasized that Heaven did not speak, but showed its intention through acts and events (Mengzi, 5A:5). Since Confucians believe that humans must follow the Way of Heaven, it is natural for them to refrain from talking and to tell their students not to be talkative. In the Israelite tradition, speech is highly valued only if it appears in the forms of extolling the LORD or singing praise to his name. This involves 'telling the glories of God' and proclaiming 'his creation' in which 'Day to day pours forth speech, and night to night declares knowledge'; just because of the nature of these speeches, however, they do not appear like speech: 'There is no speech, nor are there words; their voice is not heard; yet their voice goes out through all the earth, and their words to the end of the world' (Psalm 18:49; 19:1–4). As far as wisdom is concerned, the Israelites reserve the right of speaking to YHWH who is believed to have uttered wisdom and from whose mouth comes knowledge and understanding (Prov. 2:6–7). Therefore what humans need to do is only to open their eyes to see and to lend their ears to listen, in doing this, wisdom will come to their hearts (Prov. 2:10). Israelite wisdom teachers put it clearly: 'God is in heaven and you are on earth, therefore let your words be few' (Eccl. 5:2). For those who are suspicious of the possibility that humans can know the ultimate truth and the created order, not only the oral tradition but also written texts would not be of particular help for us to know the seemingly unknowable: 'The multiplication of books is endless, and the study of them yields only exhaustion' (Eccl. 12:12).

Secondly, the preference for silence over speaking is due to their perception of the gap between wisdom and language. Wisdom is deeper understanding of, and insight into, the overall situation and the cause of things, while language is an artificial means by which we represent what has happened and make connections between things. What we say therefore is not necessarily what really happens, and when we try to describe something it does not necessarily mean that we have understood it or properly described it. True knowledge therefore lies in the quality of words, not in their quantity. The Israelites view understanding as manifested in one's deep insight and not in rushing words, and 'he who has a cool spirit is a man of understanding' (Prov. 17:27). For them one of the criteria for judging the wisdom of men is that the wise know when to speak and when to be silent: 'Even a fool who keeps silent is considered wise; when he closes his lips, he is deemed intelligent' (Prov. 17:28). Confucius has a deep suspicion about the people who talk nicely, and believes that these people would find it difficult or impossible to be benevolent (*Analects*, 1:3); so do Israelites teachers who caution their audience to guard against a man of an evil intention, and 'when he speaks graciously, believe him not' (Prov. 26:25). Therefore the use of language can be justified only by the moral character of the user: 'He who speaks the truth gives honest evidence, but a false witness utters deceit'; 'Truthful lips endure for ever, but a lying tongue is but for a moment' (Prov. 12:17, 19).

Thirdly, that Confucians and the Israelites give priority to silence rather than speaking reflects their practical wisdom in dealing with the human situation, in which bad consequences and transgression often result from an open mouth. Words are a necessary tool in communicating but are equally a means to bring about disasters. It is in this sense that Israelite teachers take it as a life or death issue whether or not one can control one's mouth: 'Death and life are in the power of the tongue' (Prov. 18:21). Fully aware of the danger one's words can bring about, 'A prudent man conceals his knowledge' (Prov. 12:23) and 'He who guards his mouth preserves his life; he who opens his mouth comes to ruin' (Prov. 13:3). A fool is a fool because he cannot control his mouth: 'A fool's lips bring strife, and his mouth invites a flogging. A fool's mouth is his ruin, and his lips are a snare to himself' (Prov. 18:6–7). 'When words are many, transgression is not lacking, but he who restrains his lips is prudent' (Prov. 10:19). Therefore loquacity is a sign of lacking sense, while silence signifies understanding (Prov. 11:12). Confucius sets it as one of the necessary qualities of a gentleman that he is 'quick in action but cautious in speech' (*Analects*, 1:14). Considering the strong effect of bad words, Confucius even tends to agree that 'a saying can lead the state to ruin' (*Analects*, 13:15). Xunzi also makes a strong comment on the danger and harm boastful words can bring about: 'The danger to every step of the traveller lies generally with words' (Xunzi, 4:1).

Pursuit of Wealth and Making Friends

We live both in a natural environment and in a social context, and the quality of our life depends, at least partially, on what we can employ to satisfy our needs and what kinds of people we come to associate with. Human needs are manifested through multiple facets and are satisfied at various levels. In terms of material prosperity, we need a certain amount of goods to lead a decent life, without suffering the terrible hardship of hunger and cold, and, in terms of interpersonal relationship, we need to be associated closely with some people while distancing ourselves from others. Therefore how to deal with the issues of poverty and wealth, and how to make the right people our friends have naturally become part of Confucian and Israelite wisdom of life.

Poverty and Wealth

Both Israelite and Confucian masters realized that a certain level of wealth or possessing sufficient means to meet one's desires is a necessary guarantee of a good life, while poverty can often lead to a distorted character. For the Israelites it is apparent that 'The wealth of the rich is their fortress; the poverty of the poor is their ruin' (Prov. 10:15),[27] while for Confucians, it is no surprise at all that 'Wealth makes

---

[27] For a detailed discussion of poverty and wealth in the book of Proverbs, see R.N. Whybray's *Wealth and Poverty in the Book of Proverbs*, JSOT Press, 1990.

a house shining and virtue makes a person shining' (Daxue, 6) and that a man in extreme poverty has no home to go back to (Mengzi, 5Λ:1). Although later Confucians frequently refer to wisdom as the extinction of desires, in early Confucian classics, meeting physical needs and having a decent material life are an integral part of the right way of life, in which regulated passion is needed for the attainment of wisdom.[28]

Wealth not only provides us with necessary life-provisions and prevents us from suffering from hunger and cold, but also is an important condition for a respectable social life, because it is often the case that 'Wealth brings many new friends, but a poor man is deserted by his friend' (Prov. 19:4). Contrary to the commonly accepted view that ancient Chinese and Israelites view wealth as corrupting human spirit, whilst poverty can produce good qualities, Confucian and Israelite teachers argue that wealth itself does not necessarily lead to evil or immoral attitudes.

Confucius was quoted as saying that the head of the state should not worry about poverty but about instability (*Analects*, 16:1) and in the *Book of Mengzi* we read a quotation from Yang Hu that 'If one's aim is wealth one cannot be benevolent; if one's aim is benevolence one cannot be wealthy' (Mengzi, 3A:3). These remarks have been taken as evidence that Confucians believe in a diametric opposition between the rich and the virtuous. However, in the same section, Mengzi also points out that 'Those with constant means of support (*heng chan*, permanent property) will have constant hearts' and confirms that a certain level of wealth is necessary to ensure the pursuit of the moral way of life. Confucius has repeatedly said that being rich and being morally good do not necessarily constitute a contradiction and that being poor does not necessarily lead to good, for poverty would prevent people from being virtuous: 'It is more difficult not to complain of injustice when poor than not to behave with arrogance when rich' (*Analects*, 14:10). Therefore one of the key policies Confucius promoted is 'to make the people rich' (*Analects*, 13:9).

This attitude is also echoed in the Israelite texts where, although lust or unrestrained desire for riches is disdained, wealth acquired by proper means is praised, and living comfortably is said to be the sign of blamelessness and intelligence, as can be seen from the example of Job before he was struck down by heavenly punishments (Job 1:1–3). Having studied Israelite wisdom literature, James Crenshaw confirms that

> At the very heart of the wise's search for knowledge lay a value judgment: *life* was the supreme good. The word 'life' is used here in its pregnant sense – a long existence characterised by robust health, an abundance of friends, a house full of children, and sufficient possessions to carry one safely through any difficulty.[29]

---

[28] 'Before the feelings of pleasure, anger, sorrow, and joy are aroused it is called equilibrium (*chung*, centrality, mean). When these feelings are aroused and each and all attain due measure and degree, it is called harmony. Equilibrium is the great foundation of the world, and harmony its universal path' (Zhongying, 1; in *A Source Book in Chinese Philosophy*, vol. 1, p.98).

[29] James L. Crenshaw, 1998, p.66.

Believing that a good life must be supported by sufficient possessions, the Israelite sages praised the diligent and condemned the lazy, because diligence can generate wealth, while poverty results from laziness. In the eyes of the ancient Israelites, the poor would have nothing to be proud of: 'The lazy do not roast their game, but the diligent obtain precious wealth' (Prov. 12:27), and this reflects only how lazy and unskilful they are: 'A slack hand causes poverty, but the hand of the diligent makes rich' (Prov. 10:4). Poverty is the necessary result of ignoring wise teachings: 'Poverty and disgrace come to him who ignores instruction' (Prov. 13:18).

Pursuing wealth is not only socially sound but also morally justifiable. Confucius once said that 'If wealth were a permissible pursuit, then I would be willing even to act as a guard holding a whip outside the market place' (*Analects*, 7:12). The moral problem with pursuing wealth does not lie in wealth itself, but is tangled up with the means by which one gets rich. While highlighting the value of wealth, the Israelites place an emphasis on righteousness and justice, and strongly oppose the pursuit of wealth by immoral or unjust means: 'Ill-gotten treasures are of no value, but righteousness delivers from death' (Prov. 10:2). A similar attitude is also found in Confucius when he says that 'Wealth and rank attained through immoral means have as much to do with me as passing clouds' (*Analects*, 7:16). Although he admits that 'wealth and high station are what all people desire', and that 'poverty and low station are what all people dislike', he declares that, unless he became rich and ranked highly in the right way he would not remain in them, and if he did not become poor and ranked lowly in the right way he would never try to escape from them (*Analects*, 4:5).

Morally permissible means for wealth creation was more likely to have existed in a well-governed society, while in a chaotic society people more frequently seek after wealth through unjust ways. It is in this sense that Confucius comments that 'It is a shameful matter to be poor and humble when the Way prevails in the state. Equally, it is a shameful matter to be rich and noble when the Way falls into disuse in the state' (*Analects*, 8:13). Similarly, Israelite wisdom also permits individuals to adapt themselves according to political changes, and observes that, 'When the righteous triumph, there is great glory, but when the wicked rise, men hide themselves (Prov. 28:12).

Not only must wealth be acquired through moral means, but Confucians and Israelite teachers also demand that it be used according to ethical requirements. In any society where there exists a polarity of the rich and the poor, a wise and morally good way to safety and harmony is generosity of the rich towards the poor and moderation of the poor in their life (Xunzi, 7:1). While praising the rich in their wisdom, the Israelite and Confucian teachers remind their students again and again that rich people must do their duties towards the poor: 'A generous man will himself be blessed, for he shares his food with the poor' (Prov. 22:9). A poem quoted in the *Book of Mengzi* claims that 'Happy are the rich; but have pity on the helpless' (Mengzi, 1B:5) and Mengzi defines 'generosity' as 'sharing one's wealth with others' (Mengzi, 3A:4).

Where does poverty or wealth come from? Why have some people become rich and others poor? Confucian and Israelite answers to these questions range from theological consideration to the practical account of the means one happens to be able to employ, in which we find the diversity between a more humanistic reasoning and a more theocentric way of thinking. For Confucians and Israelites alike, poverty results from ignorance and disregard of wise teaching, while wisdom can overcome poverty and bring people wealth. In the book of Proverbs we read that 'Poverty and disgrace come to him who ignores instruction' (Prov. 13:18). Wisdom openly claims that 'Riches and honour are with me, enduring wealth and prosperity' (Prov. 8:18), and that 'I walk in the way of righteousness, in the paths of justice, endowing with wealth those who love me, and filling their treasuries' (Prov. 8:20–21). This total confidence and trust in the divine wisdom is rooted in the Israelite belief that poverty is brought about by the unfaithful, while righteousness generates prosperity: 'prosperity rewards the righteous' (Prov. 13:21); 'In the house of the righteous there is much treasure, but trouble befalls the income of the wicked' (Prov. 15:6). Determined by its theocentric theology, however, Israelite wisdom eventually does not emphasize the difference between the rich and the poor; rather it views them equally, because whether one is rich or poor is completely in the hands of YHWH: 'The rich and the poor meet together; the Lord is the maker of them all' (Prov. 22:2), and with the faith that all things in human life and the world are determined by YHWH, it is natural for the Israelites to believe that 'Good things and bad, life and death, poverty and wealth, come from the Lord' (Sir. 11:14).

In contrast, Confucians take a humanistic view of the rich and the poor. They admit that to be rich is the desire of all the people, but owing to the different situations in which they are born and live, not all the people can be rich. There is no shame on the poor, but disgrace is on those who become rich by immoral means and on those who are too lazy to make an effort to change their dire conditions. To the question whether it is possible for a poor man to become rich, Xunzi's answer is positive, believing that poverty can be overcome and the misfortunes of the poor can be reversed through 'learning' (Xunzi, 8:7). However, Confucian learning is not merely an accumulation of knowledge. In fact knowledge itself does not necessarily bring about a wealthy and prosperous life, as it is apparent that 'for all their breadth of knowledge' some people would be 'reduced to poverty because of their penchant for slander' (Xunzi, 4:2). More important is that one has a good character and leads a life of virtue and wisdom.

Because of the complexity of social conditions and personal circumstances, it is possible that, whatever one does, one may still remain poor. However, there is a sharp contrast between the wise and the foolish in their attitude towards poverty. The wise accept poverty easily while the foolish would be overwhelmed by a dire life situation. Confucius compares a gentleman who in poverty acts as a gentleman (*jun zi*), with a small man (*xiao ren*) who in extreme straits would throw over all restraint (*Analects*, 15:2). Confucian wisdom concerning the issues of poverty and wealth is that one should not allow the conditions of being rich or poor to damage the integrity of one's character: Mengzi praises the great man in that he cannot be led to excesses when wealthy or honoured, nor can he be deflected from his purpose when poor and obscure (Mengzi, 3B:2; 5B:1). When facing the rich and the poor, a correct attitude recommended by Xunzi is not to be arrogant in treating the rich and the eminent, nor to demean oneself before the poor and humble (Xunzi, 3:14).

Making Friends

As social beings, humans live in interpersonal relations. It is therefore important for the quality of life not only that one does not unnecessarily offend other people but also that one has some people as close companions and friends. In all wisdom traditions making friends and guiding people in friendship are an important element of the wise way of life. Confucians take the principle for the intercourse between friends as one of the five universal ways (*da dao*, Zhongyong, 20), and Xunzi explicitly defines the way of a gentleman as to 'esteem his teachers and to be intimate with his friends' (Xunzi, 2:1). The Israelite teachers employ every means to convince their students that friends are one's castle and true friends are the most effective protection and the most valuable treasure: 'A faithful friend is a sturdy shelter; he that has found one has found a treasure' (Sir. 6:14). Friends are thus in stark contrast to foreigners and strangers, and wisdom students are frequently warned against associating with the latter because they represent temptation personified and a departure from Wisdom's ways (Prov. 2:16; 5:3, 20; 6:24; 7:5; 23:27).

Valuing highly the importance of friendship for the way of life, Confucians and Israelite teachers do not recommend one to keep the company of all sorts of people; rather, they ask their students to choose carefully the people they associate with. How to keep a distance from the fool and the unworthy, and how to be a friend with the wise and the good are not only an important part of wisdom but also an art of life. There is consideration of the relation between wealth and friendship. The Confucian and Israelite attitude towards wealth, as discussed above, determines that the rich or the poor should not be a criterion in one's choosing friends, because there is no necessary contradiction between wealth and friendship and a certain level of wealth is a precondition for making friends, as we can see from the book of Proverbs, which says that 'The poor are disliked even by their neighbours, but the rich have many friends' (Prov. 14:20).

Primary concern in Confucianism about whom one should be associated with is given to one's personality and moral virtues. Confucius taught his students that in order to benefit from friendship, they must carefully choose their companions, who must be morally good and be more advanced in moral cultivation (*Analects*, 9:25). Xunzi explains why it is important for the common people to be careful in choosing their friends. For him, friends are those with whom one has mutual interests. One therefore must choose those who pursue the same way as one's own, because 'If their way is not the same, how can there be mutual interests?' (Xunzi, 27:102). The Israelite teachers are also aware of the importance of friendship with the right people, but they place less emphasis on the moral effect friendship may bring about and are more concerned with whether or not one would become wise in one's contact with other people. They require their students to 'leave the presence of a fool, for there you do not find words of knowledge' (Prov. 14:7), and advise 'Do not talk much with a foolish man, and do not visit an unintelligent man' (Sir. 22:13), for the same reasons as those provided by Confucian teachers.

It is clear for Confucians and Israelites that the importance of having friends or choosing the right people as friends arises from the benefit one can take from them. The reason why Confucius advises his audience to 'make friends with the most benevolent gentlemen in a state' (*Analects*, 15:10) is that they would benefit from these benevolent gentlemen. He goes even further, to define three kinds of people as beneficial, and another three as harmful: 'To make friends with the straight, the trustworthy in word and the well-informed is to benefit. To make friends with the ingratiating in action, the pleasant in appearance and the plausible in speech is to lose' (*Analects*, 16:4).

The Israelite teachers tell how one can become wise by making friends with the wise and become a fool by staying together with the fool: 'He who walks with wise men becomes wise, but the companion of fools will suffer harm' (Prov. 13:20). It is believed that friendship makes one stronger and enables one to gain more reward, as claimed in an Israelite text which says that 'Two are better than one, because they have a good reward for their toil … A threefold cord is not quickly broken' (Eccl. 4:9–12). The benefit can be in terms of material gains, but more importantly it is judged in moral and intellectual terms. Confucians give primary consideration to the beneficial influence of moral virtues between friends, while the Israelites take into account the mutual stimulation: 'Iron sharpens iron, and one man sharpens another' (Prov. 27:17).

True friendship not only benefits our social and moral life, but can also make our life more pleasant. The first sentence of the *Analects* records Confucius as saying, 'Is it not a joy to have friends come from afar?' (*Analects*, 1:1). However, a joyful thing can easily be turned into distress if we do not cultivate friendship in a right way: 'Is it not a grief to the death when a companion and friend turns to enmity?' (Sir. 37:2). A significant part of the Confucian and Israelite wisdom is devoted to the discussion of how to appreciate and maintain friendship. It is believed among the late Jewish community that 'There is nothing so precious as a faithful friend', and they compare a good friend to an elixir of life (Sir. 6:15–16). This is a continuation of the earlier tradition on friendship, where conventional wisdom is provided to protect and nurture friendship, and to ward off anything that may alienate or damage it, for example, gossip (Prov. 16:28), garrulousness (Prov. 18:9) and the denouncing of friends for reward (Job 17:5). Confucian wisdom is to promote and enhance friendship through virtuous attitude and behaviour. Although there is an element of mutual (material) benefit in friendship, Confucians define it primarily as an ethical relation. Therefore when we make friends with others, we must not rely on any perception of taking material and social advantages from them. Rather, in taking someone else as a friend the only consideration is his virtue (Mengzi, 4B:3). The same is also true in maintaining friendship. It is important to establish trust between friends, because without trustfulness they would easily lose confidence in each other. Many of the close disciples of Confucius defined 'trustfulness' (*xin*) as the criterion for maintaining friendship (*Analects*, 1:4, 7), and Mengzi first raised 'trust' between friends to the level of the five constant virtues (*wu chang*, Mengzi, 3A:4), and this has become one of the most important moral teachings in China.

Joy and Wisdom

As the way of life, wisdom consists of maxims on how to conduct oneself in speech and deportment so as to dispose others favourably towards you, to foster one's own success and advancement, and, more importantly, how to live free of anxiety which arises from hostility, opposition and failure. Living a life without anxiety, worry and pressure is, in other words, to lead a life of joy, pleasure and happiness. In both Confucian and Israelite traditions there is an intrinsic link between wisdom and joy. The joyful character makes Confucian and Israelite wisdom diverge from that of ascetics who believe that wisdom comes only from enduring physical and mental suffering.

Joy in Confucian and Israelite traditions

We have no doubt that joy or delightfulness is characteristic of the early Confucian perception of wisdom. Confucius is recorded as having commented on the two dimensions of the ideal life, *zhi* (wisdom) and *ren* (virtue or benevolence), claiming that

> A person of wisdom delights (*le*) in water.
> A person of benevolence delights in mountains.
> A person of wisdom is active.
> A person of benevolence is in quietude.
> A person of wisdom is joyful (*le*).
> A person of benevolence is long-lived. (*Analects*, 6:23)

This poetic verse draws us a picture in which a person of wisdom demonstrates a distinctive character, different from, but not unrelated to, a person of benevolence. The former is joyful, active and fond of water, while the latter delights in [the image of] mountains, is fond of quietude and lives a long life. These characteristics have a fundamental effect on the Confucian paradigm of wisdom. Wisdom and joyfulness interact, supplement and strengthen each other. For Confucians, the wiser one has become, the happier one will be; in turn, the more one enjoys life and its richness, the more likely one is to be able to ascend the ladder of wisdom.

It seems clear that early Confucians have rejected the paradoxes that, to gain wisdom, one must give up consciously enjoying oneself, and that the older, less joyful and more serious one is, the wiser one will be considered to be. Instead, they take the view that the ageing process serves to increase knowledge and understanding,[30] that understanding of life will naturally bring joy and happiness, and that the wiser one is, the more joyful one will be.

In the Confucian tradition, wisdom is demonstrated in two aspects of a moral life: in one's carefulness and seriousness in fulfilling responsibilities[31] and in the joyfulness and delightfulness one has experienced. In his conversations with students, Confucius has clearly cast a distinctively joyful mark on his concept of wisdom, that is, wisdom is meant to bring about joy or is essentially related to delightfulness; it is understood that the wise are wise at least partly because they can take joy in all activities and throughout all time. When Confucius described his own character, he made a special reference to his joy in learning: 'He is the sort of man who forgets to eat when trying to solve a problem that has been driving him to distraction, who is so full of joy that he forgets his worries and does not notice the onset of old age' (*Analects*, 7:19).

One of Confucius' favourite disciples, Yan Hui (511?–480BCE), is highly praised for his conscience and moral character, because he loved learning so much that he would remain joyful even when having little for food and plain water for drink. In the later Confucian tradition, this kind of joyfulness is identified as one of the defining qualities of a wise and good man (*xian zhe*).

With a theocentric foundation, the Israelites tend to be more serious in their attitude towards the way of life, particularly in comparison with the more relaxed attitude espoused by Confucius. They associate wisdom with the creation and therefore with the human fulfilment of their duties towards the creator, and suggest that the way of life is no more than a demonstration or reflection of YHWH's knowledge and wisdom. However, this does not mean that there is no joyful element in the Israelite concept of wisdom. In the book of Proverbs we read,

> Happy are those who find wisdom, and those who get understanding.
> …
> Long life is in her [wisdom's] right hand;
> in her left hand are riches and honour.
> Her ways are ways of pleasantness,
> and all her paths are peace.
> She is a tree of life to those who lay hold of her;
> those who hold her fast are called happy. (Prov. 3:13, 16–18)

In this paragraph we can see a number of points underlying the Israelite view of wisdom and happiness. First, wisdom is the source of, and the reason for, a joyful life,

---

[30] 'Age is thus an ordering and sequencing principle. A distinctive feature of Confucian ethics is to accept seniority as a value in setting up social hierarchy', in Wei-Ming Tu: 'Probing the "Three Bonds" and "Five Relationships"'; see *Confucianism and the Family*, ed. Walter H. Slote and George A. De Vos, Albany, State University of New York Press, 1998, p.127.

[31] For example, Zengzi, the youngest disciple of Confucius, described his attitude towards life as 'In fear and trembling, as if approaching a deep abyss, as if walking on thin ice' (*Analects*, 8:3).

and only those who have found wisdom can have joy and happiness. Wisdom provides a person both with insightful understanding and with necessary conditions such as riches and honour, by which one follows a wise way of life. Secondly, the way of wisdom is not merely an external requirement; it is by nature the way of happiness, and brings pleasantness to those who have followed it. It is therefore the path to peace, internal as well as external. Thirdly, wisdom is the fountainhead of the life stream, and is a tree of life. Wisdom enables one to have a long life; those who possess wisdom can therefore be free of anxiety about death and illness, and enjoy a happy life.

The Nature of Joy

Why must joyfulness or happiness, rather than seriousness or stressfulness, be characteristic of the concept of wisdom? To answer this question, Confucians and the Israelites follow different routes to reach their conclusion that wisdom is by nature closely related to joy and happiness.

For Confucians, the answer lies in wisdom itself. Confucian wisdom is an insight into the essence and ultimate meaning of life, which is gained through a virtuous course of life and through the process of learning and self-cultivation. In the words of Xunzi, learning is the means by which humans are set apart from animals: 'Those who undertake learning become men; those who neglect it become as wild beasts' (Xunzi, 1.8). Success in effectively engaging in learning is essential to one's wisdom, and only when enjoying learning can one constantly pursue it: 'To be fond of something is better than merely to know it, and to find joy in it is better than merely to be fond of it' (*Analects*, 6:20). Joyful are those who, having learned something, put it into practice constantly (*Analects*, 1:1). Confucians also consider joyfulness to be a genuine by-product of virtue, insisting that wisdom entails the bringing of joy to people and enables people to be content with hardship.[32]

For the Israelites, the reason why wisdom is joyful lies in their overall view of the world. There is a logical connection between wisdom and the way YHWH is pleased. When they say that wisdom is the first created, the Israelites mean that the purpose of wisdom is to enable the creature to please the creator by following wise instructions. In this sense it can be said that joy is embedded in the nature of the divine wisdom. According to Israelite theology, what pleases YHWH also pleases humans, because YHWH alone can ensure that humans lead a happy life, as stated in the book of Proverbs: 'happy is he who trusts in the LORD' (Prov. 16:20) and again in

---

[32] As far as the relation between wisdom and joy is concerned, we find that Confucianism and Daoism have a common ground. Both place joy in deeper wisdom rather than in superficial knowledge. Daoist masters also highly value joyfulness in wisdom. To be one with the Way is not a miserable journey. It is a personal experience. 'He who conforms to the Way will be delightedly accepted by the Way; he who conforms to virtue will be delightedly accepted by virtue' (Daode jing, 23). Both Confucians and Daoists emphasize the importance of being contented with what one has had, believing this is the guarantee of a happy life.

Ecclesiastes, 'to the man who pleases him God gives wisdom and knowledge and joy' (Eccl. 2:26). Those who have embraced wisdom will 'find gladness and a crown of rejoicing' (Sir. 15:6).

True joy is related to wisdom, and without understanding, it is not possible for anybody to have real joy. Real joy is carefully differentiated from the joy of a fool because 'folly is a joy to him who has no sense' (Prov. 15:21). To have joy is to be free from fear and anxiety. How to expel fear and how to be safe are therefore central to the Israelite exploration of wisdom and are the key to their understanding of the function of wise teaching. Since joy is based on wisdom, it is natural for the Israelite teachers to require that individual humans receive instruction and follow wise teachings, as advised in the book of Proverbs:

> Keep sound wisdom and discretion;
> let them not escape from your sight,
> and they will be life for your soul and adornment for your neck.
> Then you will walk on your way securely and your foot will not stumble.
> If you sit down, you will not be afraid;
> when you lie down, your sleep will be sweet. (Prov. 3:21–4)

To emphasize the importance of wise teaching for happiness, it is claimed that 'whoever listens to me will live in safety and be at ease, without dread of evil' (Prov. 1:33).

Instead of intending to dissolve fear and reduce the threat from evil, Confucian wisdom strives for an intellectual solution of the perplexity and worry that are caused by the complicatedness and ambiguity of social and moral problems, insisting that wisdom enables one to be exempt from uncertainty about right and wrong, good and bad, and pointing out that 'a person of wisdom has no doubts in his mind' (*Analects*, 9:29). Consistently with his humanistic view of the world, Confucius believes that to be free from perplexities and worries one has to be engaged in self-cultivation. Self-cultivation underlies the Confucian way to freedom and courage, and therefore to joy and wisdom, and gaining freedom is the sign of one's breaking through the finitude of the self. Confucius says that after seventy years' untiring learning and practice he gained a total freedom in his self; whatever he does in following his desires, he would not violate the norm (*Analects*, 2:4). Interpreted as such, Confucian self-cultivation is no longer a dull and boring 'job', but a joyful and pleasant process of personal engagement in moral growth, which will bring about great joy and deep insight into life.

Dimensions of Joy

There are different kinds of joy. Confucian joy is expressed both in internal happiness and in external achievements. Internally, joy is attained when one's heart is not troubled by ambiguity and perplexity any more. The process of gaining internal joy involves many steps, each of which is an important link in the continuous chain of learning. According to the *Great Learning*, it starts with investigating things and affairs, moves to expand one's knowledge, then aims at establishing a sincere will, and consequently makes one's mind correct. A rectified mind is free of worries and anxieties (Daxue, 7), and is therefore full of joy. Confucius has noted that only upon examining oneself, and finding nothing to reproach oneself for, would one be without worry and fear (*Analects*, 12:4), while Mengzi claims that 'All the ten thousand things are there in me. There is no greater joy for me than to find, on self-examination, that I am true to myself' (Mengzi, 7A:4).

For a Confucian, internal joy can also come from what one has achieved in one's conscious activity. According to Mengzi, a gentleman would delight in three things, related to the three major areas of human conscience. The first delight is that his parents are alive and his brothers are well. The second delight is that, above, he is not ashamed to face Heaven; below, he is not ashamed to face other people. The third delight is that he has the good fortune of having the most talented pupils in the Empire (Mengzi, 13:20). However, Confucian joy is more than what we call personal happiness. It is to be extended to human communities and to 'delight on account of the world' (*le yi tian xia*, Mengzi, 1B:4). It is argued that, when self-cultivation has been carried out, one is able successfully to regulate the family, govern the state and bring peace and order to the world. This is, according to Confucians, the highest grade of joy and happiness (Daxue, 10).

For the Israelites joy is first the pleasantness of the heart or soul, while what makes the heart or soul happy is not power or wealth but good understanding and knowledge, as the proverb says that, if one understands righteousness, justice and equity, then 'wisdom will come into your heart, and knowledge will be pleasant to your soul' (Prov. 2:10). The manifestation of the joy is in the appreciation of familial and social life: 'My soul takes pleasure in three things, and they are beautiful in the sight of the LORD and of men: agreement between brothers, friendship between neighbours, and a wife and husband who live in harmony' (Sir. 25:1). The Israelite teachers value more at a personal level, and claim that 'There is no wealth better than health of body, and there is no gladness above joy of heart' (Sir. 30:16). In a clear contrast to Confucians, who believe that the source of joy lies in self-cultivation, however, the Israelites insist that like wisdom that is first created by the LORD, the final source of joy is also from the gift of YHWH. This theme runs consistently through almost all books in Hebrew wisdom literature, for example, in the book of Psalms it is claimed that YHWH has made known to humans the path of life, and filled them with joy and eternal pleasures (Psalm 16:11), and the book of Ecclesiastes quotes from conventional wisdom that YHWH gives to the one who pleases him 'wisdom, knowledge and joy' (Eccl. 2:26).

On the human side, true joy can only be found when YHWH accepts one's prayer (Job 33:26). Faith and wisdom are two in one and are the precondition for humans to have joy, because those who are foolish and do not hold faith in YHWH and his creation cannot have true and lasting joy, as it is stated in the book of Job that 'the joy of the godless is but for a moment' (Job 20:5). Based on this, the Israelites believe that only the people who are faithful and just can have real joy, while those who are wicked and wrongdoers will only suffer: 'An evil man is ensnared in his transgression, but a righteous man sings and rejoices' (Prov. 29:6). There is a difference between good joy and bad joy, which is compared to the contrast between the light of the righteous and the lamp of the wicked: the former rejoices while the latter will be surely be put out (Prov. 13:9). Good joy is for those who are just and moral, as it is stated that 'those who plan good have joy', in contrast to those who embrace deceit in their hearts and devise evil (Prov. 12:20). Bad joy is immoral, unfaithful and foolish, and so has been categorically excluded from wisdom. Seduced by a lustful woman, for example, a fool would seek joy in making love with her and delight in committing adultery. However, Israelite teachers warn that this is a foolish joy as the adulterer does not know that he 'follows her as an ox goes to the slaughter' and 'it will cost his life' (Prov. 7:18–23).

Like the Israelites, Confucians also differentiate long-term joy from short-term joy and define wisdom joy in moral terms. For them, long-term joy comes from benevolence and wisdom, and therefore endures, while joy resulting from immoral and unwise activities is temporary and superficial. It is in this sense that Confucius said that only a person of benevolence and wisdom has true and lasting joy. 'One who is not benevolent cannot for long endure adversity, nor can he for long stay in joyfulness' (*Analects*, 4:2).

Joy, Virtue and Wisdom

In both Confucian and Israelite texts, joy which arises from wisdom is not, primarily, physical pleasure. Although there is no rejection of bodily enjoyment, the wisdom texts in Confucian and Israelite traditions do reveal to us a tension between pursuing wisdom and taking pleasure by satisfying one's corporeal needs. While wisdom makes a diligent person wealthy, seeking pleasure will lead to folly and poverty: 'He who loves pleasure becomes poor' (Prov. 21:17).[33] Confucians have also seen the tension, admitting that, necessary as it is to live a life without worrying about food and clothes, possessing a large amount of material wealth does not necessarily bring about joy; as Mengzi points out: 'wealth is something every person wants, yet the wealth of possessing the whole Empire was not sufficient to deliver him from anxiety' (Mengzi, 5A:1). In terms of the consequences joy may have brought about, Confucius makes a distinction between beneficial joy and harmful joy; the former brings benefits to oneself and others, while the latter brings harm to the self and

---

[33] The only exception to this is probably from the book of Ecclesiastes. Owing to his suspicion about traditional wisdom, the author of this book attempts to reverse the conventional Israelite view, believing that the real joy is to fulfil what YHWH has given to humans, using their wealth and abilities to enjoy eating, drinking and all other pleasures, as well as to accept their lot and find enjoyment in their toil. This is justified because this is the gift of YHWH and because the human life span is very short (Eccl. 5:18–20). Joy and sadness, internal happiness and external pleasure do not make any difference: 'all was vanity and a striving after wind' (Eccl. 2:10–11). This highly hedonic and sceptical attitude, however, was produced in a specific historical context and did not necessarily reflect what we can call Israelite wisdom.

community. For him, beneficial joys are manifested in taking pleasure in the correct regulation of rites and music, in singing the praises of other men's goodness and in having a large number of excellent men as friends, while harmful joys are brought about by taking pleasure in showing off, by living a dissolute life and by indulging in food and drink (*Analects*, 16:5).

Joy results from one's appreciation of things and matters, and one and the same thing would appear to be joyful to some people, but unpleasant to others. Wisdom of life enables one to see the joyful nature of things and to find joy in a variety of life situations. The Israelites give priority to the interaction between justice and joy by which the righteous are differentiated from the wicked, as explained in a proverb: 'When justice is done, it is a joy to the righteous, but dismay to evildoers' (Prov. 21:15). Wisdom and justice will bring about joy, while foolishness and injustice will generate unhappiness, as is demonstrated in the case of parents who rejoice for the righteous and wise behaviour of their children while regretting their unfaithful and stupid choices (Prov. 23:24–5).

Confucians have listed two conditions under which humans can rightly appreciate joy. First, virtue is a precondition of enjoying, and only a virtuous person can have true joy. A person of a noble character is full of wisdom and enjoys a pleasant life, while a person of a vile character is full of worries and anxiety, and can therefore never have true pleasures (*Analects*, 7:37). When discussing what kind of people would really enjoy natural beauties, Mengzi argues that 'Only if a man is good and wise is he able to enjoy them. Otherwise he would not, even if he had them' (Mengzi, 1A:2). Secondly, a personal joy must not be in contradiction with the joy of other people. Mengzi contrasts his contemporaries with ancient rulers who, according to him, had true joy and were recognized as true kings because they shared their enjoyments with the people and were whole-heartedly delighted when other people were joyful (Mengzi, 1B:4).

From what has been examined above, we can see clearly that, although Confucian wisdom and Israelite wisdom are based on different theoretical foundations, one theocentric and the other humanistic, they converge in the way of life and in the appreciation of joy in life. Both of them seek, not only to enable the people to lead a happy life, but also to connect their personal joy and the joy of others and the human community. This makes their understanding of joy essentially an ethical concept: only those who delight in the joy of others can have joy themselves.

In summary, we confirm that in China and Israel wisdom is an important path to a meaningful and valuable life. A significant number of the sayings as recorded in Confucian and Israelite texts are concerned with such questions as what the wise way of conduct is and how to lead a wise course of life. Through examining the different aspects of life above, we have noted in this chapter that, while there are significant differences between the Israelite and the Confucian answers, which may well be explained by the difference between the theocentric and the anthropocentric traditions, some experiences are also found common to both of them, in which wisdom and the way of life become interdependent and interactive. To reveal fully the differences and similarities in wisdom thinking between the Confucians and early Israelite wisdom teachers, we turn now to Chapter 5, where wisdom is seen to play an important role concerning moral and ethical issues.

CHAPTER FIVE

Virtue, Moral Training and Wise Man Images

The study of wisdom in Confucian and Israelite traditions has to a great extent concentrated on the implications for individuals, defining wisdom as life experience or as a way in which individuals lead a good life. Indeed, Confucian and Israelite wisdom is based on personal appreciation of the world order and individual understanding of life situations, and is crystalized as mental characteristics and attitudes towards oneself and others. It is believed that wisdom must be gained either through self-cultivation as the way to break through one's intellectual and moral finitude, or by personal acceptance and conviction of YHWH's creation. However, unlike many mystic philosophies and religions where wisdom is defined purely as contemplation-like activities and their result, and the only path to wisdom is said to be one's mystic union with its ultimate source such as Dao in Daoism, Confucians and Israelite teachers view human beings as substantially leading a 'moral' existence, and define wisdom in ethical contexts, although they interpret what is moral in significantly different ways. For them, there is no doubt that wisdom is manifested, at least partially, in one's knowledge of social norms and consciously following this knowledge in dealing with interpersonal relationships.

'Ethical' in Confucian and Israelite Contexts

'Ethic' comes from the Greek word *ēthos*, 'nature, disposition' or 'custom', denoting 'the characteristic spirit of a culture, era, or community as manifested in its attitudes and aspirations'.[1] When we say wisdom is 'ethical', we mean that wisdom is concerned with moral principles and that wisdom knowledge is, to a great extent, involved with the knowledge of ethical norms and rules. Despite their deliberation on the spiritual source and nature of moral norms, Confucian and Israelite traditions hold a strong conviction that 'moral principles' are rooted in the existence of human beings and manifested in human relationships, which are then internalized as personal disposition, aspiration and conscience. The two dimensions of the 'ethical', external rules and internal awareness, are lucidly expressed in Chinese, where its meaning is often expressed through two phrases, '*dao de*', inner moral qualities and virtues, and '*lun li*', moral principles governing human relationships, by which an

---

[1] *The Concise Oxford Dictionary*, 10th edn, revised, ed. Judy Pearsall, Oxford University Press, 2001, p.490.

ideal personality is produced and social harmony and world peace are brought about.[2] In the early Hebrew tradition, there is much less deliberation on the internal cultivation of human nature; attention is paid there primarily to the hierarchical rules that have their source in the commandments of YHWH. This has become a characteristic way of moral thinking in Israel, as is stated in the *Eerdmans Dictionary of the Bible*, 'The ethical thought of ancient rabbinic Judaism focused on *halakhah*, the rules of behavior found in the written Torah interpreted by the tradition of the oral Torah.'[3] However, this does not mean that ancient Israelites lacked interest in inner moral qualities; rather, they explored this dimension through a number of other terms, such as wickedness and righteousness, to reflect the need for humans to be guided by the law of God and to manifest the ethical nature of religious faith and conduct. The internal and the external were combined in the images of the wise and the righteous. Therefore, a discussion of 'ethical wisdom' in Confucian and Israelite traditions cannot but deal with the following four issues: a profound understanding of human nature, the association of wisdom and virtue, the appreciation of moral disciplines, and the model persons who in their understanding and attitude demonstrate ethical wisdom, particularly the wise and *zhizhe* (the man of wisdom), the righteous and *junzi* (the gentleman).

A number of attempts have been made to examine differences and similarities between Israelite and Confucian perceptions of wisdom, either by bringing together the Israelite wise man and the Confucian sage,[4] or through studying the Confucian image of the sage alongside the Israelite man of righteousness,[5] or by comparing Confucian masters (sages) and Israelite prophets.[6] These works have widened our horizons about wisdom in biblical Israel and classical China, and highlighted the chief features of Israelite and Confucian images of the ideal man. However, they have not sufficiently explored the subtleties of the wise and the ethical implicit in Confucian and Israelite wisdom texts, and improperly put in pairs different images, particularly the Israelite wise and the Confucian sage.

On the surface, the Israelite wise man can also be called a 'sage' and it seems right to rank him with a Confucian sage. However, there is a fundamental difference

---

[2] *Shuowen jiezi* (Explanation of Words and Characters) defines *dao* and *de* as follows: 'The *dao* is that way along which one walks; once obtained one calls it the Way', and '*De* is what is won from others outside and from the self inside' (Zhang Dainian: *Key Concepts in Chinese Philosophy*, trans. and ed. Edmund Ryden, New Haven and London: Yale University Press, Beijing: Foreign Language Press, 2002, pp.12, 318). *Dao de* in Chinese therefore means what one has gained from the appreciation and understanding of the Way. *Lun li* is a binome comprising *lun*, human relationships and *li*, principles, which together refer to the moral principles that govern human behaviour and attitudes towards one another.

[3] *Eerdmans Dictionary of the Bible* (David Noel Freedman, editor-in-chief), Grand Rapids, Michigan: William B. Eerdmans Publishing Company, 200, p.431.

[4] For example, Nathaniel Yung-tse Yen: 'Prophet sage and wise man: a comparative study of intellectual tradition in ancient China and Israel', PhD thesis, Madison: Drew University, 1977.

[5] For example, Sung-Hae Kim: 'The righteous and the sage: a comparative study on the ideal images of man in biblical Israel and classical China', PhD thesis, Harvard University, 1981.

[6] For example, H.H. Rowley: *Prophecy and Religion in Ancient China and Israel*, Jordan lectures in comparative religion, University of London/The Athlone Press, 1956.

between the Israelite sage who is wise in understanding and quick in action and the Confucian sage who is the totality of all the sublime qualities human beings can possibly attain. This difference cannot be illustrated more clearly than in the *Book of Mengzi*, where Mengzi defines sagehood as something great and divine:

> The desirable is called 'good'. To have it in oneself is called 'true'. To possess it fully in oneself is called 'beautiful', but to shine forth with this full possession is called 'great'. To be great and be transformed by this greatness is called 'sage'; to be a sage and to transcend the understanding is called 'divine'. (Mengzi, 7B:25)

Like the Confusian view of the world that is structured hierarchically, the Confucian view of human cultivation is also constructed step by step, each of which signifies particular progress in becoming an ideal person and a necessary preparation for the next one. Confucian images of the ideal person constitute a hierarchical ladder, as Xunzi has explained:

> One who has such learning and puts it into practice is called 'scholar' [*shi*]; one who fervently loves it is a 'gentleman' [*junzi*]; one who knows it fully is a 'sage' [*shengren*]. What could prevent me from become either at most a sage or at the least a scholar or a gentleman? (Xunzi, 8:5)

By comparison, the Israelites do not have such a hierarchical ladder in their images of human beings. The wise, the righteous, the faithful and the prophet each demonstrate a different way to satisfy the overall requirements of the Israelite ideal, and all are by nature theocentric, converging in faith in YHWH. In this sense, an Israelite wise man, righteous man or prophet only corresponds to part of the Confucian ideal of sage. To avoid oversimplifying the Israelite ideal and Confucian sagehood, therefore, we approach their perceptions of wisdom in this chapter by comparing the Israelite wise man and the Confucian *zhizhe* or man of wisdom, and then examining the Israelite righteous man and the Confucian *junzi* or gentleman. We take these images as ethical models for humans to follow, and compare them in the context of Confucian and Israelite ethical wisdom, while leaving to the next chapter the political dimension of Confucian sagehood in relation to the Israelite image of wise kings.

Human Nature

The individuality and communality of human existence are two dimensions of human life that dominate the Confucian and Israelite definitions of human beings and human nature. Neither Confucians nor Israelite teachers looked at human nature from a single point of view; they both attempted to bring the two dimensions together, and make them mutually supplementary rather than remain separated from each other.

The Israelite understanding of human beings is profoundly theocentric, defining their origin, nature and destiny in relation to YHWH, and communal, placing human individuals in community and social relationships. Human nature, from the Israelite point of view, lies therefore in 'the totality of human being out of lived experience' and in 'different social locations and contexts as shapers of that experience'; modern scholars have explored in depth a number of words used in the Hebrew scriptures for human beings such as *nepeš* (soul/person), *bāśār* (flesh/body), *rūaḥ* (spirit/breath), *lēb* (*heart/feelings*) and *kᵉlāyōt* (kidneys/emotions), from which they have found that *nepeš* which occurs 755 times in the OT refers to what we today call 'the totality of the person'.[7] The early Israelite totality of human experience is hardly an isolated phenomenon, nor is a human person a totally independent being; rather the experience and the person must be shaped and reshaped through their relationship with the divine and with the community. It has been argued that 'human beings in the OT do not have a "soul"; they are a "living soul/*nepeš*" (Gen. 2:7)'; that 'individual consciousness and morality' 'emerged later with the classical prophets'; that 'humans are creatures of God dependent upon their Creator for life (as Psalms 104, 147, 148 also attest)', and that 'God created human beings as part of the natural world but with a special relationship to that world, to each other, and to God, the One who gives human life meaning.'[8] In these relationships humans are both individuals, personally responsible for their own behaviour, and members of the community, taking collective responsibility for their history and behaviour, and the Israelite 'person' can be understood only in his or her relationship with the Creator and with other people. This understanding is reflected in the wisdom literature in a variety of ways, but the key point is made clearly that one cannot become wise unless one has served YHWH and followed his commands, on the one hand, and unless one has served other people well and followed the moral rules, on the other.

Similarly, Confucian views of human beings are also both individualistic and communal. On the one hand, Confucius initiated the awareness of individual value and meaning, shaking off the traditional bondages that attached individual human beings to the spirits (*gui shen*) and to their social classes. For him, any individual had his or her own value, the only criterion for which was not birth or rank but the moral effort made and the learning gained. He was the first major Chinese thinker in history to elevate *ren* (human being) to a fully conscious and responsible being, referring to each individual, with physical life that must be cherished (*Analects*, 10:17), having desires that should be satisfied (*Analects*, 4:5), as an individual who should be treated with 'love' (*Analects*, 1:5; 12:22), and as a person who should be helped to become established and prominent (*Analects*, 6:30). On the other hand, Confucius did not see

---

[7] *Eerdmans Dictionary of the Bible*, p.615.

[8] *Eerdmans Dictionary of the Bible*, p.615. The Israelite emphasis on the theocentric and communal nature of human beings can be supported by what Ludwig Köhler found in the composition of the names of the Israelites. According to him, there are 1400 names we know from the Old Testament, and 'more than half the surviving names are theophoric', and 'consist of two parts, of which either the first or the second is the name or the designation of a deity'. He further explained, 'besides these theophoric names, there are many which ask some quality for the bearer', 'with which the parents desired to keep always present a wish for the nature or the fortune of their child' (Ludwig Köhler, 1956, p.65).

the individual as totally independent of others; rather he defined a person in terms of human relationship networks; for example, as a son to his father, a member of his community, or a subject to his lord. It was in these relationships, Confucius believed, that an individual could fully become a responsible person, and that human nature would be recognized both as a psychological structure and as a moral setting. Confucius placed great emphasis on the role of human relations for human nature, and gave priority to the association of humans with one another as the source of wisdom. When faced with the challenge that the best way of life was not to refine human nature but to retreat from society, Confucius counter-attacked his critics by pointing out that 'One cannot associate with birds and beasts. Am I not a member of this human race? Who, then, is there for me to associate with?' (*Analects*, 18:6)

Individuality and communality constitute two of the most important elements for a being to be human, yet there is a third dimension of human nature in Confucian and Israelite traditions, which is formed in human relationship with the divine. It is the different understandings of the divine and human relationship to the divine that sets Confucians and the Israelites apart. Although early Confucians also held a strong belief that human beings were 'born' (produced or generating, *sheng*) by the divine power of Heaven and that wisdom was perceived from the enlightened awareness of heavenly nature and heavenly mission, their discourses on human nature diverged significantly from the Israelites owing to the difference in their view of the divine. For the Israelites the divine is YHWH, the creator of the world and of human beings, and YHWH is the sole source of human nature and wisdom, as explained in the Book of Ben Sira:

> He [YHWH] gave to men few days, a limited time, but granted them authority over the things upon the earth. He endowed them with strength like his own, and made them in his own image … he filled them with knowledge and understanding, and showed them good and evil. (Sir. 17:2–7)

In this theocentric view, humans are in the image of the divine, and wisdom is nothing but an appreciation of the good will of the Creator. What differentiates humans from other animals is their understanding of the created order, which is possible because YHWH has 'filled them with knowledge and understanding'. The difference between a human and a beast is therefore said to be having or lacking understanding: 'a man without understanding (*lō' yābhīn*) is like a beast that perishes' (Psalms 49:20), the understanding whose object is primarily the divine order.

Early Confucians also insisted that humans came from Heaven, the spiritual power or natural law of the world and beyond. However, in contrast to the actual creation of the first man and woman in the image of YHWH in the Israelite narrative, the Confucian notion of Heaven's 'producing' humans is more a metaphor than a reality; and the creation of humans by Heaven signifies moral value and meaning, rather than physical and psychological functions. Unlike the book of Genesis in the Hebrew Scriptures, none of the major Confucian scholars explained in any detail why and how humans were produced. Rather they took the existence of humans as a given precondition for their anthropocentric speculations. To make their view of human nature more complicated, Confucians went into the moral evaluation of human nature, arguing among themselves whether humans were born with a good or bad nature. While Confucius understood the difference between humans as the result of practices and learning by which some became gentlemen while others become 'small men' (*xiao ren*), his followers advanced two opposing theories. Mengzi argued that, endowed with moral senses by Heaven, humans could make themselves distinctive only by cultivating these senses, and those who failed to do so would degenerate into the category of wild animals. Xunzi insisted that, as a natural animal, humans did not have any inborn moral senses; rather they were born with desires and instincts which, if not properly restricted and guided, would lead to the violation of moral principles and were therefore evil by nature. Despite these differences, Mengzi and Xunzi did agree upon a number of points. First, both argued that the difference between a human and a beast was actually very small, either in terms of moral senses (Mengzi) or in terms of intelligence (Xunzi);[9] secondly, both agreed that humans were able to cultivate or capable of developing this initial substance within, through proper training or discipline (Xunzi) or moral cultivation (Mengzi), to make it substantial and manifested. These have rendered the Confucian view of human nature substantially moral and educational rather than religious and philosophical.

Wisdom and Virtue

It seems apparent that, apart from their differences in interpreting the 'divine' element of human nature, early Confucians and Israelites are both convinced that human nature is rooted in the existence and activities of individuals both internally and in association with other people and larger communities. Because wisdom does not arise merely from acknowledging what human nature is, but from the exercising and functioning of *the* nature, the Confucian and Israelite discourses of ethical wisdom necessarily lead to the manifestation of humanity through personal and interpersonal activities. The two-in-one nature of being a human determines that ethical wisdom is essentially related to what we call 'virtue', the excellence, whose value is defined in personal as well as communal life.

'Virtue' as an English word is derived from the Latin '*virtus*' meaning 'valour, merit, moral perfection', which initially referred to male strength and power ('virility' shares the same root, *vir*, man), but soon came to be associated with physical courage and thence moral fibre. The word 'virtue' still retains the less

---

[9] 'What is it that makes a man human? I say that it lies in his ability to draw boundaries ... these characteristics man is born possessing, and he does not have to wait to develop them' (Xunzi, 5:9). Here 'draw boundaries' does not fully express what is said. '*Bian*' means actually the intellectual capability to differentiate and to judge.

common meaning of inherent power or efficacy, but its interpretation is constantly under the influence of the Greek '*arete*', whose

> central meaning in Greek philosophy was excellence of any kind, but from the beginning it was also associated with the idea of fulfilment of function: excellence, whether in animate or inanimate objects, consists in the fullest performance of the object's function or its power to achieve the fullest performance.[10]

This means that, for Greek philosophers, *arete* is a fulfilment of one's function and so a kind of 'efficiency'. Virtues are of different kinds. Ancient Greeks often talked about the four cardinal virtues: justice, bravery, fortitude and moderation. Thomas Aquinas separated human virtues from divine virtues, and based the four cardinal virtues on the three divine virtues of faith, love and obedience.

A variety of virtues are discussed and praised in Confucian and Israelite wisdom texts, which demonstrate the close connection between wisdom and virtue. Since virtue is often manifested as an inner quality and a stable habit of behaviour, it can be roughly classified into different categories, such as personal, social and religious, although some of the virtues, such as justice transcend the division and penetrate all aspects. Personal virtue is about the morally desirable and commendable qualities demonstrated in a person's behaviour and attitudes, such as honesty, benevolence and faithfulness. Social virtue defines how society should treat its members and how people should treat each other, and this is demonstrated in a series of social norms and principles such as justice. Religious virtue signifies spiritual pursuits, involving devotion and discipline, such as faith and humility. As we have noted in Chapter 4, the Israelites believed that pride was the path to stupidity, while humility led to true wisdom. Indeed, a significant number of Confucian masters and Israelite sages claimed that they were not as worthy as they were frequently regarded as being.

Unlike the Greeks who used general terms such as 'fulfilling function' and 'efficiency' to define virtue, early Confucians and the Israelites tended to be more specifically ethical in their discourse on human excellence. For them virtue has a moral nature and will produce ethical consequences. Since humans must be responsible for the consequences of their attitude and behaviour, it is natural for Confucians and the Israelites to believe that there is a close link between virtues and wisdom.

Virtue or *ḥayil* in early Israelite texts refers to an ability or disposition towards excellence, usually in the moral sense.[11] In the book of Proverbs it is stated that virtue leads to admirable consequences, while the lack of virtue is blamed for personal and familial shame: the virtue of a wife brings honour to her husband and she is therefore said to be the crown of her husband, in contrast to the wife who brings shame (Prov. 12:4). There is no doubt that wisdom is a gift from the divine. The divinity of wisdom

---

[10] *The Encyclopedia of Philosophy*, ed. Paul Edwards, Macmillan, 1967, vol. I, pp.147–8.
[11] *Eerdmans Dictionary of the Bible*, p.1359.

does not, however, discourage the Israelites from believing that wisdom must be manifested in moral virtues: truthfulness, moderation, chastity, kindliness, honesty, diligence (Prov. 10:4; 26:14), self-control (Prov. 14:17; 15:1) and a sense of responsibility (Prov. 10:26; 27:23–7). The contrast between the wise and the foolish parallels that between the just and the unjust: 'A characteristic and striking move within the Wisdom Literature is the identification of the righteous (*ṣaddīq*) with the wise person (*ḥākām*)' and 'wisdom is identified with virtue and its awards'.[12] For this we can find ample proof among Israelite proverbs, such as wisdom 'dwells in prudence' (Prov. 8:12). Identifying wisdom and virtue, in other words, means that wisdom is the antithesis of an immoral character: 'wisdom will not enter a deceitful soul, nor dwell in a body enslaved to sin' (Wisd. 1:4). Wisdom and virtue (for example, righteousness) are therefore interlocked, and are taken as the foundation of human life: 'The fruit of the righteous is a tree of life' (Prov. 11:30).

In the Confucian tradition, *zhi* (wisdom) and *de* (virtue) are considered to be two most important dimensions of the way of life, both religious and ethical in meaning and implication. *De* was traditionally seen as a gift from Heaven, transmitted to noble individuals at birth because of their inherited social and religious positions, or seen as a boon by ancestors in reciprocal response to sacrificial rituals.[13] It was more a political position than a personal characteristic, because *de* was quintessentially the quality evinced by sages and great rulers. By the time of Confucius, however, the reference of *de* had been changed to something an individual could personally manifest and enhance. Confucius was himself most concerned with cultivating his *de* (*Analects*, 7:3), and placed *de* in a close relationship to all recognized virtues such as benevolence (*ren*), wisdom (*zhi*), courage (*yong*), reliability or faithfulness (*xin*), reverence (*jing*), duty or righteousness (*yi*), ritual propriety (*li*), respecting parents or filial piety (*xiao*) and loyalty and obedience (*zhong*) to superiors and rulers. In the network of human virtues, Confucius constructed a corporate notion of being truly human.

To understand why Confucian masters regard *de* as the root of wisdom, we must examine what is meant by '*de*' in a Confucian context. It is difficult to find a single English word to translate *de* throughout this chapter. 'Virtue' is only a convenient, but not necessarily accurate, rendering. In one sense, *de* is what one has obtained in the practice of *dao* (the Way) and in the accumulation of good deeds. It is therefore similar to 'virtue', in the sense of moral excellence demonstrated in one's behaviour and attitudes. For Confucius, as an inner power, virtue is a potent and powerful quality, not only making someone morally strong, but also exerting sweeping influence over others: 'The virtue of the gentleman is like the wind. The virtue of the small man is like grass. Let the wind blow over the grass and the grass is sure to bend'

---

[12] *The Anchor Bible Dictionary* (editor-in-chief: David Noel Freedman), New York: Doubleday, 1992, vol. VI, p.926.

[13] David S. Nivison, 'The Classical Philosophical Writings', in *The Cambridge History of Ancient China*, ed. Michael Loewe and Edward Shaughnessy, Cambridge University Press, 1999, p.749; Sarah Allan, *The Way of Water and Sprouts of Virtue*, Albany: State University of New York Press, 1997, p.106.

(*Analects*, 12:19). Therefore virtue enables one to be charismatic, as the ruler who possesses virtue can be like the Pole Star around which other stars revolve (*Analects*, 2:1). For Mengzi, virtue is innate in everybody's heart, but like the sprouts of a plant, virtue needs to be cultivated to grow to the full. Being one's inner quality, virtue is not confined to an individual's own internal quarters; rather it has a kind of psyche-power, enabling its owner or possessor to shine and to be equal with Heaven and Earth.[14] On many occasions in the *Book of Mengzi* and the *Doctrine of the Mean*, virtue is used to refer to the inner power or force that is taken to be the source of wisdom, and it is believed that wisdom appears only when virtue is abundant.

Functioning in relationships, wisdom is manifested as virtues. There are many kinds of relationships, and there are many different virtues based on wisdom. According to the nature of these relationships, we may classify wisdom virtues into the following categories: virtues towards the natural environment, virtues towards other humans and social institutions, virtues towards one's self, and virtues towards the spiritual authorities. In the Confucian and Israelite traditions, virtue as one of the defining factors for human wisdom is spiritual by nature. All virtues in the Israelite texts are from YHWH who determines what is good and what is bad, and it is believed that by following his commandments one becomes virtuous while in disobeying his commands one becomes immoral and sinful. The Confucian virtue is closely associated with Heaven, the spiritual author of virtues. In Confucian classics, which contain some passages predating Confucius, we read:

> The people of our race were created by Heaven … and what they admire is virtue (*de*); and Heaven had compassion on the people of the four quarters; its favouring decree lighted on our earnest founders. Let the king sedulously cultivate the virtue of reverence.[15]

Inheriting these traditional beliefs, Confucius made it clear that virtue had a divine source: 'Heaven is author of the virtue (*de*) in me' (*Analects*, 7:23).

Compared with the Israelites, Confucians demonstrate a unique characteristic in their discourses on wisdom by confirming that wisdom is not only manifested in virtue but also comes from the power of virtue. Confucius explains wisdom in terms of *wuyi*, diligently performing one's duties towards the people: 'He who devotes

---

[14] 'This is an inner power (*qi*) which is, in the highest degree, vast and unyielding. Nourish it with integrity and place no obstacles in its path and it will fill the space between Heaven and Earth.' 'It unites righteousness and the Way. Without it, man is in a state of starvation.' 'It is produced by the accumulation of righteous deeds; it is not to be obtained by incidental acts of righteousness. If the mind does not feel complacency in the conduct, it becomes starved' (Mengzi, 2A:2). Although Mengzi here discusses the nature of inner energy, he is actually referring to one's inner nature and therefore inner virtue.

[15] Arthur Waley (trans.), *The Book of Songs: The Ancient Chinese Classic of Poetry*, New York: Grove Press, 1960, p.141; James Legge (trans.): *The Chinese Classics. Vol. III, The Shoo King or the Book of Historical Documents*, London: Trübner & Co. 1865, p.426.

himself to working for the things the common people have a right to have, who by respect for the Spirits keeps them at a distance, may be termed as a man of wisdom' (*Analects*, 6:22). Confucius believes that a person who does not practise virtue earnestly is the one without wisdom: 'How can the man be considered wise who, when he has the choice, does not settle in benevolence?' (*Analects*, 4:1). When nothing stands in the way and yet one fails to behave benevolently, Mengzi argues, this is evidence of the lack of wisdom (Mengzi, 2A:7). To be virtuous, one must engage in long-term practice and learning with a strong will and inspiration. This is what is said in the *Doctrine of the Mean*: 'To be fond of learning is to be near to wisdom. To practise with vigour is to be near to benevolence. To possess the feeling of shame is to be near to courage. He who knows these three things knows how to cultivate his own character' (Zhongyong, 20).

Unlike the Israelites who have their source of wisdom in YHWH and draw their inspiration for virtue from their faith in the created order, Confucians load humans themselves with the responsibility for the ultimate wisdom. It is believed that, when one's self-cultivation reaches the highest point, one will gain the knowledge of Heaven and Earth, of the past and of the future. In this sense, we may well say that for most Confucian masters one's insight and wisdom comes from the cultivation of virtue, and foreknowledge is essentially derived from inner cultivation rather than from external observation or religious commitment. Following this argument, Confucians go a further step by concluding that wisdom is not only closely associated with virtue, but is also itself one of the virtues. To be wise is essentially to know how to live a moral life or, in Confucius's words, to know how to become a benevolent person.

Moral Discipline

However differently Confucian and Israelite teachers taught about 'virtue', they were in agreement that true knowledge and insight came from 'virtue', by which they rendered their discourse on human nature and behaviour in the form of ethical wisdom. How can humans who are individuals gain ethical wisdom, that is, become social beings equipped with practical abilities to deal with life's problems? Confucians and the Israelites answered this question from the point of view of education, or more specifically, moral training, believing that humans must be trained to be virtuous since ethical wisdom would not come unless proper disciplines were followed.

In the Confucian and Israelite traditions, training is of great importance for the accumulation and growth of wisdom, where discipline that exercises a binding power over the people, especially the young, is understood in a much wider sense than its use in a contemporary context. The Confucian discipline is in most cases delivered and practised through '*li*' (rites, ritual, or the codes of conduct), a comprehensive system of norms covering all aspects of life, individual and social, religious and secular, personal and familial,[16] central to which are the 'established rules' which one should follow in everything one does (Mengzi, 4A:1). Israelite discipline is frequently defined as *tōrā* (instruction, guidance, law), the codes of conduct arising from the divine commandments, and *miṣwāh* (law, rule, commandment, obligation) which both bind individuals in their personal life and govern religious, familial, social and political practices.[17]

The discipline Confucians and the Israelites took as an important tool for the growth of wisdom consisted not only of secular rules or norms, by following which people became accustomed to communal, social and political requirements; Confucian and Israelite codes of conduct were also essentially of a divine origin, and had their justification in the human relationship with Heaven or YHWH. For Israelite teachers, discipline comes from the divine commandment, and 'the commandment is a lamp, while the teaching is a light, and the reproofs of discipline are the way of life' (Prov. 6:23). Discipline is therefore the path to wisdom: 'Whoever loves discipline loves knowledge' (Prov. 12:1).

For Confucians, the binding power of rites comes from the commanding force of Heaven and Earth. Although Confucius himself did not talk much about the spiritual root of rites, his followers revealed to us a unique understanding of how the rites came into being. The *Book of Rites*, for example, describes the origin and function of sacred rites:

> While the rules of ceremony [*li*] have their origin in heaven, the movement of them reaches to earth. The distribution of them extends to all the business (of life). They change with the seasons; they agree in reference to the (variation of) lot and condition. In regard to man, they serve to nurture (his nature). They are practised by means of offerings, acts of strength, words, and postures of courtesy, in eating and drinking, in the observances of capping, marriage, mourning, sacrificing, archery, chariot-driving, audiences, and friendly missions.[18]

---

[16] Although '*li*' is often translated as 'rites', its meaning and reference range widely from decorum in daily life and ritual in religious ceremonies, not only denoting 'politeness' or 'courtesy' but also the customary requirements of all social and political institutions. Its extension was further pushed to metaphysical principles that governed all evolutions, movements and changes in the world, as defined in the *Zuo's Commentary on the Spring and Autumn Annals*, the *li* constitutes the 'regular procedure of Heaven, the right phenomena of earth, and the actions of men' (James Legg, trans. *The Confucian Classics, Vol. V, The Ch'un Ts'ew, with the Tso Chuen*, London: Trübner & Co., 1872, p.708).

[17] 'Torah' is often ascribed to the first division of the Hebrew canon, the five books of Moses, the Pentateuch. However, 'in a more general sense, torah indicates the divine law or instruction according to which Israel was to live as stipulated in the covenant' (*Eerdmans Dictionary of the Bible*, p.1321). Torah (root *yrh*) carries very generally the notion of teaching, and its participle is equal to 'teacher'. YHWH and humans, equally, can teach, but for the Israelites, YHWH teaches 'truth' and perfection, and his teachings are the ultimate and must/should be obeyed. *Miṣwāh* (commandment) (root *ṣwh*) means to firmly 'command' (God and humans). Therefore, the two words, torah and *Miṣwāh* are used on many occasions as synonymous. The 10 commandments are simply as 'Ten Words'.

[18] James Legge (trans.): *The Li Ki or the Collection of Treatises on the Rules of Propriety or Ceremonial Usages*, in *The Sacred Books of the East*, ed. F. Max Müller, Oxford: Clarendon Press, vols 27–8, 1885, reprinted Delhi: Motilal Banarsidass, 1968, vol. 27, p.388.

Xunzi also extends the meaning of the rites to the principle that governs the universe, and says that the order and peace of the world depends upon ritual principle. The ritual principle or codes of conduct governing human relationships are of a sacred nature because they are generated by Heaven and Earth (Xunzi, 10:7).

Apart from their spiritual source and nature, disciplines in Confucian and Israelite traditions are considered sacred also because they are said to have come from the ancients. Confucian rites are regarded as handed down from the ancients, or, in Xunzi's words, as having been brought to their completion by ancient sages. Xunzi believed that there were three roots of the sacred rites, of which ancestors were one:

> Ritual principles have three roots. Heaven and Earth are the root of life. Forebears are the roots of kinship. Lords and teachers are the root of order … Thus, rituals serve Heaven above and Earth below, pay honour to one's forebears, and exalt rulers and teachers. (Xunzi, 19:4)

The *Book of Rites* asserts that the principle of rites is that by which the ancient kings embodied the laws of heaven and regulated the expressions of human nature. 'Therefore he who has attained *li* [the principle of rites] lives, and he who has lost it, dies.'[19]

Israelite authors of wisdom texts frequently used parents or, more frequently, the father to function as the representative of the ancients; we read in Proverbs the teaching, 'keep your father's commandment, and forsake not your mother's teaching', and the commandment, 'Bind them upon your heart always; tie them about your neck' (Prov. 6:20–21). The young became mature and morally responsible not only by being disciplined through the explicit instructions from parents and the elders but also by being trained through the implicit 'rules' of living in communities. According to Ludwig Köhler, the early Israelites grew up in close communities, 'in which everyone knows everyone else, observes, judges, has contact in friendship or hostility. One is never alone. One does what everybody else does. One sees what everyone else does.'[20] In this intense interpersonal community a comprehensive training programme was provided and exercised.

For the Israelites the training was primarily one of honouring the deity: 'the sacred places and times, which must be attended to with caution and with the observance of definite, strict rules',[21] and this was believed to generate a sense of the holy in the heart/mind of the young. Religious training was carried out frequently in association with the conducting of rituals. Ritual in early Israel had a variety of meanings and functions. Reflecting the rhythms of the annual harvests, ritual told people to present

---

[19] LinYu-tang (ed. & trans.): *The Wisdom of Confucius*, Random House, 1938, reprinted in Taipei: Zhengzhong Shuju, 1994, p.493.

[20] Ludwig Köhler, 1956, p.70. Although this description may be suited more to the earlier tribe life than the society as the wisdom literature has depicted, we can see it as a model of Israelite social life.

[21] Ludwig Köhler, 1956, p.79.

first fruits and offerings to symbolize a response of thanksgiving to the blessings of YHWH and to gain continuing divine blessings. It also carried with it a sacred history, providing occasions for the 'remembering' of YHWH's saving acts on behalf of the Israelite community. Engaging the divine, ritual was also a dynamic means to approach the holiness of the world, functioning to bring into being aspects of the very good order of creation (Leviticus 8, 9), to maintain the already existing order (Numbers 28–9) or to restore order when it had been disrupted through sin or impurity (Leviticus 13–14, 16).[22]

Israelite disciplines were established on the basis of theological convictions and had strong ethical implications. In ancient Israel the value and importance of fulfilling one's legal and moral obligations as contained in Torah were primarily based on the recognition of Israel's contractual obligations to YHWH. According to the covenant theory, people and YHWH are bound in a two-way obligation: people must fulfil the covenant made between YHWH and their ancestors (for example, Abraham and David), while YHWH protects and blesses them if they are faithful, and punishes them if they have become wicked. On the other hand, particularly in some of the wisdom texts, moral norms are expected to be followed, based on universally applicable standards of justice and uprightness. In this sense the Israelite training was more than theocentric disciplining, because it involved all aspects of personal and communal life and because in early Israel '[t]he whole of life is accompanied, restricted, regulated by observances, customs, prohibitions, festivals and recitals'. In this social and moral environment, training not only cultivated a proper sense of moral responsibility but also produced a symmetric view of one's own position in history and in the community: 'Recognition of traditions handed down from the distant past gives consciousness of one's own special place; descent from ancestors, with whom God has done great things, gives a feeling of nobility.'[23]

Training and discipline were conducted in ancient China primarily by means of *li*, rites, rituals or codes of conduct. Confucians were well-known masters of rituals, rites and moral codes in their own time. *Li* is a character portraying a sacred ritual vessel, and its original meaning is 'to arrange ritual vessels'; hence 'serving gods and praying for good fortune'.[24] Rites had a specifically religious dimension, when they were used to conduct ceremonies in relation to the spiritual others, including the power of Heaven and Earth, the spirits of ancestors and the spirits of natural phenomena and human beings. While recognizing the importance of religious rites for the Confucians, we must make clear that Confucian rites were of a much wider application than simply being religious ceremonies, and were a means by which people were regulated, families harmonized and the state was supported.[25] Thus rites

---

[22] *Eerdmans Dictionary of the Bible*, p.1131.

[23] Ludwig Köhler, 1956, pp.80, 81.

[24] Duan Yucai: *Shuowen jiezi zhu*, Hangzhou: Zhei jiang Guji Chubanshea, 1981, p.2.

[25] Patricia Buckley Ebrey: *Confucianism and Family Rituals in Imperial China: A Social History of Writing about Rites*, Princeton, New Jersey: Princeton University Press, 1991, p.26.

became a collective term for all codes of conduct, and were therefore the foundation on which individuals stood and the state was established (*Analects*, 8:8); different systems of rites even differentiated one era from another (*Analects*, 2:23). Confucius reiterated in his conversation with his son that, without a proper understanding of rites, one would be ill-equipped to take a stand in society (*Analects*, 16:13). Rites thus became a carefully constructed web in which everyone was located in, and assigned to, a specific position in family, community and society, which in turn enabled each member of these communities to assess what he or she should or should not do in a particular circumstance and to formulate his or her words and choose a particular course of action accordingly. For some idealist Confucians, training in rites was essential to the peace and harmony of the world, because if everybody acted in accordance with the codes, then the state would be peaceful and orderly, ruled without ruling, governed without governing, and ordered without ordering. In the complex moral training system, Confucius considered the training and discipline by rites to be the final stage in which virtues were made perfect:

> What is within the reach of a man's understanding but beyond the power of his benevolence to keep is something he will lose even if he acquires it. A man may be wise enough to attain it and benevolent enough to keep it, but if he does not rule over them with dignity, then the common people will not be reverent. A man may be wise enough to attain it, benevolent enough to keep it and may govern the people with dignity, but if he does not set them to work in accordance with the rites, he is still short of perfection. (*Analects*, 15:33)

Moral rules or rites are not merely external binding rules, visible codes that regulate people and discipline their behaviour; more importantly, they must be taken into one's inner realm where the sense of rites becomes conscience and a self-disciplining force. It is the case that some people may abide by rules when they are forcefully imposed, and may well cast them aside when nobody watches over them. On the surface these people seem to be 'wise' as they do not have to follow 'inconvenient' rules. However, conventional wisdom in Confucian and Israelite traditions teaches us that, in the long term, wrongdoers will certainly suffer from the consequences of their cheating and dishonesty.

Is the world as we live in it really bound by such a causal law? In a theocentric tradition this would not be a serious problem, because even without being exposed, one's sinful act would not evade the eyes of the divine power. The Israelite teachers indeed told their audience with confidence that nobody would escape from YHWH's discerning and punishment. For a semi-spiritual system such as Confucianism, this would present a great difficulty. When we say Confucian tradition is 'semi-spiritual', we mean that, although for Confucians the ultimate judgment of human wrongs lies with Heaven, their solution is different from that of the theocentric tradition, and leads to an anthropocentric discipline for human transgressions. Confucius also resorted to the power of Heaven when dealing with private offences, and believed that, wherever one was and whatever one did, if one offended against Heaven, there would be nowhere one could turn to in one's prayers (*Analects*, 3:13). Probably because of his awareness of the ineffectiveness of the spiritual power in keeping human errors in check, Confucius explored human sides of moral disciplining, including utilitarian interfering and self-cultivating. While recognizing the spiritual authority of Heaven, Mengzi turned his attention away from heavenly punishment and identified the observance of Heaven with the requirements of people, and used a verse from the *Book of Documents* to illustrate this: 'People's eyes are the eyes of Heaven; people's ears are the ears of Heaven' (Mengzi, 5A:5).

Utilitarian and political consequences might be effective leverages to restrain the people in power from transgressing, but how about the common people? Confucian training was designed to enable everybody to be self-disciplined, and to be good out of their own heart. The author(s) of the *Doctrine of the Mean* thus turned to the moral mechanism of conscience as the reason why one must follow the rules and exercise self-discipline when alone: 'There is nothing more visible than what is hidden and nothing more manifest than what is subtle. Therefore the superior man is watching over himself when he is alone' (Zhongyong, 1). In this kind of self-disciplining, it was believed that training would produce a complex of moral rules within, and a respectful attitude in one's relations to other people, by which following rules would become self-generated respectfulness. It was in this sense that Confucius claimed that 'To be respectful is close to being observant of the rites in that it enables one to stay clear of disgrace and insult' (*Analects*, 1:13), and that to be really observant of rites, one must follow not only external rules (rites) but also internal conscience (*Analects*, 3:3). Moral training in Confucianism thus started with rites and ended up with that order and harmony being realized internally. The full function of the seemingly external rites could reach their highest perfection only when both emotion and form were fully realized internally in all individuals.

In both Confucian and Israelite traditions the orientation of the ethical system is not theoretical but practical, and wisdom is intended to guide action and behaviour rather than meditating on matters metaphysical and mysterious. Moral discipline and training are not themselves the end of wisdom. Rather they are intended to pave the way for understanding and insight, provide guidelines for personal choices, and help people, especially young students, in their examination of various situations, anticipating possible results and analysing motivations. In these processes, Confucians and Israelite teachers demonstrate a character close to that of utilitarianism. An action is good because it will bring about good results, either for the short-term interests or the long-term benefits of the person involved. However, because of their awareness of the existence of the world order, Confucian and Israelite training is also deontological in nature: an action is good not only because it can produce the maximum good result for the agent and his immediate family, but also because it is desired by YHWH (for the Israelites) or is in line with the spiritual principles of Heaven and Earth (for Confucians), while a wrong action is wrong because it has transgressed the venerated rules handed down from the spiritual ultimate and ancestors. In their discussion of being more careful when alone,

Confucians extend the authority of moral rules to internal conscience and take it as the criterion for judging disposition and behaviour. In this utilitarian–deontological system, ethical wisdom is gained through making choices between the way of evil (stupidity, foolishness, recklessness) and the way of righteousness (uprightness, intelligence). Students are therefore constantly asked to be aware of the existence of two paths, one to the bright realm of wisdom and the other to darkness. Choice means freedom; however, this freedom is not arbitrary, doing whatever one wants to do; rather it involves huge responsibilities, having an impact not only on one's own welfare but also on the communities one lives in.

Moral training and education are a means by which a good character can be cultivated and shaped, and understanding and knowledge can be gained and accumulated. The core of Confucian and Israelite ethical thinking is how to enable people to be wise and to manifest the heart and manner of wisdom. Against this background, we see that a large portion of wisdom teaching in China and Israel is concerned with model persons and their characteristics, by which an ideal of the worthy is set up for common people to follow. As far as ethical wisdom is concerned, Confucian and Israelite authors/compilers are particularly interested in two kinds of model person, the wise or *zhizhe* and the righteous or gentleman (*junzi*). Through taking them as an exemplary model for educational or moral training purposes, Confucians and Israelite teachers call people to follow them and to strive to become them. These models have a dual function in ethical wisdom. On the one hand, they demonstrate good qualities (good moral senses, unique religious visions, insightful understanding and knowledge and so on), are admired by and attractive to common people; on the other hand, they are said to be the source of wisdom by which people are educated and become prudent and insightful.

The Wise Man as an Ethical Ideal

Given the complex usage of 'the wise' (wise men) in Israelite wisdom literature, it is necessary for us to differentiate the wise as authors or compilers of wisdom texts and the wise as exemplary models for Israelite people. Almost all scholars on wisdom in ancient Israel have come to the view that wisdom texts were shaped in the hands of wise men or sages or the educated elite, but they differ regarding such questions as whether or not this group was connected with the royal court, formed a 'definite class' and led a powerful wisdom movement in the pre-exilic era. Whoever they were and whatever they accomplished, we can safely assume that wisdom teachers, such as the 'men of Hezekiah' (Prov. 25:1), were very important in causing earlier oral traditions to be edited and transmitted as wisdom texts, and therefore represented, at least partially, the wisdom ideal revered in Israelite history. However, what we seek to investigate in this section is primarily not how these so-called 'wise men' did their work; rather we shall concentrate on what the texts have revealed to us, namely, the wise as moral and religious figures who embodied Israelite wisdom.

There is no doubt that the wise man is depicted differently in a Confucian context from an Israelite context. For Confucians, the wisdom of a person is measured by his achievements in fulfilling moral responsibilities and is demonstrated in his knowledge, intelligence and conduct, while for the Israelites a wise man is first of all a religious man with a firm faith that wisdom comes from YHWH. Having said this, we must add that in general Confucians and the Israelites would agree that the wise are exemplary persons who have met the requirements of epistemological and ethical qualifications of wisdom. As an intellectual achievement, the wise have a superior ability in reasoning, reflecting and foreseeing, while, as a virtue, they have followed wise teachings, cultivating a character and leading a morally admirable way of life.

'The wise' as we use the term in this section is of a general meaning, referring to the people of wisdom who are revered as teachers and who, in their behaviour and words, demonstrate a high degree of wisdom. Various models of the wise are presented for us in Confucian and Israelite wisdom texts, each reflecting a series of specific expectations of social and political reality, while together manifesting moral and religious requirements in particular cultural settings. The wise are referred to by different terms. In Israelite texts they are 'the wise' or wise men (*ḥāḵām*, pl. *ḥᵃḵāmīm*), while in early Confucian writings we find an expression specifically for a man of wisdom (*zhizhe*). *Ḥāḵām* and *zhizhe* correspond to, yet are distinguishable from, each other, and in examining each in the light of the other we will be able to identify some wisdom images with distinct features.

The original meaning and reference of the wise in Hebrew is simple, referring to those who have 'superior mental ability or special skill'; Ludwig Köhler confirms that

> The man who is wise (*ḥāḵām*) is in the first place in Hebrew thought a man who understands a thing, and understands it properly. He is one who has experienced much and therefore knows for himself how one should act in a given situation.[26]

It is argued that 'The saying in Prov. 21:22 about the superiority of the wise over mere physical strength gives expression to a simple experience that is still based on the non-specific concept of being clever or knowledgeable.'[27] However, this primarily epistemological perception of the wise went through dramatic changes, under the influence of theological and philosophical construction, and thus became complex and profound, carrying with it ethical, political and educational implications, and being associated with a specific moral paradigm, professional teacher and statesman.

In Israelite wisdom texts, wise men have eyes on secular matters, commonly considered clever, shrewd and skilful, which characterize their profession and life style. The qualities of a wise man are described or interpreted, frequently in contrast

---

[26] Ludwig Köhler, 1956, p.104.

[27] *Theological Dictionary of the Old Testament*, ed. G. Johnnes Botterweck and Helmer Ringgren, trans. David E. Green, vol. IV, Grand Rapids, Michigan: William B. Eerdmans Publishing Company, 1980, p.379.

to the fool (*'ewīl*) or the foolish (*nābāl*) or the stupid (*keŝīl*), as being such that he embodies all dimensions of traditional wisdom, as G. von Rad has suggested: 'In the majority of instances, the wise man is not the representative of a position, but simply the wise man who is contrasted, as a type, with the fool.'[28] For example, the wise man knows well that experience is the best source of wisdom and that teaching of others guides one in life; therefore he takes advice to his heart, while the fool inflates himself and this prevents him from doing so (Prov. 12:15). Teaching or advice may not always be in agreement with how one thinks, but a wise man knows that in knowing how to treat this disagreement lies wisdom, and he thus loves instruction, in contrast to a scoffer or babbler who 'does not listen to rebuke' (Prov. 13:1). Conducting himself in social life, a wise man engages other people in the most proper way, and knows how to answer discreetly and always holds back his wrath (Prov. 26:16; 29:8). The wise person also demonstrates other good qualities such as trustfulness in words, as when one of Job's friends asked him if 'a wise man should answer with windy knowledge' (Job 15:2).

It is evident that Israelite wise men were not only clever or 'prudent' (Prov. 1:5; 17:28) individuals, but also professional teachers;[29] they themselves led a wise way of life, and were also able to have a significant effect on other people. Those who did not listen to the voice of their teachers or not incline their ears to their instructors, it is warned, would have nothing other than regret and ruin (Prov. 5:11–14). A number of scholars have made the point that there is a close connection between *ḥākām* (the wise) and *yā'aŝ* (to counsel, advise) and *'ēŝā* (counsel, advice) and that the wise men in Israel played the role of giving counsel, especially on statesmanship: 'the recognized crafts of political negotiation and diplomacy'.[30] It seems correct to say that wise men gave counsel or advice not only to statesmen but also to their students and other ordinary audiences. The value of the counsel or advice is first seen in its good consequences, and Hebrew proverbs confirm that the teaching of the wise is able to bring 'long life', 'riches' and 'honour' (Prov. 3:16). In a hierarchical society, the wisdom texts nevertheless raise wisdom above social rank, justifying the view that the power of a man is in his wisdom, not in his position, because 'wisdom gives strength to the wise man more than ten rulers that are in a city' (Eccl. 7:19). Those who follow the teaching of the wise are believed to be surely gaining benefit, while those who follow the nonsense of a fool will suffer: ''The words of the wise heard in quiet are better than the shouting of a ruler among fools' (Eccl. 9:17). Because of the qualities of the wise and the beneficial effect of his teaching, it is natural for Israelite teachers to exhort their audience or students to be wise, which becomes a distinct

---

[28] G. von Rad: *Wisdom in Israel*, Nashville: Abingdon, 1972, p.20.

[29] Prov. 17:16 seems to indicate that a student was expected to pay a fee to his teacher, and wisdom teaching could be bought at a price, although such a conclusion has not been supported materially.

[30] M. Noth and W. Thomas (eds): *Wisdom in Israel and in the Ancient Near East*, Leiden: E.J. Brill, 1955, pp.42–71; W. McKane: *Prophets and Wise Men*, London: SCM Press, 1965, pp.13, 115; *Theological Dictionary of the Old Testament*, vol. VI, 1990, pp.171–3.

style of many Israelite proverbs.[31] For example, 'Hear, my son, and be wise, and direct your mind in the way', or 'Listen to advice and accept instruction, that you may gain wisdom for the future' (Prov. 23:19; 19:20).[32] Through contrasts between the wise and the fool, the Israelite teachers encourage their audience to be associated with the wise, because this is the only path to wisdom: 'He who walks with wise men becomes wise, but the companion of fools will suffer harm' (Prov. 13:20).

Wise men are not always depicted positively in the Hebrew Bible. From the fact that wise men and their counsel were under the condemnation and scorn of the Prophets who claimed that their supposed wisdom was in opposition to the divine will (for example, Isaiah 29:14–16), it is easy to assume that the wise in Israel represented conventional wisdom, and formed a recognizable camp different from those called prophets who proclaimed that they were more authentic in delivering divine messages. However, there is no evidence that wise men were totally outside the religious realm. Rather, wise men consciously aligned themselves with traditional beliefs, and there is no lack of references in the wisdom literature to wise men acknowledging that wisdom comes from YHWH. The wise are wise only because they subject themselves to divinity, and it is in this sense that the Israelites believe that the knowledge that comes through wisdom can 'save' or 'deliver' (Prov. 2:12, 16), because 'The teaching of the wise is a fountain of life, that one may avoid the snares of death' (Prov. 13:14). However clever one is, one still needs to be guided and corrected by the divine, as we can see from the Wisdom of Solomon: 'May God grant that I speak with judgment and have thoughts worthy of what I have received, for he is the guide even of wisdom and the corrector of the wise' (Wisd. 8:15). Criticism made by prophets, therefore, cannot be reasonably interpreted as showing that wise men had departed from the religious tradition, but it may point to a division between different professions; the distinctiveness of Israelite wise men lay, as von Rad argues, in their intensive search for a reliable order in the form of rules and in their acquiring knowledge from their environment and experience, by which they sought something 'eternally valid' in contrast to, for example, Israelite theologians who were interested in establishing theological meanings which were unique to Israel.[33]

It is apparent that there is a fundamental openness in early Confucian and Israelite traditions that anyone can choose to lead a life of wisdom or become wise. This is typically expressed by two short phrases, respectively: those who 'walk in the way of insight' would be recognized as men of wisdom (Prov. 9:6), and 'To be fond of learning is close to becoming the wise' (Zhongyong, 20). Differences between these two traditions do exist, however, not only in who can be called the wise, but also in

---

[31] *Theological Dictionary of the Old Testament*, vol. IV, pp.373–4.

[32] 'My son' occurs 22 times in the book of Proverbs. The words 'father' and 'son' are not solely for a familial relation in Hebrew texts; rather they are often used figuratively in a pedagogical context, father implying an authoritative figure in the sense that 'he who is master over' with 'my son' referring to 'my pupil' or 'disciple'.

[33] G. von Rad: *Wisdom in Israel*, p.289.

what characterizes the wise, and how these characteristics contribute to the meaning and happiness of life.

The profession the Israelite wise engaged in (counsellors, teachers and authors) corresponds, roughly, to that taken by *ru* (Confucians) or *shi* (scholars) in early China who advised the ruler and taught at schools. Whether or not Confucius, Mengzi, Xunzi and their followers were specifically called 'wise men' or 'sages' in history,[34] we have material evidence that these masters demonstrated a significant similarity to their counterparts (wise men) in Israel, travelling from state to state to offer their advice to the rulers. Confucians invested heavily in their counselling activities in the hope that their political blueprint would be adopted by those in authority, and oriented their education more towards character development than towards professional training, enabling their students to gain moral and political insight rather than practical skills.

Like the wise in Israel who functioned as teachers or instructors in schools or communities, Confucians engaged in education by opening private schools in which students were taught six arts (history, poetry, rites, music, maths and archery).[35] The Confucian teacher endeavoured to know what was new by keeping fresh in his mind what he was already familiar with, namely pioneering the knowledge and understanding while transmitting the tradition of the past (*Analects*, 2:11). They were proud of their profession, and they praised the contribution of the teacher to the continuation of culture and civilization. Confucius became recognized as the sage primarily because of his excellence in education. According to Xunzi, 'the teacher is one who makes his own person an erect gnomon indicating the proper standard of development and who values what is at peace with him' (Xunzi, 2:11). The teacher is not only responsible for transmitting the Way, but also capable of bringing order to the world, but most importantly, manifesting all virtues such as loyalty, faithfulness, love and beneficence among the people (Xunzi, 8:3).[36]

---

[34] In a Confucian context, 'wise men' (*zhizhe*) and 'sages' (*shengren*) are two different categories and represent two stages of personal achievement in the Confucian tradition. The latter is in a higher position than the former. However, we have no intention to separate them this way. Rather we take their intellectual activities as representing the ideal of wise men, as will be discussed below, while combining their political teachings with historical kings in which Confucians furthered a particular wisdom in politics that will be examined in the next chapter.

[35] Confucius was no doubt the first man in China who established private schools, opened them to all who sought education and had the potential to learn, and aimed at bringing about an ideal person who possessed wisdom, free from covetousness and well versed in courtesy, ceremonial and music. While having his own school, Mengzi also advised the Duke of Teng to 'establish *xiang, xu, xue* and *xiao*' – educational institutions with different purposes (Mengzi, 5:3).

[36] For Xunzi, esteeming the teachers or not is to separate a gentleman and a small man. Xunzi required students to obey and follow their teacher as the way to wisdom: 'To oppose your teacher is the same as being without a teacher. Not to hold correct your teacher and the model, but to prefer instead to rely on your own notions is to employ a blind man to differentiate colours or a deaf person to distinguish sounds – you have nothing with which to reject confusion and error' (Xunzi, 2:11). Primarily because of Xunzi's advocacy, teaching became a more respected profession, standing together with Heaven, Earth, Ruler and Parents to enjoy the highest possible position in imperial China.

The Confucian wise are differentiated from the ignorant or stupid (*yu*). Unlike the fool in an Israelite context who is unwilling to follow the teaching of the wise and therefore behaves against YHWH's will, ignorance or stupidity for Confucians comes primarily from one's unwillingness to learn. In terms of intelligent faculties, there may be some people who are born stupid and there may be different grades of human intelligence. However, what Confucians are most concerned with is the foolishness that results from the underdevelopment of the human mind due to the lack of learning (*Analects*, 17:8); in other words, a person becomes wise through learning or else becomes stupid or foolish because of improper education.

At this point there is a difference in emphasis between Confucian and Israelite perception of the wise. For Confucians, the faculty of knowing is present in everybody, and so can then be cultivated and developed through learning to enable its possessor to grasp the principles of the world and the norms of social life. In other words, wisdom can be learned, and by learning people become wise, and when one's learning reaches the highest point, one can understand the ultimate truth and principle. For Israelite teachers, learning is also important because it develops human intellectual faculties and improves understanding, by which the learner becomes wiser. However, gaining wisdom is not as simple as that. There is much more than the development of one's intelligence. A man may be prudent and clever in daily life, but this does not mean he is a wise man. A true wise man is the one who possesses wisdom by faith and by heart, because the highest wisdom is with the divine rather than in the hands of humans.

Israelite texts depict an ethical image of the wise man who carefully manoeuvres his way through personal and communal life, while the Confucian concept of the wise reveals well developed qualities of intellectual faculties. However, this does not mean that the Confucian ideal of wise men is not practical. Confucians endeavour to combine the intellectual and the practical into their image of the wise, whose knowledge is essentially about the world and life. Unlike Daoists who believe that a wise person is the one who has reduced his knowledge to the minimum, Confucians highlight the importance of wide learning for one to become wise. Confucius calls for a gentleman to gain 'a wide range of knowledge concerning culture', and his disciple further confirms that 'learning widely' is one of the most important conditions that enable one to become a benevolent man (*Analects*, 6:27; 19:6). Mengzi openly says that 'A wise man knows everything' (Mengzi, 7A:46). However, wide learning is not the only, nor the most important, criterion for Confucians to judge whether a person is wise; having knowledge but not knowing how to use it, this kind of person cannot be said to be wise. In this sense, Xunzi directly refuted the view that the more knowledge one has the wiser one is, pointing out that 'when a gentleman is termed "wise", this does not imply that he can know all that knowledgeable men know' (Xunzi, 8:3). Instead, a wise man is wise because he knows where his knowledge is required most urgently and how to concentrate his attention on the issues he must sort out first: 'A wise man ... considers urgent only that which demands attention ... Even Yao and Shun did not use their wisdom on all things alike; this is because they put first things first' (Mengzi, 7A:46).

Further, Confucian knowledge is not primarily factual but moral by nature, and, by employing knowledge, a wise man knows what is right and what is wrong, so that his mind is never perplexed (*Analects*, 9:29). How to use knowledge is a practical matter; a wise man must be skilful in conversation, speaking to those who are capable of benefiting from his words, while not speaking to those who are incapable of benefiting, so that he does not let men or words go to waste (*Analects*, 15:8). Furthermore, a wise man is judged by his success in completing his tasks, which results in his sincerity: 'The wise man is clear in regard to his tasks and comprehensively employs his calculations; so it would be impossible for him to be insincere in his understanding (Xunzi, 27:104). Thanks to the intimate connection between wisdom and virtue, a wise man is naturally attracted to benevolence, because he finds it to his advantage (*Analects*, 4:2). Ultimately a wise man in Confucian contexts is one who actively participates in political administration. As a politician, he stipulates norms and establishes rules that can be used to enforce order; as the head of a state he stands in awe of Heaven, knowing how to submit himself to a state bigger than his own when necessary, which enables him to possess his state (Mengzi, 1B:3). Wise men make 'distinctions' and 'separations', instituting names to refer to objects, making distinctions to make clear what is noble and what is base and separations to discriminate between things that are the same and those that are different (Xunzi, 22:2b).

Just as the wise man in Israel has his shortcomings and weaknesses, Confucians are not overconfident in the ability and capability of the wise. Splendid and admirable as a wise man is, he is not always able to complete his task successfully. First, it is possible that a wise man does not know how to employ his knowledge in administration, which results in his failure. Secondly, a wise man often tends to be single-minded in reaching his target, which causes him to be disliked by the people in the world; in this sense, Confucians call for the wise to learn something from the way that the ancient sage–king Yu guided the water by imposing nothing on it that was against its natural tendency (Mengzi, 4B:26).

Can wise men be further classified into different categories? In other words, can there be some people wiser than others under the overall umbrella of the wise? It seems that the Israelites tend to separate the true wise from the false wise, the former having faith in the wisdom of YHWH, the latter trusting only his own intelligence: 'He who trusts in his own mind is a fool; but he who walks in wisdom will be delivered' (Prov. 28:26). The Israelites also differentiate the man with knowledge and the man who claims to possess knowledge, and recommend keeping a distance from those self-professed wisdom teachers.

It is apparent that, while demonstrating goodness and wisdom for personal and communal life, the wise only represent specific qualities that a Confucian and Israelite ideal person is expected to have, not the ideal itself. In terms of one's achievements in personal cultivation, the wise in the eyes of Confucians can demonstrate different aspects of ethical wisdom, in accordance with the levels they have achieved; in other words, the Confucian concept of the wise contains many dimensions, and different people may have demonstrated only one or two of them. In conversations with his students, for example, Confucius was said to have divided them into three categories according to their understandings of what is wise and benevolent: Zi Lu was called 'a scholar–knight' (*shi*), because he suggested that 'the wise man causes others to know him, and the benevolent man (*ren ren*) causes others to love him'; Zi Gong was named a scholar–gentleman (*shi junzi*), because he thought that 'the wise man knows others, and the benevolent man loves others'; Yan Yuan was entitled an enlightened gentleman (*ming junzi*) because he believed that 'the wise man knows himself, and the benevolent man loves himself'.[37] Following his intellectual interpretation of wisdom, Xunzi associates the level of the wise with different professions, and makes four categories of the wise to correspond to four social classes: the understanding of the sage, that of the scholar–gentleman, that of the petty man, and that of the menial servant (Xunzi, 23:6). This hierarchical view of wisdom, that the knowledge of the wise man is attached to the social class he happens to be in, is most likely unacceptable to the minds of Israelite wisdom teachers, or at least fundamentally different from the image of the wise as depicted in Israelite wisdom texts.

The Righteous and *Junzi*

The wise man in Confucian and Israelite texts is never an isolated model; rather he is a constituent element of the ideal image for perfect morality, righteousness and foresight. Being wise in personal circumstances is only part of the overall ethical requirements, or one of many qualities necessary for one to become a culturally appraised person. It is therefore no surprise that the wise are closely related to, and on many occasions interchangeable with, another ethical model, called respectively 'the righteous' (*ṣaddīq*, pl. *ṣaddīqīm*) in the Israelite tradition and 'gentleman' (*junzi*) in Confucianism.

In Hebrew wisdom texts, righteousness (*ṣeḏeq*) is a virtue, referring to the state of being upright, right and just, and, by extension, innocent and blameless.[38] Like many other virtues of the Israelites, however, righteousness is first of a divine character, belonging to YHWH, and humans are expected to be righteous, because their Lord is righteous (2 Chronicles 12:6), and so the righteous person is primarily defined as the one who practises a wholehearted piety towards YHWH. Compared with the wise, therefore, the righteous person is more a religious than an ethical figure. It may be possible for one to proceed from being unwise to being wise through learning and

---

[37] This conversation is found in the *Book of Xunzi* (29:7). It is most likely that what it reveals is not representative of Confucius's own understanding, but that of Xunzi.

[38] As a virtue Hebrew righteousness is not only an inner quality, but also has a substantial communal qualification, and righteous refers to the one who has 'recognized and fulfilled claims made upon him by the community to which he belongs' (G. von Rad: *Wisdom in Israel*, p.79).

following advice; however, from unrighteousness to righteousness, one must submit oneself to YHWH. The book of Job identifies having faith in YHWH and becoming righteous, and likens 'returning to the Almighty and humbling oneself' to 'removing unrighteousness far from one's tents' (Job 22:23). The favourable position of the righteous is due to the love and care of YHWH who is said not to 'withdraw his eyes from the righteous' (Job 36:7) and, in figurative words, not 'to let the righteous go hungry' (Prov. 10:3).

Righteousness is also used in a moral and legal sense, a sense of 'proper order, proper comportment' and 'doing the "right" things' in a right way, which is manifested through one's behaviour and thought. The righteous is in sharp contrast to the wicked (*rāšāʿ*, pl. *rᵉšāʿîm*),[39] or a man of evil. In the ethical realm, there is room left for individuals' choice to become righteous or wicked, and the audience are taught again and again that they must keep in mind the instruction, 'do not enter the path of the wicked, and do not walk in the way of evil men', because 'the path of the righteous is like the light of dawn, which shines brighter and brighter until full day. The way of the wicked is like deep darkness' (Prov. 4:13–14, 18–19). The way of the righteous is good or essential for humans to lead a good life, while the way of the wicked will bring them nothing but disaster, as wisdom teachers admonish their audience:

> So you will walk in the way of good men and keep to the paths of the righteous.
> For the upright will inhabit the land, and men of integrity will remain in it; but the
> wicked will be cut off from the land, and the treacherous will be rooted out of it.
> (Prov. 2:20–22)

On many occasions in Israelite wisdom texts, wisdom and righteousness, and the wise and the righteous, are identifiable, frequently complementing each other in parallel, although with different emphases. In terms of knowledge growth, the righteous or upright is almost equal to the wise, as both benefit from wisdom teachings and are able to increase their wisdom through accepting teaching and instruction: 'I have taught you the way of wisdom; I have led you in the paths of uprightness' and the wisdom teachers are confident: 'Give instruction to a wise man, and he will be still wiser; teach a righteous man and he will increase in learning' (Prov. 4:11; 9:9). In terms of human relationship to God, the righteous and the wise are synonymous, for 'the righteous and the wise and their deeds are in the hand of God' (Eccl. 9:1), and 'The LORD's curse is on the house of the wicked, but he blesses the abode of the righteous … The wise will inherit honour, but fools get disgrace' (Prov. 3:33, 35). In a family context, the righteous and the wise bring happiness to the family, in contrast to the wicked and fool who make their parents suffer, and it is said that 'the father of the righteous will greatly rejoice; he who begets a wise son will be glad in him' (Prov. 23:24). On many other occasions the comparability between the righteous and the wise is also implied, sometimes hidden

---

[39] One form of the verb *rāšāʿ* is certainly legal – it means 'to find not guilty'.

in phrases; for example, in the book of Job we read that 'The righteous holds to his way, and he that has clean hands grows stronger and stronger. But you, come on again, all of you, and I shall not find a wise man among you' (Job 17:9–10).

Like the wise, a man of righteousness is able not only to benefit from wisdom but also to provide wisdom teaching, as is clearly indicated in the proverb, 'The mouth of the righteous is a fountain of life' (Prov. 10:11). A good life is a life without troubles, which can be guaranteed only through being righteous, because it is believed that 'The righteous is delivered from trouble, and the wicked gets into it instead' (Prov. 11:8). There seems no doubt at all in the minds of the Israelites that the righteous will be able to realize their wishes and lead a pleasant life because of their uprightness: 'The hope of the righteous ends in gladness, but the expectation of the wicked comes to nought' (Prov. 10:28). Some people may want riches more than righteousness. However, Hebrew wisdom cautions against this, because the Israelites believe that 'He who trusts in his riches will wither, but the righteous will flourish like a green leaf' (Prov. 11:28) and that 'Treasures gained by wickedness do not profit, but righteousness delivers from death' (Prov. 10:2). Some people may wish to cut corners in their business dealing, either by cheating or by transgressing, but this will certainly lead to severe punishment and even death, as the Proverbs say, 'The fruit of the righteous is a tree of life, but lawlessness takes away lives' (Prov. 11:30). The Israelites take the righteous man as the seeker of truth, in contrast to the wicked man who always hides himself in falsehood. They depict the righteous not only as behaving but also thinking in a right way, as it is said, 'The thoughts of the righteous are just' (Prov. 12:5) and 'A righteous man hates falsehood' (Prov. 13:5).

Although there may be some dissonant tunes here and there in emphasis between the divine nature of righteousness and its human applications, the conventional Israelite wisdom texts are nevertheless attempting to harmonize righteousness as YHWH's activity and righteousness as human behaviour. The pious attitude of the righteous towards the divine is the foundation on which moral qualities and behaviour that follow are built. There is a special relationship between the righteous and the divine, and a righteous person behaves according to his own standards that are derived from this relationship. The wisdom texts admit that this would cause him to be seen as not particularly popular, or more likely strange, astray or even weird. Through the mouth of King Solomon, the composer of the Wisdom of Solomon has drawn us a picture to illustrate how the righteous person appears to be strange and to go beyond ordinary people's comprehension:

> He reproaches us for sins against the law, and accuses us of sins against our training. He professes to have knowledge of God, and calls himself a child of the Lord. He became to us a reproof of our thoughts; the very sight of him is a burden to us, because his manner of life is unlike that of others, and his ways are strange. We are considered by him as something base, and he avoids our way as unclean. (Wisd. 2:12–16)

The book goes on to explain that these perceptions are generated, not because the righteous are wrong, but because the people are blinded by their wickedness or ignorance which prevents them from knowing the secret purpose of God. In the end, people must come to terms with the righteous, not the other way around, for it is righteousness that will triumph. Although composed under the influence of Hellenistic philosophy, this book presents an understanding of the righteous that is in line with the central theme of Israelite proverbs that the way of righteousness is the way of eternity awarded by YHWH, while that of the unrighteous leads to dire consequences: 'In the path of righteousness is life, but the way of error leads to death' (Prov. 12:28).

Roughly corresponding to the righteous in biblical Israel, we have a morally appraisable model in classical Confucianism called '*junzi*', translated variously as 'gentleman', 'princely man', 'superior man', 'noble man', 'good man' or 'virtuous man'. The original meaning of *junzi* is the 'son of the ruler', referring to the social status of the ruler or nobility. While this meaning is still retained on a number of occasions in the *Analects*, it is evident that Confucius has transformed it into a moral ideal in the sense that a man is a gentleman only when he has demonstrated superior moral qualities and stable patterns of admirable moral behaviour,[40] and it is in the sense of being a man of civility and high morals that we adopt 'gentleman' as a translation of Confucian *junzi*.

In contrast to the essentially religious image of the righteous in Israel, a Confucian gentleman is first of all a moral man, namely, a man of virtues, in sharp contrast to a small man (*xiao ren*), a morally and intellectually underdeveloped person. The difference between a gentleman and a small man is due, not to their birth, but to their learning and cultivation. However, this difference results in two different characters, one noble and the other base, of totally different attitudes and behaviours, for example, 'While the gentleman cherishes virtue, the small man cherishes his native land'; 'The gentleman helps others to realize what is good in them; he does not help them to realize what is bad in them. The small man does the opposite'; or 'The gentleman is at ease without being arrogant; the small man is arrogant without being at ease' (*Analects*, 4:11; 12:16; 13:26).

Through these contrasts, Confucius promoted an image of the virtuous person whose action is free from violence, whose bearing is completely sincere and whose speech lacks all vulgarity. According to his description, the gentleman 'seeks neither a full belly nor a comfortable home', is 'quick in action but cautious in speech' and 'free from worries and fears', and would be ashamed of his word outstripping his deed (*Analects*, 1:14; 12:4; 14:27). All these appearances reflect a character of virtue that is the foundation or roots of the gentleman. 'The gentleman devotes his efforts to the roots', for he knows that 'once the roots are established, the Way will grow therefore' (*Analects*, 1:2). In cultivating virtues, the gentleman differentiates himself from ordinary people because he knows how to nurture his nature by means of

---

[40] In the *Book of Mengzi*, the term *junzi* has 81 occurrences, of which 22 refer to the ruler or a member of the ruling class, and 52 to a virtuous being who follows the way of the gentleman.

benevolence and the rites, and by his introspective conscience in the sense that he always examines himself for reasons when treated improperly by others (Mengzi, 4B:28). The gentleman broadens his sense of purpose in times of hardship, and comports himself with respectfulness in times of prosperity and honour. He is able to achieve a perfect character because he can fully make use of 'a sense of common good to triumph over merely personal desires' (Xunzi, 2:14).

A Confucian gentleman is also a wise man who has a wide learning, and a practical man who puts his words into action before allowing his words to follow his action (*Analects*, 2:13). Since wisdom and virtue are interrelated, a gentleman combines them in his own self in a perfect way. A gentleman may not know everything; however, his wisdom enables him not to offer an opinion when ignorant; in other words, he does not widely comment on things he does not understand, but when 'he names something the name is sure to be usable in speech, and when he says something this is sure to be practicable' (*Analects*, 13:3). The wisdom of a gentleman enables him to seek the Way or truth sincerely, even at the price of suffering poverty: 'A gentleman seeks the Way and not mere living … worries about the Way and not about poverty' (*Analects*, 15:31). Being wise, a gentleman may engage himself in the teaching profession. His pedagogical methods are distinctive, and there are five ways by which he teaches his students: by a transforming influence like that of timely rain, by helping the student to realize his virtue to the full, by helping the student to develop his talent, by answering his questions, and by setting an example others not in contact with him can emulate (Mengzi, 7A:40). More importantly, the wisdom of a gentleman is the totality of knowledge about his self and his environment which guides behaviour. To do so, it is necessary for him to widen his learning as much as possible and to engage in self-examination on a daily basis, as Xunzi has explained: 'In broadening his learning, the gentleman each day examines himself so that his awareness will be discerning and his actions without excess' (Xunzi, 1:1).

In contrast to the righteous person in Israel who is only a man of character and is seldom involved in politics, a Confucian gentleman is above all a noble statesman, in the sense that his wisdom and learning would be enthusiastically put into governing practice. Because of his virtue and wisdom, a gentleman can be entrusted with the destiny of the whole state, and he willingly bears such a heavy burden as serving the state and the people (*Analects*, 8:4, 6, 7). In carrying out his administrative responsibilities, he is respectful in the way he conducts himself, reverent in the service of his lord, generous in caring for the common people, and just in employing their service (*Analects*, 5:16). As a good official or minister, 'In serving his lord, a gentleman has only one aim that is to put him [his lord] on the right path and set his mind on benevolence' (Mengzi, 6B:8). Being engaged in governmental matters, a gentleman bases his political activities on his self-cultivation. Confucius highly values 'bringing peace and security to the people'. However, this is achievable because of self-cultivation and achieving reverence (*Analects*, 14:42). A gentleman manages the state through his moral influence, rather than by punishing, and is able to transform the people through his knowledge and understanding. Confucius even said that, as soon as a gentleman lived among the barbarians, then all the uncivilized manners and customs of the barbarians would be transformed (*Analects*, 9:14). Confucians were convinced that 'order was born of the gentleman and chaos was produced by the small man', as Xunzi said in confidence that he had not yet heard of a case, from the most distant past to the present day, where there was a gentleman in charge of the government but chaos ensued (Xunzi, 9:2).

There is no doubt that the Confucian gentleman is a morally virtuous man, distinguishable from the Israelite righteous man who is fundamentally judged by his piety towards YHWH. Divine and human righteousness in Israel are not separable, although there is a clear tension between them, and the righteous man is not only religious but also recognized as the one who has fulfilled his duties towards communities and as ethically good. In a similar way, the gentleman in Confucianism is not only moral in its narrow sense, but he also possesses spiritual qualities that enable him to conduct a mission in the world. Confucius clearly states that the gentleman has a purpose higher than any secular achievement when he says that 'The gentleman gets through to what is up above' (*Analects*, 14:23). 'What is up above' here may sound like a purely mundane matter, referring to a higher grade of learning or something similar. However, in the Confucian worldview, the moral does not end at temporary matters; rather it goes on to something more permanent and spiritual. When saying that the gentleman stood in awe of three things, Confucius specified that the decree of Heaven was the first of which the gentleman should stand in awe, and when explaining why he was not understood by his fellow countrymen, he claimed that the gentleman could be understood only by Heaven (*Analects*, 14:35). If the gentleman carries out moral responsibilities because of his belief in the mandate of Heaven and his fear of the power of Heaven, and if he expects to be understood only by Heaven, then it is apparent that what one is and what one does are not purely moral in its narrow sense, but religio-ethical with a specific spiritual value, and it is this special spiritual value that enables the Confucian gentleman to be a moral and 'saintly' model, bearing a spiritual mission that is to be realized through his personal efforts in studying and in executing administrative responsibilities.

CHAPTER SIX

Family, Politics and the Sage–King Paradigm

In one's journey to ultimate understanding, wisdom is required not only to deal with a variety of personal problems, to become more experienced and skilful in coping with life, and to refine personal character and virtues, but also to operate in a much larger context, involving familial and political norms and activities, by which one gains knowledge of, and insight into, complex human relationships. However personal it is, wisdom must be cultivated and acquired in communal life and in social interaction. In this sense wisdom can be defined as a communal product, gained through bringing together collective knowledge and past experiences, in the contexts first of all of clans and then of political communities, by which a special type of family and political wisdom is cultivated. The people who possess familial and political wisdom are both recognized as successful in managing life because of their superb skill and ability, and respected as charismatic and exemplary in reshaping community life and social customs, at the top of which stands the figure of the sage–king or the wise king who is taken as the Confucian and Israelite paradigm of wisdom.

Familial Wisdom

Family occupies a central position in both early China and Israel, and familial wisdom is an important constituent part of Confucian and Israelite wisdom. Family is composed of various and complex relationships which require knowledge and skill to deal with; understanding and insight concerning family matters and situations can be obtained only from proper training and disciplining. Familial relations are both the first test and the first manifestation of family members' virtues. Based on a proper understanding of human nature and destiny, familial wisdom is gained through an efficient exercise of familial duties and is in turn a necessary pathway leading to social and political wisdom.

Family in Early China and Israel

Family is designated by different terms in Chinese and Hebrew, which are derived from the description of a house where residents formed between them intimate relationships. In Chinese, the most frequently used character for family is *jia*, referring originally to the shelter under which domesticated animals or pigs were raised, which was then extended to mean a household (*ju*) in which family members live together to become recognized as a distinctive unit.[1] An ordinary Chinese family included grandparents, parents and children, as evidenced in the *Book of Mengzi*, the chief requirements for the head of a household were 'to take care of parents' and 'to support wife and children', and the family of that time seemed not normally extended to include other non-intimate members, to judge from Mengzi's reference to there being 'eight people in one family' (Mengzi, 1A:7). The family, or in Hebrew, *bēt-'āb*, literally meaning the house of the father, was what today could be called 'extended family'; 'Close examination of the biblical materials, in the light of comparative anthropological research, suggests that the family and the clan tended to be more basic to the structure of the society than the tribe.'[2] Compared to an ordinary family in ancient China, a typical Israelite family as revealed in biblical texts was much larger, and was often further extended to include slaves and other people, among them 'the patriarch and his wife, unmarried children, married sons and grandsons with their families, slaves and their families, and resident aliens'.[3]

Confucian and Israelite families shared a number of features. A family was a place where the tradition, both religious and ethical, was maintained, the young were educated, and the old were respected as the embodiment of traditional values. In terms of the material side, the family was the means by which family members of different generations supported and protected one another. However, the Israelite family was distinctive in the following two aspects: 'First, it was the primary means of maintaining the link between faith and ethnicity, and second, there was no distinction between the domestic and public spheres of religion.'[4] Apart from this, there is another notable difference between Confucian and Israelite views of family. On the Confucian side, the emphasis is on the middle-aged man who headed the household and was given responsibilities to support the old parents and to take care of the young children, by which he demonstrated traditional wisdom, while in an Israelite family the chief responsibilities were placed on the shoulders of the patriarch or 'father', who, however old, was in charge of the family's affairs and regarded as the fountainhead of family wisdom.

In contrast to the modern concept, the family in early China and Israel was in its full size, and incomplete families such as single-parent or childless families or

---

[1] Duan Yucai: *Shuowen jiezi zhu*, 1992, Hangzhou: Zhejiang Guji Chubanshe, p.337.

[2] J. Maxwell Miller and John H. Hayes: *A History of Ancient Israel and Judah*, London: SCM Press, 1986, p.91.

[3] *Eerdmans Dictionary of the Bible* (David Noel Freedman, editor-in-chief), Grand Rapids, Michigan/Cambridge, UK: William B. Eerdman's Publishing Company, 2000, p.457. This difference may be due to the different emphasis of Confucian and Israelite authors when talking about family. It is possible that a household of the upper class in Confucian China was as extended as that in Israel, including not only intimate family members and secondary relatives but also slaves and other people; on the other hand, the core of the Israelite family was similar to that of the Confucian family, as Ludwig Köhler comments, 'Man and wife and children form the smallest but also most natural community' (*Hebrew Man*, trans. Peter R. Ackroyd, London: SCM Press, 1956, p.89).

[4] *Eerdmans Dictionary of the Bible*, p.613.

orphans were not really valued. Both Confucian and Israelite teachers highlighted the importance of forming a full family, and considered the untimely passing-away of parents or childlessness to be unfortunate cases. When the author(s) suggested in the Wisdom of Solomon that a childless family with virtue was far better than an unlawful union and its offspring this was merely to emphasize the evil nature of the latter, not to indicate that the former was appreciated in Israelite society (Wisd. 4:1). Unmarried men or women were not natural in early Israelite communities, as Ludwig Köhler's study has indicated: 'The Arabs still call the bachelor "*azab*", "forsaken, lonely". The Old Testament has no word for this at all, so unusual is the idea. Nor is there known the woman who is felt single.'[5] In the Confucian classics, incomplete families were taken as a shame on the society and 'old men without wives, old women without husbands, old people without children, young children without parents' were considered to be the most destitute and had to be properly taken care of (Mengzi, 1B:5).

Being a social, religious and educational unit, the family requires wisdom to be properly maintained and to function well, and indeed a large part of Confucian and Israelite wisdom teachings is concerned with family and family relations. Following their understanding that there existed a universal order, divine or metaphysical, early Confucian and Israelite teachers insisted that a particular order also existed in the family and was crucial for family harmony and prosperity, and that the core of family wisdom was to understand and maintain that order. The relationship between husband and wife was the foundation on which the order was established and maintained, while the core of the order was that between parents and children. Governing all the various family relationships was the principle of hierarchy and patriarchy, in which the senior and male held a dominant position over the junior and female; the former required following and obedience from the latter. This view is well illustrated in Hexagram 37 of the *Book of Changes*, where the parents are said to be the authoritative ruler (*yan jun*), while the relationship between husband and wife is its foundation, and this is said to be the great law (*da yi*) of Heaven and Earth. Every member of the family has its own duties and rights, and when they are all in the right position and perform their own duties, then the family has a right order, and 'When the family is in order, all the social relationships of mankind will be in order.'[6]

Hierarchical and patriarchal as the Confucian and Israelite families were, their views about parents–children and husband–wife relationships contain, on different foundations, some ideas that would suggest equality between parents and children, and between husband and wife. For the Israelites, parents and children, husband and wife were each subject to the will and wish of the Creator, who alone is the source of wisdom and life. Parents may have more life experience and a higher grade of knowledge than their children, and a husband may have the advantage of physical

---

[5] Ludwig Köhler, 1956, p.89.

[6] Yijing (Text: 37). *I Ching or the Book of Changes,* The Richard Wilhelm Translation, London: Arkana, 1967, pp.143–4.

and spiritual power over his wife; however, as humans they are all creatures of YHWH, and have no way to the secrets of the world unless YHWH so wishes. This we may call theological equality. For Confucians, parents and children, husband and wife are each bearers of moral duties and possessors of moral virtues. Irrespective of whether one is a parent or a child, a husband or wife, one must fulfil one's particular moral duties when playing a particular role. This is the same for all, as was the basis on which Confucians, arguably, established their concept of moral equality.

Parents–Children

The relationship between parents and children stands at the centre of the family order. In the Confucian and Israelite structure of the family, the parent–child relationship was the starting point of the formation of a family. From the vertical point of view, parents and children held a central position: from parents the family was extended upwards to grandparents, great-grandparents and eventually to the forebears who were regarded as the fountainhead of the family tradition, and from children it was extended downwards to grandchildren, great-grandchildren and to all future generations who were the future of the family.[7] From the horizontal point of view, parents and children also form the core of the family: parents have their own brothers and sisters who may stay in the same compound to make an extended family, or when married may become heads of new branch families, while children get married and bring outside members into the family.

Parents and children were interlocked in Confucian and Israelite wisdom transmission chains, and from parents to children was considered the most natural and effective way to connect traditional wisdom and current knowledge. In the chain linking parents and children, the hierarchical relation was crucial for the family, and it was believed that only when children learned the discipline of obedience would they understand how to exercise authority over others and over their own children. In the Israelite tradition, parents represented the authority, wisdom and tradition, whose instruction was believed to enable children or the young in general to 'gain insight' (Prov. 4:1). The Israelites and Confucians insisted that the governing principles for family relations were affectionate rather than determining. Even parents must teach children and admonish them when they are wrong; their teaching is given with love: as the Israelite proverb goes, 'the LORD reproves him whom he loves, as a father the son in whom he delights' (Prov. 3:12). Wisdom is attached to the tradition of one's parents, and this makes it possible for wisdom to be transmitted smoothly from ancients to later generations; consequently children are required to 'keep your father's commandment, and forsake not your mother's teaching. Bind them upon your heart always; tie them about your neck' (Prov. 6:20–21). Confucians also took parent–child as the central line for transmitting ancient wisdom, and Confucius

---

[7] The value of lineage is clearly presented in Israelite proverbial wisdom teachings: 'Grandchildren are the crown of the aged' (Prov. 17:6).

defined a good son as the one who followed the way of his parents and continued to do so even after their death (*Analects*, 1:11).

Traditional Confucian and Israelite families were hierarchical, and the parent–child relationship was fulfilled primarily through children performing duties for their parents. The hierarchical order of Confucian and Israelite families reflected the social reality and moral requirements of the time. The proper order between parents and children was part of the world order, and was taken as essential for social and political peace and harmony. Confucian and Israelite justification for the authoritive model of the parent–child relationship ranges from theological and biological to moral.

In terms of theological reasons why parents must take the lead while children must follow, the Israelites appealed to YHWH and his authority: 'For the Lord honoured the father above children, and he confirmed the right of the mother over her sons' (Sir. 3:2). The Israelite teachers argued that it was YHWH's will that being a son meant to listen to one's father's instruction and not to forsake one's mother's teaching (Prov. 1:8–9). Although Confucians did not stress much the creation order of Heaven, they nonetheless took Heaven or Heaven and Earth as the reason for a hierarchical order in the family, as stated in a later Confucian text entitled the *Book of Filial Piety* (*Xiao jing*) 'The Way of parent and child is rooted in the Heavenly moral nature ... Parents give one life; no bond could be greater.'[8]

In terms of the biological and social sequence, parents as the ones first created were in turn the 'creators' of children; parents nurtured and educated children, and were therefore to be taken as the authority. Since one's parents were one's benefactors in the sense that one was reared by them in one's early life, one must repay one's parents by following their orders and serving them with care and respect. This was both biologically and socially significant. 'Hearken to your father who begot you, and do not despise your mother when she is old' (Prov. 23:22). The *Book of Ben Sira* specifically spelled this out: 'Honour your father with all your heart and do not forget your mother's birth-pangs. Remember that your parents brought you into the world; how can you repay them for all that they have done?' (Sir. 7:18–28). A similar idea was also uttered by Confucius who when criticizing one of his disciples who suggested abolishing the three-year mourning rites, argued that the three year rites were simply a means by which one could repay the three years' love parents gave to children in their early years (*Analects*, 17:21).

In terms of moral justification, Confucians and Israelite teachers employed consequentialist arguments to show that fulfilling one's duties to parents would enable one to harvest spiritual and material benefits. 'Whoever honours his father atones for sins, and whoever glorifies his mother is like one who lays up treasure. Whoever honours his father will be gladdened by his own children, and when he

---

[8] *Xiao jing*, Chapter 9, in *Sources of Chinese Tradition – From Earliest Times to 1600*, vol. 1, compiled by Wm Theodore de Bary and Irene Bloom, 2nd edn, New York: Columbia University Press, 1999, p.328.

prays he will be heard. Whoever glorifies his father will have long life, and whoever obeys the Lord will refresh his mother; he will serve his parents as his masters' (Sir. 3:3–7). Conversely, dishonouring one's parents or bringing blame or shame on them was to bring about disasters to oneself and to one's family: 'Honour your father by word and deed, that a blessing from him may come upon you, for a father's blessing strengthens the house of the children, but a mother's curse uproots their foundation' (Sir. 3:8–9). In the Confucian tradition, the dire consequences of being undutiful to parents are also highlighted, as in the Xunzi where we read that 'to be young and yet unwilling to serve one's elders, misfortune will follow' (Xunzi, 5:3).

However, there is a difference in terminology between Confucians and the Israelites. *Shi*, serving or fulfilling one's duties, is a common word for Confucians to express their requirements from children. One of Confucius's disciples, Zi Xia, described as a properly educated gentleman one who 'exerts himself to the utmost in the service of his parents' (*Analects*, 1:7), and demanded that in serving their parents children must act in accordance with properly proscribed rules of propriety (*li*) (*Analects*, 2:5). Mengzi considered serving parents to be the most important of all services (Mengzi, 4A:19). In emphasizing the service to parents, Confucians developed the moral virtue of *xiao*, filial piety or filial love, which has become the backbone of Confucian family wisdom. In the Israelite tradition, 'honouring' is used to prescribe the kind of attitude children should have towards their parents. As a prime theological term, 'honour' is both for (Psalm 29:2) and from YHWH (Eccl. 6:2). By applying this word to the parent–child relationship, the Israelites linked their attitude towards parents with their faith in YHWH; it is significant that, listed after the commandments regarding YHWH, the fifth commandment is 'Honour your father and your mother, that your days may be long in the land which the Lord your God gives you' (Exodus 20:12). It has been argued by some modern scholars that, for some ancient Israelite teachers, to honour one's parents came directly after honouring YHWH, and some have even suggested that the honour due to one's parents is equivalent to that due to YHWH.[9]

However different the words used by Confucians and the Israelites, the teaching concerning parents and children is more or less the same or at least similar. The Confucian filial piety and the Israelite honouring of parents both require that children support, respect and bring honour to their parents, and take care of them when they are old. In a pre-modern society, parents were both the providers of the family's needs and were themselves in need of support when old. Abandoning one's duties towards aged parents would create serious problems for society. Therefore the first requirement of Confucian and Israelite family wisdom was that children serve their old parents and satisfy their physical needs. Of the services children owed to their parents, providing food and clothes (*yang*) was regarded as significant (*Analects*, 1:7; 2:5, 7). Mengzi lists five categories under which a son was seen as an undutiful son; of these the core is his negligence of his duties towards parents since he thus brings

---

⁹ J.D. Cohen (ed.): *The Jewish Family in Antiquity*, Atlanta, Georgia: Scholars Press, 1993, p.65.

harm, shame or humility on his parents:

> First, the neglect of one's parents through laziness of limb. Second, the neglect of
> one's parents through indulgence in the games of *bo* and *yi* and fondness for
> drink. Third, the neglect of one's parents through miserliness in money matters
> and partiality towards one's wife. Fourth, indulgence in sensual pleasures to the
> shame of one's parents. Fifth, a quarrelsome and truculent disposition that
> jeopardises the safety of one's parents. (Mengzi, 8:30)

The Israelites also stressed the help and support children must provide to their
parents,[10] and this was accepted as part of their wisdom teaching. In Proverbs 10:1 we
read, 'A wise son brings joy to his father, but a foolish son grief to his mother'. It is
required that 'help your father in his old age, and do not grieve him as long as he lives'
(Sir. 3:12). From an Israelite standpoint, whoever abandoned their parents in their old
age was like a blasphemer (Sir. 3:16), directly violating the will and wish of YHWH.

The second requirement for Confucians and the Israelites was to respect and please
parents and not to bring dishonour on them. Apart from being responsible for the care
and material support of their aged parents, and for arranging a proper funeral for
deceased parents, children were expected to respect and please their parents. It is clear
that the Israelite family wisdom emphasized honouring and obeying one's parents (Sir
3:1–4) in deed as well as in word (Sir 3:8), serving them as one's masters (Sir. 3:7).
Confucius highly valued respect for parents with sincerity and reverence (*jing*) as the
underlying principle of filial piety (*Analects*, 2:7), while Mengzi even declared that
'When one does not please one's parents, one cannot be a human; when one is not
obedient to one's parents, one cannot be a son' (Mengzi, 4A:28). For Xunzi the
goodness of a young man can be defined by nothing other than respecting, and
submitting himself to, his parents: 'if you are straightforward and diligent, obedient and
respectful of your elders, you are properly called a good youth' (Xunzi, 2:12). This kind
of filial piety became the main theme of later Confucian texts. For example, in the *Book
of Rites*, Zengzi, one of Confucius' disciples, is recorded as saying that 'There are three
kinds of filial piety: the greatest filial piety is to respect one's parents, the second is not to
bring shame on them, and the third is to support them by providing food and clothes.'[11]

The third requirement specified in Confucian and Israelite teachings was concerned
with what children should do in the case of disagreement between parents and children,
especially when the parent went astray. Being given a status of superiority and
authority, parents naturally assumed a higher position in the hierarchical order. The
difference in education and life experience frequently led to disagreements between
parents and children. When this happened, what were children expected to do? The
emphasis was on the virtues of patience and obedience: 'even if he [father] is lacking in
understanding, show forbearance' (Sir. 3:13). Carefully safeguarding family privacy

---

10 Leo G. Perdue *et al.: Families in Ancient Israel*, Louisville: Westminster John Knox Press, 1997,
pp.104–62.

11 Sun Xidan: *Liji Jijie*, vol. 3, p.1225.

and requiring that children should not reveal their parents' wrongdoing, Confucius promoted 'dissuading with respect' as a way to deal with this problem:

> In serving your father and mother you ought to dissuade them from doing wrong in the gentlest way. If you see your advice being ignored, you should not become disobedient but remain reverent. You should not complain even if in so doing you wear yourself out. (*Analects*, 4:18)

Israelite teachers and Confucian masters adopted similar teaching in respect of the parent–child relationship, believing that bringing joy and providing service to parents was wise and the opposite foolish. However, when we closely examine these two kinds of filial teaching against the theoretical bases of Confucianism and the Israelite tradition, we find that their basic motivations are quite different. For Confucians filial piety is *the* most important duty of one's life, and abandoning one's duty to parents is the most unforgivable crime. But for the Israelites, serving and honouring parents can be fully explained only if it is placed in the context of the overall commands of YHWH, and honouring one's parents was simply an example of how one should follow the divine discipline. Confucian filial piety came from the law of Heaven and Earth, and was an anthropocentric norm guiding human behaviour, while the Israelite honouring of parents came from the commandment of the Creator, and was therefore a theocentric ruling that humans must obey.

Husband–Wife

In a traditional society such as that of ancient China or Israel, husband and wife provided the foundation on which a full family was able to come into being. Although parents and children played a leading role in maintaining the family order, husband and wife were biologically prior to them, and their relationship was therefore properly regarded as the pillar supporting all other family relationships. This is illustrated clearly in the book of Genesis where the union of Adam and Eve, the first man and woman, gave birth to Cain and Abel and so the first human family was formed (Genesis 4:1–2). Confucian authors have also made this point in their examination of the family. For example, in the Confucian commentary on the sequence of hexagrams in the *Book of Changes*, it is said that the relationship between husband and wife is the basis of the family: by their union male and female become husband and wife, and by extension they cause parents and children to exist; therefore 'The way of husband and wife must not be other than long-lasting.'[12] Xunzi goes further in arguing that the relationship between husband and wife is the source from which all social and familial relations spring: 'The Way of relations between husband and wife cannot be allowed to be incorrect, for it is the root source for the relations between lord and minister, father and son' (Xunzi, 27:40). For him, when

---

[12] *I Ching or the Book of Changes*, pp.540, 545.

this relation becomes disrupted, it will certainly cause chaos in the family and society: 'then father and son distrust each other, the ruler and the ruled will be in conflict and divided, and invasion and disaster will arrive at the same time' (Xunzi, 17:7).[13]

In the context of Confucian and Israelite family wisdom, the relationship between husband and wife involves the roles husband and wife are each assigned in the family, how to understand gender difference and division in the family, and what virtues should be prescribed to them. In all these aspects, Confucian and Israelite teachings demonstrate substantial similarities as well as subtle divergences. On the whole, both are traditional, hierarchical and patriarchal, with a measure of inequality between husband and wife since the husband is placed on a higher level of the family administration ladder. Specifically, they promote a primeval labour division in which the wife is assigned to internal housework, while the husband assumes a governing position as the head of the family. The wisdom of the wife is seen in her conscious performing of duties towards other members of the family and in her demonstration of female virtues in relation to her husband.

Confucians strongly emphasize the importance and significance of the husband–wife relationship for the family's prosperity and harmony. In Hexagram 37 of the widely circulated version of the *Book of Changes*, the relation between husband and wife is said to be the foundation of the family, while the wife's loyalty and perseverance are defined as the tie that holds the family together. In the following hexagram (No. 38) it is said that the husband–wife relationship is formed in accordance with the universal principle by which two opposites are united and harmonized, and the union of man and woman to become husband and wife is the way of Heaven and Earth: 'Heaven and earth are opposites, but their action is concerted. Man and woman are opposites, but they strive for union.'[14] It is clearly stated in the *Book of Mengzi* that a man and a woman living together is the most important of human relationships (Mengzi, 5A:2). The Israelites understood this from the point of view of creation, viewing the husband–wife union as essential to human nature: since both man and woman were created by YHWH, and particularly since woman was originally part of the man, they were naturally longing for each other: 'a man leaves his father and his mother and cleaves to his wife, and they become one flesh' (Genesis 2:24).

The hierarchical nature of the Confucian and Israelite family means that their wisdom is inevitably biased towards the husband at the expense of the wife. This is in line with their understanding of parents' roles in the household. Of the parents who are considered to be superior to children, the father is clearly given a more authoritive role than the mother; this makes the Confucian and Israelite family not only hierarchical but also patriarchal. It was the father, rather than both father and mother,

---

[13] For this passage, the translation of Wing-tsit Chan is adopted (Wing-tsit Chan: *A Source Book in Chinese Philosophy*, Princeton: Princeton University Press, 1963, p.121).

[14] Yijing (Text: 37). *I Ching or the Book of Changes*, pp.570, 575.

who took charge of moral and educational matters. Modern scholarship has confirmed that, in early Israel, 'The education of the growing youth rests entirely upon the father', and 'Together with actual work and methods of executing it, the son also learnt from his father a wealth of practical wisdom.'[15] This patriarchal tradition inevitably led to a kind of gender discrimination in the husband–wife relationship, allocating a higher position and more important function to the husband, but a lower position and less significant function to wife. The wife was said to help her husband, and this was the intention of YHWH who created Eve from the rib of Adam and called her the 'helper' of the man. In the eyes of the Israelite teachers, the proper family order was that a husband supported his wife, not the other way around: if a wife had to support her husband then there would be 'wrath and impudence and great disgrace' (Sir. 25:22). A wife was expected to follow her husband, and Israelite wisdom even taught that, 'If she does not go as you direct, separate her from yourself' (Sir. 25:26).

Following the model of Heaven and Earth, the Confucian husband–wife relationship also demonstrates a discriminatory tendency, with the husband being taken as a dominant power in the family and the wife obeying and following. The way of a wife is said to be 'obedience and docility' towards her husband (Mengzi, 3B:2). However, in contrast to the vertical patriarchal relation between father and son, where, although affection governed their relationship, a father assumed a much higher position than his son, it seems that Confucians did not particularly emphasize the hierarchy between husband and wife; rather, they viewed the husband–wife relationship as horizontal, and therefore the principle governing this relationship was not 'authoritative' but 'differentiating' (Mengzi, 5A:4), in the sense that husband and wife must be assigned different duties and different roles. This differentiation, according to Xunzi, was the criterion by which the union of man and woman had added values that male and female animals lacked: 'Even though wild animals have parents and offspring, there is no natural affection between them as between father and son, and though there are male and female of the species, there is no proper separation of sexes' (Xunzi, 5:9).

Drawing a proper distinction between the duties of husband and wife was not an invention of Confucians. It prevailed in almost all traditional societies, including that of Israel. It must first be understood as a way of life by which the correct place of the wife was said to be within the family, while that of the husband was without. The wife was confined to household work, while the husband was active in community life and sat 'among the elders of the land' (Prov. 31:23). As part of the social and labour division, Confucians considered the separate duties of husband and wife to have been instituted by the wise, and therefore central to family wisdom. We presume that originally there was no separation between male and female and between husband and wife; however, as human wisdom developed, it was found necessary to have proper rules regulating the male–female and the husband–wife relationships

---

[15] Ludwig Köhler, 1956, pp.73, 74.

within the family, in order to maintain family harmony and prosperity, as Xunzi made clear: 'If there were no ritual principles governing the union of man and woman, the separation of duties between husband and wife … people would suffer the grief of losing any means to marital union and the calamity of contention for sex' (Xunzi, 10:1).

Separating husband and wife was also taken to be a necessary means to ensure that men and women would not mix unnecessarily, thus violating proper codes and laws. These codes and laws were already extremely strict and delicate in pre-Confucian China and were widely accepted as the norm. In the *Book of Mengzi* we read, 'in giving and receiving, men and women should not touch each other' (Mengzi, 4A:17), and in the *Book of Xunzi* the separation between men and women is said to be one of the criteria by which humans beings are distinguished from wild beasts (Xunzi, 5:10). Similar observation can also be found in ancient Israelite society and family, where there were 'strict custom, religious attitudes concerning the taboos on everything sexual'.[16] However, Confucians and the Israelites did not go to the extreme of instituting a code of conduct totally separating husband from wife; rather they saw the couple in a mutually supplementary relation. The emotional needs of husband and wife for each other had to be met, and the Confucian moral code for the relationship was not only one of separating, but also 'rejoicing' (*huan*, Xunzi, 10:6). As in Israel happiness in the family was valued, and a husband was taught to 'enjoy life with your wife, whom you love' (Eccl. 9:9), and a good wife is good because she 'rejoices her husband' (Sir. 26:2). However, this rejoicing must be guarded against slipping into a 'promiscuous' relation (*yin luan*, Xunzi, 17:7), and against improper contact between men and women, and so the Israelite proverb makes it clear that whoever touches his neighbour's wife will be severely punished (Prov. 7:29).

A proper separation of the duties of husband and wife points in an ethical direction. There is a long list of moral requirements for the Confucian and Israelite woman and wife. A wife was expected to have a noble character, to which the man was attracted, and indeed the Israelites considered such a wife 'her husband's crown' (Prov. 12:4). Of the noble character such virtues as silence, discipline, modesty and steadfastness are particularly praised by Israelite wisdom teachers (Sir. 26:13–18), while Confucian masters emphasized that a wife 'must be respectful and circumspect. Do not disobey your husband' (Mengzi, 3B:2). This is further extended in the *Book of Rites* to include such virtues as 'following' (*ting*) her husband, 'faithfulness or chastity' (*xin*) to her husband, and 'obedience' (*cong*) to her husband and in-laws.[17] The noble character of the wife was seen in her contribution to family life, for example, providing food for the family, working diligently, carefully planning the family economy, being generous to the poor and 'the needy' (Prov. 31:10–20). A wife of noble character was also expected to be wise and she 'opens her mouth with wisdom, and the teaching of kindness is on her tongue' (Prov. 31:26), and is in stark

---

[16] Ludwig Köhler, 1956, p.94.

[17] Sun Xidan: *Liji Jijie*, vol. 2, Beijing: Zhonghua Shuju, 1989, pp.607, 707, 709.

contrast to a foolish one 'who is noisy, wanton and knows no shame' (Prov. 9:13). While a wise wife was expected to fulfil her responsibilities towards her husband, a man had parallel, but much fewer, moral requirements towards his wife. First, a wise man should marry a woman of noble character and not to be attracted solely by charm and beauty, because he knew that 'charm is deceitful, and beauty is vain' (Prov. 31:30), and that 'happy is he who lives with an intelligent wife' (Sir. 25:8). Secondly, a husband was expected to 'praise' his faithful wife and 'give her the rewards she has earned' (Prov. 31:28–31).

A moral concept of the union between a man and a woman will necessarily require a safeguard against abusing or improperly engaging in it. Therefore both Confucians and the Israelites placed great importance on certain moral rules or rites governing marriage and contact between male and female. As in many other ancient societies, early China and Israel saw marriage primarily as the means of social connections, not something resulting from sexual attraction. In Israel 'Marriages were more the affair of the family and of convention, than matters of strong personal inclination and individual choice',[18] and improper contact between man and woman was always condemned as an immoral sin or fault. For this reason strict rules were instituted to confine young women to certain boundaries: 'Keep strict watch over a headstrong daughter, lest, when she finds liberty, she use it to her hurt' (Sir. 26:10). In China, marriage must be arranged through the command of the parents and the mediation of a go-between, while those who met illicitly were condemned; Mengzi made clear that although all parents wanted their sons and daughters to be married one day, this must proceed according to proper rites: 'Those who bore holes in the wall to peep at one another, and climb over it to meet illicitly, waiting for neither the command of parents nor the good offices of a go-between, are despised by parents and fellow countrymen alike' (Mengzi, 3B:3).

Both Confucian and Israelite masters were worried that men in general were more attracted to the beauty and charm of women than to their good character, and warned that unregulated male–female relationships would lead to nothing but disaster. To prevent it from happening, they adopted two strategies. On the one hand, they suppressed women by arguing that women were less virtuous in their character than men. Confucius thus equated women and morally underdeveloped people or 'small men' (*xiao ren*), believing that they were most difficult to deal with (*Analects*, 17:25), while a wisdom teacher of Israel made the claim that 'I found one "upright" man among a thousand, but not one "upright" woman among them all' (Eccl. 7:28), and kept alive the traditional belief that 'From a woman sin had its beginning, and because of her we all die' (Sir. 25:24). On the other hand, Confucians and the Israelites warned men against being attracted by the beauty of women. Confucius deplored the fact that he had not yet met a man who was fond of virtue as much as beauty in women (*Analects*, 15:13), and called on young men to 'guard against the attraction of the feminine beauty' (*Analects*, 16:7), while the book of Proverbs warns

---

[18] Ludwig Köhler, 1956, pp.90–91.

men or particularly young men to keep away from 'the immoral or loose woman': 'Do not lust in your heart after her beauty or let her captivate you with her eyes' (Prov. 6:24–5), because 'her house is the way to Sheol, going down to the chambers of death' (Prov. 7:27).

Social and Political Wisdom

The political landscapes of early China as envisaged in Confucian conversations and of Israel as perceived by its wisdom texts were quite different. In China under the kings of the Zhou dynasty, there were dozens of semi-independent states which developed sophisticated administrative systems, both corresponding to the Zhou codes of rites and accommodating the actual needs of each state, while in Israel such a system did not exist. For most of Israelite history the 'state' was indeed no more than 'a kind of confederacy', where the political infrastructure as frequently referred to in the texts was not well developed. As scholars have pointed out, the 'kingdom established by Saul and David was more a community created by necessity than a living unity', and the split after the death of Solomon did not make either of the two states any more strongly unified than before, which proves again that in Israel 'there was only a framework, and not a pattern which really bound together all the members into one whole'.[19] By comparison, political wisdom as a systematic way of thinking in Israel was much less developed and played a much less important role than that in China. In terms of political wisdom, the Israelite teachers gave much more attention to the practical dimension of politics, placing emphasis on juristic and administrative skills, while Confucians inclined more to the theoretical aspects of politics, laying down metaphysical–ethical principles for political governing.[20]

Having said this, one must not fail to notice a similarity of political thought between these two such geographically distant countries and dramatically different cultures, where Confucians and the Israelites developed and promoted knowledge and understanding in the field of political relations and activities, and demonstrated political wisdom of a similar nature.

In traditional Confucian and Israelite societies, political insight grew out of their appreciation of the family and family relations, and there was a close connection between household management and state administration, and between familial and political wisdom, albeit in different ways. This point is not made particularly explicit in Israelite texts, although it is evident that there are plenty of proverbs that maintain that things bad for the family would also destroy the rulers of the state (Prov. 31:3),

---

[19] Ludwig Köhler, 1956, p.150.

[20] What we are discussing as Confucian wisdom is drawn from their theoretical ideas. However, as has been pointed out, 'the existence of a theory influences one's perception of reality', which in turn guides both how history is written and how real government is constructed (June Teufel Dreyer: *China's Political System – Modernization and Tradition*, 3rd edn, revised and updated, London: Macmillan Press, 2000, p.25).

and there is widespread agreement that the family and the state are governed by the same principles and norms (Sir. 10:1). By contrast, the association of family and political wisdom is the most significant part of the Confucian way of thinking. In the *Analects of Confucius* it is said that a son good to his parents and brothers at home will never transgress against his superiors and have any inclination to rebel (*Analects*, 1:2), while Mengzi defines good sons as those who 'in the family serve their fathers and elder brothers, and outside the family, serve their elders and superiors' (Mengzi, 1:5). In practice, Confucian political parameters were set up in correspondence to the requirements of the family, by which the ruler (king or lord) and the father assumed the highest position, respectively, within the state and the family, as stated in the *Book of Xunzi*: 'The lord is the most exalted in the state. The father is the most exalted in the family' (Xunzi, 14:8). Consequently, the same moral principles were applied to both family and political relationships, and it was strongly believed that failing to do so would corrupt people's hearts and result in chaotic situations: 'between lord and minister there is no honoured position, between father and son no affection; between elder and younger brother no submissiveness, and between husband and wife no rejoicing' (Xunzi, 27:41). In this sense, we may say that Confucian politics is essentially an ethic, while its political wisdom is based on ethical wisdom. As Mengzi summarizes, its aim is to educate individual persons into moral agents, by which the familial and social harmony can be maintained: 'The Empire has its basis in the state, the state in the family, and the family in one's own self' (Mengzi, 4A:5).

Although in different ways addressing political problems, Confucian and Israelite political wisdom both aimed to provide justifiable means to enable the state to function well and to enable peace and harmony to last. To reach this goal, Confucian masters and Israelite teachers pioneered two interconnected pathways by which they hoped to construct a good government: revering the tradition and ordering society.

Revering Tradition

Both Confucians and Israelite teachers held on to tradition, believing that the tradition of the past provided a blueprint for personal and social life in the present. The Confucian and Israelite traditions were inherited from oral and written histories, each with a clear hallmark of its own culture and spirituality. However, 'tradition' for them does not mean everything historical. Rather, it represents the 'good' part of the memorable past, while the bad elements are used as a contrast to illustrate why the good tradition must be honoured and carried on. Taking 'revering tradition' as the primary tool to solve contemporary political problems and to engage state administration makes Confucian and Israelite wisdom clearly diverge from many other political thought systems, where penal laws and punishment are taken as an effective enforcement of order.

Studies of ancient Israel reveal that 'The Hebrew depends upon tradition. He holds to what has been handed down. A man learns from his father and ancestors what he should do'; the Israelites adhered to tradition which was seen not only as past experience but also the living experience of the present, and this mentality fundamentally shaped how everyday life was ordered and communal activities were regulated, because 'Where tradition is firm and is respected by all, everything follows automatically.' Ancient Israel was not particularly well known for its civil and penal law system, which was indeed 'not comprehensive in its regulations, nor is it unified in the principles of its selection', again because 'When tradition is sufficiently alive and clear, there is no need for legal regulation.'[21] What was the tradition? The answer to this question makes 'revering tradition' in Israel stand out as a distinctive doctrine and practice. To ancient Israelites, tradition was associated with the conviction that YHWH favoured their ancestors, made covenants with them, and enabled them to establish 'Israel' on the promised land.[22] Israelite wisdom converged again on the authority and power of YHWH, who 'appointed a ruler for every nation, but Israel is the Lord's own portion' (Sir. 17:17). In this tradition, the codes of conduct and 'law' were all sacred, in the sense that they were either directly given by God or were derived from divine commandments. Because of the sacred nature of rules, norms and laws, for humans to follow them was not only a political requirement, but also a religious necessity. Therefore, in Israel politics was always interwoven with religious faith; the two were never separated from each other.

For the authors or compilers of the Confucian texts the sacred past was represented by the golden age of the three dynasties when sage–kings ruled the world and when the empire was in peace and harmony. This tradition was cultivated in the belief that through their intelligent observation and insight, the sages or sage–kings had instituted a wide range of norms that not only enabled humans to be distinguished from animals, but also refined human emotions and intelligence, and that by following these codes of conduct human relationships were dealt with appropriately and state administration was carried out most effectively. In this sense, 'revering tradition' was identified with honouring sagely instruction or teaching. Although sagely or sage–kings' teachings were also thought to be 'holy', originally full of religious meanings in the sense that they manifested or revealed the will or mandate of Heaven (*tian ming*), the connection between the 'tradition' and the religious ultimate was so loosely made that it became possible for Confucians to separate 'revering tradition' from religious faith practices, and to define political wisdom as following the tradition of the ancient past. In this way, 'revering the tradition' is redefined as a moral and political matter of concern. It was through their moral and

---

[21] Ludwig Köhler, 1956, pp.138, 141, 142.

[22] In the Hebrew texts there is a 'genitive phrase *yôm* YHWH, "day of Yahweh"', representing the divine tradition. OT scholars have interpreted this phrase in a variety of ways; some suggest it refers to 'a very ancient complex of eschatological ideas involving salvation and deliverance, rooted in nature mythology'; some point to 'Israel's traditions of (theological) history as a better interpretative background', and others propose that it has a specific connection with 'traditions associated with the ancient holy war' (*Theological Dictionary of the Old Testament*, ed. G. Johannes Botterweck and Helmer Ringgren, trans. John T. Willis, Grand Rapids, Michigan: William B. Eerdmans Publishing Company, 1977, vol. VI, p.29).

educational reinterpretation of the tradition that Confucians put great emphasis on 'revering the past': to honour the remote past was to enable the 'virtue of common people' to incline towards fullness (*Analects*, 1:9). At the same time, revering tradition also defines how Confucian politics operates in society, which in Xunzi's words is to establish moral models for people to follow, because

> If things are assigned to their proper position on the basis of the model of the sage kings, one will know what is valuable; if a sense of moral rightness is used to regulate undertakings, one will know what is beneficial ... Thus, those who honoured sages became kings; those who valued the worthy became lords-protector; those who respected the worthy survived; and those that scorned them were destroyed. (Xunzi, 24:5)

Confucian and Israelite ways of political thinking have many commonalities, but are nevertheless distinguishable from each other. Different understandings of the sacred past lead further to their differences in political applications of how the state should be governed. This makes their political wisdom both convergent and divergent, with differences in similarity and similarities in difference.

For the Israelites, political matters must be placed on a religious foundation to be understood and sorted out. Therefore revering tradition was identified with revering wisdom that had a sacred source and was of a sacred nature. Wisdom was thus considered to be the most important factor in personal life as well as in political construction; as was said, 'the desire for wisdom leads to a kingdom' (Wisd. 6:20). Between secular forces and sacred wisdom, wisdom determined the fortune and destiny of the ruler, as 'A king is not saved by his great army' (Psalm 33:16), and without conforming to the commandments of YHWH, a king was doomed. Since 'The LORD by wisdom founded the earth; by understanding he established the heavens' (Prov. 3:19), human rulers must also honour wisdom in their ruling of the world: 'If you delight in thrones and sceptres, O monarchs over the peoples, honour wisdom, that you may reign for ever' (Wisd. 6:21). From this belief it seems natural for the Israelite teachers to reason that the state must be ruled in wisdom and by wisdom, and only the wise should be given the right to rule, because with wisdom one will have counsel and sound knowledge, insight and strength. The personalized divine wisdom declares, 'By me kings rule, and rulers decree what is just; by me princes rule, and nobles govern the earth' (Prov. 8:15–16). Wisdom is more important than the ruling power and more precious than wealth; in comparison to wisdom, any priceless gem becomes devoid of value; gold is a little sand, and silver clay. Wisdom is also more needed than health and beauty; we enjoy them only because all good things are brought about by wisdom (Wisd. 7:7–12). Wisdom enables the ruler to set a good example for the people to follow: 'A wise magistrate will educate his people, and the rule of an understanding man will be well ordered. Like the magistrate of the people, so are his officials; and like the ruler of the city, so are all its inhabitants' (Sir. 10:1–2).

Following the moralization of ancient history and culture, Confucians took virtue as the core of the tradition. Confucius strongly disagreed with the legalistic politics which required the state to be guided by edicts or penal laws and kept in line with punishments. He argued that, although these measures or policies would make the common people not dare to commit crimes or stir up trouble, the people refrained from doing so, not because they were ashamed of these wrongdoings, but because they were afraid of punishment, and as soon as the risks of being punished were lessened, they would go on rebelling again. By contrast, Confucius argued, if we guided them by virtue and kept them in line with the rites, they would, besides having a sense of shame, reform themselves (*Analects*, 2:3). In the same vein, Confucius redefined political governing as exercising exemplars of moral influence. For him administration required nothing other than setting up good examples for the people to follow, and a ruler or the superior of a virtuous character would be naturally followed by his subjects or the junior. Confucius thus compared the rule of virtue with the Pole Star that would remain at its own place while the multitude of stars paid their homage to it (*Analects*, 2:1). Among various virtues, Confucius particularly emphasized the effectiveness of *xin* (faith, faithfulness or trust) for political administration. When being asked what was government, Confucius listed three elements as essential to the existence of government: providing people with sufficient food, equipping the state with sufficient military force, and establishing faith or trustfulness among the people. When further pressed as to which of these three was the most important, he ruled out food and military force, insisting that, without faith or trust, 'the common people would have nothing to stand on' (*Analects*, 12:7).

Ordering Society

Just as they believed that the world was predetermined by the (religious or natural) cosmic order and that the family was functional through the family order, early Confucians and the Israelites were convinced that the political realm must also have an order that was based on the cosmic order and closely associated with the family order. Does the early Confucian and Israelite concept of wisdom imply a 'unity' or 'harmony' between these different presentations of the world order? Although it is generally agreed that the authors of the wisdom literature in the Old Testament used 'cosmic order' and 'social order' to illuminate one another, which implies the influence of one order upon the other, there is a disagreement concerning whether or not these orders were believed to impinge upon each other. The paradigm of wisdom in Israelite wisdom literature highlights questions regarding symmetries between the underlying order of the world and the regulation of human society, as well as issues concerning diverse strategies for disseminating wisdom within the different layers of society.

Instead of taking the Way of Heaven as purely externally transcendent, most Confucians understood it as immanent in humans, so that the Way of Heaven was closely related to the way of humans, and was manifested in personal, familial and political life. Early Confucians strongly contested the belief that humans must behave in accord with the cosmic order, and the Way of Heaven was the underlying reason for social harmony. However, they did not proceed to argue that there was a strictly corresponding relationship between human action and Heaven. The mutual responsiveness between Heaven and humans became the underlying principle of Confucian political wisdom only in the much later Han period (206 BCE–220CE).

As far as the political realm is concerned, Confucian and Israelite texts reveal a belief that social problems are nothing more than problems caused by the disruption or corruption of the social order, and that the only way to social peace and harmony is through restoring the order. The order in Confucian and Israelite politics was hierarchical, in the sense that political and social life was sustained as a social ladder on which each of the social classes, groups, professions and individuals was allocated a specifically defined position with corresponding rights and responsibilities. The primary task of government was thus to set up state regulations to define these positions, rights and duties, and to enforce their fulfilment in an orderly way.

In contrast to a common misunderstanding that a hierarchical order merely means the dominating power of the higher classes over the lower, Confucians and the Israelites taught that a properly functioning hierarchy placed a greater responsibility on the shoulders of the superior who had, in one way or another, undertaken leadership, and specified different but corresponding requirements for the superior and the junior so that they fulfilled their own responsibilities to each other. Therefore two features make Confucian and Israelite wisdom distinctive. First, the higher one is on the hierarchical ladder, the heavier the responsibilities one carries. Second, however low one is on the ladder, performing one's duties requires that all others including those above also fulfil their duties.

In Israelite wisdom literature, as regards the consequential considerations, the inferior or the poor or the weak are reminded again and again that they must heed authority, but at the same time the superior or the rich or the strong are also reminded that they must fulfil their responsibilities. This is, in the mind of the Israelite teachers, the justice of YHWH. In a similar way, Confucian wisdom also promotes the mutuality of political requirements and responsibilities. On the one hand, Confucius disapproves strongly of those people who resist 'the authority of their superiors' (*Analects*, 1:2), and almost all Confucian masters take 'loyalty to one's superior or ruler' as one of the prime virtues. On the other hand, loyalty must not be given without a price, and should only be offered to a ruler or king when he is virtuous and benevolent. Confucius insists that the moral responsibility of the ruler is to employ the service of his subjects in accordance with the rites, while a subject should serve his ruler in loyalty (*Analects*, 3:19). Mengzi directly requires that, if a prince wants to achieve great things, he should go to his subjects and consult them, and declares that if 'he does not honour virtue and delight in the Way in such a manner, he is not worthy of being helped' (Mengzi, 2B:2). For Xunzi, the superior must be able to love those who are inferior to him, and the inferior must be able to honour and respect his superior. Otherwise, 'To occupy a superior position and yet be unable to love those inferior to him or to occupy an inferior position and to be fond of condemning his superior – this is the first way to bring certainty of dire need' (Xunzi, 5:3).

Confucians and the Israelites reveal a significant agreement in their diagnosis that social and political problems arise from the fact that people in their positions do not perform their responsibilities, and that the wrong people are put in wrong positions. However, their prescriptions are different, one attempting to rectify all political chaos and disorder by a moral and educational approach, while the other extending religious solutions to the social and political realm. Different as they are, the two prescriptions are nevertheless mutually translatable in the light of hermeneutical principles, as set out in Chapter 1.

Central to Israelite political wisdom is the conviction that 'righteousness exalts a nation' (Prov. 14:34). It is believed that the prosperity of the state and happiness of the people come from wisdom and uprightness, as Proverbs says, 'When it goes well with the righteous, the city rejoices; when the wicked perish there are shouts of gladness. By the blessing of the upright a city is exalted, but it is overthrown by the mouth of the wicked' (Prov. 11:10–11). At this point we find an interesting comparison with Confucian understanding of the political function of the words. When asked if there is a saying that can lead a state to prosperity, Confucius responded that, although not every word would produce such a dramatic effect, the ruler must understand the difficulties of being a ruler, and, if he can do so, he will be careful about what he says and his word will naturally lead the state to prosperity. When again asked if there was a saying that could lead the state to ruin, Confucius replied that if no one went against whatever the ruler said, the words of the ruler would no doubt lead the state to ruin (*Analects*, 13:15).

Wisdom attracts people from all other nations to the state: 'Through one man of understanding a city will be filled with people' (Sir. 16:4). Modern scholars have observed that 'The profoundest content of the tradition, of the ordering of practice, law and custom, is righteousness', which at the individual level means that 'each man should give the other his rights'.[23] In other words, righteousness is equated with justice when all people are given what they deserve and are expected to do what their responsibility requires. Each person has the position and rights he deserves. If all the people are in their right positions and enjoy their proper rights, the world is at peace; otherwise, chaos and evil will inevitably follow. Maintaining hierarchy is thus taken as the way to maintain social order. Israelite proverbs tell us that there are four things that the earth cannot bear, of which the first two are 'a slave when he becomes king, and a fool when he is filled with food' (Prov. 30:21–2). The disrupted hierarchy leads to misplacing people or putting them in wrong positions, which is intolerable in the eyes of the author of the book of Ecclesiastes: 'There is an evil which I have seen under the sun, as it were an error proceeding from the ruler: Folly is set in many high places, and the rich sit in a low place. I have seen slaves on horses, and princes walking on foot like slaves' (Eccl. 10:5–7).

If we understand the Israelite principle of social righteousness essentially as different people being put in different positions and fulfilling their respective responsibilities, it can be roughly translated into the Confucian principle of rectifying

---

[23] Ludwig Köhler, 1956, p.148.

names and behaviour. Confucius regarded the rectification of names as the first thing he would do if he had the chance of administering the state. 'To govern means to rectify' (*Analects*, 12:17). The prescription Confucius made for his time was 'Let the ruler be a ruler, the subject a subject, the father a father, the son a son' (*Analects*, 12:11), which means, in plain language, that all people must think and behave as they are socially required and fulfil their own responsibilities as politically defined. Rectifying names and behaviour was seen not only as a secular necessity but also as a spiritually justified norm, because all familial and social relationships were based on the universal principle of Heaven and Earth and their forms would last forever, as Xunzi pointed out: 'The relationships between lord and minister, father and son, older and younger brother, husband and wife, begin as they end and end as they begin, share with Heaven and Earth the same organizing principle, and endure in the same form through all eternity' (Xunzi, 9:18).

Israelite political wisdom is to establish a just society based on the righteous hearts of the people.[24] A just society is established on the rule of justice and on the goodness of the people, and the Israelites believe that 'Lawlessness will lay waste the whole earth, and evil-doing will overturn the thrones of rulers' (Wisd. 5:23). To overcome evil and to rectify the wrong, a king or ruler must rule and administer righteously, not only securing the social order, but also protecting the rights of weak classes, as the mother of the king of Massa taught her son: 'Open your mouth for the dumb, for the rights of all who are left desolate. Open your mouth, judge righteously, maintain the rights of the poor and needy' (Prov. 31:9). To maintain a just society, a king or ruler must also be wise and gain understanding, which cannot easily be done through secular means, but must be achieved by religious faith: 'Evil men do not understand justice; only those who seek the LORD understand it completely' (Prov. 28:5). Politics and religion are thus converged or, in other words, Israelite political wisdom is essentially religious wisdom, because both are extensions of faith in YHWH, the creator of the world as well as political order: 'The government of the earth is in the hands of the Lord' (Sir. 10:4).

Confucian masters also believe that the root of chaos and disorder is in human hearts and minds. However, unlike their counterparts in Israel, who resort to the spiritual ultimate for the final solution, Confucians explore two interrelated ways to root out the source of evil or wrongdoing. Inwardly, Confucius calls people to restrain or overcome themselves (*ke ji*) and, externally, he demands the full observation of the rites (*fu li*). By these two means Confucius has transformed

---

[24] Political wisdom in Israel is very much associated with skill and ability in running a government, whether a small tribe or a big political entity. It refers to skills and abilities in running the state (Genesis 41:39) and it is the prudence of the chieftain of a tribe or the leader of community (Deuteronomy 1:13, 15). It can be morally neutral, to say the least; the devious plan which Jon'adab suggested by which Amnon might rape Tamar is called wise or crafty (2 Samuel 13:3), and so is the craft by which Solomon is expected to create a trap for Joab (1 Kings 2:9). David is said to have wisdom 'like the wisdom of the angel of God to know all things that are on earth' (2 Samuel 14:20). Wisdom to render judgement is required in the judge (1 Kings 3:28) (John L. McKenzie, S.J.: *Dictionary of the Bible*, London/Dublin: Geoffrey Chapman, 1980, p.930).

politics into ethics, and intertwined political wisdom with ethical wisdom. The self is located in the central position in the Confucian ethical system and is held to be responsible for the kind of people we are. Through moral cultivation, Confucians believe, the virtues of the self are extended to the family, community, society and the world, and all problems are sorted out morally. The importance of the self for political peace and harmony explains why Confucians call for all people to take self-cultivation as their foundation. Self-cultivation is a conscious activity within. However, it is not totally separated from the so-called teaching and discipline we have received. We need external rules and norms to help guide our action and support our internal transformation. This is the role of the rites or codes of conduct. When Confucius explains how the world can achieve virtue, justice and order, he makes use of the rites as binding norms for all thinking and behaving: 'Do not look unless it is in accordance with the rites; do not listen unless it is in accordance with the rites; do not speak unless it is in accordance with the rites; do not move unless it is in accordance with the rites' (*Analects*, 12:1). For Confucians, rites or ritual principles or moral codes are the primary means by which the social order is maintained: 'a man without ritual principle will not live, an undertaking without ritual principle will not succeed, and a nation without ritual principle will not be tranquil' (Xunzi, 27:43).

Wisdom and the Wise King Paradigm

Conforming to a particular political order does not come automatically; it must be either enforced by coercive means or brought about through teaching and example. Both Confucians and the Israelites have excluded the former from their political wisdom. In line with the political strategies of revering tradition and ordering society, they particularly idealized and reconstructed history and took some of the ancient kings as exemplary sages, wise kings or sage–kings, from whose reigns or wise teachings a ruling paradigm was created as a model for the way the state should be ruled.[25] A significant part of Confucian and Israelite teaching concerning the ruling paradigm was focused on two themes: what patterns are those of the expected kingly behaviour; in other words, how should a king behave to meet the criteria of wisdom, and what attitudes are ordinary people expected to adopt towards their rulers?

---

[25] The creation and function of the sage–king paradigm was perhaps more indigenous to the Confucian way of thinking than to Israelite religion. When examining the paradigm in China, Julia Ching comments, 'I speak of the *paradigm* because the institution of kingship goes back, in principle, to the sages of a mystical past, and became, for later generations, an ideal of striving, embodying all the virtues of humane government, as well as of a humanity open to the beyond'; 'And the ancient texts that supported the sage-king paradigm were all enshrined in a canon of Confucian classics, becoming thereby also a repository of sagely authority, to be manipulated by the scribes and exegetes who interpreted them under the supervision of the state' (*Mysticism and Kingship in China: The Heart of Chinese Wisdom*, Cambridge University Press, 1997, pp.xiv–xv).

Wise Kings and Sage–Kings

A number of the kings in Chinese and Israelite history are drawn upon to provide such a ruling paradigm. Comparatively speaking, far fewer Israelite figures are particularly introduced in the wisdom texts as exemplary kings; in fact only King David (1000–965 or 961BCE), King Solomon (965/961–922BCE) and King Hezekiah (715–687BCE) make their appearance in the Hebrew texts,[26] while in Confucianism a good number of ancient kings are called 'sages'[27] or 'former kings' and their reigns and teachings are believed to be *the* source of wisdom. Among these legendary or historical figures are Yao, Shun and Yu of the remote past, and the founding kings of the Zhou dynasty (1045?–256BCE), King Wen (Wen Wang, 1099/56–1050BCE) and King Wu (Wu Wang, 1049–1043BCE), with the Duke of Zhou (Zhou Gong, 1042–1036) as the royal regent for his nephew, the young King Cheng (Cheng Wang, 1042/35–1006BCE).[28]

For the purpose of examining Confucian and Israelite wisdom paradigms, it is not important whether these kings actually behaved in a particular way or not, or if the people under their rule were as reverent as they were said to have been. In most cases we have insufficient evidence either to prove or disprove what is said about them, and must issue a primary caution in the following two ways. First, these kings themselves might not have played a role as vital as is claimed in Confucian and Israelite wisdom texts in wisdom transmission. We should understand them more as part of the reconstructed paradigm than as actual historical figures, and take them as the models that are used to illustrate the kinds of behaviour and attitude that are morally, politically and religiously justified, either for the ruler in treating his subjects or for the people in dealing with their king. Secondly, while it is important for us to note the kingly way of behaviour and wise teaching attributed to them underlying the Israelite and Confucian ruling paradigm, we must take into consideration the question of Katharine Dell, when she examines the role played by King Solomon in Hebrew wisdom texts: 'How far are these sayings specific to a royal context? Are they simply

---

[26] 'Chronological Tables of Rulers' in *The New Oxford Annotated Bible*, New York: Oxford University Press, 1977, pp.1548–79. For details of these kings and their reigns, see J. Maxwell Miller and John H. Hayes, 1986.

[27] Julia Ching has explained, 'The term *sheng* or "sage" refers to a wise and virtuous man, usually a ruler in a remote antiquity. Etymologically, the oracle bone graph is made up of a big ear and a small mouth. It is closely associated with acute hearing, perhaps hearing the voice of the spirits, and perhaps also communicating something of what has been heard' (Julia Ching: *Chinese Religions*, London: Macmillan Press, 1993, p.23). For this word in oracle bonze inscriptions, see Xu Zhongshu's *Jiaguwen zidian* (*Dictionary of Oracle Bonze Inscriptions*), Chengdu: Sichuan Cishu Chubanshe, 1990, p.1287.

[28] Dates are from Michael Loewe and Edward L. Shaughnessy (eds): *The Cambridge History of Ancient China – From the Origin of Civilization to 221 B.C.*, Cambridge University Press, 1999, p.25. For a philosophical discussion of the wisdoms of these sages or sage–kings in China, see Julia Ching, 1997.

reflections on wider wisdom principles, the king being used in an exemplary role?'[29]

Whether deriving from the royal tradition or from general life experience, Confucian and Israelite masters conscientiously created a wisdom paradigm by using figures of the past, and applied this paradigm to their political thought and practice. First, the wise king paradigm was a way to swing people's moral and religious attitude. Holding the highest position on earth, the value of Confucian sage–kings and Israelite wise kings was not seen in their enforcing order upon the people; rather they were taken as educational models to encourage all people to imitate and to follow, by which political wisdom is gained, as Mengzi asked, 'Can one be deemed wise if, in governing the people, one fails to take advantage of the way of the Former Kings?' (Mengzi, 4A:1).

Secondly, the paradigm was deeply imbedded in their mentality of revering tradition. The wisdom of wise kings or sage–kings was associated with their ancestors, and glories they brought themselves and the state were said to be due, at least partially, to the merits of their fathers or forefathers. Confucians were essentially ancestors-oriented in deliberating on the source of wisdom; the Israelites also implicitly stressed that ancestors were instrumental to the wisdom of the wise king, as indicated in the Book of Ben Sira which asserts that Solomon 'overflowed like a river with understanding' and was loved for his peace; there was not the slightest doubt in the mind of the author that Solomon's wisdom was an award God gave in consideration of his father David's merits (Sir. 47:12–17).[30]

Thirdly, the invoking of ancient kings was a way to lend authority to the wisdom teaching of the present. It was clearly more effective to quote from the most respected figures in history to admonish the ruler than directly to blame him for his failures. This functioned not only as an encouragement of contemporary kings, but also as a warning for those who were, potentially, going to rebel or who contemplated becoming wicked. The wisdom of ancient kings exerted a positive influence over the people and punished rebellion or transgression to protect the peace and security of the state. In China the sage–kings were frequently contrasted with evil kings or usurpers, and in Israel the wise ruling of a king was in direct contrast to foolish policies and strategies. While, through the former, glory and prosperity were brought about, from the latter, disaster and punishment were bound to result.

---

[29] Katharine Dell, 'The King in the Wisdom Literature', in *King and Messiah in Israel and the Ancient Near East – Proceedings of the Oxford Old Testament Seminar*, ed. John Day, *Journal for the Study of the Old Testament*, Supplement Series 270, Sheffield: Sheffield Academic Press, 1998, pp.163–86.

[30] Here we find a negative image of King Solomon who despite his intelligence and wisdom, failed to maintain the peace: because 'you laid your loins beside women, and through your body you were brought into subjection'; therefore 'You put a stain upon your honour, and defiled your posterity' (Sir. 47:19–20). While we find it interesting how the positive (intelligence) and the negative (body) were divided in the case of King Solomon and left two different legacies, it is not our primary concern in this book.

The Wise King Paradigm and the King–People Relationship

There is a strong tradition of upright and wise kings in the deuteronomic history where David is conceived as the upright king *par excellence* and Solomon is praised because his 'wisdom surpassed the wisdom of all the peoples of the East, and all the wisdom of Egypt' (1 Kings 4:30). Inheriting, or in line with, this tradition, the wisdom texts explore the wisdom images to expand wise teachings, and take wise kings as the ruling paradigm. Even later wisdom works also make the effort to strengthen the paradigm; for example, the Wisdom of Solomon explicitly attributes its teaching to King Solomon, the paragon of Hebrew wisdom, and in the Book of Ben Sira a section is particularly devoted to the praising of ancient kings and ancestors who ruled in their kingdoms and were renowned for their power, and credits them with cultural innovation such as composing 'musical tunes' and setting 'forth verses in writing' (Sir. 44:5).

Of all the Israelite kings, Solomon is an outstanding figure for Hebrew and Greek wisdom texts. Modern scholars agree that 'Solomon is a major biblical figure' and a not-insignificant part of several Old Testament books is concerned with 'his wisdom and his great success, the building of the Temple'.[31] Whether directly or indirectly, in the wisdom texts the ideal of the wise king was lent narrative form in the figure of Solomon. There is a double role Solomon plays in the Israelite paradigm. On the one hand; Solomon is taken as the model itself, and his reign is said to be a period of remarkable social and political development, of economic organization and expansion, of centralized power, court life, and successful international relations: 'Solomon's reign was "the golden age" of Israelite and Judean history ... The compilers of Genesis–II Kings depicted Solomon as exceedingly wise, exceptionally wealthy, and extremely powerful.'[32] On the other hand, more importantly, Solomon is central to transmission of wisdom, and it has been suggested that 'the success of the Solomonic attribution ... was fixed and edited more or less definitely during the post-exilic period'.[33] There are constant references to Solomonic patronage and even authorship of wisdom texts.[34] For Proverbs, 'the attribution to Solomon, the wise king, is the thread that holds together the whole work'; although Ecclesiastes is not directly attributed to him, that is, his name does not appear in the actual text, it identifies Qoheleth and 'Son of David, king of Jerusalem' (Eccl. 1:1, 12), which some scholars believe 'to have been naturally linked with Solomon', and can be viewed 'as

---

[31] 'The first mention of Solomon in the Bible is 2 Samuel 12:24. It narrates the birth of the second son of King David, who is called Solomon by David and Jedidah by Nathan' (Pablo A. Torijano: *Solomon The Esoteric King – From King to Magus, Development of a Tradition*, Leiden: Brill, 2002, p.8).

[32] J. Maxwell Miller and John H. Hayes, 1986, p.189.

[33] Pablo A. Torijano, 2002, pp.20–21.

[34] Among the five wisdom texts we examine in this book, only the book of Job is not attributed to any king and does not include Solomon's name. Katharine Dell argues that the fact that both general references to the activities of kings and the use of king imagery are minimal in Job could be seen to add to her argument over whether or not Job should be classified as a wisdom text (Katharine J. Dell: *The Book of Job as Sceptical Literature, Beihefte zur ZAW*, 197; Berlin: W. de Gruyter, 1991, pp.57–88).

referring to *the* king and *the* Son of David *par excellence*.[35] The Greek texts of wisdom 'reinterpreted the figure of Solomon in the light of the newly formed Hellenistic monarchies and their royal representatives',[36] where the traditional image of the wise king was developed or reshaped in the Hellenistic wisdom transmission context.[37]

In her examination of the king in the wisdom literature, Katharine Dell discusses the kingship's theological implications for the Israelite proverbs, paying particular attention to the issue of God–king relation and king's power. She concludes,

> There is no absolute power to monarchs, since all are subject to God and to the principles of justice and righteousness on which their leadership is founded … the king is primarily in the role of maintainer of justice, the ultimate human court of appeal before God himself. He has God-given power to effect good, power which can, if used wrongly, corrupt himself and others.[38]

Using her examination, we will further argue that the Israelite paradigm of wise king is in fact built upon three interrelated teachings: YHWH's gifts of power and wisdom to the king, the king's authority derived from righteousness and justice, and people standing in awe and obedience to the king. The first is the foundation because without YHWH's support and favour no king would have been established, or effectively exercised his power; the second is built upon the special relationship of the king to the divine, and sets the king as the upholder of divine as well as secular justice and righteousness; and the third is the natural consequence for a wise and just king who rules the state.

It is a fundamental Hebrew belief that the wisdom of the king is a special award from YHWH.[39] The king was the highest authority within the state. However, this authority could not be established unless YHWH wished it, a theme echoed in the

---

[35] Pablo A. Torijano, 2002, pp.22–3. In his summary of the three pieces of texts, Proverbs, Ecclesiastes and Song of Songs, Torijano concludes, 'The principal traits that all the three works share is their attribution to Solomon. As the sapiential contents are not common to all, this attribution was not necessarily and primarily made on the ground of Solomon's fame as a wise man, but on his fame as king. Somehow, Solomon is depicted first as king, and only later and secondarily as wise king.' However, as Torijano himself admits, 'Proverbs is a clear exception where both traits are totally intertwined' (ibid., p.23), it is in this combination of the two traits that the wisdom texts regenerate an image of political wisdom – the wise king.

[36] Pablo A. Torijano, 2002, p.26.

[37] However, we will primarily explore below the Israelite wise king paradigm as revealed in the post-exilic texts, primarily that of the book of Proverbs.

[38] Katharine Dell, 1998, p.185.

[39] In presenting her case, for example, the woman in front of King David openly declared her faith that 'my lord has wisdom like the wisdom of the angel of God to know all things that are on the earth' (2 Samuel 14:20). The reason why Solomon became king was because YHWH loved him (2 Samuel 12:24), and his image as divinely appointed successor of David and as embodiment of wisdom became the main theme of the wise and just Solomon legend. After Solomon rendered a judgment over the case of mothers and child, for example, the people were said to stand 'in awe of the king, because they perceived that the wisdom of God was in him, to render justice' (1 Kings 3:28).

book of Job where it is said that the throne of earthly kings was established by heavenly YHWH: 'with kings upon the throne he sets them for ever, and they are exalted' (Job 36:7).

Built into the ruling paradigm is that the wise king demonstrates the traditional virtues of being righteous and just.[40] The book of Proverbs prescribes that the king must be righteous: 'It is an abomination to kings to do evil, for the throne is established by righteousness' (Prov. 16:12). Whether this proverb is directed against evil done by the king or speaks of evil of others, it shows clearly that a wise king is depicted in the wisdom text as a righteous king who is opposed to evil. Being righteous and faithful is the condition for the king to preserve his throne, while at the same time his rule must strengthen and encourage these virtues among the people, as it is said, 'Loyalty and faithfulness preserve the king, and his throne is upheld by righteousness' (Prov. 20:28). The righteous character of the king is believed to be able to bring happiness to the people, as the proverb says, 'When the righteous are in authority, the people rejoice; but when the wicked rule, the people groan' (Prov. 29:2). Only when the righteous king rules the country can the state become prosperous, and the corrupt character of the king will definitely bring about disasters: 'By justice a king gives stability to the land, but one who exacts gifts ruins it' (Prov. 29:4).

In Hebrew proverbs, the interdependent relation between the king and the people is emphasized: 'In a multitude of people is the glory of a king, but without people a prince is ruined' (Prov. 14:28). It seems that the king and the people or subjects are locked in a circle: on the one hand, 'obeying the king's command' (Eccl. 8:2) plays an important part in Israelite political wisdom, and it is taught that 'he who angers him [the king] forfeits his life' (Prov. 20:2). However, on the other hand, this obedience does not stand alone; the king is particularly required to be religiously and morally just and virtuous. While the people should be in awe of a king's authority, the king can strengthen his position only through love and faithfulness: 'Love and faithfulness keep a king safe, through love his throne is made secure' (Prov. 20:28). Although interrelated, there is nevertheless a difference between the king and the people. While the king is required to be responsible primarily to YHWH, the people or subjects are demanded to be responsible to their king. In the book of Proverbs there are verses saying that the king's servants must serve him wisely, since then they will enjoy his favour like dew upon the grass, and they must not behave in a wrong way because this would definitely bring punishment from the king (Prov. 14:35; 19:12). Although the relationship between a servant and the king is emphasized here, it can also be applied to that between the ruler and the people, as Whybray has suggested, ' '*ebed* has a very wide range of meanings, and in fact any or all of the king's subjects can be described as his "servants"'.[41]

---

[40] These virtues are in particular 'referring to politics, administration and life in general' of a wise king, and the two collections of sayings introduced in Proverbs 10:1 and 25:1, seem 'to reflect the image of Solomon in 1 Kgs 5:12' (Pablo A. Torijano, 2002, p.22).

[41] R.N. Whybray: *Wealth and Poverty in the Book of Proverbs*, Sheffield: JSOT Press, 1990, p.49.

To be righteous is a divine command. However, here it has also become a requirement from the king: 'Righteous lips are the delight of a king, and he loves him who speaks what is right' (Prov. 16:13). It is apparent that through righteousness a hierarchy is inserted into the king–people relationship. In this relationship, people should follow and obey their kings: 'What can the man do who comes after the king? Only what he has already done' (Eccl. 2:12). Scholars have advanced different interpretations for this verse and those that follow, against the general tone of the book that 'nothing is new under the sun'. However, from my point of view, they illustrate well what a hierarchical king–people relationship means to the Israelites, and we can read several significant implications into them. First, the king is expected to take the lead, accomplishing things so that his subjects can follow suit. Secondly, a subject is expected to do what his king asks him to do, repeating what the king has already done either in content or in manner. Thirdly, in this relation, wisdom is revealed, which overcomes folly, just as light excels darkness.

Confucian Paradigm of Sages

The political wisdom of Confucianism is aimed at two targets: first, the government must endeavour to bring about the welfare and happiness of all the people, meeting their needs and satisfying their requirements; secondly, the ruler or king or officials must be competent in their posts and appoint men of capacity and good character to corresponding positions, the selection criteria of which should be their virtue rather than family or wealth. These two aims are subsequently used to measure ancient kings and contemporary rulers, a process by which early Confucians created a political paradigm of sage–kings (*sheng* or *sheng wang*) or former kings (*xian wang*), who were instrumental in the peace and harmony of the golden past, and believed that by exalting them the world would rectify its chaos and disorder; as Xunzi pointed out, it was only with the establishment of intelligent kingship that the inhabitants of a kingdom had regulations (Xunzi, 9:3).

The meaning and implication of the Confucian sage is much wider than the sage in Israel. In Israelite texts a sage means a wise man or more precisely a teacher of wisdom, while in Confucian contexts the sage is the sublime model of humanity. There is also a difference between the Confucians and the Israelites when we come to the question of whether the sage becomes a sage because of his knowledge and wisdom, or he attains wisdom and knowledge because he is a sage. According to Israelite understanding, humans are not capable of wisdom, which is in the realm of the divine. Therefore, before one can know the ultimate truth, one has to be given by YHWH the gifts of knowing and understanding; that is, sagehood is the gift from the above, by which the sage gains wisdom. Not confined by the theistic view of the world, Confucian masters reverse the order: a person can become a sage only when he has gained wisdom knowledge and has grasped the principles of Heaven and Earth, a form of knowledge that transforms an ordinary person's way of life into a sagely presence on earth.

Different authors of Confucian texts place an emphasis on different aspects of sagehood or sageliness, from cultural invention, to social institution design, to perfect personality, but our attention here will be confined to the sages or sage–kings whose wisdom has profound implications for a wise ruling. To qualify as a sage in Confucian contexts, one must have achieved great success in administering the state, either in person or by teaching, while to be regarded as a sage–king, one must have been a ruler in the past.[42] The qualifications required for sage–kings have added two important features to the Confucian paradigm. First, the sage–king paradigm demonstrates that Confucian political wisdom was devoted to the search in the past for the formality of the present. Both Israelite teachers and Confucian masters took the wisdom of past kings as a model to combat the evils they perceived and to rectify the life of the state. However, there is a difference between them. For the Israelites, wisdom of the past was a tool useful for realizing the Golden Age, a kingdom of YHWH in the future, which was proclaimed by prophets and also implied in the works of Israelite wise men. For Confucians, the past was itself the Golden Age and what could be realized was no more than the restoration of the kingly rule of that age. This has fundamentally shaped the Confucian mentality of the older being the better, in which looking to the past for the model of contemporary society became dominant.

Secondly, the Confucian sage–king model reflects the hierarchical structure of the Chinese political world as well as Confucian wisdom transmission. By appealing to the ancient kings, the wisdom teachings given by Confucian masters were not only justified but also gained authority. In contrast to biblical Israel, where a number of images co-exist in an equal relation among them, the wise, the faithful, the righteous, the king and the holy form a circle, bound together by the law of YHWH at the centre,[43] the sage or sage–king of Confucianism stands at the top of a clearly laddered structure, as the sublime ideal for the ethical and political world. The hierarchy of the ignorant, the scholar, the wise, the gentleman, the benevolent and the sage is primarily an ethical one, with each representing a further step in learning and personal cultivation. It also has fundamental implications for political hierarchy, because it is believed that good government is that in which the right person fills the right rank and the top seat is preserved for the sage, and that only in this way can benevolent influence be brought upon society as a whole.

---

[42] This explains why it was important for later Confucian followers to believe that Confucius was the 'acting prime minister', even very briefly, in his home state, which was most likely fabricated to lend him an authority position during the Han dynasty. Without actually being the ruler of the empire or state, few people could be ranked among former kings. Even Confucius was revered only as the 'Uncrowned King (*su wang*), because he did not ever head the state' (*Han shu*, Beijing: Zhonghua Shuju, 1997, p.2509).

[43] The Israelite images also include the prophet. There has been an extensive discussion of what 'prophet' means in Hebrew. Some suggest that it is related to a particular behaviour, ecstatic and strange, which generates a primary meaning of the one who is carried away by a supernatural power, while others believe that it is associated with 'call', and that it refers to the people who call or proclaim their messages (H.H. Rowley: *Prophecy and Religion in Ancient China and Israel*, University of London/The Athlone Press, 1956, p.4). For our purpose in this book we have no intention to introduce the figure of the prophet into our comparison.

A tension has been built up in the Confucian paradigm of the sage or sage–king, between the confining of the term 'sage' to a few ancient kings and the universality of sagehood. On the basis of humanistic principles, Confucians believe that all people have the same nature and are open to the same possibilities. This is also applicable to the issue of sagehood. However sublime and authoritative, ancient sage–kings were not significantly different from the people of today or from all the people of all times, as far as their nature was concerned. They were not men of superhuman endowment; rather they 'were the same as anyone else' (Mengzi, 4B:32). What made them distinctive was only that they were exceptional individuals who knew how to perfect their inborn nature, and who identified with the order of the world and applied themselves to accomplish it. This has effectively opened the door of sagehood to all people and promised them that it is possible to become sages if they cultivate themselves to the utmost: 'All men are capable of becoming a Yao or a Shun' (Mengzi, 6B:2). However, it seems clear that this optimistic promise was not realistically possible because the Confucian sages were in fact all confined to a very small group of 'mystical' or ancient figures, as C.K. Yang has pointed out:

> In spite of the Confucian theory that through cultivation and effort such qualities are attainable by men, history showed no such examples. Setting up such standards resulted only in lengthy imperial titles given to rulers through the centuries, titles that claimed sagely wisdom, unusual abilities, and perfect virtues, all in order to create an aura of superhuman qualities around the imperial personage.[44]

The gap between theoretical possibility and actual situation was disappointing to Confucians, too. Confucius himself admitted he did not expect to meet a sage, and what he hoped was to meet a person of virtue: 'I have no hopes of meeting a sage. I would be content if I met someone who is a gentleman. I have not hopes of meeting a good man. I would be content if I met someone who has constancy' (*Analects*, 7:26). However, it is not fair to conclude from this that Confucius had totally lost his confidence in the perfectibility of humans. Hidden in these passages was an implication that, if one were constant (*heng*), it would be possible for one to become a good man, and if one continued to be good, there was no reason why one could not become a sage. This kind of solution reflects an ethical and political expectation of the people and a belief in the effect of morally oriented self-cultivation: although it is possible for everyone to become a sage, it takes time and effort to do so; and people can penetrate as far as spiritual intelligence and form a Triad with Heaven and Earth, if and only if they can engage in study, focus their minds on this single aim, unify their intentions, ponder these principles and, more importantly, accomplish them each day over a long period of time (Xunzi, 23:5).

This is, doubtless, too far away from everybody's reach. Apart from the requirement of constant effort and a strong will, there is also a material condition for

---

[44] C.K. Yang: *Religion in Chinese Society*, Los Angeles: University of California Press, 1967, p.131.

one to achieve and a spiritual qualification for one to possess before becoming a sage. As far as the material side is concerned, Confucius specified that the sage was a man who 'gave extensively to the common people and brought help to the multitude', which, he believed, even ancient kings such as Yao and Shun would have found it difficult to accomplish (*Analects*, 6:30). However hard ordinary people had tried, it was not their task to bring wealth and security to the people, and peace and harmony to the state. They must first have been in the right position and have had administrative means available. According to the Confucian political view, positions were awarded to those whose virtue and ability matched up to their requirements. However, the highest social post was reserved only for those whom Heaven appointed, and this added a spiritual dimension to kingship. Therefore the sage could not possibly be an ordinary person; rather he was the one who had been 'set by Heaven on the path to sagehood' (*Analects*, 9:6), or the one who had received 'a great task' (*da ren*) from Heaven (Mengzi, 6B:15). The sage also had a mission to awaken and arouse the people, as the border official of Yi told the followers of Confucius: 'The Empire has long been without the Way. Heaven is about to use your Master as the wooden tongue for a bell' (*Analects*, 3:24).

Strict conditions and requirements have therefore totally transformed Confucian perception of the sages. It is true that sages had the same nature as everybody else; however, through their personal effort and spiritual qualifications, they were actually 'divine beings', which very few would be able to become. In this way the early Confucian sage–king paradigm was turned into a metaphysical speculation. The essential conviction Confucians held was that, because sages reached the 'culmination of humanity' (Mengzi, 4A:2), they would manage the world as easily as turning up their hands, and because they were the 'ultimate paragon of the Way' (Xunzi, 19:2; 31:2), their rule would 'achieve order without taking any action' (*Analects*, 15:5). Such sages were not only able to transform the world but also to assist 'the transforming and nourishing powers of Heaven and Earth' and to form 'a triad with Heaven and Earth' (Zhongyong, 22).

Wise Kingship and Benevolent Government

Established on different grounds, the paradigms of Israelite wise kings and Confucian sages were used to enhance governmental exercises, calling the rulers of the present times to follow ancient models, providing a wise rule for the people and for the state. Ruling wisely is therefore the concrete requirement of Confucian and Israelite political wisdom. As far as the principles of government are concerned, Confucians and the Israelites each demonstrate their own distinctive features, in many aspects clearly distinguishable from each other, but in many others comparable. Fundamental to Israelite kingly rule was righteousness or justice, and Israelite teachers held that the wise king was the upholder of rightness; while essential to Confucian sage–kings' rule was benevolence and rites, and Confucians believed that sage–kings were the upholders of culture (civilization) and transmitters of wisdom. When Confucius said in confidence that 'With King Wen dead, is not culture (*wen*) invested here in me?', he implied that King Wen was one of the culture inventors and transmitters, and after him Confucius himself was given such a mission (*Analects*, 9:5).

Both Confucian and Israelite rulers were regarded as pathfinders, inventing or discovering moral rules and social norms as administrative tools. However, differences exist between Israelite wise kings and Confucian sages. For the Israelites the way of YHWH was righteous and just; to be righteous meant to employ righteousness in governing practices, loving those who spoke the truth and abominating evildoers. Holding to it, the king would be able to make 'inspired decisions' and not 'sin in judgment' (Prov. 16:10). He could detect wrongdoing and make right judgments, as it is said that 'A king who sits on the throne of judgment winnows all evil with his eyes'; and before a wise king, it was not possible for any dishonest man to escape detection and juristic punishment: 'A wise king winnows the wicked, and drives the wheel over them' (Prov. 20:8–9, 26). In more general terms, what a wise king was expected to do was to reveal the divine (the hidden and secrets of the world) to the people: 'It is the glory of God to conceal things, but the glory of kings is to search things out' (Prov. 25:2).

Confucian sage–kings were also the explorers and upholders of the Way. The way of Heaven and Earth was believed to be benevolent and beneficent; correspondingly, the way of ruling was to make the people rich and faithful, reduce poverty and uneven distribution, and do away with cruelty and killing (*Analects*, 13:11). In the *Book of Mengzi* we read that the rule of a sage–king was beneficent, providing support to the helpless; that his rule was benevolent, not extending punishment to 'the wife and children of an offender' (Mengzi, 1B:5). As a consequence of the sage–king's benevolent government (*ren zheng*), the people would have 'no old folk who were cold and hungry' (Mengzi, 7A:22).

In an authoritive state, kings held absolute power, and the authority of the kings was the centre of gravity of the state. The Israelite wisdom texts explore the power of the king from their divine source, and by placing the king and God in parallel they make the people aware of the dire consequences of the wrath of the king. The theocentric politics justified the power of the king and meant that the king possessed something sacred. Therefore the commonsense wisdom was to understand that 'A king's wrath is a messenger of death, and a wise man will appease it' (Prov. 16:14). The wisdom of a king is the prerequisite of a well-governed state, and a wise king knows how to discipline himself as well as his people: 'An undisciplined king will ruin his people, but a city will grow through the understanding of its rulers' (Sir. 10:3). To enhance the authority of the king on earth, wisdom teachings put him in parallel with God in heaven: 'My son, fear the LORD and the king, and do not disobey either of them; for disaster from them will rise suddenly, and who knows the ruin that will come from them both?' (Prov. 24:22). By likening the power of the king to that of YHWH, the author of this verse pointed to the dire consequence of disobeying the spiritual and the earthly ultimate power, as Katharine Dell explains:

'Whichever translation one follows, the gist of the maxim seems to stress obedience to those in power – to God as supreme authority and to the king as temporary authority.'[45]

In a Confucian context, the authority of government comes from the gravity of an excellent character, which will inspire awe among the people, and it is believed that, thanks to his moral power, the sage–king did not have to do more than 'holding himself in a respectful posture and face due south' (*Analects*, 15:5). However, on occasions the powerful rage of the sage–kings was also claimed to be instrumental to the peace and prosperity of the people. A poem from the *Book of Poetry* paints a vivid picture of how the rage of King Wen brought peace to the country, to which Mengzi added, 'This was the valour of King Wen. In one outburst of rage King Wen brought peace to the people of the Empire' (Mengzi, 1B:3). The only criterion the sage–kings followed to decide whether or not to engage in war was pleasing the people or not antagonizing the people, and Mengzi said this was exactly what King Wen and King Wu did when they considered whether or not to engage in warfare (Mengzi, 1B:10).

Any good government must be able to achieve peace for the state, prosperity for the people and an efficient governing mechanism for the king, but different political entities require different approaches. The Israelite paradigm follows its theocentric blueprint for kingly rule, where the king has total dependence upon divine control: 'The king's heart is a stream of water in the hands of the LORD, he turns it wherever he will' (Prov. 21:1). While the LORD watches over the king, the king will also watch over his officials, and so on and so forth. This generates a hierarchical structure, and all people are both the governing and the governed, as the author of Ecclesiastes points out: 'the high official is watched by a higher, and there are yet higher ones over them' (Eccl. 5:8). However different the responsibilities these officials hold, they are all responsible to the righteousness and justice of YHWH, by which the earthly hierarchy is totally broken. In the governing chain of the state, the most important thing is to govern by justice at all levels. The punishment of the wicked and the upholding of the righteous are central to a harmonious society: 'When a scoffer is punished, the simple becomes wise; when a wise man is introduced, he gains knowledge' (Prov. 21:11). For the Israelites, the key to political prosperity is to rule in justice, because this will make the good overwhelm the evil: 'When justice is done, it is a joy to the righteous, but dismay to evildoers' (Prov. 21:15).

The Confucian paradigm is part of its moralistic outline for a benevolent government. As an impersonal power, the Confucian Heaven does not directly instruct how to govern, and Confucian sages have to use the heavenly way as the guiding principle to design their own policies to maintain or restore political order. For example, King Wen praised the worthy and tolerated opponents; Mengzi, quoting from the *Book of Poetry*, describes King Wen: 'He neither dispelled the dislike of others, nor did he lose his own reputation' (7B:19). Xunzi believed that ancient kings acted to control the people by dividing society into classes, creating

---

[45] Katharine Dell, 1998, p.178.

thereby differences in status between the noble and base, disparities between the privileges of age and youth, and the division of the wise from the stupid, the able from the incapable. All of this caused men to perform the duties of their station in life and ensured that each received his due (Xunzi, 4:14).

CHAPTER SEVEN

Secularity and Sacredness of Wisdom

Wisdom comes from a skilful combination and application of knowledge and experience, past and present, ethical and political. However, in early Confucian and Israelite traditions it is not simply seen as conventional knowledge, instructions or witty sayings which are distilled from past experiences and are employed to guide present life and action choices. It is also to be understood in the context of the human search for the ultimate meaning of the world and for breakthroughs in personal, social and spiritual life. The search is undertaken in a variety of forms, which are related to particular languages, cultures and belief systems. Whatever forms it may take there is, as John Eaton has rightly observed, a common core, associated with 'watching and listening for the One, whom they refer to with such words as the Truth, the Way, the All, God'.[1] This common core of experience invariably underlies wisdom as a sacred enterprise, while the variety of forms determines how to understand the source and key element of ultimate wisdom. It is indeed the case that, without a full appreciation of its spiritual dimension and without taking into account the interaction between 'spiritual seekers' and wisdom, our hermeneutical interpretation of early Confucian and Israelite wisdom thinking that is demonstrated in epistemological, personal, moral and political spheres would be a construction without a solid basis, nor would our interpretative findings fit in well with the overall framework of early Confucian and Israelite worldviews.

For Israelite thinkers, wisdom is sacred because it comes from YHWH and is revealed to human beings in the divine creation. Therefore the sacredness of Israelite wisdom is rooted in divinity and is primarily 'holiness'.[2] In early Confucian discourse there is also a 'holy' aspect to wisdom. The 'holy' is related to the concept of 'the Mandate of Heaven' that makes it necessary for human understanding to go beyond temporal matters. However, the Confucian sacredness of wisdom is not primarily rooted here, but in the profundity of knowledge, the transmission of ancestral teachings and the mysterious link between the human mind and the way of the cosmos. In this sense the relationship between the secular and the sacred is manifested differently in Confucian wisdom and Israelite wisdom. In the Israelite

---

[1] John Eaton: *The Contemplative Face of Old Testament Wisdom in the Context of World Religions*, London: SCM Press/Philadelphia: Trinity Press International, 1989, p.1.

[2] In Hebrew *qādōš* (holy) has the basic meaning of 'separate'. It properly signifies divinity, the essence of deity itself (John L. McKenzie, S.J.: *Dictionary of the Bible*, London/Dublin: Geoffrey Chapman, 1965, p.365). The holy is primarily associated with YHWH and his creation, who is regarded as 'the Holy One of Israel'. Owing to the fact that they were selected by, and belonged to, YHWH, the Israelites became a 'holy nation'. Therefore holiness is a gift or reward from the divine: 'You shall be holy for I am holy' (Lev. 11:44; 19:2; 20:7, 26). Though we are aware that in conventional English usage the holy and the sacred both refer to dedication to the deity and have more or less the same meaning, we attempt in this chapter to differentiate the 'holy' from the 'sacred': the 'holy' comes from a proper separation from the profane and is related fundamentally to 'spiritual otherness', while the 'sacred' refers to the venerable meanings and values that are added to the secular through ethical, religious or spiritual means.

tradition, wisdom is with the Creator and is part of the creation, and creatures including humans do not have the sacred nature. No matters, events or things, however important they appear to be, can become sacred unless they are made so in the divine. In early Confucian discourse, wisdom is partly derived from the 'mysterious unity' between humanity and the universe that enables humans to appreciate the seemingly 'unfathomable' nature of the world. All secular phenomena in the three realms of Heaven, Earth and humans by nature partake, partially or wholly, of sacredness from the very beginning. To understand the sacredness of Confucian wisdom, we must set it in the moralized picture of the world which Confucian masters drew for us: the world – composed of Heaven, Earth and humans – would reveal itself in certain 'ways', and by observing and discerning these 'ways' sages or sage–kings were able to set up 'principles' or 'rules' for humans to follow; whether or not a particular person can find the ways and follow the principles is determined primarily by education and practice.

It is therefore important for our appreciation of Confucian and Israelite convergence and divergence in wisdom thinking to explore the sacredness of wisdom after examining its manifestations in epistemology, and as the way of individual, social and political life. With this in mind we will in this chapter examine how ancient Confucian masters and Israelite teachers elaborated on the ultimate origin of wisdom, how they justified the existence of the sacred order and explained away the disorder of the contemporary world, and how much they had confidence in human wisdom to secure a successful life.

Theocentric and Anthropocentric Wisdom

Where is the origin of wisdom? This question must have been asked in all religious and philosophical traditions. How to answer it reveals the character of a particular way of wisdom thinking, and often distinguishes one way from another in its search for wisdom. As far as the answers to this question are concerned, there are at least three types of wisdom thinking: theocentric, anthropocentric and nature-centric.

Theocentric wisdom thinking places the origin of wisdom in theistic being(s) or power(s), of which the most prevalent format is the belief that human wisdom is the result of revelation from God or gods. Because of the different conceptions of theistic being or power, theocentric thinking can be further classified into two categories. The first is monotheistic, that is, a belief that wisdom comes from a supreme creator either named 'God' or something else, who is recognized as the only deity, omnipotent and omnipresent, and whose revelation is regarded as the sole source of what we call wisdom. The second is polytheistic, that is, a belief that wisdom comes from the collective power of deities or gods or spirits, who assume various forms such as heavenly bodies, earthly forces or ancestral spirits. The difference between monotheism and polytheism is that in the strictest sense the former believes in or worships only the high god as the sole source of wisdom, and denies the existence of divinities other than this high god, while the latter admits, and encourages, worship of or making sacrifices to a pantheon of gods or spirits, who are either ranked or in parallel, in harmony or in conflict.

Anthropocentric wisdom thinking is characterized by the conviction that wisdom comes primarily from human intelligence, reflection and knowledge. As for questions regarding where wisdom exists and how humans gain knowledge and insight, anthropocentric wisdom can also be further divided into the idealistic anthropocentric and the rationalistic anthropocentric. Idealists believe that humans are born with the heart/mind in which all knowledge concerning the world innately exists; through proper cultivation and retrospection we will find wisdom, and there is no need for us to look for wisdom knowledge in the external world or in the interaction between the internal and the external realms. Rationalists argue that wisdom is not innate; rather, humans are equipped with faculties of observing, reflecting and thinking; to gain wisdom, namely profound knowledge of the world and life, we must apply these faculties to observation of the external world, and to rational reasoning and analysis of what we have observed.

Nature-centric wisdom thinking prefers the thesis that wisdom is in the (natural) world itself, and is embedded in the secret operations or laws of nature. Since wisdom is external to human beings, a question arises concerning whether or not humans are capable of grasping the secrets of nature. Those who take a positive stand on this question can be regarded as 'cognitive nature-centric', because they are optimistic about human success in achieving unity with nature, in which the human mind operates well, along with the laws of nature, and understands ultimate wisdom. Those who answer this question in the negative, and believe that it is not possible for human beings to have ultimate wisdom, can be regarded as 'non-cognitive nature-centric', because they believe that, although humans may experience nature and observe the structure and patterns of natural movements, they are unable fully to appreciate the underlying principles because the secrets or hidden principles of nature are far beyond human comprehension. According to this way of thinking, human language and rationality are not sufficient for the wisdom of natural laws, and all they do is provide us with a distorted image of nature. This pessimistic view of wisdom is a kind of 'nature mystery'; a typical expression may be found in early Daoist mystic teachings, where the first sentence of the first chapter of the *Daode jing* states that 'The Dao (Way of Nature) that can be spoken of is not the eternal Dao' (Daode jing, Chapter 1).

It is clear that Israelite wisdom belongs to the category of theistic tradition, even if earlier Israelite thought was probably not as exclusively monotheistic as the Jewish theology of a later age. Although of the Ten Commandments the first four are based on the requirement that the Israelites worship only YHWH their only God, and although scholars have shown that starting from 'the ninth century BCE Israelites began to distinguish YHWH from other gods',[3] we can still read in various passages

---

[3] Bruce M. Metzger and Michael D. Coogan (eds): *The Oxford Companion to the Bible*, New York and Oxford: Oxford University Press, 1993, p.526.

of wisdom literature, which might have come from an earlier source and/or have been influenced by polytheistic religions prevailing in the then Near East, that God or YHWH is not the only spiritual being and that other gods or deities may also have played a part in the formation and function of wisdom. For example, it is said that YHWH presided over the divine council of the sons of God among whom Satan also came, who reported to and suggested strategies to YHWH, and that YHWH entrusted the work of inspecting people on the earth to Satan: 'Behold, he is in your power; only spare his life' (Job 1:6–2:6). In some of the texts, wisdom is described or addressed as a goddess or 'Lady Wisdom', a title which may reflect the influence of worship of a female deity of reproduction in earlier Israelite history.[4] However, most scholars agree that in the context of the wisdom literature the goddess of wisdom is only used as a metaphor of YHWH's supreme power or a demonstration of wisdom's holiness, and that she should not be considered to be a separate deity parallel to YHWH himself.

In almost all early Israelite wisdom texts there is a consistent theme that wisdom can come when and only when YHWH reveals himself to human beings. In this sense, the overall solution to the origin and source of wisdom for ancient Israelites points in a clearly monotheistic direction; or, in the mouth of goddess wisdom, wisdom was the first creation of God: 'The Lord created me at the beginning of his work, the first of his acts of long ago. Ages ago I was set up, at the first, before the beginning of the earth' (Prov. 8:22). To the question, 'Where shall wisdom be found?' (Job 28:12), characteristic of the Israelite tradition are answers such as that 'God understands the way to it' (Job 28:23), or that 'the Lord gives wisdom; from his mouth come knowledge and understanding' (Prov. 2:6), or that 'The fear of the Lord is the beginning of wisdom' (Prov. 9:10). In the Book of Ben Sira the first sentence unmistakeably locates the source of wisdom in divinity: 'All wisdom comes from the Lord' (1:1). This indicates that, for the Israelites, wisdom is primarily a vertical movement from YHWH above to the Israelites below: being holy, transcendent and totally other by nature, unlike anything else in creation, YHWH's revelation is made in his relation to his world, his people and humanity as a whole. However, the language used to describe this vertical movement is metaphorical rather than realistic. Thus the relationship between YHWH and his people must be described in such social and familial relationships as those of king–subject, judge–litigant, husband–wife, father–child and master–servant. An appropriate appreciation of these relationships has thus become the primary source from which the Israelites draw their wisdom. Since the Israelites identify themselves as 'the people of YHWH' (Judges 5:13) from the outset, to gain wisdom, they must behave in the manner of subjects,

---

[4] In a recent popular literature presentation, this point has been stretched to the effect that 'Early Jews believed that the Holy of Holies in Solomon's Temple housed not only God but also His powerful female equal, Shekinah … The Jewish tetragrammaton YHWH – the sacred name of God – in fact derived from Jehovah, an androgynous physical union between the masculine *Jah* and the pre-Hebraic name for Eve, *Havah*' (Dan Brown: *The Da Vinci Code*, London: Transworld Publishers/Corgi Books, 2004, p.411).

children, brides and servants. The monotheistic discourses on the divine source of wisdom and on the way to wisdom lead to the praises of the faithful and the righteous. Wisdom is possible only in the person of the righteous and through the faithful, as shown in the saying that 'The mouth of the righteous utters wisdom, and his tongue speaks justice' (Psalm 37:30).

Early Confucian wisdom is essentially anthropocentric. For most of the Confucian masters, wisdom does not dwell in gods or spirits, but in human working in the world and in human pursuit of knowledge. This was clearly expressed when Confucius explained what wisdom was to his students: 'He who devotes himself to the duties of the people, and who while revering the spirits and gods, keeps away from them can be called wise' (*Analects*, 6:22). On the one hand, Confucius believes that there is no 'abstract' wisdom; wisdom must be experienced in one's work for the benefit of people. On the other hand, he disregards the view of traditional shamanism that wisdom came from one's communication with spirits and gods. Confucius chose a middle way between totally throwing out the spiritual content of wisdom and seeking wisdom in spirits, and argued that true wisdom lay in 'keeping a distance from spirits', but 'showing them reverence'. This has become the cornerstone of Confucian wisdom thinking, and has determined the Chinese understanding of the relationship between wisdom and the spiritual world.

Humanistic by nature and yet transcending the wholly secular realm in function, Confucian wisdom does not concentrate on grace or revelation from God or gods, as many theocentric systems do, or on intellectual achievements, as some philosophical traditions tend to do. Instead, it starts with the search for ordinary knowledge and ends up informing the ultimate fulfilment of humanity. This is characteristic of the Confucian search for wisdom, and has been illustrated by Confucius's description of his own progress in learning: 'I start from below and get through to what is above' (*Lunyu*, 14:35). To reach what is above is, in later Confucian terminology, to be sagely or to become a sage, the self-transformed and transformative ideal embodying profound knowledge and functioning as a central figure linking the ultimate and the ordinary, the past and the future. It is the central position of the sage and the importance of wisdom in Confucianism that has led some scholars to define the Confucian tradition in terms of a wisdom religion.

From what we have said above it seems reasonable to say that ancient Confucians and Israelites departed from each other in terms of their thinking on the source of wisdom; one was totally theo-centred and the other primarily anthropo-centred. However, the line between anthropocentric wisdom thinking and theocentric thinking cannot be easily drawn. Having originated in the power of YHWH, Israelite wisdom also demonstrates an important trait of the anthropocentric way of thinking. This may be further elaborated from the following three points of view. First, anthropomorphism prevails throughout the Israelite wisdom literature. YHWH, the supreme and only deity the Israelites are allowed to worship, is portrayed as a human figure, with 'eyes, mouth, lips, arms, bowels (as seat of compassion) and heart'. In addition to these physical traits, he is endowed with 'human emotions: kindness, love, anger, but not the ignoble emotions'. Consequently, just like any normal human being, YHWH 'lives, speaks, hears, thinks, plans, desires, loves, hates, commands, moves from place to place, dwells'.[5] YHWH is thus a living person, and his teaching and instructions are characteristic of personal wisdom that humans can accept, share and reflect upon.

Secondly, in contrast to other types of texts in the Hebrew Scriptures, the wisdom literature does not concern itself much with traditional themes such as the covenant or the salvage history of Israel. It is devoted primarily to the human understanding of life and its structure and orders, and is concerned essentially with human conditions, human relationships and human choices, especially in the face of life difficulties and dilemmas. The basic tone of these texts is that humans must seek understanding for themselves, and must find their answers in a variety of relations between individuals, between human beings and the world around them, and particularly between human beings and YHWH. This makes Israelite wisdom very much akin to the wisdom thinking in an anthropocentric tradition. Thirdly, humans-inclined though it may appear to be, Israelite wisdom is fundamentally centred on YHWH as the source of wisdom. In the Wisdom of Solomon we see how the chain of wisdom teaching leads to the acknowledgment of YHWH's sovereignty:

> The beginning of wisdom is the most sincere desire for instruction, and concern for instruction is love of her, and love of her is the keeping of her laws, and giving heed to her laws is assurance of immortality, and immortality brings one near to God; so the desire for wisdom leads to a kingdom. (Wisd. 6:17–20)

Confucianism demonstrates a clear tendency towards the anthropocentric understanding of wisdom, and in general the Confucian discourse on the interaction between the Way of Heaven and human wisdom takes the form of cosmic rather than theological ethics, providing an ethical–cosmological solution to human puzzles over the nature and source of wisdom. However, early Confucians did not completely turn away from the spiritual source of wisdom. Their queries about the source and nature of wisdom led them to a more profound layer of human knowledge: wisdom is of more than a secular nature, and humans cannot always comprehend the mysteries of the world. Apart from the phenomenal world that can be grasped, there exists the transcendental reality that is beyond our immediate knowledge, and wisdom will not be possible unless we have entered this reality. This is where the sacred aspect of Confucian wisdom thinking first comes in. To fully appreciate the sacredness of wisdom we must consider the Confucian view of *tian* or Heaven. By evoking Heaven Confucians add a mysterious and yet immanent meaning to their concept of wisdom. They admit that wisdom is the result of observing and following the laws of Heaven and Earth. The laws or ways of Heaven and Earth are not apparent to the human mind, yet knowledge of them, the most profound of all kinds of knowledge, is what constitutes the foundation of wisdom. The commentators of the *Book of Changes*, for

---

[5]   John L. McKenzie, S.J., 1965, p.35.

example, believe that the ancient sages looked up to observe the pattern of Heaven, and looked down to examine the order of Earth, so that they gained knowledge about the causes of various affairs and understood the circle of life and death.[6]

What then is the Confucian Heaven? How does it function as the source and content of wisdom? To answer these questions we have to look more closely at the Chinese character itself.[7] 'Heaven' as we have used the word in this book is only a convenient interpretation of the Confucian ultimate, called *tian*, that is traditionally defined as the 'Supreme Ultimate (*zhigao wushang*)'.[8] Modern renderings of this character varies from the 'ONE above man', to 'the rulers of the past, collectively conceived as living in heaven', to the 'Sky-god' to the 'ultimate transcendence'.[9]

Whatever interpretation *tian* is given, it has a fundamentally spiritual connotation above or besides its material and natural meanings, and is essentially regarded as the primary source of wisdom in the early Confucian tradition. However, we must take into account the changes of meaning by which the term *tian* is employed in the history of Confucian texts. The earlier the context in which *tian* is used, the more likely it is that it refers to a personal power or spiritual being who controls the world and who provides humans with insights into the secrets of the world and of life. It is thus no surprise that references to *tian* in the *Book of Poetry*, the *Book of Documents*, parts of the *Book of Rites*, *Zuo Zhuan* or *Zuo's Commentary on the Spring and Autumn Annals* and *Guo Yu* or the *Conversations of the States*, 'seem generally to designate the ruling or presiding anthropomorphic "Imperial Heaven Supreme Emperor"',[10] who could bestow the mandate on a virtuous ruler.[11]

In Confucius's conversations there is a transitional change: while the theological *tian* is used and referred to as the source of human wisdom, a new metaphysical

---

[6] *A Source Book in Chinese Philosophy*, trans. and compiled by Wing-tsit Chan, Princeton: Princeton University Press, 1963, p.265.

[7] The Confucian Heaven is substantially different from the Israelite heaven or heavens, although both have the two meanings of 'sky' and 'the place where God/gods dwell'. In the Hebrew Scriptures the word *šāmayim* is plural, and the English translation is 'heaven' or 'the heavens'. Heaven in the Scriptures depicts 'an overarching vault resting on pillars at the end of earth'. Above it is the celestial ocean and above this the dwelling of God who 'looks down from heaven upon the children of men' (Psalm 14:2). Sometimes it refers to 'the expanse' in which the birds fly (Genesis 1:20), sometimes to 'the starry heavens' which are 'a witness to God's being and creative power' and tell 'the glory of God' (Psalm 19:1). YHWH says 'Do not I fill heaven and earth?' (Jeremiah 23:24).

[8] Duan Yucai, *Shuowen jiezi zhu*, Hangzhou: Zhejiang Guji Chubanshe 1998, p.1.

[9] Robert Eno: *The Confucian Creation of Heaven: Philosophy and the Defense of Ritual Mastery*, Albany: State University of New York Press, 1990, pp.181–9.

[10] Fung Yu-lan: *A History of Chinese Philosophy*, trans. Derk Bodde, Princeton: Princeton University Press, 1952, vol. 1, p.31.

[11] In a later forged chapter *Da Yu Mo* of the *Book of Documents*, we find a passage concerning how an earlier sage–king was believed to become the ruler of the world: 'The virtue of Emperor Yao was so broad and profound, so wise and sacred, so wonderful and mysterious, so brilliant and powerful, and so magnificent and splendid, that August Tian bestowed him his Mandate and made him the sovereign of the world within the four seas' (see James Legge (trans.): *The Chinese Classics Vol. III: The Shoo King or the Book of Historical Documents*, London: Trubner & Co., 1865, p.54).

understanding of *tian* as the provider of political and moral standards is added. Confucian texts gradually dilute the religious or spiritual context of *tian* and are more devoted to the discussion of its significance for human life. *Tian* is still considered the source of supreme wisdom, but it no longer acts in person, does not 'speak', but is the Way, the ultimate cosmic law or mandate, regulating the four seasons, the laws of growth and declining, and the rules of human success and failure. This generates a tension in some Confucian discourses between the human origin of wisdom and spiritually oriented wisdom. On the one hand, for example, Confucius upholds that 'the fear of the Mandate of Heaven' is an integral part of wisdom and thus gives a spiritual orientation to wisdom. It is evident that he is aware of his special relation with *tian*, and claims that he has a mission that has been endowed by *tian* to transmit the ancient wisdom tradition. On the other hand, however, he never clearly spells out that wisdom can come directly from *tian* or any other spiritual power; rather, as we have noted, he admonishes his students to keep a distance from spirits in order to become wise.

Wisdom is believed to have been embedded in the cultural tradition that ancient sage–kings established and must be transmitted to later generations. Mengzi goes for an idealistic way for the source of wisdom, arguing that if one wants to know *tian* or *tian*'s will, one must first know one's inner self, because *tian* is none other than the innate heart/mind humans are born with. It seems clear to Mengzi that it is not possible for wisdom to come from one's intimate relation to the external world, or even from the spiritual and moral ultimate without personal cultivation of what one already has, and that worship of the spiritual authority is not sufficient to make a person wise. Strongly disagreeing with Mengzi, who holds to the moralized conception of *tian*, Xunzi substantializes *tian* as a natural reality, not a moral agent or spiritual power, demonstrating to a degree a cognitive nature-centric wisdom thinking way. For Xunzi, the ways of *tian* are constant and do not change in accordance with human behaviour. To have good knowledge of the natural world, humans must study, observe and calculate; and to lead a good life humans must respond to the ways of nature wisely, and apply knowledge to human government and social life (Xunzi, 17:1). Therefore, for Xunzi, the origin of wisdom is in the interaction between human intelligence and natural laws. However, he also recognizes that *tian* operates in a mysterious way which, owing to its formlessness, humans are not capable of perceiving. What we can perceive is only its results and completed forms. Therefore the knowledge of *tian* is to know what we can do and what we cannot, and it is in this kind of knowledge that 'sacred' wisdom is gained (*zhi tian*), by which the sage 'knows what is his to do and what is not his to do. Then Heaven and Earth perform the work of officers, and the myriad things serve him as foot soldiers' (Xunzi, 17:4).

Sacred Wisdom and the Power of Spirits

The otherness of wisdom not only comes from the association of knowledge and the spiritual ultimate, but is also concerned with the power or influence of spirits, whether in the form of supernatural beings subordinate to the spiritual authority or as ancestors who are taken as the embodiment of the sacred tradition and experience. What place have spirits had in early Confucian and Israelite wisdom traditions? How much is the sacredness of wisdom due to the influence of spiritual others?[12] These questions take us to another dimension of the sacredness of wisdom.

As discussed above, Confucius's definition that wisdom is devoting oneself to the benefit of the people, and revering spirits but keeping them at a distance provides an anthropocentric outline for the nature and extent of the sacredness of wisdom. Here he clearly specifies that wisdom has two kinds of sources, or must be defined by two criteria. First, wisdom must come from the fulfilment of our duties towards human beings, in which our devotion to what is right and our working for the well-being of the people play a key role, because devotion and working of this kind are believed to provide us with experience and knowledge that shape the form of wisdom. Secondly, it is reflected in correct attitudes towards spirits, that is, we must have a highly reverent attitude towards 'spiritual others', but at the same time must not be possessed by them or too much under their influence. Traditionally, spirits were revered through rites, offerings and ritual music.[13] Although placing much emphasis on the value of ritual, Confucius himself saw the true function of ceremonies as cultivating the internal reverence towards otherness, and therefore strongly disapproved of those who participated in ritual but lacked reverence within: 'Ritual, Ritual! Does it mean no more than presents of jade and silk? Music, Music! Does it mean no more than bells and drums?' (*Analects*, 17:11). For him people who performed ritual but had no reverence within did not really take part in ritual at all. An inner attitude of reverence, sincerity and self-disciplining rather than the external arrangement of ritual items is the essence of rites, and is therefore considered the proper source of knowledge and wisdom.

How can our attitude towards spirits come to be associated with wisdom? A possible answer lies in what Confucians believe to be the power and function of spirits. In the Confucian tradition, spirit, *shen* as a general term, represents the power of the 'wholly other', who stands outside the human world but at the same time is capable of intervening in the affairs of the world. In the oracle bone inscriptions *shen* appears in a pictographic form representing the force of lightning, a frightening brightness suddenly erupting from the firmament or horizon of the sky with a

---

[12] The term 'spirit' is used here in the sense of 'spiritual others' referring to the supernatural beings that have the power to control, or have an impact on, natural and human courses; it also refers to spirits or ghosts that are believed to have survived after the death of the body, and to the ultimate spiritual being or power that is both transcendent and immanent in the human world. Its Chinese, Hebrew, Greek and English origins and meanings will be discussed below.

[13] In Confucianism sacrificial rituals are an important part of the tradition. For example, during sacrifice to Confucius there is a three-offering ritual (*sanxian*): three times a cup of libation and other offerings are offered to the spiritual tablet of Confucius and to other gods and spirits (Xinzhong Yao (ed.): *Routledge/Curzon Encyclopedia of Confucianism*, London: Routledge, 2003, vol. 2, p.524).

formidable striking power. *Shen* thus particularly represents the power of heavenly spirits, although in later writings it has become a general term for all spiritual beings and powers, including human deities and earthly gods. In some early Confucian classics, such as the *Book of Documents* and the *Book of Poetry*, the highest of all heavenly spirits is *Tian* (Heaven) or *Di* (Lord), who controls and oversees both the spiritual and the human worlds. Changes of weather, natural disasters or social upheavals were all attributed to the favour and disfavour of Heaven or the Lord on High or High God (*Shang Di*).[14]

However, as Laurence Thompson has rightly pointed out, *Shang Di* or *Tian* is primarily concerned with human actions rather than with nature: 'From Shang Ti [Shang Di] or T'ien [Tian] come blessings and punishments. But there is no hint that he is the creator of the Universe or the cause of its functioning.'[15] The world order established through the Mandate or Destiny of Heaven (*Tian ming*) was both spiritual and political, in which the good were rewarded while the bad were punished. When facing the order of Heaven, human action determines their own situation; those who follow the order and are virtuous will 'win victory' without difficulty, while those who are against the order are doomed, however numerous they are. This is exactly the picture painted in a poetic eulogy of the *Book of Poetry* where the founding father of the Zhou dynasty (1045?–256BCE) was said to be the bearer of the Mandate of Heaven, and thanks to this, the Mandate of Heaven that had been bestowed upon the powerful Shang dynasty (1600?–1045?BCE) was replaced:

> August was King Wen, continuously bright and reverent.
> Great, indeed, was the Mandate of Heaven.
> There were Shang's grandsons and sons, Shang's grandsons and sons.
> Was their number not a hundred thousand?
> But the High God gave his Mandate, and they bowed down to Zhou.[16]

From this poem and many other early sources it seems that the spiritual power of *Tian* or High God determines, primarily, the political fortune and misfortune of the nation, and some scholars have therefore argued that traditional Chinese religion was monotheistic. However, this is only one side of religious culture in early China, a tradition preferred and then significantly transformed by court educators and ritual masters who were the forerunners of Confucians. When we examine the overall setting of religious culture in which early Confucians operated, we can easily see that

---

[14] See James Legge (trans.): *The Chinese Classics, Vol. IV, The She-King,* London: Trubner &Co., 1871, pp.448–9: 'Great is God, Beholding this lower world in majesty. He surveyed the four quarters [of the kingdom], seeking for someone to give settlement to the people. Those two [earlier] dynasties had failed to satisfy Him with their government; so throughout the various States, He sought and considered, for one on which he might confer the rule.'

[15] Laurence Thompson: *Chinese Religion: An Introduction*, Encino, California: Dickenson Publishing Corporation, 1975, p.5.

[16] *Sources of Chinese Tradition*, compiled by Wm Theodore de Bary and Irene Bloom, 2nd edn, vol. 1, New York: Columbia University Press, 1999, p.38.

the religious beliefs and practices of ancient China were much more polytheistic or even pantheistic than monotheistic. The association of *shen* with sky gods made this term (*shen*) a natural one to represent the spiritual essence of both celestial and meteorological phenomena. The sun, moon, stars, and the forces of cold and heat were all considered spirits, and were given thanksgiving offerings, but the scope of Chinese spirits was much wider than heavenly phenomena, and this was accepted, to an extent, in Confucian deliberation on the world and life. In a number of classical texts we find descriptions of *shen* as the spirit or transformative numinous power or mysterious forces of natural phenomena, living creatures and human beings. There are indications that Confucians recognized that there were many different categories of spiritual beings and powers,[17] and that human beings could somehow communicate with the spiritual forces external to themselves through ritualized votive offerings, which Confucius called '*ji shen*', making sacrifices to the spirits. The belief seems to have been that humans can draw spirits nearer as if they were present, a process in which humans learn about the mysterious power of the 'spiritual others'. In the *Book of Mengzi* we find a term, '*bai shen*', a hundred gods and spirits or myriads of spiritual beings. It is said that a man or a ruler cannot possibly be wise unless he is accepted and supported by gods and spirits. Being asked how the ancient sage, Shun, was accepted by Heaven and how he was accepted by the people, Mengzi explained that

> When he was put in charge of sacrifices, the hundred gods enjoyed them. This showed that Heaven accepted him. When he was put in charge of affairs, they were kept in order and the people were content. This showed that the people accepted him. (Mengzi, 5A:5)

However, compared with earlier pantheistic beliefs, there is already a significant change in the use of the term '*shen*'. In many passages in Confucian texts *shen* is no longer confined merely to spiritual beings and powers; it is also used as an adjective to refer to the spirit-like, supranormal, or 'divine' talents or power of human beings and their incalculable abilities. Humans can develop a kind of miraculous character or a transformative power within themselves through various methods of self-cultivation. Therefore Mengzi defines *shen* in terms of something mysteriously beyond normal knowledge: 'To be great and be transformed by this greatness is called "sage"; to be sage and to transcend the understanding is called "*shen*"'

---

[17] In early Chinese writings the spiritual world is composed of three parts, the heavenly spirits (*tian shen*), earthly gods (*di zhi*) and human ghosts (*ren gui*), each having a different sphere and requiring a different kind of ritual; hence the 'three religious ceremonies'(*san li*), the first of which is called 'si', the second 'ji', and the third, 'xiang' (the *Book of Documents*, see James Legge (trans.), *The Shoo King or the Book of Historical Documents*, 1865, p.47). Gradually the demarcation between them was blurred and ethical meaning was later introduced into the spiritual world: the good were called '*shen*' while unfriendly gods were named '*gui*'. As far as human spirits are concerned, a *shen* is the spirit of a person who had passed away normally and was sacrificed according to rituals, while a *gui* is the one whose death was irregular in some way and who had no family to conduct sacrifices.

(7B:25). The *Doctrine of the Mean* extends human virtues to the domain of spiritual quality, explaining that 'One who has absolute sincerity is like a spirit' (Zhongyong, 24), and partakes of the knowledge of spiritual beings. The authors of these texts demonstrate a clear tendency to associate spiritual beings and powers with human beings and human qualities, in which it seems natural for the knowledge of these powers and qualities to be recognized as part of Confucian wisdom.

The humanization trend in the issue of wisdom's sacred source gained momentum through early Confucians' emphasis on the spirits and power of ancestors and the passing-away forefathers. Ancestral worship was central to Chinese wisdom thinking, and Confucians undoubtedly believed that ancestors represented the sacred past and that by performing certain rites and honouring the glories of the past, ancient wisdom would be transmitted to later generations. All these practices were based on the belief that ancestors, though passing away, were still alive. To understand this, we must consider religious belief about life after death. Following earlier traditions, the majority of Confucian scholars of pre-Qin China believed that the life of a human being came from a combination of two kinds of essence which were later labelled 'yin' and 'yang': *hun* (composed of one radical referring to clouds (*yun*) and another to ghost (*gui*), the spirit from Heaven), and *po* (composed of one radical for white or daylight (*bai*) and another for ghost (*gui*), the soul from the earth). When a person was born, these two kinds of essence combined and thus a life began. When a person died, they departed, with the *hun* or the spiritual soul going up to Heaven and *po* or the animal soul descending to the earth.[18]

Therefore, life did not come from nothingness, and death was not viewed as a total end of life, but as a transformation from being with the family to their residing in heaven and earth. There was no specification about where the spirits were in heaven, although sometimes it was said that (royal) great ancestral spirits sat beside the Lord on High and were able to exercise an influence over the decisions of the Lord to bless or punish their descendants.[19] In *Zuo's Commentary on the Annals of Spring and Autumn* (*Chunqiu Zuo zhuan*) there is a passage relating how a spirit from Heaven visited a man in his dream: 'Ying dreamt that Heaven sent [a Spirit] to him, "Sacrifice to me, and I will bless you."'[20] This suggests that Heaven was believed to be the

---

[18] Sun Xidan: *Liji Jijie*, Beijing: Zhonghua Shuju, 1985, vol. 2, p.714. 'The intelligent spirit returns to heaven; the body and the animal soul return to the earth; and hence arose the idea of seeking (for the deceased) in sacrifice in the unseen darkness and in the bright region above' (James Legge (trans.): *The Li Ki*, in *The Sacred Books of China*, Part III, p.444, in *The Sacred Books of the East*, ed. F. Max Müller, vol. 27, reprinted Delhi: Motilal Banarsidass, 1968.

[19] 'King Wen is on high. Oh, he shines in Heaven! Zhou is an old people, but its Mandate is new. The leaders of Zhou became illustrious, was not God's Mandate timely given? King Wen ascends and descends, on the left and right of God' (*Sources of Chinese Tradition*, p.38).

[20] The Fifth Year of Duke Cheng of the *Zuo Zhuan* or the *Zuo's Commentary on the Spring and Autumn Annals*. See James Legge, *The Chinese Classics*, with a translation, critical and exegetical notes, prolegomena, and copious indexes, vol. V, London: Trubner & Co., 1872, p.356.

place where the spirit would go after death, and that the spirit in Heaven had the power and ability to move from the heavenly realm to the earthly realm.

The heavenly realm is sometimes termed 'the bright region' which is in contrast to the 'dark region', the place where the animal soul would go.[21] A specification is also made to refer to the 'dark region' where the soul went: it is said that the soul would go to a place called '*huang quan*', the Yellow Springs, the darkest and deepest place under the earth.[22] The Yellow Springs are often described by modern scholars as a shadowy underworld.[23] However, there is a joyful quality about this place; Needham quotes the *Zuo's Commentary* as referring to the Yellow Springs as a place where 'joy and concord will be found'.[24] If we take into account the features of springs that are often associated with life, renewal and immortality, then the Yellow Springs might be a place where the dead could be continually refreshed and revived, and this is in stark contrast to Buddhist hell, popular in the later history of China.

Either in Heaven or under the earth the spirits of the ancestors were believed to be an important source of knowledge and wisdom. It was of a moral and spiritual significance to consult the spirits of the dead, to worship ancestors and to praise the great achievements of the ancients, because it was believed that ancestors were not only alive, but also powerful in determining the destiny and welfare of the living community. Furthermore, ancient spirits were considered the embodiment of wisdom, and calling them to return was regarded as a unique occasion on which descendants could consult them on many important issues.

The focus on ancestors in early Confucianism developed further in two directions. In one direction it led to a familial type of religion, through which every traditional Chinese home became 'a religious shrine, for it contained spirit tablets of the ancestors, and pictures and idols of many household deities'.[25] In the other, it developed into an ethical education system, by which ancestral worship was rationalized or secularized as a moral commemoration, and sacrifices were made as a means of showing one's reverence towards the ancestral tradition. Confucius once commented that 'Making sacrifices to spirits as if they were present' (*Analects*, 3:12), which can be interpreted literally – spirits were there, and can also be explained figuratively – an ancestor who was present during the process of sacrifice rituals provided a moral model for teaching the young. Ancestral worship was thus transformed as the source of ancient teaching and wisdom, which in turn prescribed the right way for the people. The dual meaning of honouring ancestors, religious and

---

[21] James Legge (trans.): *The Li Ki*, 1968, p.444.

[22] In the First Year of Duke Yin of the *Zuo Zhuan* or the *Zuo's Commentary on the Spring and Autumn Annals*, there is a reference to the Yellow Spring (*huang quan*) where the dead went (Hu Zhihui (trans.): *Zuo's Commentary*, Changsha: Hunan Renmin Chubanshe, 1996, vol. 1, p.7).

[23] Joseph Needham: *Science and Civilization in China*, vol. V, pt. II, Cambridge University Press, 1974, p.81; Mu-Chu Poo: *In Search of Personal Welfare: A View of Ancient Chinese Religion,* Albany: State University of New York Press, 1998, p.158.

[24] Needham, 1974, p.84.

[25] C.K. Yang: *Religion in Chinese Society*, University of California Press, 1961, p.16.

ethical, is important for us to understand why Confucians highlighted the ancestral tradition. We can read from the *Book of Poetry*:

> Ah! Ah! Our meritorious ancestor! Permanent are the blessings coming from him, Repeatedly conferred without end: – They have come to you in this place.[26]

Blessings are the religious ensuring that ancestral virtues would be carried out through generations. However, honouring ancestors was also for us to honour our own beginning. For Confucians, all things originated from heaven and all men originated from their ancestors. The necessity of sacrifices was in expressing gratitude towards the originators and in recalling our beginning.

Honouring the beginning implies the importance of offspring, and Mengzi even directly regarded reproduction of children, especially the male heir, as the most important element of filial piety: 'There are three things which are not filial piety, and having no posterity is the greatest of them' (Mengzi, 4A:26). The *Doctrine of the Mean* supports this point of view:

> Confucius says that, to remember the ancestor, to perform the same rites, and the same music which they performed when living, to revere what they revered, to love what they loved, to serve them after death as they were served during their life, – that is perfect filial piety. (Zhongyong, 21)

Confucius once described a person as a filial son if he had followed his (deceased) father's way without deviation (*Analects*, 1:11). One of his disciples, Zengzi (Zeng Shen, 505–435BCE), was recorded as saying, 'When proper respect towards the dead is shown at the end and continued after they are far away, the virtue of the people will reach its highest point' (*Analects*, 1:9). It is in the following of the ancestral way that Confucians invested a sacred meaning on wisdom and knowledge.

Confined within the overall framework of monotheism, the Israelite idea of wisdom does not leave much room for the influence of spirits. In early Israelite writings there is not even a specific word for 'spirit'. The English word 'spirit' comes from the Latin word for breath (*spiritus*), which comes in turn from the verb *spirare* 'to breathe' (the Greek word *pneuma* has a similar derivation). In referring to spirit, the Hebrew word *rūᵃḥ* was used in a metaphorical sense, originally signifying literally wind and breath:[27] 'Wind is an invisible, unpredictable, uncontrollable force, which bears down on everything in its path ... Breath is a miniature wind, and from this the metaphorical use of the term acquired a more precise and positive direction, for breath is essential to life' (Genesis 6.17).[28]

---

[26] James Legge (trans.): *The She-King or the Book of Odes*, 1871, p.634.

[27] The three words, 'spirit', 'breath' and 'wind' used in English translation all render the one Hebrew word *rûah* in Ezekiel 37: 5–14.

[28] *The Oxford Companion to the Bible*, p.287.

In this respect, the usage of 'spirit' or *rū^aḥ* is similar to that of a Chinese character '*qi*'. *Qi* primarily means 'breath', 'air', 'vapour', but can also refer to the power or force that brings about life and maintains life. Since breathing is the symbol of life, and ceasing to breathe means the end of life, *qi* has obtained a spirit-like quality that powers life, and all spirits or ghosts are manifestations of the spirit-like power. It is recorded in the *Book of Rites* that, when one of his students, Zai Wo, asked about the meaning and references of ghosts and spirits (*gui shen*), Confucius explained them in terms of *qi* from heaven and earth, and believed that a proper understanding of spirits and ghosts was the highest of all his teachings.[29] *Qi* is the essence of the spirit and the soul, and it is *qi* that sustains a life. Since the status of *qi* determines the status of life, Confucians call for *qi* to be cultivated and nourished. Mengzi said that he was good at cultivating his 'flood-like *qi*', which is in the highest degree vast and unyielding. 'Nourish it with integrity and place no obstacle in its path and it will fill the space between Heaven and Earth' (Mengzi, 2A:2). Used in a spiritual sense in later literature and religious texts, both '*spirit*' and '*qi*' can be independent of the body, become something above one's life and control one's thought and action, and are therefore regarded as an important source of sacred knowledge.

Although the religious sense of 'spirits' was underdeveloped and the word for 'spirit' does not play a major role in defining the sacred source of wisdom in the early Israelite tradition, we can still read in the Hebrew Scriptures various descriptions of the nature and power of spirits. A spirit may drive people into an ecstasy and empower them to behave with miraculous strength. Spirits in early Israel, however, were not all of a good nature. Indeed, there are references to spirits acting in an evil way, enticing, lying or misleading. There seems to be a contrast between the Spirit of YHWH, who gives a person power and intelligence, and an evil spirit, who torments him (1 Samuel 16:13–14); the Spirit of YHWH can make a person a prophet and can change him into a totally different man (1 Samuel 10:6), while an evil spirit can lead a person into error. For example, when YHWH asked who would be enticing Ahab into attacking Ramoth Gilead and going to his death there, 'a spirit came forward' and said 'I will go out and be a lying spirit in the mouths of all his prophets' (1 Kings 22:20–22). How to understand the nature of evil spirits and the relationship between evil spirits and YHWH has raised serious challenges for traditional scholarship in the study of early Israelite religion. No clear explanation has been offered concerning such questions as whether an evil spirit is part of the Spirit of YHWH or is only a

---

[29] Sun Xidan: *Liji Jijie*, Beijing: Zhonghua Shuju, 1985, vol. 3, pp.1218–19. 'Zai Wo said, "I have heard the names Kwei [gui] and Shan [Shen], but I do not know what they mean". The Master said, "The (intelligent) spirit is of the shan nature, and shows that in fullest measure; the animal soul is of the kwei nature, and shows that in fullest measure. It is the union of kwei and shan that forms the highest exhibition of doctrine. All the living must die, and dying, return to the ground; this is what is called kwei. The bones and flesh moulder below; and hidden away, become the earth of the fields. But the spirit issues forth, and is displayed on high in a condition of glorious brightness"' (James Legge (trans.): *The Li Ki*, Part IV, vol. 28, 1968 reprint, p.220.

derivation from YHWH, or whether it is sent deliberately by YHWH to test people's faith or it comes of its own will and desire. It seems clear that, to some Israelite authors at least, music (such as playing the harp) could sooth the pain and injuries caused by an evil spirit and even compel it to leave (1 Samuel 16:16–23), but no satisfactory theological explanation has been made for this.

Comparatively speaking, the term 'spirit' is more frequently, if not exclusively, used in many books of the Hebrew Scriptures for YHWH, the creative power and the source of wisdom. After the heavens and the earth were created, according to Genesis, 'the Spirit of YHWH was hovering over the waters' (Genesis 1:2), implying that all subsequent life came from the Spirit. The Spirit is taken as the source of power in individuals, as it is taught that 'The spirit of the Lord will come upon you in power' (1 Samuel 10:6), and it is believed to be the life-giving 'wind' or 'breath'. In the book of Job, Elihu claims confidently that 'The Spirit of YHWH has made me; the breath of the Almighty gives me life' (Job 33:4); that the spirit of human beings comes from the 'breath' of YHWH, the sole source of wisdom and understanding: 'it is the spirit in a man, the breath of the Almighty, that makes him understand' (Job 32:8; 33:4). In Ezekiel, it is stated clearly that YHWH causes breath to enter dry bones and give them life and that YHWH can raise the dead from their graves, put his Spirit within them, and make them live again (Ezekiel 37:5, 13–14). Like their counterparts in the Confucian tradition, Israelite writers did not confine their use of 'spirit' to a spiritual being, in the way the term is used in a modern religious context. It is frequently used in the sense of 'miraculous' power or 'mysterious' trait or ability, of which wisdom is one. In the book of Deuteronomy it is said that, since Moses laid his hand on Joshua, 'Joshua son of Nun was filled with the spirit of wisdom' (Deuteronomy, 34:9). From this we may infer that, in the Israelites' mind, wisdom can pass from one person to another, and that its spirit embodies precious faith and knowledge. Of this we find a further illustration in a paragraph in Isaiah, where the Spirit of YHWH is said to be 'the spirit of wisdom and understanding, the spirit of counsel and might, the spirit of knowledge and the fear of the LORD' (Isaiah 11:2).

Even the most rational Confucians would not have denied that there was a life after death, although they tended not to speculate much about it but concentrated their attention on this life. Confucians venerated the spirits of great ancestors, but preferred to interpret the meaning and significance of ancestral worship in terms of moral education and wisdom transmission. In this way Confucians added anthropocentric sacredness to wisdom concerning life and death. By contrast, the worship of ancestors does not play an important role in the Israelite transmission of wisdom, and the concept of death is much less prominent than that we would find in many other cultures. It seems that ancient Israelites did not have a clear idea about, or did not believe in, life after death. For example, Job contrasts human life and death with those of a tree: cut down, a tree will sprout again and its new shoots will not fail, but humans die and are laid low; they breathe their last and are no more. Therefore to the question 'if a man dies will he live again?' the answer probably is 'no' (Job 14:7–10, 14). It is explained more vividly in the Wisdom of Solomon that 'there is no return from our death': 'our life will pass away like the traces of a cloud, and be scattered like mist that is chased by the rays of the sun and overcome by its heat' (Wisd. 2:4–5).[30] This does not, however, mean that ancient Israelites totally disregarded their ancestors' influence on human wisdom. Israelite wisdom thinking was engaged in its tradition, culture and religion, which were under the strong influence of the religious ideas and practices of the Near East at that time in relation to their understanding of ancestors and their power, and modern scholars have recognized that, 'Israelites invoked the ancestors for aid in matters familial, agricultural, and political. The ancestral spirits could intervene with YHWH, to the benefit of the family, and landholding corporation that inherited its resources from the fathers.'[31] We assume that all these were based on the belief that, although dead, ancestors were still, to a certain degree, powerful in terms of determining or at least influencing the course of the living.

'In the OT various terms like *šeʾōl* ("Sheol"), *māwet̲* ("death"), *ʾereṣ* ("earth"), *šaḥat̲* ("pit"), *bôr* ("pit"), and *ʾăbaddôn* ("place of destruction") could refer to the netherworld or abode of the dead.'[32] The most frequently used Hebrew word for the abode of the dead is '*sheol*' (corresponding to the Greek word '*hades*'), which is described as the lowest place imaginable (Deuteronomy 32:22; Isaiah 7:11), and is therefore also called 'the pit' (Isaiah 38:18). *Sheol* is often contrasted with the highest heavens (Amos 9:2; Psalm 139:8; Job 11:8); it is also said to be a deep grave, sometimes associated with engulfing water images (Jonah 2:3–6). These descriptions are reminiscent of the 'Yellow Springs' in the Chinese religion, which is also characterized by darkness, deep into the earth and water.

It seems that for the ancient Israelites the soul upon death would go to *sheol,* the underworld or hell, through its gates, where it was imprisoned in a place from which there was no return (Job 7:9; 38:17) and that *sheol* was the destination all people must go to, where 'there is no work or thought or knowledge or wisdom' (Eccl. 9:10). However, there is an ambiguity when the immoral and unfaithful are called the path to *sheol*: a lustful woman's house 'is the way to Sheol, going down to the chambers of death' (Prov. 7:27), while the righteous, the faithful and the wise can avoid it: 'The wise man's path leads upward to life, that he may avoid *Sheol* beneath' (Prov. 15:24). It seems apparent for the Israelites that in the underworld there is no possibility of knowledge, as implied in the following questions: 'Are your wonders known in the place of darkness, or your righteous deeds in the land of oblivion?' (Psalm 88:12).

---

[30] Influenced by Greek philosophy, later wisdom texts, especially the Wisdom of Solomon, seemed to attempt to insert into the Hebrew religion the idea of the eternal soul: 'The righteous man who has died will condemn the ungodly who are living' (Wisd. 4:16). Even in this book, however, physical immortality is not a concern of the Israelites; rather they take it as God's award, from which they go out to the consequences of being righteous: 'In the memory of virtue is immortality', and confirm that 'The righteous live for ever, and their reward is with the Lord' (Wisd. 4:1; 5:15).

[31] *The Oxford Companion to the Bible*, pp.525–6.

[32] *Eerdmans Dictionary of the Bible* (David Noel Freedman, editor-in-chief), Grand Rapids, Michigan: William B. Eerdmans Publishing Co., 2000, p.25.

However, we have clear evidence that the idea of going to *sheol* being regarded as a punishment of sinners was not developed in most parts of early Israelite writings, and only became accepted in later Judaism and in the New Testament. The underdevelopment of belief in life after death meant that the Israelites did not link knowledge with their respect of their ancestors, because ancient Israelites believed that a dead person could still feel the pain of his own body, but was not aware of or did not 'perceive' what happened to his children (Job 14:21–2), and was not able to remember and praise God: 'For in death there is no remembrance of thee; in *sheol* who can give thee praise' (Psalm 6:5). If dead ancestors were unable to perceive what happened to the living, their influence over their descendants was limited.[33] This might explain, at least partially, why the Israelites did not pay much attention to ancestral worship, a religious practice prevailing in many other cultures and civilizations.

Believing that in one form or another ancestors still existed after death, however, ancient Israelites felt it necessary to hold ceremonies to mourn the dead, although it is not entirely clear whether the main reason for such mourning was to relieve grief, or to comfort the dead, or to commemorate their achievements. There are not many descriptions of mourning the dead in Israelite wisdom literature, but from some paragraphs in other writings we can deduce that the tradition in this area was powerful and that the Israelites may therefore have been under its influence. For example, when Moses died, 'The Israelites grieved for Moses in the plains of Moab thirty days, until the time of weeping and mourning was over' (Deuteronomy 34:8); and, believing his son Joseph was dead, Jacob said, 'I shall go down to Sheol to my son, mourning' (Genesis 37:35). From this we can see that there was an agreed period for mourning, which was 30 days, and that mourning was a necessary rite for the dead.

Apart from their civil, moral and psychological functions, mourning and burial rites in many cultures also have a clear religious purpose, namely, hoping the spirits of the dead would in turn look after or protect the well-being of the living generations. Therefore, from the fact that the Israelites believed it necessary for people to mourn the dead, we can deduce that there might have been a belief, however shadowy it was, in a life after death in early Israel. Whether or not the Israelites had an undefined idea about the soul of the dead, however, it is certain that the Israelites did not attribute to mourning rites the power to save the soul, nor did they believe that by mourning rites the dead could be lifted from a lower layer (for sinners) to a higher layer (for the righteous) of hell. The Yahwism that emerged later

---

[33] The Israelites also believed that 'The dead could show themselves to the living' and 'the appearance of the dead then produces a terrifying, uncanny effect'. This explains the real meaning of the observances and customs of mourning: they are settlements with the dead, methods of release from them. However, 'The dead man remained in the not-land [*shoel*] only for a certain time … it was for just as long as there were still men to whom he appeared, who still knew his name. When that time was over, then it was as if he had never been. The life of the Hebrew was at an end. Only God knows of him always' (Ludwig Köhler: *Hebrew Man*, trans. Peter R. Ackroyd, London, SCM Press, 1956, pp.112–13).

condemned the worship of the deceased and any form of necromancy (Leviticus 19:26–32; Deuteronomy 14:1; 18:10; 26:14), and it was believed that the almighty power of YHWH would be able to destroy the evil power of *sheol*, to rescue a pious soul from death and hell. YHWH is believed to be everywhere including *sheol* to save the faithful, as one psalm sings, 'If I ascend to heaven, thou art there! If I make my bed in Sheol, thou art there!' (Psalm 139:8). Therefore we may conclude that the spirits of ancestors did not play a major role in the Israelite transmission of wisdom; rather it is in the power and spirit of YHWH that wisdom becomes sacred.

It is apparent that in searching for the sacredness of wisdom Confucians and Israelites draw different conclusions from their understanding of the spirits and ancestors. For Confucians, the existence of spirits and reverence for ancestors paves the way for a holistic view of wisdom: sacred wisdom must be found by humans themselves and can then be transmitted through human efforts. For Israelite teachers the situation is not so simple. They see a great deal of dualistic tension between the supreme source of wisdom and what humans can do about it. Although there is evidence that they believe in spirits and ancestors, this belief bypasses their central concern in religious life and is therefore not regarded as having anything to do with the sacredness of wisdom.

Theodicy and 'Knowing Destiny'

Wisdom is essentially a relationship, by which humans learn how to deal properly with themselves, nature, communities and transcendental power(s), and how to find patterns of meanings and regularities among natural and social phenomena as guidance to their choice of action. The prerequisite for formulating guidance for rational choices by either a group of people or an individual is the existence of an invisible but powerful order: by following certain rules and laws with proper understanding and knowledge we will achieve our purpose, but in disobeying or deviating from them we will fail. Behind this conventional wisdom is a religious belief that the spiritual ultimate is capable of rewarding the good and wise, and of punishing the evil and foolish. For the Israelites, YHWH protected the righteous and punished the unfaithful: 'The LORD does not let the righteous go hungry' (Prov. 10:3); for Confucians the Way of Heaven was to bless the good and bring disasters to the immoral.[34] Many wise teachings in the Confucian and Israelite texts are therefore functional, based on the anticipation of the balance between punishment and reward and between success and failure: the wicked, the fool, the sluggard or the evildoer will suffer 'punishment' of some kind, while to the wise, the upright, the hard-working and the diligent will come 'rewards', as is said in the Proverbs: 'Understanding is the fountain of life to those who have it, but folly brings

---

[34] 'The way of Heaven is to bless the good and to punish the bad' (the *Book of Documents*, James Legge, 1865, p.186).

punishment to fools' (Prov. 16:22). The rewards can be in either spiritual or material terms. In Confucianism the reward can be in the form of praise of a virtuous character, but can also be one's entitlement to a high-ranking position. In the early Israelite tradition people had no doubt that wealth was the result of wisdom and sincerity, while poverty came from foolishness and cheating, as it says in the Proverbs, 'A man of crooked mind does not prosper, and one with a perverse tongue falls into calamity' (Prov. 17:20).

However, in reality the just order that operates on the basis of a balance between punishment and reward seems not always to prevail, and order and disorder, peace and chaos, success and failure, happiness and misery, and so on, do not come in their due place, just as Job complains that, while a blameless man suffers, 'The tents of robbers are at peace, and those who provoke God are secure' (Job 12:6). Is this because of a lack of order or due to the fact that the metaphysical and religious order is always hidden behind the apparent state of affairs and events? If it is hidden, then when and how will its power be shown and be seen? In dealing with these questions early Confucian and Israelite thinkers explored a number of experimental and contemplative solutions. Based on their own understandings of the nature and function of the world order, they considered conventionally plausible and acceptable explanations.

First, it was suggested that disorder or undue punishment was merely a temporary phenomenon, and would not last long. It is a firm belief among Confucian and Israelite teachers that, although unjust people or unrighteous persons might enjoy for the moment their undeserved share of wealth and power, justice and righteousness will eventually triumph. Confucius confidently states that a man who is not benevolent cannot for long enjoy prosperity (*Analects*, 4:2). This implies that a cruel man might have gathered a great amount of wealth for the moment, but he will not always be able to do so and will not draw much benefit from the ill-gotten assets. When he says that the benevolent lives a long life (*Analects*, 6:23), Confucius may also be indicating that there is a causal relation between living a life of benevolence and longevity, and between the immoral way of living and a shortened span of life. In the same vein the book of Proverbs speaks: 'The getting of treasures by a lying tongue is a fleeting vapour and a snare of death' (Prov. 21:6). This implies that for the Israelites the wicked can enjoy a good life only for the time being, and that their wealth and treasures will eventually disappear like a vapour.

Secondly, punishment may be a means of testing or cultivating one's integrity, and a divine discipline for one to grow stronger and firmer. Mengzi taught obedience to the will of Heaven by quoting from the *Book of Poetry*: 'Obey forever Heaven's mandate; And seek much blessing for yourself' (Mengzi, 2A:4). He examined the cause of seemingly undeserved suffering and concluded that this might have come as a test and form of training Heaven had specially arranged: 'When Heaven is about to confer a great office on any man. It first exercises his mind with suffering, and his sinews and bones with toil. It exposes his body to hunger, and subjects him to extreme poverty' (Mengzi, 6B:15). Having endured these difficulties and suffering, one would prove one's value and courage, and would be able to take upon oneself a huge responsibility. Therefore there is nothing here one should complain about. A similar way of thinking is also found in the Israelite wisdom texts, in which personal suffering and undeserved treatment are explained as the discipline of YHWH, as we see in the book of Job when some of Job's friends argue that punishment should be taken as a means to make him stronger: all sufferings are for discipline and discipline cleanses a person from sin and guilt (Job 5:17–27).

Thirdly, in terms of quantity, reward and suffering can be measured by more or less, and an amount of unjust suffering can be compensated by the similar amount of reward, which is essential to judicial justice as practised in ancient China and Israel. However, reward and suffering are also measured by their quality, in which a difference between real and false and between the higher and the lower are of importance. The one who seeks material profit by immoral and wicked means causes more problems for himself and the reward is therefore false and temporary. Confucius once commented: 'If one is guided by profit in one's action, one will incur much ill will' (*Analects*, 4:12). For Mengzi there are two kinds of honours, one bestowed by Heaven, the other by humans. The former exists in the form of benevolence, righteousness, sincerity, truthfulness and so on, while the latter is shown in the ranks of duke, minister or high official. Mengzi seriously criticized his contemporaries because they exerted great efforts in pursuing the honours bestowed by humans and disregarded those of Heaven. He believed that this was surely the way to perish. By contrast, people of antiquity were different: they pursued honours bestowed by Heaven, while honours bestowed by humans followed as a matter of course (Mengzi, 6A:16). Israelite wise men also taught that no ill-perceived action would be truly respected, and only the righteous could enjoy real reward: 'The wicked earn no real gain, but those who sow righteousness get a true reward' (Prov. 11:18); and 'The wise will inherit honour, but fools get disgrace' (Prov. 3:35). In an Israelite context, nothing is higher and more important than the reward of YHWH in terms of forgiveness and blessing, and no material gains can be more appreciated than wisdom. Therefore the book of Proverbs repeatedly tells the reader that 'wisdom is better than jewels' (Prov. 8:11).

All these deliberations and contrasts, implicitly or explicitly, point to a more fundamental issue that is concerned with the disparity between the sacred and the secular elements of wisdom. However we think of the imbalance of action and its results, undeserved suffering exists. This causes great concern among Israelite and Confucian teachers. Recognizing that not all punishments are deserved, they approached the question concerning the justification of unexplainable disorder with a positive, rather than negative, attitude, in which the sacredness of wisdom arose from a successful resolution of the tension between human knowledge and the ultimate meaning of events, and between the invisible order, principle or law and the apparent social and personal consequences. The question regarding the limitations of human knowledge is actually twofold: first, can humans come to know the real intention of YHWH or *tian*; if they can, how? Secondly, can humans thoroughly grasp the secrets of the world that is external to their own existence?

As we have pointed out in Chapter 3, in both Confucian and Israelite traditions wisdom has a double nature, human knowledge and divine knowledge, and both recognize a clear difference between ordinary and profound knowledge. In Israel, 'wisdom' stands both for the divine wisdom through which YHWH created the cosmos and for the human wisdom with which rational creatures explore and master the divine creation, opening up paths of discovery above and below the earth (Job 28:20–28). Therefore in Israel faith and knowledge are two in one, as von Rad has rightly put it: 'It is perhaps her greatness that she did not keep faith and knowledge apart. The experiences of the world were for her always divine experiences as well, and the experiences of God were for her experiences of the world.'[35]

In the Confucian tradition there is less emphasis on the oneness of world experience and divine experience, but more on the unity between what we can know and what we are expected to know.

However, tension between knowledge of the world and knowledge of the spiritual ultimate does exist, and humans cannot always easily understand what is intended for the world, if there is an intention behind phenomena. Both Confucians and Israelites confirm that true wisdom is to admit that humans cannot possibly control all human events and affairs, and human intelligence alone is not sufficient to comprehend the consequences of their action and explain every phenomenon that happened in the world. They see the limitations of human intelligence and of human ability to understand fully what order lies behind changing events and what certainty humans can possibly seek. Therefore, like the proverb in the West, 'Man proposes; God disposes', there is a popular Chinese expression, 'How to plan is up to humans, but whether or not the plan can be realized depends on Heaven.' We may take these proverbs as a continuation of earlier wisdom traditions of which Confucian and ancient Israelite wisdom were important parts. And indeed, in the book of Proverbs on the Israelite side, we read that 'A man's mind plans his way, but the Lord directs his steps', or that 'The plans of the mind belong to mortals, but the answer of the tongue is from the Lord' (Prov. 16:9; 16:1), while in the Confucian texts we see a fundamental belief that Heaven 'knows' all we do, and cannot be cheated, as when Confucius denounced some of his disciples and asked if 'they would be deceiving Heaven' (*Analects*, 9:12).

What kind of function does human experience perform in the formation of wisdom, and how is it related to transcendental knowledge? How can we explain the disasters that overtake human societies or personal miseries that come as a surprise? In a polytheistic culture, it may be believed that disasters or suffering might have been caused by a disagreement between deities, or by the malevolence of particular spirits towards human beings. In a monotheistic system such as the ancient Israelite tradition, however, proving the justice of God in the face of injustice of the world is no easy task, and was indeed an essential challenge for wisdom thinking in ancient Israel. The search for possible answers, conceptualized as theodicy in later Christian

---

[35] Gerhard von Rad: *Wisdom in Israel*, Nashville: Abingdon, 1972, p.62.

theology, was first undertaken in the book of Job, which has been regarded as the most consistently theological work in the Hebrew Scriptures, even if there are problems concerning interpreting the meaning of some parts of the book owing to the imperfect preservation of, and certain later editorial revisions to, the original text and the difficult Hebrew it was written in. The book was composed in the historical setting of the post-exile era. After returning to their homeland from exile in 538BCE, the Jewish people found the life situation, both for individuals and for Jews as a nation, extremely harsh. They had endured punishment which, according to the prophets, was a result of their sin, but they could not see any prosperity that, again according to earlier prophets, should have followed. Conventional wisdom was unable to explain this, and this caused widespread pessimism and discontent. Sensitive minds attempted to make sense of the seeming incongruities of life, and searched for an explanation of the sufferings that fell upon the faithful and righteous. The author of the book of Job made the most outstanding of these attempts; he composed poetic dialogues to address the problems of a particular 'righteous sufferer', Job. According to the book, Job suffered what he believed to be undeserved punishments: his property was destroyed and his children were killed; his relatives and friends deserted him; he himself was inflicted with unbearable diseases, and he was indeed 'left with nothing but skin and bones'.

The questions underlying the dialogues of the book are significant and wide-ranging: why did such a righteous and faithful person as Job suffer? Why did God, omnipotent and just, allow evil and injustice to exist? How can we humans understand unjustified punishments? The book of Job sets out, more importantly, the tension between divine meaning and human comprehension, which, according to Katharine Dell, is 'between God's control, legitimated by his acts in creation, and human attempts to comprehend the unfathomableness and power of God' and is 'at the heart of both the figure of wisdom and of the wisdom enterprise itself'.[36] This tension is reckoned as one of the underlying reasons for the disunity between virtue and happiness, and is taken by some Israelite teachers for the 'inexplainability' of the suffering of the innocent.

Unlike the case in other religious systems such as Buddhism and Hinduism, where the accepted concept of reincarnation makes it easier to explain why in this life a person suffers, ancient Israelites did not have this kind of solution, because they lacked a clear concept of life after death. Because there was no belief in life after death, for any particular person fairness and justice must be realized in this life; otherwise it would not be realized at all! Various attempts are made in the book of Job to identify the true reasons or causes for the punishments Job endured, and most of them followed the traditional thinking way and regarded punishment as exclusively a result of sin: 'Who, being innocent, has ever perished? Where were the upright ever destroyed? Only those who plough evil and sow trouble reap the same' (Job 4:7–8).

---

[36] Katharine Dell: *'Get Wisdom, Get Insight' – An Introduction to Israel's Wisdom Literature*, Macon, Georgia: Smyth & Helwys Publishing, Inc., 2000, p.42.

These arguments, however, as we have noted above, do not really answer the question concerning unjust suffering.

So what wisdom has the book of Job found? It is the need to understand that there are things in this life and in this world that can never be understood or explained by humans, because they belong to the world order and can be explained only in the greatness of YHWH. For example, to the questions 'Who can understand (*byn*) how YHWH spreads out the clouds, how he thunders from his pavilion?' the wisest possible answer for the author can only be that this is YHWH's intention and, by scattering lightning about him, he judges peoples (Job 36:29–31). It seems to Israelite teachers that the only solution to the perceived tension between what is known and what can be known is to separate the divine wisdom and the human knowledge: what belongs to YHWH cannot be fully grasped by humans; and humans must admit that their intelligence is limited, which has been evidenced by the fact that there are 'things too wonderful to be known' (Job 42:3), and by the experience that the normal process of perception cannot deal with things that are great, hidden, dark, deep or new. The solution of the tension caused by the double nature of wisdom is consistent with the overall view of the Israelites: the sacredness of wisdom can be, and can only be, found in trust and faith in YHWH, rather than in human views, which is already well summarized in the book of Proverbs: 'Trust in YHWH and do not rely on your own insight' (*bīnā*, Prov. 3:5). The only possible solution is to turn to YHWH and ask him 'let me know' (Job 10:2).

Substantially anthropocentric and not particularly fond of the dualistic separation between the divine and the human, Confucians seek a humanistic approach to wisdom in their attempt to understand the problem of undeserved suffering and disorder. They admit that there is a disparity between what humans do and what they deserve, but they attribute this to the invisible hand of the Way. To further examine the cause of the success or failure of an individual, or disaster or peace and harmony of a particular society, Confucian masters developed a special concept, namely, *ming* or Destiny. Composed of *kou* (the mouth) and *ling* (to order or command), *ming* was initially interpreted as '*ling*', 'to command or order (somebody to do something)',[37] and was then extended in the Confucian classics to refer to the 'commandment of Heaven' (*tian ming*), and the life and fate of an individual. According to Confucian understanding, everything or every being has a destiny before coming into existence that predetermines its lot in the world, and this is ultimately related to the command or mandate or Destiny of Heaven that underlies and determines all individual destinies or fates, and predetermines the direction of human courses and the result of individual efforts. While it is possible for us to understand the reasons and causes behind an individual action, there is something more fundamental than what can be

---

[37] *Ming* and *ling* are the same word in the oracle bones and bronze inscriptions, composed of a mouth (representing giving an order) above and a kneeling person who accepted the order. From this it refers to an order that was given by a higher authority to a person who is to carry it out (Duan Yucai: *Shuowen jiezi zhu*, 1998, p.57; *Hanyu da zidian*, 1993, pp.47, 254).

seen in its results. The causation is not brought about by humans, because it is in the hands of Destiny. Confucius attributed peace or disharmony to the power of Destiny that is beyond human control: 'It is Destiny if the Way prevails; it is equally Destiny if the Way falls into disuse' (*Analects*, 14:36). Mengzi explains the unaccountability of the cause clearly when he defines the work of Heaven and Destiny: 'When a thing is done though by no one, then it is the work of Heaven; when a thing comes about though no one brings it about, then it is the work of destiny' (Mengzi, 5A:6). Xunzi, a fundamentally rationalistic philosopher, has also pointed out that 'the Destiny of humans lies with Heaven (Nature)' (Xunzi, 16:1), although for him knowing one's fate or destiny merely enables one not to complain against Heaven: 'Those who know themselves do not resent others; those who know fate do not resent Heaven' (Xunzi, 4:5).

Confucians in general were confident of human ability to understand and interpret the world, but at the same time they, or at least some of the early Confucian masters, saw the limitations of this ability and wondered how much the way *tian* produced things could be fully interpreted. Together with Confucian beliefs in fate or destiny (*ming*), the admission of human limitations poses a serious challenge to its general anthropocentric outlook. As a way out of the dilemma, Confucius suggests that true wisdom lies in our honestly admitting what we know and what we do not know (*Analects*, 2:17). To know what one can know and what one cannot is the beginning of knowledge and is the essence of Confucian wisdom. The *Great Learning* explains that 'knowing where one should stop (*zhi zhi*)' will lead to stability, tranquillity and deliberation. For Confucians there are peace and chaos in society and there are good and bad fortune for individuals. However, there is no particular reason why we must question their final cause, nor must we provide an explanation. Instead they recognize that good or bad fortune has its justification in the operation of the Way. When the way prevailed there was peace, harmony and justice, but when the way failed, then chaos and disorder took over the society and individuals suffered from injustice. It seems to be the Confucian wisdom that, because all these are part of the predetermined destiny, we humans do not have the capacity to explain and understand them.

Although all events in life were believed to be predetermined, Confucians nevertheless maintained their final trust in Heaven, and believed that Heaven's Way would finally prevail and that Heaven was the true witness to one's innocence. This can be illustrated by an anecdote recorded in the *Analects*. In the State of Wei, the Duke Ling's wife, Nanzi, was a notorious woman. When Confucius and his disciples stayed there, Confucius had to deal with her. One day he visited her again, and this caused great displeasure among some of his disciples. To counter this Confucius felt that there was no other way to prove his innocence but by invoking Heaven's witness: 'If I have done anything improper, may Heaven avert me, may Heaven avert me!' (*Analects*, 6:28). The repetition of 'May Heaven avert me' reflected, on the one hand, that he did not really have any other means but Heaven's witness to prove his innocence and, on the other hand, that he was determined to seek justice from Heaven rather than from any individual. For him, although some people might be able to make undeserved accusation appear justifiable, Heaven was always there to watch us, and final justice would be done only through a particular relation between us and Heaven. It was also true that, when Confucius felt that there was no one else who could understand him, he did not complain against Heaven nor did he blame other people. Instead, he held a strong belief that, if he was ever understood at all, that must be by Heaven (*Analects*, 14:35). That was, for him, the highest wisdom we humans would ever be able to master. One might be able to cheat other people, but one can never evade the eyes of Heaven.

When Confucius was seriously ill, one of his disciples arranged for their students to serve Confucius as his retainers. Since Confucius was no longer holding an office and should not have retainers, Confucius felt that this was cheating. He asked in great discontent, 'Who would we be deceiving? Would we be deceiving Heaven?' (*Analects*, 9:12). In all these cases we find the wise teaching of a higher degree that Confucians tried to deliver to their students or audience: we might not be able to understand fully the reasons and causes for injustice in the world; holding faith in Heaven and submitting ourselves to Destiny is the only way to get over a life crisis and have a positive attitude towards the future.[38]

When we reflect on this kind of wisdom we find that it demonstrates a remarkable similarity to that of the traditional wisdom teachings in Israel. Israelite prophets and teachers of all generations aimed to deliver a single message to their people: YHWH was fair and just, and humans must accept what had come from him. Therefore a person who suffered from mistreatment must not abandon his or her faith in YHWH, as in the case of Job, where his friend repeated: 'Blessed is the man whom God corrects; so do not despise the discipline of the Almighty. For he wounds, but he also binds up; he injures, but his hands also heal' (Job 5:17–18). Perhaps it was this conviction that enabled Job to believe in his 'redeemer',[39] and to hope that in the end the Lord's justice would prove him innocent of any charges of evil that deserved the suffering that he had experienced (Job 19:19–25).

In contrast to the Israelite teachers who ended their search for the cause of suffering in faith in YHWH, however, the Confucian search for wisdom did not stop at the unaccountable force or power. Instead, they went a step further to ask about the Way of Heaven, in the attempt to understand their own destiny. In the knowledge of

---

[38] In the *Analects* it is recorded that, when under siege in Kuang, Confucius demonstrated his faith in the Mandate of Heaven and experienced joy even when facing danger (9:5). This anecdote was also used in the *Book of Zhuangzi* to illustrate how a wise man would do in a dangerous situation: Confucius sang to his lute in enjoyment. When asked why, Confucius was supposed to explain that everybody has his own fate and time, and that a sage fears nothing because he knows that hardship is part of life, knows that success depends upon the times (The *Book of Chuang Tzu*, trans. Martin Palmer with Elizabeth Breuilly, London: Arkana, 1996, p.144).

[39] 'To redeem' is a translation of the Hebrew word *gā'al,* that is related to the whole concept of justice and making things right in this world, involving something on behalf of others because they are unable to do it for themselves (*The Oxford Companion to the Bible*, pp.643–4).

destiny and Heaven, Confucian wisdom reached its highest degree. It is one of the fundamental Confucian teachings that, although ordinary humans are not naturally able to know their own destiny, they must nevertheless be trained to gain this kind of knowledge, by which they would be able not only to know their own destiny but also to understand the destiny of Heaven. It is in knowing destiny that we find the sacredness of Confucian wisdom, in the sense that this knowing means seeking an explanation for the unexplainable, because it is intended to make a breakthrough in one's limitations, in terms both of intelligence and of capabilities. Since all things have their roots and branches, and all affairs have their beginnings and ends, the knowledge of what is first and what is last concerns our own destiny and the destiny of all things and events. Although we may never be able to see the final cause of life problems, knowledge of our destiny will enable us to understand the mechanism and process of life, and to make progress in our moral cultivation. This is why Confucius repeatedly told his students that without a proper knowledge of destiny, they would not be able to become gentlemen (*Analects*, 20:3). He also proudly claimed that by the age of fifty he himself had come to the full knowledge of Destiny of Heaven (*Analects*, 2:4).

Identifying Destiny as the cause of one's suffering or problems is not the end of Confucian wisdom, and Confucian masters would not agree that humans should totally surrender human responsibilities to Destiny. In earlier Chinese history, questions concerning the suffering of the innocent led to the distancing of Heaven from human comprehension, and complaints arose such as 'What is my offence against Heaven?'[40] While complaining against or lamenting seemingly unjust and unkind Heaven, it was observed that the Way of Heaven was 'inexplicable'.[41] Acknowledging the fact of retribution in which ultimate innocence and success were to be judged by Heaven and Destiny, Confucius and his followers nevertheless refused to base moral cultivation on the principle of rewards and punishments (*Analects*, 4:25). Contrary to the early Israelite agnosticism which held that the creation of YHWH was too wonderful for human minds, by which the created and the Creator were finally separated, Confucians went for an antithesis that, although individuals were not always able to comprehend what happened to and resulted from one's action, the world was knowable and human wisdom was able to grasp the secrets and mysteries of the world, by which the limitations of humans in intelligence, morality and action could be overcome. In this process, humans are always in a positive and active position, without which knowledge of the world is impossible. It is in this sense that Confucius proposed that 'it is humans that are capable of making the Way great, not the Way that is capable of making humans great' (*Analects*, 15:29).

As human beings we have our limitations or finitude. To find the solution to the problems caused by the finitude of the self and to grasp the ultimate truth, we must

---

[40] James Legge (trans.): *The She-King or the Book of Odes*, 1871, p.336.

[41] Ibid., p.325.

know ourselves. It is not a particularly Confucian doctrine that we come to understand our destiny through knowing ourselves. Socrates, for example, calls for 'knowing yourself', while Laozi, the supposed compiler of the *Daode jing*, gives a preference to 'being enlightened' over 'being wise', insisting that 'He who knows others is called wise, while he who knows himself is named enlightened' (Daode jing, 33). For Confucians, knowing ourselves is important, not only because it enables us to know better our limitations, but also because it can lead us to the knowledge of the Way. Acknowledging that the ultimate is beyond our comprehension or that the finitude of humans prevents them from fully comprehending the Way of Heaven, some Confucian masters nevertheless argue that the only way to the knowledge of Heaven and Destiny is to know one's own self and one's own nature. Differently from idealist Confucians, Xunzi emphasizes that, as a kind of rational knowledge, wisdom distinguishes what belongs to humans from what belongs to Heaven. Interpreting Heaven as Nature, Xunzi is nevertheless positive that the ultimate wisdom exists in the knowledge of the distinctive functions of Heaven and humans.[42]

However, Confucians are not blind optimists contending that humans are capable of acquiring sacred wisdom. Their limited positivism requires three conditions by which humans can finally understand the secrets of destiny and the final cause of the world. First, humans must share the divine nature of Heaven. Without sharing the same nature as Heaven and Destiny, humans cannot possibly truly comprehend what is disclosed to them. Confucians assume that all humans come from Heaven, as we can see from many sayings in the classics, such as 'Heaven gives birth to the people' (*tian sheng min*); 'Heaven produces the teeming masses' (*tian sheng zheng min*), and 'Heaven populated the earth below' (*tian jiang xia min*).[43] Since humans are born from Heaven, the nature of humans is the same as that of Heaven, and it is reasonable to presume that humans can know Heaven or the Way of Heaven through internalizing what Heaven imparts to them.

Secondly, comprehension will not come unless one has fully cultivated oneself, through moral experience in life, both internally and externally. Confucius said of himself that he did not comprehend the 'destiny of Heaven' till he was fifty years old, and Mengzi set it as the condition of knowing Heaven that one has exerted one's mind and nature to the utmost.

Thirdly, there must be an unbroken chain of moral efforts through which wisdom can be fully manifested to human beings as a whole. There is a limitation on what an individual can do in his life. Concerning the question whether or not humans can really comprehend the transcendent Heaven, Confucians provide two answers, one

---

[42] *A Source Book in Chinese Philosophy*, p.117.

[43] Shangshu (*Book of Documents*), Changsha: Human Publishing House, 1997, p.324. Mengzi quoted from the *Book of Poetry*: 'Heaven produces the teeming masses, And where there is a thing there is a norm. If the people held on to their constant nature, they would be drawn to superior virtue' (Mengzi, 6A:6) and quoted from the *Book of Documents*: 'Heaven populated the earth below. Made a lord for them and made him their teacher that he might assist the Lord on High in loving them' (Mengzi, 1B:3).

partial and the other whole. The partial answer is that an individual may not be able to fully grasp the Destiny of Heaven in his life, but he can know the essence of that destiny which should be sufficient to guide his own life choices, and although exerting one's mind to know one's nature cannot enable one to grasp the whole meaning of the Mandate of Heaven and the Way of Heaven, it at least can prove and secure its moral implications, proving and securing it as the essence of creation. For a whole revelation of human destiny, Confucians come to the transmission of wisdom through cultural and historical links. Thus knowing Destiny is not a journey of one generation only; rather it is pursued in history and in cultural transmission. It is in this sense that Confucian veneration of ancestors and emphasis on cultural transmission become an important part of Confucian wisdom, in the sense that, without the wisdom of the ancients, we would not have a start in our knowledge, and we would never come to a comprehensive knowledge of the world and the destiny of humankind.

Confucians advanced an anthropocentric approach to personal problems or suffering. What is essential in this approach is that one concentrate on one's duties as a human, by which one can come to a new understanding of one's destiny. We can make this clearer by analysing the following dialogue between two of Confucius's disciples, Sima Niu (?–?BCE) and Zi Xia (507–?BCE). Sima Niu felt aggrieved, complaining that everyone else had brothers, and that only he himself was alone. It was clear to him that life was unfair to him and he had good reasons to make a complaint. How would this be explained? Zi Xia looked at this issue from a different point of view and then provided an answer. Zi Xia quoted a saying he had heard (probably from the Master Confucius) that 'Death and life are the Destiny (of Heaven); wealth and rank depend upon (the will of) Heaven.' He further deliberated that Sima Niu should really not have been distressed by this, because he could have all men in the world as his brothers if he was reverent, unfailingly courteous towards them, and observant of the rites (*Analects*, 12:5). Mengzi went further in an anthropocentric direction when coming to explain the cause of disasters and calamities. For him there were two kinds of calamities, one natural, and the other human-made. Mengzi quoted from the *Book of Documents* to illustrate that the most serious of all disasters are those caused by humans themselves, because

> When Heaven sends down calamities,
> There is hope of weathering them;
> When humans bring disasters upon themselves,
> There is no hope of escape. (Mengzi, 2A:4)

For Mengzi all real disasters could be explained by the failure of human beings. It was so for society and it was the same for an individual. He therefore placed the responsibility for a good life on the shoulders of each individual, and rejected taking knowing destiny as an excuse for human failure. Mengzi was eager to establish a concept of the proper destiny, to differentiate this from the destiny that was caused by human errors. The former would be fulfilled by human endeavours to meet their own responsibilities, while the latter would occur when people failed to follow the Way of Heaven: 'Whatever befalls one is predestined. One should accept fittingly one's proper destiny … One who dies after having done his best in following the Way dies according to his proper destiny. It is never anyone's proper destiny to die in fetters' (Mengzi, 7A:2). If one can know one's proper destiny while shunning improper destiny, then one is fulfilling one's destiny and can therefore be said to have wisdom.

Conclusion

In terms of the sacredness of wisdom the Israelite tradition is fundamentally theocentric and Confucianism anthropocentric. However, both are faced with the tension caused by the hidden nature of the world order, and both are determined to find answers from their own understanding of the tension. However, owing to the differences in their metaphysical understanding of the world and life, they diverge in their methodology and final solution, one developing further in the direction of wisdom dualism, and the other searching for a holistic concept of wisdom. The Israelite tradition is fundamentally dualistic in terms of the sacred nature of wisdom, and separates sacred wisdom from secular wisdom, bestowing the former on the divine, while leaving the latter to humans. To reduce the tension between them, Israelite teachers propose that humans must commit themselves totally to trust and faith in YHWH, the only true source and guarantee of sacred wisdom.

By contrast, Confucians do not need to be dualistic in their understanding of the sacred nature of wisdom. Like the Israelite tradition, in the Confucian thinking humans are not totally identified with the divine, and the order behind events and affairs cannot be fully appreciated, and so tension arises. This tension might have led Confucian masters in the theistic direction, had they not had a different perception of the world and destiny. They do not have a fundamental commitment to the divine creation; rather, they view the world as it is, and in it each being and each thing has its own position, value and destiny, which if fully explored and extended enables humans to see the secrets of the world order and understand their own destiny. Therefore, in the Confucian world, the divine (the realm of Heaven (*tian*), ancestors, spirits and destiny) and the human (events, affairs, justice and unjust suffering) cannot be totally separated; rather, in their connection and communication, the sacredness of wisdom is born.

Wisdom as Breaking Through Human Finitude

In the Preface we have suggested that, although wisdom has a very practical focus, it should not be regarded merely as a collection of practical advice; the attainment of wisdom should be more properly understood as a personal or collective journey taken by intellectual and spiritual seekers to reach their goal. Through subsequent chapters we have examined different aspects of Confucian and Israelite 'travellers' on the path to wisdom through the lens of hermeneutical comparison, and reconstructed their discourses on wisdom as recorded in a defined number of Confucian and biblical texts, discovering that the wisdom path does not end with its travellers becoming more skilful and knowledgeable; rather, it goes on to break through human finitude. To reach this ultimate goal, Confucians and the Israelites follow different, separate routes, due to the influences of different cultures, faith systems and languages. In concluding our investigation, we must further our hermeneutical reconstruction of Confucian and Israelite wisdom, and advance a number of arguments crucial to our understanding of wisdom as an intellectual and spiritual journey, during which the limitations of human individuals or groups are gradually surmounted; thus the temporary gains the meaning of the eternal and the particular is endowed with the value of the universal.

Common Features of Confucian and Israelite Wisdom

By examining these two ways of thinking together, we have discovered certain key differences in the way the Confucians of pre-Qin China and the Israelites of the post-exilic era follow the path to wisdom, the chief of which being that the Israelites are primarily theocentric, while the Confucians are essentially anthropocentric. However, we have also discovered many similarities in these differences, with each system demonstrating its own characteristics, while sharing a number of fundamental principles with the other; thus the two together present a way of wisdom distinct from many other wisdom theories and practices.

We first examined the epistemological foundation of wisdom, in which wisdom presents itself as a kind of knowledge: the knowledge that enables its possessors to know or understand the universal and particular laws of the world, natural as well as social, and to foresee what is to happen on the basis of what has happened. Thus a wise course of action may be determined. Similar to many other epistemological products, wisdom knowledge is learnable and transmissible through education. In defining wisdom as knowledge, Confucians and the Israelites differentiate themselves from mystics who deliberately rid wisdom of intellectual content, and identify it with the mysterious union of the intuitive mind and the supposed origin of wisdom hidden behind phenomena.

We then investigated the practical side of wisdom, in which wisdom functions as a way of life, guiding individuals through complex life situations. As a practical tool, wisdom demonstrates itself as skills and capabilities by means of which personal and social problems and difficulties are successfully tackled or solved. Through highlighting the practicality of wisdom, Confucians and the Israelites show a similar mentality, believing that wisdom is not only abstract principles or guidelines, but also has very concrete elements, enabling those who have gained wisdom to sail through rough seas together and to steer their voyage in life. This makes Confucians and the Israelites distinct from a variety of purely philosophical wisdom pursuers who indulge themselves in the speculations of universal truth and sublime goals, while shunning any practical involvement.

Considering that wisdom and morality are closely related, we have examined the ethical nature and application of Confucian and Israelite wisdom. In Chinese and Hebrew wisdom, a significant part of knowledge and skill is concerned with moral deliberation and choice, and wise abilities and capacities are measured primarily by a person's success in understanding and unfolding ethical dilemmas. Although having different emphases on the divine and the secular and different understandings of what is moral, Confucian and Israelite moral wisdom share a circular reasoning that a person cannot be truly wise unless he is a person of virtue, and that a person cannot be truly virtuous unless he is a person of wisdom. Wisdom is thus entwined with virtues, the most important of which in Israelite wisdom texts is righteousness and in Confucianism benevolence (*ren*). Thus Confucian and Israelite wisdom diverges significantly not only from the so-called amoral doctrines that define wisdom in terms of intelligence only and view the wise merely in terms of IQ, but also from the consequentialists who justify the means merely by the ends, considering whatever enables one to garner a desirable result as wisdom.

Confucian and Israelite wisdom operates in a communal context, primarily that of the family and political community. The family is the core of society both in ancient China and in biblical Israel, and is structured in a hierarchical and patriarchal way in both, while the political community or the state can normally be compared to an extended family, where the function of the king in the state is similar to that of the father in the clan or family. Therefore, like the father who disciplines his family members, the king has authority and power over his subjects. However, Confucian and Israelite society do not consider the authority of the king to be absolute, nor do they believe that authority is an automatically generated quality of a king or a father. The people in these two societies believe that the political authority of a king must be based on righteousness or benevolence; in other words it can only result from the wise execution of a king's responsibilities to the divine and to the people. Understood as such, the Confucian and Israelite king stands at a point between the divine and the people, and functions as an exemplary model for society. The Confucian and Israelite wise/sage kingship provides a ruling paradigm that differs significantly from the authoritive one that, by vesting absolute power in the kingship, deprives the kingly way of any accountability or any real necessity for political wisdom and moral justification.

There is a fundamental spiritual orientation in Confucian and Israelite doctrines, and their paths to wisdom, although taking different routes, demonstrate a commonly recognizable sacredness. The sacredness of wisdom is primarily seen in its association with the spiritual ultimate, YHWH and Heaven, respectively, although Confucian and Israelite traditions interpret this association in significantly different ways. There is also an implicit link between wisdom and the spirits, the most significant of which are the spirits of ancestors. However, both Confucians and the Israelites see ancestors primarily, not as the agents from the other world who wield the power to determine the life of this world, but as the prototypes of wisdom, faith and moral tradition, the source from which these values are transmitted and the model by which the human way of life can be positively influenced. More importantly, the sacredness of wisdom is derived from human understanding of the matters that seemingly transcend understanding; hence the Israelite theodicy and the Confucian knowing of destiny. It is in this transcending of understanding that we find the ultimate meaning of sacredness in Confucian and Israelite wisdom, a sacredness which distinguishes their wisdom from the purely secular pursuing and employing of skilfulness and knowledge.

The Goal of Wisdom Journeys

Having completed our examination of various routes or dimensions of the wisdom journey, we can now say with confidence that, although different in emphasis, early Confucian and Israelite discourses demonstrate again that wisdom is essentially aimed at breaking through human finitude. Humans are born with limitations, natural as well as social, and are therefore confined to finitude. However, having intelligence and an emotional longing for freedom, humans are never completely content with these limitations and thus constantly seek to break through the finitude or at least to expand to the maximum the space allowed within it. This is one of the most powerful motives for humans to pursue wisdom, knowledge, skill and understanding. Human limitations are various, as are the methods for breaking through them. Among these methods the most important for Confucians and the Israelites are spiritual and moral approaches.

For the Israelites, the finitude of human beings is predetermined by YHWH who alone can free them from the limitations by awarding them special gifts, of which wisdom is one. Therefore humans cannot break through their finitude unless YHWH wishes it, but YHWH will not wish it unless humans have a total faith in and reliance on him, and have followed the path of righteousness as he has commanded. This feature determines that the Israelite wisdom journey is theocentrically circular, with

YHWH at the centre radiating wisdom to those who are surrounding him. For the Israelites, the wisdom journey begins with the divine gift of intelligence and ends with the divine gift of wisdom, although human experience, understanding and knowledge are also necessary for moving the wheel and for accelerating the journey.

Confucian wisdom is also intended to break through human finitude, and also has confidence in the Way of Heaven as its primary method. However, Confucian Heaven does not interfere with human matters directly; rather, it operates through the efforts and pursuits of humans. To break through finitude humans must engage in moral cultivation and must extend their virtues to other people in community life. Humans cannot be truly free in their actions unless they are truly wise, but they cannot be truly wise unless they are morally good. In this sense, the Confucian journey for overcoming human limitations is anthropocentrically open, starting from the self and self-cultivation and aiming at becoming the sage who by his wisdom and morality will have surpassed human finitude and become part of the eternal course of Heaven and Earth. Based on human wisdom, however, this essentially 'ethico-centric' understanding of the wisdom journey is in fact also open to spiritual interpretation, albeit in a form of spirituality quite different from that of the Israelites.

Paradoxes in Wisdom Discourses

Throughout our examination we are frequently confronted by paradoxes in which the two sides both contradict and rely on each other to function. These paradoxes constitute the main themes of the Confucian and Israelite doctrines of wisdom, or, more precisely, it is in dealing with these paradoxes that the Confucians and Israelites unfold their discourses on wisdom. Of these paradoxes the important ones are those between the changeable and the unchangeable, between the particular and the universal, and between the secular and the divine.

Changeability and Unchangeability

Conventional wisdom presents itself as knowledge and skills that are important for human practical living. It therefore must change as life progresses, adding new understanding to the old, and refreshing past experience with updated information. The same can also apply to human wisdom as a whole. Each generation and each era has its own 'new' understanding, which causes the course of wisdom to change constantly in terms of form and content. Both Confucian and Israelite wisdom thinking demonstrates this character clearly. Formulated in the post-exilic period, Israelite wisdom texts accepted oral or written traditions from the past as their sources, but transformed them into something relevant to the life of their own times. Confucians venerated the past and took the ancient era as their model for the present and the future. The way they did this was through adding new interpretations to the already extant teaching, in the form of annotations and commentaries, which in turn became an important means by which new paradigms of thinking and reconstruction evolved.

However, the changeable is only part of the picture; there is also the unchangeable element within the boundary of the wisdom paradigm. Wisdom is in essence an understanding or appreciation of the world order. Whether called the 'created order' by the Israelites or the 'moral way' by Confucians, the order itself is perceived as not changing, which reflects the permanent structure of the universe and the constant requirements for humans to conform to it. As part of the order or as the way to adjust consciously to it, wisdom is therefore also unchangeable.

Particularity and Universality

Wisdom must be particular in order for it to be practised and applied; however it must not be so particular that it loses its universal appeal. On the one hand, wisdom is a way to cope with the problems of life, which each individual must find his/her own ways to grasp and apprehend. On the other hand, wisdom provides a universal path for all people to follow; a path of wisdom is not worthy of transmission unless it has value for the universal needs of humanity. However, it is difficult, if not impossible, for wisdom teaching to be both particular and universal at the same time, and one is achieved often at the expense of the other; hence the paradox.

The paradox of the particular and the universal is presented in Confucian and Israelite wisdom texts in two ways. In terms of cultural settings, some of the Confucian and Israelite wisdom teachings are particular, in the sense that each concentrates on the problems particular to its own culture and tradition and does not have direct appeal to the culture and tradition of the other. For example, the Confucian deliberation on the relationship between the duke and his ministers, between the ministers and his knight–scholars is unique to the social and political contexts of pre-Qin China, which are not found in biblical Israel, while the Israelite depiction of the beauty and attraction of Lady Wisdom, as a way to lure men to pursue wisdom, does not have any correspondence in Confucian texts. However, the underlying themes of these particular teachings seem to transcend cultural barriers. In terms of historical settings, some of the Confucian and Israelite teachings are confined to their own times, particularly to the special requirements of the societies of more than 2000 years ago. However, there are reasons to suggest that advice on how to lead a wise course of life may be universal across races, and moral criticism of unwise behaviour may be valid throughout the ages. For example, Confucians and the Israelites taught men to be on guard against sexual seduction and women to be cautious about the 'loose way' of life; they educated the young to respect the old and the old to provide proper training to the young; they warned of the danger of being covetous while praising generosity as the sign of faith or morality. These kinds of teaching have a universal appeal because they have explored the depth of human nature and revealed the wisdom embodied in successful human social life.

Secularity and Spirituality

Wisdom in the secular realm is to enable people to cope with daily problems, personal, familial, social and political, with a major part of Confucian and Israelite wisdom teaching being concerned with this; however, if solely confined to these areas, their wisdom would appear to be no more than a collection of aphorisms and proverbs. As stated earlier, the more spiritual orientation in both Confucian and Israelite wisdom seeks a breakthrough in human finitude. In presenting these so-called 'lower' and 'higher' levels of wisdom, Confucianism and the Israelites are confronted by the paradox of secularity and spirituality.

Katharine Dell takes the tension between divine and human wisdom as the centre of Israelite wisdom thinking. If we interpret the divine as the spiritual ultimate and the human as the secular, her assertion is also applicable to Confucian wisdom. However, differences do exist in these areas between the Confucian way of wisdom and the Israelite one. Wisdom as presented in Israelite wisdom texts demonstrates the tendency to suppress the secular for the divine, but does not go to the extreme of denying the human. The Israelite tradition of wisdom is fundamentally theocentric: wisdom is a gift of YHWH, and human wisdom is subject to divine wisdom: 'No wisdom, no understanding, no counsel can avail against the Lord' (Prov. 21:30). However, the Israelites of the wisdom texts still managed to maintain a balance between the divine and the human so that a significant part of their teachings was concerned with cosmic–ethical, communal and secular matters, in a clear contrast to the extreme Yahwehism that later became popular among the Jews. For a theocentric extremist, all secular matters are totally trivial in comparison with following the call of YHWH, and there is no need at all to care about human wishes or desires. This in effect discards some of the most meaningful wisdom teaching transmitted from the past.

Confucian wisdom is essentially humanistic and yet is not without spiritual value. Based on the perception that the world and life were governed by the same moral principles, Confucian wisdom teachings concentrated on secular matters and practical issues, particularly those of the family and public administration, and explored useful skills for dealing with problems in ethical and political arenas. However, it did not develop into completely secular humanism and utilitarianism, manipulating wisdom for material gains of a particular person or group. Rather it maintained that true wisdom for humanity was derived from a human appreciation of the eternal Way, which operates in the universe and throughout time, considering that the secular could not persist without the guidance of the spiritual principles and unless it partook of the divine course of 'generation and regeneration' (*sheng sheng*). Confucius illustrates this spiritual connotation in his self-description: 'In my studies I start from below and get through to what is up above' (*Analects*, 14:35). The underlying argument can be reconstructed by considering 'what is below' to be secular. However, as the starting point of a journey to 'what is above', the learning and wisdom of the secular becomes no longer purely 'secular', but part of the spiritual.

Confucian and Israelite Solutions

The seeming paradoxes of changeability and unchangeability, particularity and universality, and secularity and spirituality exist in all systems of wisdom, but different systems tend to make a different presentation of them and to adopt a different approach in appreciating them. Different as they are in interpreting these paradoxes, Confucians and the Israelites have, in a more or less similar way, gained wisdom about how to deal with them.

The Confucian approach is related to the understanding of the interconnectedness of the Way of Heaven and the way of humans. Unlike later Confucians who claimed that the unchangeability and universality of human wisdom came directly from the Way of Heaven, early Confucians placed more emphasis on changeable and particular wisdom, insisting that there was no fixed format for wisdom, and that wisdom must change according to changes of personal, social and historical circumstances. As a result, Confucius distanced himself from four kinds of attitude: entertaining conjectures, insisting on certainty, being inflexible and being egoistical (*Analects*, 9:4). However, this does not mean that Confucius denied all possibility of permanent, universal and spiritual wisdom, like the Greek Heraclitus (540?–480?BCE) who held that 'everything is in flux'. While Confucius said that the gentleman should not be invariably for or against anything, he also set righteousness or morality (*yi*) as a 'fixed' standard (*Analects*, 4:10). He seemed to confirm that there was an unchangeable and universal standard, which should be applicable to all situations and to all people, and that, since this universal wisdom was to raise human secular existence to a morally higher level, it must be spiritual by nature and in application.

The authors or compilers of Israelite proverbial wisdom focused their attention on the constant nature of wisdom rather than its changeable character, confirming again and again that YHWH founded the earth and heavens through wisdom and wisdom was created at the beginning of God's work (Prov. 3:19; 9:22). Divine wisdom is therefore eternal, universal and sacred, or, in other words, as permanent as the creative order and the created world. However, from this we should not conclude that Israelite wisdom teaching has totally thrown out the flexibility, particularity and secularity of wisdom. Although the source of wisdom is in YHWH, everybody must discover or attain it by themselves (Prov. 3:13). Since each individual is unique and his or her relation with ultimate wisdom is special, what he or she can attain is changeable and particular; since human understanding is limited by their intelligence and capability, they can approach divine wisdom only through their secular experience. Thus the secular cannot exist totally outside the spiritual, and is a necessary step to divine wisdom.

From the above, we find that Confucians and the Israelites demonstrated different characteristics in approaching these paradoxes, but they finally resolve these issues in the same or similar ways. Confucians placed more emphasis on the flexible, particular and secular side of wisdom, requiring each individual to pursue wisdom in their own ways and through their own experiences. However, this does not mean that Confucians ignored the other side. Rather, they followed a path from the below to the above, and in dealing with changing, particular and secular matters they reached unchanging, universal and spiritual wisdom. This was the same way as Confucius dealt with the understanding of life and death, and with the service of humans and of spirits when he took the understanding of life as a route to the understanding of death and taking serving humans as a path to the service of spirits (*Analects*, 11:12). In comparison, the Israelite approaches laid more emphasis on the eternal, universal and sacred nature of wisdom, demanding that all the people follow the same path to the wisdom of YHWH. However, we should not conclude from this that the Israelites did not care about the changeable, particular and secular. In contrast to Confucians who approached the unchangeable from the changeable, the universal from the particular, the spiritual from the secular, the Israelites explored a reverse path, namely, approaching the changeable from the unchangeable, the particular from the universal, and the secular from the spiritual.

In these two different approaches to wisdom paradoxes Confucians and the Israelites demonstrate the diversity of wisdom discourses. However, through their coming to the same or similar solutions, we discover a common wisdom mentality across human cultures and traditions regarding human life and destiny, which makes it possible for us to forge a synergy of human wisdom in breaking through finitude.

Bibliography

Ames, R.T., Dissanayake, W. and Kasulis, T. (eds), *Self as Person in Asian Theory and Practice*, Albany: State University of New York Press, 1994.

Anderson, Graham, *Sage, Saint and Sophist*, London and New York: Routledge, 1994.

Aristotle, *Ethics*, translated by J.A.K. Thomson, Harmondsworth: Penguin, 1976.

Ban Gu, *et al.*, *Hanshu* 漢書 (*History of the Former Han Dynasty*), Beijing: Zhonghua Shuju, 1997.

Barton, John and Muddiman, John (eds), *The Oxford Bible Commentary*, Oxford: Oxford University Press, 2001.

Armenti, J. (ed.), *Wisdom and Knowledge: Papin Festschrift*, Philadelphia: Villanova Press, 1976.

Bergant, Dianne, *What are they saying about wisdom literature?* New York/Ramsey: Paulist Press, 1984.

Billington, Ray, *East of Existentialism – The Tao of the West*, Unwin Hyman, 1990.

Botterweck, G. Johnnes and Ringgren, Helmer (eds), *Theological Dictionary of the Old Testament*, translated by David E. Green, Volumes I–VI, Grand Rapids, Michigan: William B. Eerdmans Publishing Company, 1980–90.

Brown, William P., *Character in Crisis: A Fresh Approach to the Wisdom Literature of the Old Testament*, Grand Rapids, Michigan: Eerdmans William B. Publisshing Company, 1996.

Bryce, Glendon E., 'Omen-Wisdom in Ancient Israel', *Journal of Biblical Literature*, 94, pp.19–37, 1975.

Burkert, Walter, *Greek Religion*, translated by John Raffan, Cambridge, Massachussetts: Harvard University Press, 1985.

Chan, Wing-tsit (ed.), *A Source Book in Chinese Philosophy*, Princeton: Princeton University Press, 1963.

Charles, R.H., *Critical and Exegetical Commentary on the Book of Daniel*, Oxford: Clarendon Press, 1929.

Chen Lai 陳萊 *Gudai Zongjiao yu Lunli – Rujia Sixiang de Genyuan* 古代宗教与倫理--儒家思想的根源(Ancient Religion and Ethics – The Origin of the Confucian Thought), Beijing: Sanlian Shudian, 1996.

Chen, Ning, 'The Etymology of *Sheng* (Sage) and its Confucian Conception in Early China', *Journal of Chinese Philosophy*, 27 (4), pp. 409–27, December 2000.

Cheng, Chung-ying, 'Inquiring into the Primary Model: *Yijing* and Structure of Chinese Hermeneutic Tradition', *Journal of Chinese Philosophy*, 30 (3–4), 2003.

Cheng, Chung-ying and Bunnin, Nick (eds), *Contemporary Chinese Philosophy*, Malden, Massachusetts and Oxford: Blackwell, 2002.

Ching, Julia, *Chinese Religions*, London and New York: Macmillan Press, 1993.

Ching, Julia, *Mysticism and Kingship in China: The Heart of Chinese Wisdom*, Cambridge: Cambridge University Press, 1997.

Clifford, Richard J., *The Wisdom Literature*, Nashville: Abingdon, 1998.

Cohen, J.D. (ed.), *The Jewish Family in Antiquity*, Atlanta, Georgia: Scholars Press, 1993.

Cooley, Charles Horton, 'The Roots of Social Knowledge', *American Journal of Sociology*, 32, pp. 59–79, 1926–7.

Crenshaw, James, L., *Studies in Ancient Israelite Wisdom*, New York: Ktav Publishing House, 1976.

Crenshaw, James L., *Old Testament Wisdom: An Introduction*, revised and enlarged, Louisville: Westminster John Knox Press, 1998.

Day, John, Gordon, Robert P. and Williamson, H.G.M. (eds), *Wisdom in Ancient Israel*, Cambridge: Cambridge University Press, 1995.

de Bary, Wm Theodore and Bloom, Irene (eds), *Sources of Chinese Tradition – From Earliest Times to 1600*, vol. 1, 2nd edn, New York: Columbia University Press, 1999.

Dell, Katharine, *The Book of Job as Sceptical Literature*, Beihefte zur ZAW, 197; Berlin: W. de Gruyter, 1991.

Dell, Katharine, 'The King in the Wisdom Literature', in *King and Messiah in Israel and the Ancient Near East – Proceedings of the Oxford Old Testament Seminar*, edited by John Day, *Journal for the Study of the Old Testament*, Supplement Series 270, Sheffield: Sheffield Academic Press, 1998, pp.163–86.

Dell, Katharine, *'Get Wisdom, Get Insight': An Introduction to Israel's Wisdom Literature*, Macon: Smyth & Helwys Publishing, Inc., 2000.

Dreyer, June Teufel, *China's Political System – Modernization and Tradition*, 3rd edn, revised and updated, London: Macmillan Press, 2000.

Duan Yucai, *Shuowen jiezi zhu* 说文解字注 (*A Commentary on Explaining Simple Graphs and Analysing Compound Characters*), Hangzhou: Zhejiang Guji Chubanshe, 1998.

Eaton, John, *The Contemplative Face of Old Testament Wisdom in the Context of World Religions*, London and Philadelphia: SCM Press and Trinity Press International, 1989.

Eber, Irene (ed.), *Confucianism: The Dynamics of Tradition*, London: Macmillan, 1986.

Ebrey, Patricia Buckley, *Confucianism and Family Rituals in Imperial China: A Social History of Writing about Rites*, Princeton, New Jersey: Princeton University Press, 1991.

Efird, James M., *Biblical Books of Wisdom*, Eugene: Wipf and Stock Publishers, 2001.

Eno, Robert, *The Confucian Creation of Heaven: Philosophy and the Defense of Ritual Mastery*, Albany: State University of New York Press, 1990.

Flood, Gavin, *Beyond Phenomenology*, London: Cassell, 1999.

Freedman, David Noel (editor-in-chief), *The Anchor Bible Dictionary*, vol. VI, 1992.

Freedman, David Noel (editor-in-chief), *Eerdmans Dictionary of the Bible*, Grand Rapids, Michigan/Cambridge, UK: William B. Eerdmans Publishing Company, 2000.

Fung Yu-Lan, *A History of Chinese Philosophy*, vols 1–2, translated by Derk Bodde, Princeton: Princeton University Press, 1952–3.

Gernet, Jacques, *A History of Chinese Civilization*, translated by J.R. Foster and Charles Hartman, 2nd edn, Cambridge: Cambridge University Press, 1996.

Gammie, John G., Brueggermann, Walter A., Humphreys, W. Lee and Ward, James M. (eds), *Israelite Wisdom: Theological and Literary Essays in Honor of Samuel Terrien*, Missoula, Montana: Scholars Press, 1978.

Graham, A.C., *Disputers of the Tao: Philosophical Argument in Ancient China*, La Salle, Ill.: Open Court, 1991.

Griffiths, Paul J., *Problems of Religious Diversity*, Oxford and Malden: Blackwell Publishers Inc., 2001.

Grondin, Jean, *Introduction to Philosophical Hermeneutics*, New Haven: Yale University Press, 1994.

Hall, David L. and Ames, Roger T., *Thinking Through Confucius*, Albany: State University of New York Press, 1987.

Hansen, Chad, *A Daoist Theory of Chinese Thought: A Philosophical Interpretation*, New York: Oxford University Press, 1992.

Hanyu dazidian bianji weiyuanhui (ed.), *Hanyu da zidian* 漢語大字典 (*A Great Dictionary of Chinese Characters*), Sichuan Dictionary Publishing House and Hubei Dictionary Publishing House 四川辭書出版社 湖北辭書出版社 1993.

Heidegger, Martin, *Being and Time*, translated by John Macquarrie and Edward Robinson, Oxford: Blackwell, 1962.

Holliday, S.G. and Chandler, M.J., *Wisdom: Exploration in adult competence*, Basle: Switzerland: Karger, 1986.

Huang Hui, *Lunhen jiaoshi* 論衡教釋, vols 1–4, Beijing: Zhonghua shuju, 1990.

Hu Zhihui 胡志揮 (trans.), *Zuo zhuan* 左傳 (*Zuo's Commentary on the Spring and Autumn Annals*), Changsha: Hunan Renmin Chubanshe, 1996.

Ivanhoe, Philip, *Confucian Moral Self Cultivation*, New York: Peter Lang, 1993.

Kim Sung-Hae, 'The righteous and the sage: a comparative study on the ideal images of man in biblical Israel and classical China', PhD thesis, Harvard University, 1981.

Knoblock, John, *Xunzi: A Translation and Study of the Complete Works*, vols 1–3, Stanford: Stanford University Press, 1988, 1990, 1994.

Knoblock, John and Riegel, Jeffrey (trans.), *The Annals of Lü Buwei*, Stanford: Stanford University Press, 2000.

Köhler, Ludwig, *Hebrew Man*, trans. Peter R. Ackroyd, London: SCM Press, 1956.

Küng, Hans and Julia Ching, *Christianity and Chinese Religions*, New York: Doubleday and London: Collins Publishers, 1989.

Labouvie-Vief, Gisela, 'Wisdom as integrated thought: historical and developmental perspectives', in Robert J. Sternberg (ed.) *Wisdom: its nature, origins, and development*, Cambridge: Cambridge University Press, 1990.

Lambert, W.G., *Babylonia Wisdom Literature*, Oxford: Clarendon Press, 1960.

Lash, Nicholas, *The Beginning and the end of 'Religion'*, Cambridge: Cambridge University Press, 1996.

Lau, D.C., *Confucius: The Analects (Lun yü)*, translated with an introduction by D.C. Lau, Harmondsworth: Penguin, 1979.

Legge, James (trans.), *The Chinese Classics: Vol. III, The Shoo King or the Book of Historical Documents*, London: Trubner & Co., 1865.

Legge, James (trans.), *The Chinese Classics: Vol. IV, The She-King or the Book of Odes*, London: Trubner & Co., 1871.

Legge, James (trans.), *The Confucian Classics, Vol. V, The Ch'un Ts'ew, with the Tso Chuen*, London: Trubner & Co., 1872.

Legge, James (trans.), *The Li Ki or the Collection of Treatises on the Rules of Propriety or Ceremonial Usages*, in F. Max Müller (ed.), *The Sacred Books of the East*, Oxford: Clarendon Press, vols 27–8, 1885, reprinted Delhi: Motilal Banarsidass, 1968.

Li, Wai-Yee, 'Knowledge and skepticism in ancient Chinese historiography', in Kraus Christina Shuttleworth (ed.), *The Limits of Historiography: Genre and Narrative in Ancient Historical Texts*, Mnemosyne, bibliotheca classica Batava, Supplementum, 191, Leiden/Boston: Brill, 1999.

Li Xueqin 李学勤 (ed.), *Shisan jing zhushu* 十三经注疏 (*Annotations and Commentaries on the Thirteen Classics*), vols 1–13, Beijing: Beijing University Press, 1999.

Lin Yu-tang (ed. & trans.), *The Wisdom of Confucius*, Random House, 1938, reprinted in Taipei: Zhengzhong Shuju, 1994.

Liu, Da, *The Tao and Chinese Culture*, London: Routledge and Kegan Paul, 1981.

Lloyd, G.E.R., *Adversaries and Authorities: Investigations into ancient Greek and Chinese science*, Cambridge: Cambridge University Press, 1996.

Locke, John, *An Essay Concerning Human Understanding*, Harmondsworth: Penguin, 1997.

Loewe, Michael (ed.), *Early Chinese Texts: A Bibliographical Guide*, Berkeley: The Society for the Study of Early China and the Institute of East Asian Studies, University of California, Berkeley, 1993.

Loewe, Michael and Edward L. Shaughnessy (eds), *The Cambridge History of Ancient China*, Cambridge: Cambridge University Press, 1999.

Makeham, John (trans.), *Transmitters and Creators: Chinese Commentators and Commentaries on the 'Analects'*, Harvard University Asia Center, 2004.

McKane, W., *Prophets and Wise Men*, London: SCM Press, 1965.

McKenzie, John L., *Dictionary of the Bible*, London/Dublin: Geoffrey Chapman, 1980.

Miller, Maxwell J. and Hayes, John H., *A History of Ancient Israel and Judah*, London: SCM Press, 1986.

Metzger, Bruce M. and Coogan, Michael D. (eds), *The Oxford Companion to the Bible*, New York/Oxford: Oxford University Press, 1993.

Moore, Charles A. (ed.), *The Chinese Mind: Essentials of Chinese Philosophy and Culture*, Honolulu: University Press of Hawaii, 1967.

Munro, Donald J., *The Concept of Man in Early China*, Stanford: Stanford University Press, 1985.

Munro, Donald J., *Individualism and Holism: Studies in Confucian and Taoist Values*, Ann Arbor: Center for Chinese Studies, The University of Michigan, 1969.

Murphy, Roland E., *Wisdom Literature* (*The Forms of the Old Testament Literature* series, Volume XIII), Grand Rapids, Michigan: William B. Eerdmans Publishing Company, 1981.

Murphy, Roland E., *The Tree of Life: An Exploration of Biblical Wisdom Literature*, 2nd edn, Grand Rapids, Michigan: William B. Eerdmans Publishing Company, 1996.

Needham, Joseph, *Science and Civilization in China: volume 2: History of Scientific Thought*, Cambridge: Cambridge University Press, 1956.

Needham, Joseph, *Science and Civilization in China*, vol. V, pt. II, Cambridge: Cambridge University Press, 1974.

Nivison, David S. *The Ways of Confucianism – Investigations in Chinese Philosophy*, Chicago: Open Court, 1996.

Noth, M. and Thomas, W. (eds), *Wisdom in Israel and in the Ancient Near East*, Leiden: E.J. Brill, 1955.

O'Hara, Albert Richard, *The Position of Woman in Early China – According to the Lieh Nu Chuan 'The Biographies of Eminent Chinese Women'*, Washington, DC: The Catholic University of America Press, 1945.

Paul, Gregor S., *Aspects of Confucianism: A Study of the Relationship between Rationality and Humanity*, Frankfurt am Main: Peter Lang, 1990.

Perdue, Leo G. *et al.*, *Families in Ancient Israel*, Louisville: Westminster John Knox Press, 1997.

Plaks, Andrew (trans.), Ta Hsüch and Chung Yung, *The Highest Order of Cultivation* and *On the Practice of the Mean*, London: Penguin Classics, 2003.

Poo, Mu-chu, *In Search of Personal Welfare: A View of Ancient Chinese Religion*, Albany: State University of New York Press, 1998.

Queen, Sarah A., *From Chronicle to Canon: The Hermeneutics of the Spring and Autumn, According to Tung Chung-shu*, Cambridge: Cambridge University Press, 1996.

Rad, von Gerhard, *Old Testament Theology*, vol. 1, Edinburgh and London: Oliver and Boyd/SCM Press, 1962.

Rad, von Gerhard, *Wisdom in Israel*, Nashville: Abingdon, 1972.

Ralph, Margaret Nutting, *Discovering Prophecy and Wisdom: The Books of Isaiah, Job, Proverbs, Psalms*, Discovering the living word, no. 4, New York: Paulist Press, 1993.

Roetz, Heiner, *Confucian Ethics of the Axial Age – A Reconstruction under the*

Aspect of the Breakthrough Toward Postconventional Thinking, Albany: State University of New York Press, 1993.

Rosemont, Henry (ed.), *Chinese Texts and Philosophical Contexts*, Chicago: Open Court, 1991.

Rowley, H.H., *Prophecy and Religion in Ancient China and Israel*, Jordan lectures in comparative religion (University of London), University of London/The Athlone Press, 1956.

Rubin, Vitaly A. *Individual and State in Ancient China*, New York: Columbia University Press, 1976.

Rutt, Richard, *Zhouyi: the Book of Changes*, Richmond: Curzon Press, 1996.

Sailey, Jay, *The Master who Embraces Simplicity – A Study of the Philosopher Ko hung, A.D. 283–343*, San Francisco: Chinese Materials Center, 1978.

Schwarts, Benjamin, *The World of Thought in Ancient China*, Cambridge, Massachussetts: Harvard University Press, 1985.

Scott. R.B.Y., *The Way of Wisdom in the Old Testament*, New York: Macmillan, 1971.

Shankam, Steven and Durrant, Stephen, *The Siren and the Sage – Knowledge and Wisdom in Ancient Greece and China*, London and New York: Cassell, 2000.

Sharpe, E., *Comparative Religion, A History*, London: Duckworth, 1975.

Sheldon, Holly Anne, 'The problem of evil in the Zhou Dynasty', MA thesis, International School of Theology, 1993.

Shih, Joseph, 'The Notions of God in Ancient Chinese Religion', *Numen* (16–17), pp.99–138, 1969–70.

Shryock, John K., *The Origin and Development of the State Cult of Confucius: An Introductory Study*, New York: Paragon Book Reprint Corp., 1966.

Shun, Kwong-loi, *Mencius and Early Chinese Thought*, Stanford: Stanford University Press, 1997.

Si Maqian, *Shiji* 史記, Beijing: Zhonghua Shuju, 1997.

Sketan, Patrick W. (ed.), *Studies in Israelite Poetry and Wisdom*, CBQ Monograph Series 1, Washington DC: The Biblical Association of America, 1971.

Skehan, P.W. and Lella, A. Di, *The Wisdom of Ben Sira*, Garden City, New York: Doubleday, 1987.

Slingerland, Ted, 'The Conception of Ming in Early Confucian Thought', *Philosophy East and West*, 46 (4), pp.567–81, 1996.

Slote, Walter H. and De Vos, George A. (eds), *Confucianism and the Family*, New York: State University of New York Press, 1998.

Smart, Ninian, *The Phenomenon of Religion*, London: Macmillan, 1979.

Soothill, W. E., *The Hall of Light: A Study of Early Chinese Kingship*, London: Lutterworth Press, 1951.

Steele, John (trans.), *The I-li or Book of Etiquette and Ceremonial*, vols 1–2, London: Probsthain & Co.; republished Taipei: Ch'eng-wen Publishing Company, 1966.

Sternberg, Robert, 'Implicit theories of intelligence, creativity, and wisdom', *Journal of Personality and Social Psychology*, 49 (3), pp.607–27, 1985.

Sternberg, Robert (ed.), *Wisdom: its nature, origins, and development*, Cambridge: Cambridge University Press, 1990.

Thompson, Laurence, *Chinese Religion: An Introduction*, Encino, California: Dickenson Publishing Corporation, 1975.

Tjan, Tjoe Som (trans.), *Po Hu T'ung – The Comprehensive Discussions in the White Tiger Hall*, vols 1–2, Leiden: E.J. Brill, 1949: reprinted Westport, Connecticut: Hyperion Press, 1973.

Torijano, Pablo A., *Solomon The Esoteric King – From King to Magus, Development of a Tradition*, Brill: Leiden, 2002.

Tucker, Mary E. and Berthrong, John H. (eds), *Confucianism and Ecology: the inter-relation of heaven, earth, and humans*, Cambridge, Massachussetts: Harvard University Press for the Harvard University Center for the Study of World Religions, 1998.

Twitchett, Denis and Michael Loewe (eds), *The Cambridge History of China: Vol. 1: The Ch'in and the Han Empires 221 B.C.–A.D. 220*, Cambridge: Cambridge University Press, 1986.

Vollbracht, James, *The Way of Virtue: The Ancient Wisdom of Confucius Adapted for a New Age*, Lake Worth, Florida: Humanics New Age, 1997.

von Rad, Gerhard, *Old Testament Theology*, vol. 1, translated by D.M.G. Stalker, New York: Harper & Row, 1967.

von Rad, Gerhard, *Wisdom in Israel*, translated by James D. Martin, Nashville: Abingdon, 1972.

Waley, Arthur (trans.) *The Book of Songs*, Boston: Houghton, 1937.

Waley, Arthur (trans.) *The Analects of Confucius*, London: Allen & Unwin, 1938.

Wallacker, Benjamin E., 'Han Confucianism and Confucius in Han', in *Ancient China: Studies in early civilization*, ed. David T. Roy and Tsuen-hsuin Tsein, Hong Kong: Hong Kong University Press, pp.215–28, 1978.

Waltham, Clae (ed.), *Shu Ching Book of History* – a modernized edition of the translation of James Legge, London: George Allen & Unwin, 1972.

Ward, Keith, *Religion and Community*, Oxford: Oxford University Press, 2000.

Watson, Burton (trans.), *Records of the Grand Historian of China*, vols 1–2, New York and London: Columbia University Press, 1961.

Watson, Burton (trans.), *Hsün Tzu: Basic Writings*, New York and London: Columbia University Press, 1966.

Watson, Burton (trans.), *The Complete Works of Chuang Tzu*, New York: Columbia University Press, 1968.

Watson, Burton (trans.), *The Tso Chuan – Selections from China's Oldest Narrative History*, New York: Columbia University Press, 1989.

Weber, Max, *The Sociology of Religion*, Boston: Beacon Press, 1963.

Weber, Max, *The Religion of China: Confucianism and Taoism*, New York: Free Press, 1968.

Weeks, Stuart, *Early Israelite Wisdom*, Oxford: Clarendon Press, 1994.

Whybray, R.N., *The Intellectual Tradition in the Old Testament*, Berlin and New York: Walter de Gruyter, 1974.

Whybray, R.N., *Wealth and Poverty in the Book of Proverbs*, JSOT Press, Sheffield, 1990.

Whybray, R.N., *Proverbs*, New Century Bible Commentary, London: Marshall Pickering/Grand Rapids, Michigan: William B. Eerdmans Publishing Company, 1994.

Wieger, Léon, *A History of the Religious Beliefs and Philosophical Opinions in China*, translated by E.T.C. Werner, Hsien Hsien: Hsien Hsien Press, 1927.

Wilhelm, Richard (trans.), *The I Ching or Book of Changes*, English translation by Cary F. Baynes, London: Arkana, 1967.

Wright, A.F. (ed.), *Confucianism and Chinese Civilisation*, Stanford: Stanford University Press, 1959.

Wright, A.F., *The Confucian Persuasion*, Stanford: Stanford University Press, 1960.

Wu, Pei-yi, 'Self Examination and Confession of Sins in Traditional China', *Harvard Journal of Asiatic Studies*, 39 (1), pp.5–38, 1979.

Xu Zhongshu 徐中舒 (ed.), *Jiaguwen zidian* 甲骨文字典 (*Dictionary of Oracle Bonze Inscriptions*), Chengdu: Sichuan Cishu Chubanshe, 1990.

Yang Bojun 楊伯浚, *Lunyu yizhu* 論語譯注 (*A Translation and Annotations of the Analects of Confucius*), Beijing: Zhonghua Shuju, 1980.

Yang Bojun, 楊伯浚 *Mengzi*孟子譯注 (*A Translation and Annotation of the Book of Mengzi*), Beijing: Zhonghua Shuju, 1960.

Yang, C.K., *Religion in Chinese Society*, University of California Press, 1961.

Yang, Hsien-yi and Gladys Yang (trans.), *Records of the Historian*, Hong Kong: The Commercial Press, 1974.

Yao, Xinzhong, *Confucianism and Christianity*, Brighton: Sussex Academic Press, 1996.

Yao, Xinzhong, 'Self-Construction and Identity: The Confucian self in relation to some Western Perceptions', *Asian Philosophy*, Vol. 6, No. 3, pp.179–95, 1996.

Yao, Xinzhong, *An Introduction to Confucianism*, Cambridge: Cambridge University Press, 2000.

Yao, Xinzhong (ed.), *Routledge/Curzon Encyclopedia of Confucianism*, vols 1–2, London: Routledge, 2003.

Yen, Nathaniel Yung-tse, 'Prophet sage and wise man: a comparative study of intellectual tradition in ancient China and Israel', PhD thesis, Drew University, Madison, 1977.

Young, Robert, *Analytical Concordance to the Holy Bible*, London: United Society for Christian Literature, Lutterworth Press, 8th edn, 1939.

Zhu Xi 朱熹, *Sishu zhangju jizhu* 四書章句集注, Beijing: Zhonghua Shuju, 1983.

Appendix I: Glossary of Chinese Characters

Pinyin spelling	Chinese character	English meaning/references
bai	白	white
bai ji	百技	a hundred skills
bai shen	百神	a hundred gods of deities
ba zheng dao	八正道	eight orthodox paths
bian	辨	to differentiate
bo shi	博士	academician
cheng ji	成己	self-completion
Cheng Wang	成王	King Cheng (1042/35–1006BCE), the third king of the Zhou dynasty
cong	從	to obey
da dao	达道	universal ways
dao	道	the way
dao bu xing	道不行	The Way does not prevail
dao de	道德	inner moral qualities, morality
Daode jing	道德經	classic on the *Way and its Power*
Dao, suo xing dao ye	道，所行道也	Dao is the path along which one walks
dao xue	道學	the learning of the way
da ren	大任	great task
da yi	大義	great laws
Da Yu Mo	大禹謨	a chapter of the *Book of Documents*
Daxue	大學	The *Great Learning*
da xue zhi dao	大學之道	the way of great learning
de	德	virtue
Di	帝	Lord, god, emperor
di zhi	地祇	earthly gods or spirits
Dong Zhongshu	董仲舒	(179?–104?BCE), a distinguished Confucian scholar of the Former Han dynasty

Pinyin spelling	Chinese character	English meaning/references
fan shen	反身	self-examination
fu li	復禮	to observe, or return to, the rites
fu zhi dao	父之道	the way of the father
fuzi zhi dao	夫子之道	the way of the master
ge	格	investigating
ge wu	格物	investigating things
guan	觀	to observe
gui	鬼	ghosts
gui shen	鬼神	spirits
Hanshu	汉书	*The History of the Former Han Dynasty*
hao xue	好学	eager to learn or love of learning
heng	恆	constant, permanent
heng chan	恆产	permanent property
houzhi	后知	afterknowledge
huang quan	黃泉	yellow springs, the underworld, hell
hun	魂	human spirit from heaven
ji	祭	rituals in relation to earthly gods
jia	家	household, family
jiao	教	teaching, education, doctrine
jie	街	street
jing	經	classics
jing	精	vital essence
jing	敬	reverence, respectfulness
jing xue	經學	classical learning
ji shen	祭神	making sacrifices to gods, deities or spirits
ju	居	household, a place where people live
jun zi	君子	gentleman, noble man, superior man, man of virtue
jun zi zhi dao	君子之道	the way of gentlemen
ke ji	克己	to restrain or overcome oneself
Kong Fuzi	孔夫子	Confucius (551–479BCE)
kou	口	mouth

Pinyin spelling	Chinese character	English meaning/references
le yi tian xia	樂以天下	delight on account of the world
li	禮	rites, ritual, codes of conduct, rules of propriety
li	理	principle, reason
liangzhi	良知	good knowledge, innate good senses
lie zhuan	列传	individual biographies
Liji Jijie	禮記集解	*Collective Annotations on the Book of Rites*
ling	令	to order or command
lun li	倫理	moral principles, human relationships
Lüshi Chunqiu	呂氏春秋	*The Spring and Autumn Annals by Mr. Lü*
Mengzi	孟子	a Confucian master (372?–289?BCE) and the supposed author of the *Book of Mengzi*
ming	命	destiny, fate, mandate of Heaven
ming junzi	明君子	enlightened gentleman
mou	謀	seek after
ne	訥	slow to speak
nei zi xing	内自省	looking within and examining one's self
po	魄	human spirit from earth
qi	氣	vital power, breath, air
qianshi	前識	advanced knowledge
qianzhi	前知	foreknowledge
qiao yan	巧言	clever talking
Qilu xuekan	齐鲁学刊	*Academic Journal of Qilu*
ren	仁	benevolence, humanity, humaneness
ren	人	humans
ren gui	人鬼	human ghosts
ren ren	仁人	benevolent man, humane man
ren zheng	仁政	benevolent or humane government
ri xin	日新	daily renewal

Pinyin spelling	Chinese character	English meaning/references
ru	儒	Confucians
ru jia	儒家	the Confucian school or Confucianism
ru shi	儒士	Confucian scholars
san li	三禮	three religious ceremonies
sanxian	三獻	three offerings of sacrifices
Shang Di	上帝	Lord on High, High God
Shangshu	尚書	the *Book of Documents*
shang zhi	上智	people of high intelligence
shan ren zhi dao	善人之道	the way of good men
shen	神	deity, god, divinity, spirits, mysterious
shen	審	to examine
sheng	生	to produce, to give birth to
sheng sheng	生生	generating and regenerating
shen zheng biao	審癥表	examining the internal and external signs
shengren	聖人	sage
sheng wang	聖王	sage–king
sheng wang zhi dao	聖王之道	the way of sage–kings
shi	士	scholar, scholar–knight
shi	矢	an arrow
shi	事	to serve
shi dao	失道	have lost the way
Shiji	史記	the *Records of the Historian*
shi junzi	士君子	scholar–gentleman
Shisan jing zhushu	十三經註疏	*Annotations and Commentaries on the Thirteen Classics*
shou	首	head
shu er bu zuo	述而不作	transmitting but not composing
Shun	舜	a legendary sage–king
Shuowen jiezi zhu	说文解字注	*A Commentary on Explaining Simple Graphs and Analysing Compound Characters*
si	祀	rituals in relation to heavenly gods
situ zhi guan	司徒之官	ministry of education
su wang	素王	the uncrowned king

Pinyin spelling	Chinese character	English meaning/references
Tai chu you Dao	太初有道	in the beginning the way
tian	天	heaven, sky, nature
tian dao	天道	way of heaven
tian jiang xia min	天降下民	heaven populated the earth below
Tian ming	天命	mandate or decree of heaven
tian shen	天神	heavenly gods or spirits
tian sheng min	天生民	heaven gives birth to the people
tian sheng zheng min	天生烝民	heaven produces the teeming masses
tian xing you chang	天行有常	there is a constant order in the course of heaven
ting	聽	to follow, to listen to
ting qi yan guan qi xing	聽其言觀其行	observing one's words and behaviour
Wen Wang	文王	King Wen (1099/56?–1050?BCE), the founding king of the Zhou dynasty
wu chang	五常	five constant virtues
wu dao	無道	have not the way
Wu Wang	武王	King Wu (1049?–1043?BCE), the second king of the Zhou dynasty
wuyi	務義	diligently performing one's duties
wu xing	五行	five agents, five elements, five powers
xiang	享	rituals in relation to human ghosts
xiang	庠	school
xianshi	先識	foreknowledge
xian wang	先王	the former kings
xian wang zhi dao	先王之道	the way of former kings
xianzhi	先知	to foresee, foreknowledge
xiao	孝	filial piety, filial love
xiao dao	小道	small arts
xiao ren	小人	small man, inferior man, morally underdeveloped man
xiao ren zhi dao	小人之道	the way of an inferior man
xia yu	下愚	people of low foolishness
xin	信	faithfulness, trustfulness, chastity

Pinyin spelling	Chinese character	English meaning/references
xiu dao	修道	cultivating the way
xue dao	學道	to study the way
Xunzi	荀子	A Confucian master (313?–238? BCE) and the supposed author of the *Book of Xunzi*
yang	養	to support, providing food and clothes
Yan Hui	顔回	one of Confucius's disciples
yan jun	嚴君	the authorative ruler
Yao	堯	a legendary sage–king
yi	義	righteousness, rightness
yi	異	prodigies
yi ben	一本	one root
yi da wei zhi dao	一達謂之道	Dao is that by which we reach our destination
Yijing	易經	the *Book of Changes*
yin luan	淫亂	licentious and disorderly
yong	勇	courage
you	憂	to be concerned about, worry about
yu	預	to predict
yu	愚	ignorant, stupid, foolish
Yu	禹	a legendary sage–king and the founder of the Xia dynasty
yu	亏	air
yun	云	clouds
zai	災	visitations
Zhao Qi	趙啓	a Confucian scholar of the 2nd century CE
zhe	哲	wise
zhen xiang	禎祥	lucky omens
zhi	知	knowledge
zhi	知, 智	wisdom
zhi cheng	至诚	absolute sincerity
zhi de chuantong	智的傳統	wisdom or intellectual tradition
zhigao wushang	至高無上	the ultimate

Pinyin spelling	Chinese character	English meaning/references
zhi guo zhi li	治國之理	the principle of governing the empire
zhi tian	知天	knowing heaven
zhi zhi	知止	to know where to stop
zhizhe	智者	the wise
zhong	忠	loyalty
zhong dao	中道	the middle way
zhong he	中和	centrality and harmony
Zhongyong	中庸	the *Doctrine of the Mean*
Zhou Gong	周公	Duke of Zhou (1042–1036BCE), the younger brother of King Wu of the Zhou dynasty
zhuan	傳	commentaries
zi	子	master
Zi Gong	子貢	one of Confucius's disciples
Zi Lu	子路	one of Confucius's disciples
Zi Si	子思	(483–402?BCE) Confucius's grandson
Zi Zhang	子張	one of Confucius's disciplines
zong	宗	ancestral
zu	足	foot
zuo	作	to compose, write
Zuo Zhuan	左傳	*Zuo's Commentary on the Spring and Autumn Annals*

Appendix II: Glossary of Hebrew Words

Transliteration	Hebrew	English Meanings
'ōraḥ	אֹרַח	way, path
'ĕwîl	אֱוִיל	a fool
bînā	בִּינָה	understanding
bêt-'āḇ	בֵּית־אָב	literally, father's house
bāśār	בָּשָׂר	flesh/body
gōlā	גּוֹלָה	exile(d ones)
gālūt	גָּלוּת	exile(s)
da'at	דַּעַת	knowledge
dereḵ	דֶּרֶךְ	road, way
heḇel	הֶבֶל	breath, vanity
hāliḵ	הָלִיךְ	a step
hᵃlikā	הֲלִיכָה	a walk, doings, the rules of behaviour
ḥāḵam	חָכַם	to be(come) wise
ḥāḵām	חָכָם	skilful, wise
ḥoḵmā	חָכְמָה	shrewdness, wisdom
ḥoḵmōt	חָכְמוֹת	wisdom
ḥûs	חוּץ	the outside, street
ḥayil	חַיִל	virtue, power
yāḇîn	יָבִיו	(he) will understand
yāḏa	יָדַע	knowledge, knowing
yhwh	יהוה	Yahweh, God of Israel
yôm yhwh	יוֹם יְהוָה	day of Yahweh
yā'aṣ and *'ēṣā*	עֵצָה / יָעַץ	counsel, advice
yāšar	יָשַׁר	to be straight, right
kᵉlāyot	כְּלָיוֹה	kidneys/emotions
kᵉsîl	כְּסִיל	a stupid person
lēḇ	לֵב	heart, inner man
mᵉsillā	מְסִלָּה	highway
ma'gāl	מַעְגָּל	track, course
miṣwāh	מִצְוָה	law, rule, commandment, obligation
māšāl	מָשָׁל	proverbial saying

Transliteration	Hebrew	English Meanings
nāḇōn	נָבוֹן	one who discerns
nābî	נָבִיא	prophet
nābāl	נָבָל	a foolish person
nepeš	נֶפֶשׁ	soul/person
nāṯîḇ	נָתִיב	path
nᵉṯîḇā	נתיבָה	path, way
sōpēr	סֹפֵר	scribe, secretary
'āzaḇ	עָזֻב	forsaken, lonely
'ormā	עָרְמָה	prudence
ṣedeq	צֶּרֶק	righteousness
ṣaddîq	צַדִּיק	righteous, guiltless
ṣᵉḏāqā	צְרָקָה	righteousness
qādōš	קָרוֹשׁ	holy, set apart
rūᵃḥ	רוּחַ	breath, wind, spirit
rāšāᶜ	רָשָׁע	the wicked
śāḵal	שָׂכַל	to have insight
śᵉ'ōl	שְׁאוֹל	the Underworld
šūq	שׁוּק	street
tᵉbūnā	תְּבוּנָה	understanding, skill
tōrā	תּוֹרָה	instruction, guidance, law
tāmîm	תָּמִים	perfect, blameless
tāmam	תָּמַם	to be complete, finished

Index